T0271254

Building Technology Transfer within Research Universities

An Entrepreneurial Approach

Over the past several years, academic entrepreneurship has become one of the most widely studied topics in the entrepreneurship literature. Yet, despite all the research that has been conducted to date, there has not been a systematic attempt to analyze critically the factors that lie behind the creation of successful business spin-offs from university research. In this book, a group of academic thought-leaders in the field of technology transfer examine a number of areas critical to the promotion of start-ups on campus. Through a series of case studies, they examine current policies, structures, program initiatives, and practices of twelve international universities and R&D institutes to develop a normative model of successful academic entrepreneurship, with the aim of helping other universities to enhance the quality of their commercialization programs on campus. This book is a valuable resource for university research administrators, technology commercialization officers, and researchers working on innovation, entrepreneurship, and technology.

THOMAS J. ALLEN is the Howard W. Johnson Professor of Management, Emeritus at the MIT Sloan School of Management. Professor Allen served as Deputy Dean of the Sloan School of Management at MIT from 1993 to 1998. His long-term research focuses on project management and factors influencing effective communication among engineers and scientists. Specializing in organizational psychology and management, he explores the relationship between organizational structure and behavior, the role of technological gatekeepers in technology transfer, and how a building's architectural layout influences communication. He is author of Managing the Flow of Technology: Technology Transfer and the Dissemination of Technological Information Within the R&D Organization. Cambridge, MA: MIT Press (1984).

RORY P. O'SHEA is a Visiting Assistant Professor in Innovation and Entrepreneurship at the MIT Sloan School of Management. He is also a faculty member at the Smurfit Graduate School of Business, University College Dublin. His research is primarily focused on the commercialization of academic research, with particular emphasis on the optimal organizational and financial mechanisms for transferring university-based intellectual property into knowledge-based start-ups. He has published in many of the leading technology and innovation management journals and is one of the most cited scholars in the field of academic entrepreneurship.

Building Technology Transfer within Research Universities

An Entrepreneurial Approach

Edited by

Thomas J. Allen

Sloan School of Management,
Massachusetts Institute of Technology

Rory P. O'Shea

Sloan School of Management, Massachusetts Institute
of Technology
Michael Smurfit Graduate School of Business, University College Dublin

CAMBRIDGE
UNIVERSITY PRESS

CAMBRIDGE
UNIVERSITY PRESS

University Printing House, Cambridge CB2 8BS, United Kingdom

Cambridge University Press is part of the University of Cambridge.

It furthers the University's mission by disseminating knowledge in the pursuit of education, learning and research at the highest international levels of excellence.

www.cambridge.org
Information on this title: www.cambridge.org/9780521876537

© Cambridge University Press 2014

First published 2014

A catalogue record for this publication is available from the British Library

Library of Congress Cataloguing in Publication data
Building Technology Transfer within Research Universities : An Entrepreneurial Approach / edited by Thomas J. Allen, Sloan School of Management, Massachusetts Institute of Technology; Rory O'Shea, Sloan School of Management, Massachusetts Institute of Technology.
    pages cm
Includes bibliographical references and index.
ISBN 978-0-521-87653-7 (hardback)
1. Academic-industrial collaboration – Case studies.   2. Technology transfer – Case studies.   I. Allen, Thomas J. (Thomas John), 1931–   II. O'Shea, Rory.
LC1085.B85   2014
378.1'035 – dc23   2014006634

ISBN 978-0-521-87653-7 Hardback

Contents

Figures

Tables

Contributors

Editors

THOMAS J. ALLEN is the Howard W. Johnson Professor of Management, Emeritus and Professor of Organizations Studies at the MIT Sloan School of Management. His long-term research focuses on project management in the pharmaceutical and aerospace industries. Specializing in organizational psychology and management, Allen explores the relationship between organizational structure and behavior, the role of technological gatekeepers in technology transfer, and how a building's layout influences communication. As a result of his research, MIT Sloan's new building features faculty office clusters designed to promote a broad range of interaction among faculty and graduate students. Allen is also a source for stories on international technology transfer, reward systems for technical professionals, and how organizational structure affects project performance.

RORY P. O'SHEA is a Visiting Assistant Professor in Innovation and Entrepreneurship at the MIT Sloan School of Management. He is also a faculty member at the Smurfit Graduate School of Business, University College Dublin, Ireland. His research is primarily focused on the commercialization of academic research, with particular emphasis on the optimal organizational and financial mechanisms for transferring university-based IP into knowledge-based start-ups. O'Shea has published in many of the leading technology and innovation management journals and is one of the most cited scholars in the field of academic entrepreneurship. He teaches courses in the areas of new venture finance, technology strategy, and entrepreneurship. Prior to entering academia, he worked as a management consultant in the Communications and High-Technology Industry Group with Accenture.

Contributors

PETRA ANDRIES is a senior researcher at the STI Indicator Research Center (Steunpunt O&O Indicators) at KU Leuven.

JANET BERCOVITZ is an associate professor in the Department of Business Administration at the University of Illinois.

SHIRI BREZNITZ is an assistant professor at the Munk School of Global Affairs at the University of Toronto.

BART CLARYSSE holds the Chair in Entrepreneurship at Imperial College London Business School.

HARVEEN CHUGH is a Lecturer in Entrepreneurship and Strategy at Royal Holloway, University of London.

KOENRAAD DEBACKERE is Professor of Managerial Economics, Strategy and Innovation at KU Leuven.

PIERRE DESROCHERS is an Associate Professor of Geography at the University of Toronto Mississauga.

HENRY ETZKOWITZ is a senior researcher at the H-STAR Institute, Stanford University and is also a Visiting Professor at the School of Management, Birkbeck College, London University and Edinburgh University Business School.

MARYANN FELDMAN is the S.K. Heninger Distinguished Professor in the Department of Public Policy at the University of North Carolina, Chapel Hill.

IGOR FILATOTCHEV is a Professor of Corporate Governance and Strategy at Cass Business School, City University London.

ELLIOT FISHMAN is the founder and President of Astrina, Inc. Previously, he was Industry Associate Professor at Stevens Institute of Technology's Howe School of Technology Management. He obtained a Ph.D. in the History of Science from the University of Pennsylvania.

CIARA FITZGERALD is a senior postdoctoral fellow at University College Cork.

YUEN-PING HO is a research manager at the NUS Entrepreneurship Centre.

MIRJAM KNOCKAERT is Assistant Professor of Innovation and Entrepreneurship, Vlerick Leuven Gent Management School.

CAROLYN LEE is the Director of Research for Public Programs at the University of California, San Diego.

TIMOTHY LENOIR is the Kimberly Jenkins Chair for New Technologies in Society at Duke University. He was previously Professor of History and Chair of the Program in History and Philosophy of Science at Stanford University.

PHILIPPE MUSTAR is Professor of Innovation, Entrepreneurship and Public Policy at the Centre de Sociologie de l'Innovation at the École Nationale Supérieure des Mines de Paris.

COLM O'GORMAN is Professor of Entrepreneurship at Dublin City University Business School.

EDWARD B. ROBERTS is the David Sarnoff Professor of the Management of Technology at the Sloan School of Management, MIT. He is Founder and Chair of the Martin Trust Center for MIT Entrepreneurship.

FRANK W. ROCHE is the Berber Family Professorship of Entrepreneurship Emeritus at University College Dublin.

DONALD SIEGEL is Dean of the School of Business and Professor of Management at the University at Albany, SUNY.

ANNETTE SINGH is a research fellow at the NUS Entrepreneurship Centre.

BART VAN LOOY is Professor of Managerial Economics, Strategy and Innovation at KU Leuven.

MARY WALSHOK is Associate Vice Chancellor–Extended Studies and Public Service and Adjunct Professor in the Department of Sociology at the University of California, San Diego.

POH-KAM WONG is a Professor at the School of Business and the Director for the NUS Entrepreneurship Centre.

MIKE WRIGHT is Professor of Entrepreneurship at Imperial College Business School.

CHUNYAN ZHOU is Professor of Innovation at Shenyang University. She currently serves as a Director of the International Institute of Triple Helix.

Foreword

For fifty years I have been actively engaged in researching, describing, and developing policies and programs for enhancing academic transfer from research and technology-based universities all over the world.[1,2,3,4,5] I have studied academic transfer in Belgium, England, and Japan, and especially in the United States, with a primary focus on the Massachusetts Institute of Technology. My experience, and that of my esteemed colleagues Tom Allen and MIT Sloan Visiting Assistant Professor Rory O'Shea, clearly shows that what works in one university does not necessarily work in another. The many different kinds of resources both within and near the university have a great influence on what can be invented, innovated, and commercialized by students, staff, faculty, and alumni. But resources are much less important than culture, attitude, habits, role models, and even rules and regulations. In a complex feedback system of many influences, it is difficult to determine the relative strength of each factor, but my impression is that students are far more important to entrepreneurial transfers than faculty, and passion is significantly more critical than intellectual property.

Let me focus on observations from our recent publication, written with Charles Eesley, "Entrepreneurial Impact: The Role of MIT," readily accessible from our MIT Martin Trust Center for Entrepreneurship website, http://entrepreneurship.mit.edu/impact.php. The history of

---

[1] *Entrepreneurs in High Technology: Lessons from MIT and Beyond* (New York: Oxford University Press, 1991).

[2] "Policies and structures for spinning off new companies from research and development organizations" (with D. Malone), *R&D Management*, Vol. 26, No. 1, January 1996, pp. 17–48.

[3] "Overcoming weak entrepreneurial infrastructures for academic spin-off ventures" (with J. J. Degroof), *Journal of Technology Transfer*, Vol. 29, No. 3/4, Summer 2004, pp. 327–352.

[4] "Technology transfer from Japanese universities to pharmaceutical companies" (with M. Fukuda), *International Journal of Technology Transfer and Commercialisation*, Vol. 3, No. 3, 2004, pp. 243–262.

[5] *Entrepreneurial Impact: The Role of MIT* (with C. Eesley) (Kansas City: Kauffman Foundation, February 2009).

MIT described in our report provides numerous and detailed examples of how one major institution achieved significant entrepreneurial impact over its first 150 years. Early examples of engagement of the academic with the outside world, including entrepreneurial actions by senior and respected faculty and university officials, did much to capture the attention of more junior faculty members, as well as students and alumni. Technology transfer and commercialization flourished as a result of strong leadership and a culture of entrepreneurship.

MIT's history also suggests that rules and regulations need to be carefully administered to avoid creating barriers to faculty participation in industrial consulting and, more vitally, to faculty initiatives to form new companies. At MIT, active engagement between the university and the industrial community was more than just tolerated, it was the essence of an institution devoted to binding mind and hand, "mens et manus." The lesson for advocates of entrepreneurship in other institutions is to create incentives rather than barriers, with guidelines that reduce the risk of conflict that might challenge the path to commercialization.

In contrast to many other universities in the United States and abroad, MIT adopted a "hands-off" approach toward entrepreneurial engagement. With no internal incubator or venture capital fund, MIT has sidestepped internal conflicts that have plagued other academic institutions that have tried to hurry the entrepreneurship process. MIT has had the advantage of a surrounding community that performs these functions as well as providing other support for new enterprises. Most institutions have to provide active help and at least some funding to get entrepreneurial ventures off the ground, dragging the university into issues around licensing rights. MIT demonstrates that it is far better if the university can create an open door policy that provides outside financiers and business partners with a level playing field of access to faculty and intellectual property licensing opportunities. The increased interaction between the outside and inside worlds will nourish competition among the various forms of human and financial sponsorship that want to attach themselves to university programs.

Rather than launching top-down programs, MIT has created independent faculty, student, and alumni initiatives, building vibrant ecosystems that help foster the formation and growth of new and young companies. This strategy has significantly increased the number of interested and involved participants, but it is a process that evolved slowly over time. Institutions looking for a quick-fix approach to becoming more entrepreneurial must be aware that the MIT approach takes patience and self-restraint.

Educational programs inside the university can be vital contributors to educating engineers, scientists, and managers in many aspects of new company formation and growth. The best scenario is when these classes cross internal university walls to bring together the technically educated with the managerially educated students (and faculty too, if possible) in joint project courses targeted toward real problem-solving, real product development, and real new business planning. Such programs require investment and a faculty to design, develop, and teach them. The problem is that effective and well-trained academics are still scarce in most entrepreneurship-related disciplines. Fortunately, successful practitioners are available everywhere and, as MIT history indicates, they are quite willing and enthusiastic about sharing their time and experiences with novice and would-be entrepreneurs.

The long list of MIT student clubs linked to entrepreneurship and described in our report shows many ways to encourage students to become more entrepreneurial. The MIT $100K annual business plan competition is the most vibrant and perhaps most effective of these clubs. Many new companies have formed as a result of the high-profile competition. Students at other universities can learn how to get involved in starting something similar by attending the MIT $100K Global Business Plan Workshop, which MIT students conduct annually in different cities around the world. Furthermore, the MIT one-week intensive Entrepreneurial Development Program, conducted in January by MIT's Entrepreneurship Center, may well be a helpful supplement for those institutions attempting to create an overall program of education and student activities that will encourage entrepreneurship.

Alumni activities and educational and student endeavors provide a strong basis for building an entrepreneurial ecosystem, but formal institutional activities are also critical. At MIT, changing the Technology Licensing Office into a proactive and supportive-of-entrepreneurship program office has made a significant contribution to technology transfer from the research labs. This change occurred twenty years ago and has had the time to mature in its effectiveness. More recently, MIT's creation of the Venture Mentoring Service, its own modest form of incubation with coaching by interested local alumni and other "neighbors," has generated a model of help that is clearly possible in other university communities. And targeted funding of faculty research with commercial potential, exemplified by the MIT Deshpande Center, can certainly be emulated elsewhere. In this unique organization, MIT has recruited outside entrepreneurs, venture capitalists, and intellectual property lawyers to join with internal senior faculty in judging the quality of research proposals, especially from a transfer potential perspective.

The Allen–O'Shea volume has assembled a wealth of experiences worldwide in this robust area of academic transfer. In reading and learning from these chapters, one will recognize that the university is far more than its present students and faculty and their intellectual resources. All research and technology-based universities have as their principal asset the well-educated population of alumni, many of whom are ready to apply and commercialize their accumulated learning from the university and their later work experiences to new market opportunities.

EDWARD B. ROBERTS
David Sarnoff Professor of Management of Technology
MIT Sloan School of Management
Founder and Chair, Martin Trust Center for MIT Entrepreneurship

Foreword

This book addresses the managerial and policy implications of an important trend: the rise in the rate of technology commercialization at universities. While many scholars have analyzed university patenting and licensing, some researchers have assessed the entrepreneurial dimension of university technology transfer (e.g., startup formation). According to the Association of University Technology Managers (AUTM), the number of startup firms at U.S. universities rose from 35 in 1980 to 705 in 2012. This increase in entrepreneurial activity at research universities has attracted considerable attention in the academic literature.[1,2]

This volume constitutes a major advance in the analysis of academic entrepreneurship. It contains numerous illuminating case studies of private and public research universities, based on economic, sociological, and organizational perspectives, yielding important new global evidence on how research universities have stimulated academic entrepreneurship. Based on this evidence, the editors draw important conclusions on how to enhance this activity. As an economist, I tend to focus on the importance of incentives, in terms of inducing academics to be entrepreneurial. However, the book reveals that cultural and organizational factors are also critical.

The volume will also be extremely useful to university research administrators, technology transfer office directors, and others involved in the commercialization of intellectual property, as many research institutions search for ways to maximize the output and effectiveness of technology transfer. Given that academic entrepreneurship is a relatively

---

[1] Some scholars use the university as the unit of analysis, while others focus on individual entrepreneurs (see Phan, Phillip and Siegel, Donald S. "The Effectiveness of University Technology Transfer: Lessons Learned, Managerial and Policy Implications, and the Road Forward," *Foundations and Trends in Entrepreneurship*, Vol. 2, No. 2, 2006, pp. 77–144).

[2] Siegel, Donald S., Veugelers, Reinhilde, and Wright, Mike. "Technology Transfer Offices and Commercialization of University Intellectual Property: Performance and Policy Implications," *Oxford Review of Economic Policy*, Vol. 23, No. 4, 2007, pp. 640–660.

new phenomenon for many research universities, there is considerable uncertainty among administrators regarding optimal organizational practices relating to academic entrepreneurship (e.g., incentives, legal issues, strategic objectives, and measurement and monitoring mechanisms). Finally, from a broader perspective, the book also provides important new evidence on the relationship between academic entrepreneurship and technology-based economic development. This is critical from a public policy perspective, since regions are increasingly viewing their local research universities as potential engines for economic growth.

DONALD SIEGEL
President of the Technology Transfer Society
Editor of the Journal of Technology Transfer

Acknowledgments

During our time writing this book, we were fortunate in having many good friends and colleagues whose help and support was central to its completion. The first mention goes to the authors who contributed to this edited volume. Each worked tirelessly to develop a chapter that is meaningful, relevant, and of high quality. We are grateful to them for their willingness to participate in this endeavor. We would also like to thank all of the people who gave of their time and talents to providing peer reviews of papers for this volume. We are indebted to them for their willingness to provide thoughtful and timely feedback.

We would also like to pay special tribute to our editors, Chris Harrison, Phil Good, and Claire Poole, for showing unparalleled faith in our ability to deliver and for providing us with wise counsel throughout the publication process. We also appreciate the wise counsel provided by Tim Bresnahan at the commencement of this project regarding coordinating a volume of this nature and magnitude.

We would like to pay special thanks to Ed Roberts, founder and chair of the Martin Trust Center for MIT Entrepreneurship, for being such a kind and supportive colleague to us over the years. His insights into the major theoretical and empirical threads surrounding the field of university-based entrepreneurship were truly valuable in the compilation of this volume. To Lita Nelsen, Director of MIT's Technology Licensing Office, who was always available to provide us with in-depth insight about the practice of technology transfer from an MIT perspective. Special thanks also to renowned technology academic entrepreneurs Charles Cooney, Nobel Laureate Philip Sharp, Robert Langer, and Anthony Sinskey for providing us with some very valuable insights about the context and nature of academic entrepreneurship at MIT.

Acknowledgements must also go to Bill Aulet, Paul Denning, Brian Fynes, Ken Morse, Fiona Murray, Ciarán Ó hÓgartaigh, Frank Roche, Don Siegel, Vangelis Souitaris, and Mike Wright for giving their support, directly or indirectly, in the production of this volume.

On a personal note, we would like to thank our families for their unwavering support and belief in us over the years, making this book all the more worthwhile and meaningful. We would not be where we are today without their love and support, so an everlasting note of appreciation.

We dedicate this book to William Barton Rogers[1] and Richard Cantillon,[2] whose scholarly insights have provided us with much inspiration.

THOMAS J. ALLEN AND RORY P. O'SHEA

[1] William Barton Rogers believed that MIT's work should advance and develop science and then apply that knowledge to world problems. His vision for MIT was to engage with the community for the advancement and development of science and its application to industry, the arts, agriculture, and commerce.

[2] In his *Essai sur la nature du commerce en general* (1732), Richard Cantillon was credited with giving the concept of entrepreneurship a central role in economics. Cantillon held that much of the economic exchange of the State is conducted by the medium of entrepreneurs.

1   Introduction

Thomas J. Allen and Rory P. O'Shea

The increasing challenge of competing in a global economic context is forcing regions to reconsider and often revise their approaches to economic development. With knowledge now the fundamental basis of competitive advantage, regional economic development agencies are looking for ways to create and develop new and innovative technology-based start-ups. The growing acceptance of the importance of university spin-off activity to national economies has been reflected in burgeoning policy and research publications seeking to identify the drivers of spin-off activity in research universities. Interest in the spin-off phenomenon among national policy makers and university heads has been sparked largely by recognition of the emergence of the need to generate knowledge-based jobs.

Technology transfer is an important driver in innovation and the creation of sustainable growth. According to the National Science Foundation, U.S. federal government agencies allocated more than $32 billion annually to university researchers around the country to conduct scientific research.[1,2] This continuing investment expands human knowledge and helps to educate the next generation of science and technology leaders. Furthermore, this research can also have a big impact on the "discovery of innovation" element of the commercialization process (Klofsten and Jones Evans 2000; Murray 2004; Owen-Smith and Powell 2004). Mansfield has also highlighted the central role of university innovation in U.S. productivity growth. In a random sample of seventy-six major American firms in seven manufacturing industries, Mansfield (1991) investigated the extent to which technological innovations are based on

---

[1] Technology transfer is defined as "the process of transferring scientific findings from one organization to another for the purpose of further development and commercialization." (AUTM 2013).

[2] The federal government provided $32.6 billion (59%) of the $54.9 billion of academic spending on S&E R&D in FY (academic) 2009. *Sources:* National Science Foundation, National Center for Science and Engineering Statistics, Survey of Research and Development Expenditures at Universities and Colleges.

Table 1.1: *Number of university spin-offs generated in the United States (2005–2011: AUTM)*

Year	No. of spin-offs
2011	670
2010	651
2009	596
2008	595
2007	555
2006	553
2005	628

academic research. He found that about one-tenth of the new products and processes commercialized between 1975 and 1985 in some high tech industries could not have been developed without academic research.

In the United States, spin-off activity has been on an upward trajectory over the past decade. AUTM survey figures show that there has been modest growth in U.S. start-ups generated from intellectual property. The survey reveals that university start-up activity has risen from just over 628 companies in 2005 to over 670 university spin-offs in 2011 (see Table 1.1).

According to a longitudinal study of spin-off performance of U.S. universities conducted by O'Shea *et al.* (2005), the Massachusetts Institute of Technology achieved the highest ranking for all universities in the United States between 1980 and 2001, while the University of California system and Stanford University achieved second and third highest ranking, respectively, over the same period (see Table 1.2).[3] However, O'Shea *et al.* also found that 80 percent of universities spun off less than two companies in any given year over this period, despite attracting large investment from both federal and industry sources. This mean value also masks a highly skewed distribution in the data in which the most productive university, MIT, spawned 31 spin-offs in one year alone (O'Shea *et al.* 2005).

Given the growing dissatisfaction with universities' performance in commercialization, many policy makers are now investigating ways in which universities can improve their IP strategy.[4] For many institutions,

---

[3] O'Shea, Rory P., Allen, Thomas J., Chevalier, Arnaud, and Roche, Frank (2005), Entrepreneurial orientation, technology transfer and spinoff performance of U.S. universities. *Research Policy*, 34(7), pp. 994–1009.

[4] In October 2011, President Obama released a Presidential Memorandum to agencies, titled Accelerating Technology Transfer and Commercialization of Federal Research in Support of High Growth Businesses. The memorandum required agencies that

Table 1.2: *Spin-off rankings of top ten U.S. universities*

Rank 1995–2001	University	No. of spin-offs 1995–2001
1	Massachusetts Institute of Technology	132
2	University of California system	118
3	Stanford University	73
4	California Institute of Technology	67
5	University of Washington	51
6	University of Minnesota	49
7	University of Michigan	42
8	University of Georgia	41
9	University of Utah	40
10	Johns Hopkins University	35

Source: O'Shea *et al.* (2005).

the path to enhanced start-up creation has proved difficult. Successful spin-offs are difficult to initiate, if only because of our inability to make sense of the framework conditions necessary to provide assistance to universities in creating support structures, policies, and interventions to improve start-up success rates (Roberts and Malone 1996). There remains a disconnect between what researchers know about the nature of spin-off behavior and what practitioners need to know to improve the formation rates of new technology companies.[5] In the academic literature there are many models that seek to explain spin-off activity from institutions of higher education. Many of these studies have neither been effective in explaining spin-off behavior nor been particularly suited to the needs of institutional officials who seek to stimulate spin-off activity on campus. A recurring criticism is the narrow and process-driven interpretation of the technology transfer office (TTO), which establishes the primary objective of technology transfer as one of revenue generation and the primary function of the TTO as the management of university

conducted intramural research to improve their technology transfer results by "establish[ing] goals and measure performance, streamlin[ing] administrative processes, and facilitate[ing] local and regional partnerships in order to accelerate technology transfer and support private sector commercialization." Other important reports published in relation to academic commercialization included National Research Council, Managing University Intellectual Property in the Public Interest (2010); and Wendy H. Schacht, The Bayh–Dole Act: Selected Issues in Patent Policy and the Commercialization of Technology, Congressional Research Service, March 16, 2012.

[5] In June 2012, the House Committee on Science, Space, and Technology's Sub Committee on Technology and Innovation held a hearing entitled "Best Practices in Transforming Research into Innovation: Creative Approaches to the Bayh Dole Act." The session was held to learn about different approaches universities are taking in order to accelerate the transfer of results of federally-funded research to the private sector.

intellectual property rights. This, in turn, promotes short-term revenue maximization objectives and practices that neither reflect nor enhance the rich and diverse nature of university–industry collaboration (Kenney and Patton 2009; Litan *et al.* 2007; Perkmann *et al.* 2013). Therefore, the challenge lies in identifying and replicating the processes that facilitate swift movement of technology from research laboratories to the front line of industry (Allen 1984; Phan and Siegel 2006). With increasing pressure on universities to generate economic returns from government research support, policy makers and academics must find ways to stimulate technology-based entrepreneurship in universities. This book represents an effort to address this challenge and bridge the gap between research and the entrepreneurial world.

The purpose of the volume is to attempt to coordinate multiple perspectives on the issue of university spin-off creation, thereby highlighting the complexity of the phenomenon. By drawing from a multiplicity of frameworks, the aim of the book is to explore different international institutional settings and show how universities engender university-wide entrepreneurship on campus. We aim to uncover the attributes of successful spin-off programs in relation to regional context. Ultimately, we want to provide answers to the difficult questions administrators and policy makers ask about enhancing university start-up activity. The volume shares the experiences of twelve leading international research universities and R&D institutes in selected countries around the globe that have developed, or are in the process of developing, successful spin-off strategies to improve their start-up rates on campus. We aim to provide an international comparison of approaches adopted by these universities to maximize the dynamics of start-up activity. We also attempt to draw reasoned conclusions on the effectiveness of the approaches to spin-off programs and to establish what lessons might be transferable across the institutional contexts to inform approaches in this area.

This book focuses on three distinct but related goals. First, research has suggested that university spin-offs are an important aspect of regional economic development, yet scholars still debate the appropriate policies and operational structures to facilitate the creation of these ventures. A central limitation of extant spin-off literature is its failure to develop a framework to make sense of what appear to be a multitude of different commercialization approaches and their associated impacts. To address this matter, we attempt to give order to the growing body of research on spin-off research by focusing on the "individual," "organizational," "institutional," and "environmental" dimensions of spin-off behavior. Second, this work investigates what can be done to increase start-up formation from "leading" research and "mid-range" universities. We argue that a systemic and contingent approach should be undertaken to understand the full dynamics of academic entrepreneurship on campus. This volume builds on the principles of contingency theory, which suggest that different organizational arrangements are valid for different strategy conditions and that increased effectiveness can be attributed to internal consistency or fit among the pattern of relevant contextual, structural, and strategic factors. Third, in order to analyze university contributions to economic development, the study examines universities' technology transfer policies, practices, and structures and their associated economic development impact. The study examines how a university defines itself as part of a region and the impact of the local context on spin-off activity. By examining existing theories and analyzing university relationships with both government and industry, we explore ways in which universities contribute to regional economic development.

Structure of the book

The twelve university-specific studies in this volume begin with U.S.-based studies and then turn to studies based in Europe and Asia. In Chapter 14, the book also analyzes the commercialization structures of two university-affiliated technology development institutes in France and Belgium to reflect the specific institutional context of continental Europe with regard to the development and professionalization of R&D centers. The forewords for this book were authored by Professor Ed Roberts and Professor Don Siegel. Ed is the David Sarnoff Professor of Management of Technology at the MIT Sloan School of Management and Chair of the MIT Entrepreneurship Center. Ed is the author of the seminal technology entrepreneurship book *Entrepreneurs in High Technology* (Oxford University Press, 1991), and this work has been an inspiration to the field ever since. Don currently serves as the President of the Technology Transfer Society and is also editor of the *Journal of Technology Transfer*.

We selected this particular group of universities in part to represent the international diversity of research institutions. Some are large private research universities; others are public in scope and therefore are diverse in terms of mission, selectivity, size, and location. The primary purpose of the project was to discover what a diverse range of institutions across the globe do to promote spin-off success, so that other universities that aspire to enhance the quality of entrepreneurship culture and programs might learn from their example. It is also worth noting that we do not claim that all of these institutions are the "best" or the most "entrepreneurially effective" in the world. At the same time, their performance is noteworthy, and they offer many examples of promising practices that could be adapted and used productively at other institutions.

Book chapters

In Chapter 2, Etzkowitz reviews the concept of the entrepreneurial university, the various contextual issues that have shaped the nature of university start-up activity to date, and the ways universities have responded to these challenges. Etzkowitz traces the historical development of academic entrepreneurship within academic institutions and the changing role of universities in developing regional economies. He outlines how universities are becoming increasingly central players in regional and national economic development. He also postulates that academics are increasingly embracing a university–industry "engagement" model, in which firm formation as a means of knowledge transfer and contribution to society is becoming more of an accepted norm internationally.

In Chapter 3, O'Shea, Fitzgerald, Chugh, and Allen develop and integrate differing research perspectives on academic entrepreneurship to move toward a conceptualization of spin-off behavior. The chapter highlights four major streams of work that influence the rate of spin-off activity: (1) the academic's reasons for engaging in entrepreneurial activity (individual characteristics studies); (2) the attributes of universities, such as human capital, commercial resources, and institutional activities (organizationally focused studies); (3) the broader social context of the university, including the barriers or deterrents to spin-offs (institutional and cultural studies); (4) the external characteristics such as regional infrastructure that impact spin-off activity (external environment studies). In addition, the chapter incorporates two further streams of research that deal with (5) the development and performance of spin-offs and (6) the spillover effect of spin-offs on the regional economy. The authors argue that recent studies on university entrepreneurship focusing on one or the other of these dimensions have, until now, largely remained separated and ignorant of one another. As such, the literature has remained blind to some key aspects of understanding that can only be brought to the fore if the different theoretical explanations are combined.

Chapter 4, by Fishman, O'Shea, and Allen, explores the dynamic "ecosystem" factors that contribute to the success of MIT as an entrepreneurial university. The chapter explains how events within an institution can shape the process of spin-off behavior within that institution, and how external forces impacted on the institution's orientation.

In particular, the chapter reveals the importance of financial and human capital endowments specific to MIT, the historical mission of the university, and the role of key academic entrepreneurs and academic leaders in harnessing the entrepreneurial spirit within the university. The chapter also argues that spin-off success needs to be understood in the context of the regional environment. The chapter concludes that university administrators and academics can learn from the case of MIT, but efforts at transposing or replicating single elements of MIT's model may only have limited success given the interrelated nature of the drivers of spin-off activity. The chapter makes a theoretical contribution to our understanding of the self-reinforcing path-dependent processes associated with commercialization policies and activity.

Chapter 5, by Tim Lenoir, analyzes Stanford University's role in fostering both entrepreneurial activity and technical innovation at the university. Lenoir argues that Stanford has been shaped as an incubator of entrepreneurial activity largely by positioning itself as a premier research institution in a number of fields, several of which have been critical to the economy. According to the author, this "steeples of excellence" strategy of attracting and retaining the best scientific and engineering talent engaging in frontier research – as opposed to applied science – was an essential factor that contributed to the rise of entrepreneurial science at Stanford. However, while the author maintains that pursuing excellence in research is a necessary condition for entrepreneurial success, it was Stanford's ability to embed an institutional culture of entrepreneurship across campus that gave rise to entrepreneurial success within the university. The paper also documents the pivotal role that Stanford's Provost, Frederick Terman, played in setting out the economic development mission of the university to influence local and regional development.

Chapter 6, by Walshok and Lee, investigates the role of the University of California, San Diego in the creation of industrial clusters. The chapter argues that while it was essential to have top-quality academics at the university, the dynamic relationship between the entrepreneurial science community at the university and science-based entrepreneurship in the region provided a central catalyst for the emergence of high start-up activity from the university. According to the authors, having a world-class research university alone is not sufficient; there need to be institutional mechanisms that support enterprise creation both within the university and in the surrounding local community.

Chapter 7, by Feldman, Desrochers, and Bercovitz, reviews the original "hands-off" inventor ownership patent policies of Johns Hopkins University and assesses their role in promoting knowledge transfer at the university prior to the Bayh–Dole Act academic entrepreneurship.[6] From examining the Johns Hopkins and CellPro patent infringement case, the authors highlight the consequences of applying a more aggressive academic stance toward patenting and revenue generation in the context of the Bayh–Dole statute of 1980. By drawing from the Dalkon Shield case and other examples, the authors also reveal the potential reputational risks that are associated with academic institutions looking to cash in on intellectual property rights. This chapter has important implications for universities looking to devise commercialization policies.

Chapter 8, by Breznitz, describes the role of Yale University in the development of the biotechnology cluster in the New Haven region of Connecticut. Although Yale is one of the strongest universities in life sciences in the United States, its traditionally passive attitude toward the commercialization of academic research was shown to be an obstacle for transferring technologies into the region. However, after the arrival of President Richard C. Levin in the mid-1990s, the university undertook changes in personnel and structures at the Technology Transfer Office, hiring as director a senior manager from a major pharmaceutical company, to promote further biotechnology-based industrial growth in the region. Yale's approach was to implement a number of "top-down" initiatives in order to create a more entrepreneurially driven environment at the university. The author assesses the effect of these change strategies on academic commercialization at the university. In its conclusion, the chapter looks at how universities can have an important impact on local industrial and economic development.

Chapter 9, by O'Gorman and Roche, considers the commercialization programs of University College Dublin, an ambitious research university undergoing change in its technology transfer operations. They reflect on the interventions and structures that have been instituted to engender academic entrepreneurship on campus and consider the effectiveness of the introduction of "top-down" university programs, as well as a number of government interventions undertaken to accelerate the commercialization process. The authors assert that organizational interventions are a useful strategy that, when taken in concert with other multilevel government-led initiatives, can influence spin-off behavior.

Chapter 10, by Wright and Filatotchev, examines a number of entrepreneurship support mechanisms initiated by Kings College London in its drive to accelerate academic entrepreneurship on campus. The

[6] The Bayh–Dole Act (P.L. 96–517, Patent and Trademark Act Amendments of 1980) created a uniform patent policy among the many U.S. government agencies funding research. As a result of this law, universities retain ownership to inventions made under federally funded research. In return, universities are expected to file for patent protection and to ensure commercialization upon licensing.

authors highlight the range of financial and training supports employed by the university, including third-party seed funding and incubator alliances, to enable inventions to be commercialized successfully via start-up companies. The chapter also highlights the multifaceted nature of partnerships that KCL has undertaken with industry and government to enhance academic entrepreneurship on campus.

Chapter 11, by Andries, Van Looy, and Debackere, explores the complex effect of complementary university incubation processes on spin-off company formation and development. Their paper argues that universities need to move beyond providing incentive mechanisms and physical facilities, in order to foster the development of spin-offs. Drawing from the case of KU Leuven, the authors demonstrate how spin-off incubators can develop appropriate support processes that allow new ventures to experiment with and adapt their business models, while transforming their technology platforms into viable and sustainable market value propositions.

Chapter 12, by Wong, Ho, and Singh, identifies the key roles that research-intensive universities in newly industrialized regions need to play to contribute effectively to the entrepreneurial development of their economies. The chapter then analyzes how the National University of Singapore (NUS), the leading university in Singapore, adopted an integrated "global knowledge enterprise" model that involves coordination by a new organizational vehicle called NUS Enterprise. The chapter explores a number of innovative programs launched by NUS Enterprise and shows how they fit together to achieve synergies. It also discusses the critical factors necessary for such an integrated model to be successfully implemented and draws relevant lessons for universities in other newly industrialized economies facing similar challenges.

Chapter 13, by Zhou, explores how a midrange research university in China's Liaoning Province, Northeastern University, is attempting to play an increasing role in the formation of regional industries and technological innovation. The study highlights the role government can play in becoming a "regional innovation organizer" where university–industry cooperation has traditionally been weak. The chapter also highlights how a "government-pulled triple helix" made it easier to achieve large-scale innovation projects. The study also illustrates how a university, by specializing in research fields in which it holds a comparative advantage, can play an important role in kickstarting the economic development of a region.

Chapter 14, by Knockaert, Clarysse, and Mustar, compares and contrasts the commercialization structures and formal policies of two leading independent research and development institutes in Europe, IMEC and INRIA. While the central focus of the analysis is on the research institutes (i.e., rather than specifically universities), the chapter provides a useful insight as to how two leading research and development institutes in Belgium and France have developed structures and policies to help overcome the "Valley of Death" issues that entrepreneurs face in the commercialization of academic research.

The final chapter addresses the central question of what can be done to improve spin-off activity within active research universities. Drawing from previous chapters in this volume, the editors develop a "spin-off performance model" that outlines five central strategies that can be employed to promote academic entrepreneurship on campus. Using this model, the authors suggest that if academic entrepreneurship is to emerge successfully within university campuses, there is a need for policy makers to recognize that a comprehensive systems approach to the identification, protection, and commercialization of university intellectual property must be adopted. Recommendations for enhanced practices and spin-off interventions are also explained and reviewed in this chapter.

References

Allen, T.J. (1984). *Managing the Flow of Technology: Technology Transfer and the Dissemination of Technological Information within the R&D Organization.* Cambridge, MA: MIT Press.

Association of University Technology Managers. What is technology transfer? Retrieved July 2013, from http://www.autm.net/What_Is_Tech_Transfer.htm.

Bayh–Dole Act. (1980). PL 96-517, Patent and Trademark Act Amendments of 1980.

Kenney, M., and Patton, D. (2009). Reconsidering the Bayh-Dole Act and the current university invention ownership model. *Research Policy*, 38(9),1407–1422.

Klofsten, M. and Jones-Evans, D. (2000). Comparing academic entrepreneurship in Europe – The case of Sweden and Ireland. *Small Business Economics*, 14, 299–309.

Litan, R.E., Mitchell, L., and Reedy, E.J. (2008). Commercializing university innovations: Alternative approaches in A. Jaffe, J. Lerner, and S. Stern 2008. *Innovation Policy and the Economy* (eds), National Bureau of Economic Research Inc, pp. 31–57.

Mansfield, Edwin. (1991). Academic research and industrial innovation. *Research Policy*, 20(1), 1–12.

Murray, F. (2004). The role of academic inventors in entrepreneurial firms: sharing the laboratory life. *Research Policy*, 33(4), 643–659.

National Research Council (NRC). (2010). *Improving University Management of Intellectual Property in the Public Interest.* Washington, DC: The National Academies Press.

O'Shea, R.P., Allen, T.J., Chevalier, A., and Roche F. (2005). Entrepreneurial orientation, technology transfer and spinoff performance of U.S. universities. *Research Policy*, 34, 994–1009.

Owen-Smith, J., and Powell, W.W. (2004). Knowledge networks as channels and conduits: The effects of spillovers in the Boston biotechnology community. *Organization Science*, 15(1), 5–21.

Perkmann, M., Tartari V., McKelvey, M., *et al.* (2013). Academic engagement and commercialisation: A review of the literature on university–industry relations. *Research Policy*, 42(2), 423–442.

Phan, Phillip and Siegel, Donald S. (2006). The effectiveness of university technology transfer. *Foundations and Trends in Entrepreneurship*, 2(2). Available at SSRN: http://ssrn.com/abstract=1629298.

Roberts, Edward B. and Malone, Denis E. (1996). Policies and Structures for Spinning Off New Companies from Research and Development Organizations. *R&D Management*, 26, 17–48.

Rothaermel, Frank T., Agung, Shanti D., and Jiang, Lin. (2007). University entrepreneurship: A taxonomy of the literature. *Industrial and Corporate Change*, 16(4), 691–791.

Schacht, Wendy (2012). The Bayh Dole Act: Selected Issues in Patent Policy and the Commercialization of Technology. Congressional Research Service, March 16, 2012.

2 The second academic revolution: The rise of the entrepreneurial university and impetuses to firm foundation

Henry Etzkowitz

A significant number of academic scientists have broadened their professional interests from contributing to the literature to making their research the basis of a firm. These scientists have taken some or all of the steps necessary to start scientific firms by writing business plans, raising funds, leasing space, recruiting staff, etc. (Blumenthal *et al.* 1986a; Krimsky *et al.* 1991). For example, in the biology department at MIT, where surveys identified half the faculty as industrially involved in the late 1980s, an informant could identify only one department member as uninvolved at the time. The formation of firms out of research activities occurred in the late nineteenth century at Harvard, as well as MIT, in the fields of industrial consulting and scientific instrumentation (Shimshoni 1970). However, these commercial entities were viewed as anomalies rather than as a normal outcome of academic research. What is new in the present situation is that many academic scientists no longer believe in the necessity of an isolated "ivory tower" for the working out of the logic of scientific discovery.

A faculty member at Stanford University, in the mid-1980s, reviewed his colleagues' activities: "In psychiatry there are a lot of people interested in the chemistry of the nervous system and two of them have gone off to form their own company." Another Stanford professor, during the same period, estimated that "In electrical engineering about every third student starts his own company. In our computer science department it's starting as well. There is a change in student behavior and faculty acceptance because the faculty are involved in companies and interacting a lot with companies and the attitude is 'we talk to them, we teach them . . . why not try it?'"

Although this is still a limited phenomenon, except in a relatively few science and engineering departments where senior entrepreneurial faculty provide role models for their junior colleagues, the rising academic generation, many of whom have received some entrepreneurial education

as part of their graduate training, is expected to be even more amenable
to entrepreneurial pursuits. The interest in firm formation is on the rise
among Ph.D. candidates, an increasing number of whom have concluded
that organizing or joining a start-up is their best chance for a job in an era
when the availability of academic positions at a good research university
is declining (Etzkowitz 2013a). Once confined to a specialized academic
sector within the land-grant tradition, firm formation has now spread to
a broad range of universities: public and private, elite and nonelite. In
recent years, the phenomenon has become so pervasive in the biological
sciences at the University of California, San Diego that one of the very
few faculty members who had not become involved asked the director of
the University's Technology Transfer Office for advice on how to emulate
his colleagues. Indeed, associations of technology transfer professionals
have developed metrics to track this growing phenomenon and its contribution to regional development (Etzkowitz and Stevens 1995). Firm
formation is the tip of the iceberg of a broader phenomenon: the trans-
lation of academic research into economic activity through a variety of
means, such as consultation and licensing to existing firms. We focus on
the start-up phenomenon in this chapter as a key mechanism for closing
the loop between university and industry by packaging inventions in an
independent economic unit focused on innovation.

The second academic revolution

How has the university – an innovative twelfth-century collective of mas-
ters and students dedicated to passing on knowledge largely retrieved
from ancient Greece and Rome – become entrepreneurial with a remit
for economic and social development in the early twenty-first century?
We identify a series of transformations, each incorporating the previous
academic mode into a relatively compatible synthesis of existing and new
tasks: teaching and the preservation of knowledge, research and the creation of new knowledge, economic development and regional renewal.
Thus, the teaching college was incorporated into the research university
even as the research university provides a base for the entrepreneurial
university to take off from.

The acceptance of dualisms, such as patents vs. publication and basic
vs. applied research goals, was the surface expression of a theory of knowledge based on an underlying dichotomy that placed scientific advance,
i.e., development of theory, in opposition to technological advance.
Heretofore, in the hiatus between scientific discovery and application,
industry was expected to have its scientists and engineers pursue applied
research and product development. The model of separate spheres and

technology transfer across strongly defined boundaries is still common-place. However, academic scientists are often eager and willing to marry the two activities, nominally carrying out one in their academic laborato-ries and the other in firms with which they maintain close relationships.

The supersession of univalent knowledge, arising either from tradi-tional disciplines or from the context of application, has organizational consequences. During the past two decades, a broad range of universities, both private and public, have established one or more of the following mechanisms for academic–industrial relations: offices to manage patent-ing and licensing of technology; interdisciplinary research centers with industrial participation; and research parks and incubator facilities. In addition, many schools have established procedures for managing poten-tial conflicts of interest and commitment as faculty members play dual roles on both sides of the academic and industrial divide.

Thus, technology transfer is a two-way flow from university to industry and vice versa, with different degrees and forms of academic involvement:

1. the product originates in the university but its development is under-taken by an existing firm;
2. the commercial product originates outside of the university, with aca-demic knowledge utilized to improve the product; or
3. the university is the source of the commercial product and the aca-demic inventor becomes directly involved in its commercialization through the establishment of a new company.

As faculty members take on this new entrepreneurial role, they inte-grate it with their previous academic roles, just as their predecessors in the late nineteenth century combined research with teaching. In Sweden, on the other hand, when a research mission was introduced by law in 1919, a separate class of lecturers was created to allow profes-sors to concentrate on research. Given this model of separation, Swedish academics have experienced additional levels of difficulty in undertaking firm formation and other technology transfer activities as part of the uni-versity's Third Mission, established by law in 1994. Nevertheless, there is a gradual transition to drawing the various academic roles together in a single position in European universities as the model of separation is phased out. In the interim, students are trained to take the role of the entrepreneur, with faculty members as advisors to firms that emerge out of a research group. On the other hand, students increasingly take the entrepreneurial role in the United States as opportunities expand from biotechnology to computer science. A balance between separation and integration of roles, simultaneously and ad seriatim, is emerging both in the United States and in Europe as entrepreneurial tasks become an overlay on research and teaching.

Polyvalent knowledge

The first step toward an entrepreneurial university is realization that knowledge is polyvalent and that pursuit of the economic potential of research can be conducted simultaneously with its advancement. The transition from a research to an entrepreneurial university usually takes place through controversies over the conduct of the new activity, typically formulated in terms of a conflict of interest between different roles. Indeed, the acceptance of dual and then triple roles for the professor as teacher, researcher, and entrepreneur is the basis for the institutionalization of a new academic format based not only on an integration of roles but also on knowledge having simultaneous theoretical and practical consequences. Indeed, an integrated theory of knowledge, superseding Pasteur's Quadrant as a subsidiary format, is beginning to take hold. Thus, in addition to practical implications arising out of academic research and theoretical implications out of industrial research, there is also the coproduction of theoretical and practical knowledge.

If the disjuncture between theory and invention is accepted, the emergence of entrepreneurial science is an anomaly. Entrepreneurial scientists' research is typically at the frontiers of science and leads to theoretical and methodological advances as well as invention of devices. These activities involve sectors of the university, such as basic science departments, that heretofore, in principle, limited their involvement with industry. One explanation for the emergence of entrepreneurial science is that academic scientists, such as the founders of biotechnology firms in the late 1970s and early 1980s, suddenly awakened to the financial opportunities emanating from their research. Implicit in this explanation is the notion that there were recent scientific advances in molecular biology, polymers, and materials science that could be developed quickly as sources of profit. However, opportunities for commercial utilization of scientific research were often available to scientists in the past, such as the Curies, Marie and Pierre, and Louis Pasteur, who did not believe in crossing the boundary between science and business themselves, even though they evinced a strong interest in the practical implications of their findings.

Recognition of congruence between basic research and invention vitiates the ideological separation of these spheres of activity. Until quite recently, most academic scientists assumed that the advancement of knowledge was synonymous with theoretical innovation. Recent examples of research in which theoretical advances have occurred in tandem with the invention of devices or innovations in methodology in transistors/semiconductors, superconductivity, and genetic engineering have called into question the assumption of a one-way flow from basic to applied research to industrial innovation (Gibbons *et al.* 1994).

The reworking of boundaries around institutions undergoing changes in their mission occurs through a "game of legitimization." One strategy is to conflate new purposes with old ones to show that they are in accord. For example, universities legitimize entrepreneurial activities by aligning them with accepted functions such as research and service. In addition, new identifications of compatibility with other institutions are made as they move closer together. Thus, universities and corporations are found to share a common interest in putting knowledge to use (Langfitt *et al.* 1989).

The first academic revolution

The basis for the confluence of teaching and research is that students in training as researchers are highly productive of new ideas since they are not constrained by old paradigms. Moreover, as researchers in training, they are more cost-effective than the full-time employees found in the institute mode. In addition, the flow-through of students in university research groups ensures that new ideas will be generated continuously, since the stasis that tends to take place in a stable government or industry group is obviated in academia, given the fundamental nature of the university as an educational enterprise with students as temporary members who are to be sent on into the larger society after meeting specified criteria for achievement.

The research university was institutionalized from the mid- to late nineteenth century as dual professorial roles – teacher and researcher – that were initially believed to be in conflict but were reinterpreted and found to be mutually supportive of each other. The transition evoked controversy, typically formulated as a conflict of interest or obligation between the new and old modes. Complaints by traditional educators at Stanford, for example, that their research-oriented colleagues were abandoning academic ideals were dismissed by David Starr Jordan, the university's president, who strongly supported the new research mission. The transition is never complete. Inherent tensions persist and periodically reemerge when students, their parents, and legislators perceive that the pendulum has swung too far from education. Nevertheless, teaching and research, combined in a single organization, have been found to be more productive that the alternative of placing researchers in institutes without educational functions, leaving tertiary education to teaching universities.

The origins of the second revolution

The entrepreneurial university derived from a potential inherent in the introduction of research as an academic mission. As soon as secure methodologies were developed, for example, in organic chemistry, it was possible to train larger groups of students. At this point it made sense to incorporate science into an educational setting and the teaching lab, much as we know it today, was invented by Justus Liebig at the University of Giessen. Once research was systematically organized, even as a training enterprise, results were achieved that had practical uses. The question of what do with these results was addressed in the early days by academic scientists such as Liebig who founded firms to commercialize their research. Indeed, one of these early firms, Liebig's Extract, is still on the market with a product that would be conceptualized as a "functional food." Another of Liebig's enterprises, an artificial fertilizer firm, failed, as the concept on which it was based was proved wrong. Prior to scientific disconfirmation, farmers found that the "fertilizer" simply had no effect on their crops.

Firm formation was an anomaly in the late nineteenth century. Academic entrepreneurship, which primarily meant consultation at the time, was submerged by the rise of an ideology of pure research that abjured academics not only from concern with the uses of their research, but from using their academic skills to evaluate industrial processes and natural resources. Ironically, the leading proponent of an ideology of pure science had been an industrial consultant himself. Nevertheless, as industrialists such as John D. Rockefeller gave some of their fortunes to establish universities, there was a concern that control would inevitably follow provision of resources.

A strong need arose to strengthen the boundaries between the university and the external world, even as the university was emerging as a large-scale institution in its own right. An ideology of pure research emerged and an enhanced concept of academic freedom developed as organizations found themselves having to defend faculty members under attack for their views. Indeed, in a few highly publicized cases, faculty members were fired for expressing politically unpopular opinions. These firings usually occurred within the academy, perhaps out of fear of offending funders rather than from direct pressures. Nevertheless, an alternative entrepreneurial science tradition flourished in a few fields and in specialized universities, such as the land grant schools. The mechanisms of academic technology transfer, invented at MIT in the early twentieth century were transferred to Stanford, where they also, in part, had independent origins, and, from there, flowed into other liberal arts universities.

The rise of an academic entrepreneurial culture

Without sufficient finance to establish research institutes on the German model in the mid-nineteenth century, research grew up in U.S. universities on a piecemeal basis, using small amounts of funding that allowed professors to hire students and gain release time from their primary task of teaching. An entrepreneurial dynamic was built into the U.S. academic research system, later reinforced by foundation and then government funding, that made individual faculty members, both senior and junior, responsible for obtaining their own research support. As professors were successful in this effort, the number of people working with them (graduate students, undergraduates, technicians, etc.) increased. As faculty members became research managers, responsible for fundraising, personnel management, and other organizational tasks, research groups took on some the attributes of a small business or "quasi firm," save for the profit motive. Thus, when opportunities for the commercialization of research appeared, it was not a great leap for professors to move from one form of entrepreneurship to another.

The entrepreneurial nature of the U.S. academic research system helps explain why faculty entrepreneurs typically feel it is not a great leap from an on-campus research group to an off-campus firm. The U.S. format, in which each professor is responsible for raising his or her own research funds, originated in the late nineteenth century with the breakdown of the attempt to import the German chair system into the United States. There were insufficient funds to support such a system in the sciences. Even at Harvard, where a chemistry lab was built for Eben Horsford, funds to heat the building, hire assistants, and purchase chemicals were lacking. A hierarchical system of docents under the control of senior professors at the University of Chicago and Johns Hopkins was soon transformed into a professorial ladder where even assistant professors, at the first step, had the right to set their own research directions. The right to do research was dependent upon interest and the ability to find research support. For those professors who undertook to become researchers, especially in the sciences, where resources were increasingly a prerequisite for establishing laboratories to carry out serious investigation, the ability to raise funds became part of the professorial role.

There is an entrepreneurial dynamic built into the U.S. research funding system, based on the premise that faculty have the primary responsibility for obtaining their own research funds. As a faculty member described the system, "It's amazing how much being a professor is like running a small business. The system forces you to be very entrepreneurial because everything is driven by financing your group."

At least until a start-up markets its product or is able to attract funding from conventional financial sources, the focus of funding efforts is typically on a panoply of federal and state programs that are themselves derived from the research funding model and its peer review procedures. As a faculty entrepreneur viewed the situation, "What is the difference between financing a research group on campus and financing a research group off campus? You have a lot more options off campus but if you go the federal government proposal route, it's really very similar."

Entrepreneurial scientist: A new professorial role

An entrepreneurial culture within the university encourages faculty to look at their research results from a dual perspective: (1) a traditional research perspective in which publishable contributions to the literature are entered into the "cycle of credibility" (Latour and Woolgar 1979) and (2) an entrepreneurial perspective in which results are scanned for their commercial as well as their intellectual potential.

A public research university that we studied experienced a dramatic change from a single to a dual mode of research salience. A faculty member who lived through the change described the process: "When I first came here the thought of a professor trying to make money was anathema . . . really bad form. That changed when biotech happened." Several examples of firm formation encouraged by overtures from venture capitalists led other faculty, at least in disciplines with similar opportunities, to conclude that "Gosh these biochemists get to do this company thing, that's kind of neat, maybe it's not so bad after all."

Serious opposition dissipated as leading opponents of entrepreneurial ventures from academia, such as Nobel Laureate Joshua Lederberg of Rockefeller University, became involved with firms themselves – in his case, Cetus. A research group within an academic department and a start-up firm outside are quite similar despite apparent differences represented by the ideology of basic research, on the one hand, and a corporate legal structure on the other. As an academic firm founder summed up the comparison, "the way [the company] is running now it's almost like being a professor because it's all proposals and soft money."

There has been a significant change of attitude toward industrial collaboration among many faculty members in the sciences – a shift away from taken-for-granted reliance on federal funding. Three styles of participation in technology transfer have emerged, reflecting increasing degrees of industrial involvement. These approaches can be characterized as (1) hands off, leave the matter entirely to the technology transfer office; (2) knowledgeable participant, aware of the potential commercial value of research and willing to play a significant role in arranging its transfer to industry; and (3) seamless integration of campus research groups and research programs of a firm. Of course, many faculty fit into the fourth cell of "no interest" or noninvolvement. These researchers are often referred to under the rubric of the federal agency that is their primary source of support, as in, "She is an NIH [National Institutes of Health] person."

The approach of leaving it up to the technology transfer office to find a developer and marketer for a discovery precisely met the needs of many faculty members, then and now, who strictly delimit their role in putting their technology into use. A faculty member delineated this perspective on division of labor in technology transfer: "It would depend on the transfer office expertise and their advice. I am not looking to become a businessperson. I really am interested in seeing if this could be brought into the market. I think it could have an impact on people's lives. It is an attractive idea." This attitude does not necessarily preclude a start-up firm but does exclude the possibility that the faculty member will be the entrepreneur.

A stance of moderate involvement is becoming more commonplace, with scientists becoming knowledgeable and comfortable operating in a business milieu while retaining their primary interest and identity as academic scientists. A faculty member exemplifying this approach expressed the view that "In science you kind of sit down and you share ideas... There tends to be a very open and very detailed exchange. The business thing when you sit down with somebody, the details are usually done later and you have to be very careful about what you say with regard to details because that is what business is about: keeping your arms around your details so that you can sell them to somebody else, otherwise there is no point." Faculty are learning to calibrate their interaction to both scientific and business needs, giving out enough information to interest business persons in their research but not so much that a business transaction to acquire the knowledge becomes superfluous. Another researcher said, "I am thinking about what turns me on in terms of scientific interest, and the money is something; if I can figure out how to get it then it is important but it is certainly not the most important thing to me." The primary objective is still scientific; business objectives are strictly secondary.

The relatively new existence of regularized paths of academic entrepreneurship, as a stage in an academic career or as an alternative career, is only of interest to some faculty; others prefer to follow traditional career paths. However, for some members of the professoriate, participation in the formation of a firm has become an incipiently recognizable stage in an academic career, located after becoming an eminent academic figure in science. For others, typically at earlier stages of their career, either just before or after being granted permanent tenure, such activity may lead to a career in industry outside the university. As one faculty member put it, "Different people I have known have elected to go different ways . . . some back to their laboratories and some to running technology companies. You can't do both." This difficulty has not prevented other professors from trying to do both, with or without taking temporary leaves of absence.

The emergence of entrepreneurial science

A qualitative change has become a quantitative change with the availability of role models for junior faculty in the form of successful firm founders who can also act as angels and help with the provision of support mechanisms such as incubator facilities and university venture funds. Nevertheless, the emergence of entrepreneurial science has not reduced the focus on theoretical advance. If anything, it has enhanced it, as theoretical elucidation has also become a pathway to the capitalization of knowledge, as well as scientific renown. Leading academic scientists have adopted multiple objectives, "to not only run a successful company . . . and start a center here [at the university that would become] internationally recognized but to retain their traditional role as 'individual investigator,' directing a research group." An ideal-typical entrepreneurial scientist held that the "interaction of constantly going back and forth from the field, to the university lab, to the industrial lab, has to happen all the time." Moreover, a complex web of relationships has grown up between university-originated start-ups in emerging industries and older and larger firms in traditional industries. Often the same academic scientists are involved with both types of firms, managing diversified portfolios of industrial interactions (Powell 1996).

Impetuses to academic firm formation

The appearance of commercializable results in the course of the academic research process, even before scientists formulate their research programs with the intention of seeking such results or universities reorder their administrative processes in order to capture them, is the necessary cause for the emergence of entrepreneurial science. In addition to the opportunity presented by research results with commercial potential, entrepreneurial science has several sufficient causes, both proximate and long-term, that encourage academic scientists to utilize these opportunities themselves rather than leaving them to others.

Entrepreneurial impetuses in U.S. academic science include the stringency of federal research funding, a culture of academic entrepreneurship originating in the seeking of government and foundation funds to support research, examples of colleagues' successful firms, and government policies and programs that translate academic research into industrial innovation (Etzkowitz, Gulbrandsen, and Levitt 2000).

Research funding difficulties

Creating an independent financial base to fund research is a significant motivator of entrepreneurial activity. Stringency of federal research funding has led academic scientists to broaden their search for research support from basic to applied government programs and vice versa. A possible source that has grown in recent years has been research subventions from companies, including firms founded by academics themselves for this purpose, driving industrial support of academic research up from a low of 4 percent to a still modest 7 percent during the 1980s. New sources of funding for academic research have opened up in some fields that have experienced a rise in practical significance, such as the biological sciences, making the notion of stringency specific to others, such as nuclear physics, that have experienced a decline (Blumenthal *et al.* 1986a).

Although federal investment in academic R&D increased during the 1990s, academic researchers strongly perceived a shortfall of resources during this period (National Science Board, 1996). The explanation of this paradox lies in the expansionary dynamic inherent in an academic research structure, based upon a Ph.D. training system that produces research as a by-product. The expansionary dynamic is driven by the ever-increasing number of professors and by universities that wish them to engage in research. Formerly, this pressure was largely impelled by the wish to conform to the prevailing academic prestige mode associated with basic research. In recent years, expansionary pressure has intensified due to increased attention to the economic outcomes of basic research, which drew less research-intensive areas of the country into the competition to expand the research efforts of local universities as an economic development strategy.

When traditional sources of research funding were unable to meet ever-expanding needs, academics sought alternative sources such as industrial sponsors. A faculty member discussed his involvement with industry: "In some areas we have found it necessary to go after that money. As the experimental needs in computer science [increase], equipment needs build up. People realize that a small NSF grant just doesn't hack it anymore." Nevertheless, there are cultural and other barriers to overcome before a smooth working relationship can be established. A professor described the dilemma: "It's harder work with industry funding than federal funding, harder to go through the procurement process, to negotiate the terms of the contract." Industry's expectations for secrecy, for example, are sometimes unreasonable. Dissatisfaction with working with existing firms is another reason that academics start their own companies.

Nevertheless, federal research agencies are still the most important external interlocutors for academic researchers. A department chair at Cal Tech noted that "The amount of money from industry is a pittance in the total budget, therefore everybody's wasting their time to try to improve it... it's still a drop in the bucket... we were running about 3 percent total in our department. We do value our industrial ties... have good friends, interact strongly with them in all kinds of respects and... the unrestricted money is invaluable. You wouldn't want to lose a penny of it and would like to increase it a lot, but its impact vis a vis federal funding is almost non-existent." In contrast to this view, others look toward realizing greater value from the commercial potential of research.

Even without creating firms themselves, academic scientists can earn funds to support their research by making commercializable results available for sale to existing firms. As a Stanford faculty member described the process, "It's also motivating for us to try to identify things that we do that may be licensable or patentable and to make OTL [Office of Technology and Licensing] aware that 30 percent of the money comes back to the scientist, 30 percent comes back to the department and a further 30 percent goes to the University. So, almost all the computing equipment and money for my post doctorates have been funded by the work that we did. There's motivation." Earlier in the twentieth century, experiencing difficulties in the French research funding system, the Curies considered exploring the commercial possibilities of their radium discovery for just this purpose (Quinn 1995).

Tapping capital markets through a public offering of stock is an additional source of research funding, especially in biotechnology-related fields, although one not yet recognized in Science Indicators volumes! In response to the increasingly time-consuming task of applying for federal research grants, a faculty member said that "another way to get a whole bunch of money... is to start a company." After resisting the idea of starting a firm in favor of establishing an independent nonprofit research institute, largely supported by corporate and governmental research funds, two academic scientists returned to an idea they had earlier rejected of seeking venture capital funding. As one of the founders explained their motivation for firm formation, "Post docs who are really good will want to have some place that at least guarantees their salary. And that we were not able to do. It was for that reason we decided to start the company." Other scientists had the realization that they could combine doing good science with making money by starting a company. As they enhanced their academic salaries through earnings from entrepreneurial ventures, and continued to publish at a high rate, they lost any previous aversion to the capitalization of knowledge (Blumenthal *et al.* 1986b).

The industrial penumbra of the university

A surrounding region filled with firms that have grown out of the university is also a significant impetus to future entrepreneurial activity. The existence of a previous generation of university-originated start-ups provides consulting opportunities, even for faculty at other area universities. A Stanford professor noted that "In the area there's a lot of activity and that tends to promote the involvement of people." From their contact with such companies, faculty become more knowledgeable about the firm formation process and thus more likely to become involved themselves. Faculty who have started their own firms also become advisors to those newly embarking on a venture. An aspiring faculty entrepreneur recalled that a departmental colleague who had formed a firm "gave me a lot of advice... he was the role model." The availability of such role models makes it more likely that other faculty members will form firms out of their research results when the opportunity appears.

The success of the strategy of creating a penumbra of companies surrounding the university has given rise to an industrial pull on faculty members. For example, a faculty member reported that "The relationship with collaborative partners is ongoing daily. We are always talking about what project we are going to do next. What the priority is, who is involved. There are probably six projects, a dozen staff members and maybe close to a dozen people scattered around three or four different departments on campus that are doing things with them." Geographical proximity makes a difference in encouraging appropriate interaction. Such intensive interaction sheds new light on the question of industrial influence on faculty research direction and whether this is good, bad, or irrelevant. Thus, the "issue of investigator initiation is much more complicated because I am bringing my investigator initiated technology to their company initiated product. It is a partnership in which each partner brings their own special thing. That is the only reason they are talking. Do your thing on our stuff." Previous conflicts based on the assumption of a dividing line between the academic and industrial sides of a relationship are superseded as divisions disappear.

Not surprisingly, a receptive academic environment is an incentive to entrepreneurship, while a negative one is a disincentive. MIT and Stanford University are the exemplars of firm formation as an academic mission. In the 1930s the president of MIT persuaded the leadership of the New England region to make the creation of companies from academic research the centerpiece of their regional economic development strategy (Etzkowitz 1993). At Stanford, Frederick Terman, Dean of Engineering, provided some of the funds to help two of his former students, Hewlett and Packard, to form their firm just prior to World War II, setting off the entrepreneurial dynamic that was dubbed "Silicon Valley" in the early 1970s (Etzkowitz 2013b). A faculty member commented that "Because it has been encouraged here from its inception, it makes it easy to become involved [in firm formation]. [There are] . . . more opportunities . . . people come in expecting it." On the other hand, at a university noted for its opposition to entrepreneurial activity, an administrator noted that despite the disfavor in which it is held, "There have been some [firms founded] . . . it's frowned upon. It takes a lot of time and the faculty are limited . . . in the amount of time they have." Under these conditions, procedures that could ameliorate conflicts are not instituted and faculty who feel constricted by the environment leave.

Once a university has established an entrepreneurial tradition and a number of successful companies, fellow faculty members can offer material, in addition to moral, support to their colleagues who are trying to establish companies of their own. A previous stratum of university-originated firms and professors who have made money from founding their own firms creates a potential cadre of "angels" that prospective academic firm founders can look to in raising funds to start their firms. Early faculty firm founders at MIT were known on campus for their willingness to supply capital to help younger colleagues.

Normative impetus to firm formation

What are considered academic norms of sharing knowledge become more difficult to realize through conventional means as complex research techniques take on some of the characteristics of a product. Potential products are often produced as a normal part of the research process, especially as software becomes commonplace in collecting and analyzing data. As a faculty member commented in the mid-1980s, "In universities we tend to be very good at producing software, [we] produce it incidentally. So there is a natural affiliation there. My guess is that a lot of what you are going to see in university-industry interaction is going to be in the software area." This phenomenon has spread well beyond the research process, with software produced in academia outside of the laboratory and start-ups emerging from curriculum development and other academic activities (Kaghan and Barnet 1997).

In an era when results are often embodied in software sharing, research results take on a dimension of complexity well beyond reproducing and mailing a preprint or reprint of an article. Software must be debugged, maintained, enhanced, and translated to different platforms to be useful. These activities require organizational and financial resources well beyond the capacity of an academic lab and its traditional research supporters, especially if the demand is high and the software complex. As one of the researchers described the dilemma of success, "We had an NSF Grant that supported [our research] and many people wanted us to convert our programs to run on other machines. We couldn't get support [on our grant] to do that and our programs were very popular. We were sending them out to every place that had machines available that could run them." The demand grew beyond the ability of the academic laboratory to meet it.

Firm formation is also driven by the norms of academic collegiality, mandating sharing of research results. When the federal research support funding system was unable or unwilling to expand the capabilities of a laboratory to meet the demand for the software that its research support had helped create, the researchers reluctantly turned to the private sector. They decided that "Since we couldn't get support, we thought perhaps the commercial area was the best way to get the technology that we developed here at Stanford out into the commercial domain." This was a step taken only after failing to receive support from NSF and NIH to distribute the software. "The demonstration at NIH was successful, but they didn't have the funds to develop this resource." The researchers also tried and failed to find an existing company to develop and market the software. As one of the researchers described their efforts, "We initially looked for companies that might license it from us ... none were really prompted to maintain or develop the software further." Failure to identify an existing firm to market a product is a traditional impetus to inventors, who strongly believe in their innovation, to form firms themselves to bring it to market.

Chemists involved with molecular modeling, previously a highly theoretical topic, have had to face the exigencies of software distribution as their research tools increasingly become embodied in software. Since the interest in the software is not only from academic labs but also from companies that can afford to pay large sums, the possibility opens up of building a company around a program or group of programs and marketing them to industry at commercial rates while distributing to academia at a nominal cost. Academic firm founders thus learn to balance academic and commercial values. In one instance, as members of the board, the academics were able to influence the firm to find a way to make a research tool available to the academic community at modest cost. An academic described the initial reaction to the idea: "The rest of the board were venture capitalists, you can imagine how they felt! They required we make a profit." On the other hand, "It was only because we were very academically oriented and we said, 'look, it doesn't matter if this company doesn't grow very strongly at first.' We wanted to grow slow and do it right and provide the facilities to academics." The outcome was a compromise between the two sides, meeting academic and business objectives at the same time, through the support of government research agency to partially subsidize academic access to the firm's product.

Interdisciplinary collaboration

There is some evidence that firms spin out of interdisciplinary research or, at least, that some such collaborations are a significant precursor to firm formation. As one academic firm founder described the origins of his firm, "If it had not been for the collaboration between the two departments [biochemistry, computer science], intimate, day to day working [together], it never would have happened. Intelligenetics and Intellicorp grew out of this type of collaboration. We had GSB [the Graduate School of Business], the Medical School and Computer Science all working together. In this model, the various schools of the university contributed to the ability of the university to spin out firms, providing specialized expertise well beyond the original intellectual property."

Transition from consulting

Until the past two decades, a skeptical view of firm formation was the taken-for-granted perspective of most faculty members and administrators at research universities. A typical trajectory of firm formation is the transition from an individual consulting practice, conducted within the parameters of the one-fifth rule, to a more extensive involvement, leading to the development of tangible products. A faculty member described his transition from consulting to firm formation: "It got to the point where I was making money consulting and needed some sort of corporate structure and liability insurance; so I started [the company] a couple of years ago. From me [alone, it has grown] to eight people. We're still 70 percent service oriented, but we do produce better growth media for bacteria and kits for detecting bacteria." The firm was built, in part, on the university's reputation but was symbiotic in that its services to clients brought them into closer contact with on-campus research projects.

Model of integration

In another instance, an attempt was made to reconcile the various conflicting interests in firm formation and make them complementary to each other by the university having some equity in the company and holding the initial intellectual property rights. Despite the integrated mode arrived at, some separation, worked out on technical grounds, was still necessary to avoid conflicts. "There is no line. It's just a complete continuum. It is true that I have a notebook that says university name and a notebook that says firm name and if I make an invention in the company notebook then the assignment and the exclusive license goes to the firm and if I make an invention in the university notebook then the government has rights to the invention because they are funding the work. How do I decide which notebook I am going to write in? We have ways of dividing it up by compound class. In the proposals that I write to the government I propose certain compound classes. There is no overlap between the compound classes that we work on campus and the compound classes that we work on off campus so there is a nice objective way of distinguishing that." The technical mode of separation chosen, by compound classes, suggests that while boundaries have eroded as firm and university cooperate closely to mount a joint research effort, a clear division of labor persists.

Transition to the entrepreneurial university

Once the university accepted firm formation and assistance to the local economy as an academic objective, the issue of boundary maintenance was seen in a new light. An informant noted that "When the university changed its attitude toward entrepreneurial ventures, one consequence was that the administration renegotiated its contract with the patent management firm that dealt with the school's intellectual property. A new sentence said, 'If the university chooses to start an entrepreneurial new venture based upon the invention then the university can keep the assignment and do whatever it wants.' Why did the university make that change? Because the university decided that it wanted to encourage faculty to spinoff these companies." Organizational and ideological boundaries between academia and industry were redrawn, with faculty encouraged to utilize leave procedures to take time to form firms and entrepreneurial ventures noted as contributing to research excellence in university promotional literature.

Conclusion: The academic world has turned

The emergence of the entrepreneurial university is a universal phenomenon that can be identified in diverse academic traditions globally (Etzkowitz 2008). In European universities, where the professor has traditionally been a civil servant, the entrepreneurial role in firm formation is often taken by a student trained in an entrepreneurship program. In Chinese universities, entrepreneurial activities were strongly encouraged by government in an era of constrained resources (Zhou, this volume). In the United States, an entrepreneurial academic tradition was fostered during the first academic revolution, which took off from the mid-nineteenth century. As professors sought funds from diverse sources to support research, a transformation from teaching college to research university took place. The transformation from research to entrepreneurial university, a second revolution, involving the university's assumption of a mission for economic and social development, is currently under way.

As knowledge becomes a more important factor in economic development, entrepreneurial scientists and entrepreneurial universities have emerged as prestigious academic role models. The MIT/Stanford model, combining research and teaching with innovation, is displacing Harvard as the academic exemplar. Until quite recently, pursuing the "endless frontier" of basic research was the primary ideological justification of elite U.S. academic institutions. Harvard University was the model, with numerous schools identifying themselves as the "Harvard" of their respective regions. The prediction that MIT would conform to the traditional U.S. research university mode was disconfirmed as Harvard, and academic institutions that modeled themselves upon it, increasingly adopted an entrepreneurial mode (Geiger 1986). Liberal arts research universities have moved closer to the "land grant" mission of science-based regional economic development, MIT's founding purpose and historic forte (Etzkowitz 2002). Stanford University is the prototypical case of this transformation that universities worldwide wish to emulate.

A more direct role in the economy is becoming an accepted academic function and this is reflected in the way universities interact with industry. There has been a shift in emphasis from traditional modes of academic–industry relations oriented to supplying academic "inputs" to existing firms, either in the form of information flows or through licensing patent rights to technology in exchange for royalties. Utilizing academic knowledge to establish a new firm, usually located in the vicinity of the university, has become a more important objective. Indeed, the firm may initially be established on or near the campus in an incubator facility sponsored by the university to contribute to the local economy. Academic–industry relations have been transformed from a less intensive, mediated mode relying upon "knowledge flows" across strongly defended boundaries to a more intensive, integrated mode based upon technology transfer and firm formation.

A trend can also be identified of movement from an intensive academic support structure to support firm formation when regional conditions are weak to a relatively hands-off model when there is an availability of serial entrepreneurs, angel and venture financing, and informal links between academies and the entrepreneurial community. The two conditions are not alternative models but rather constitute a predictable sequence of events. When regional conditions are weak, university support will have to be strong in order to produce a take-off of entrepreneurial activity from the university. After the take-off occurs and has become self-supporting, the original conditions are typically forgotten and the model of a self-sustaining ecosystem takes hold. However, when this model runs into trouble in an economic downturn, there is typically a return to a more intensive support structure model, usually involving university–industry–government interactions.

Thus, the pendulum swings to and fro, but as we become more aware of the underlying dynamic, the gap between the two models can be reduced and they can be seen as compatible parts of a common model of academic entrepreneurial development. The entrepreneurial university incorporates and enhances previous models of academic development. Rather than entrepreneurial activity degrading research, the opposite has been found to be the case, as practice inspires theory as well as the other way around. A more profound effect has been identified: academic researchers who are leading patent filers also lead in publications (Van Looy *et al.* 2004). The classical linear model works as an assisted linear model, with a support structure to enhance innovation, even as it is itself incorporated into a nonlinear framework, with multiple complementary impetuses to theoretical advance and industrial innovation. The nineteenth-century Humboldtian academic framework, combining research with service to the state, is incorporated into a broader "triple helix" model of university–industry–government interactions.

Note

Data on academic firm formation in the United States are drawn from a series of studies conducted by the author with the support of the U.S. National Science Foundation since the 1980s.

References

Blumenthal, David *et al.* 1986a. "Industrial Support of University Research in Biotechnology" *Science.* 231: 242–246.

Blumenthal, David *et al.* 1986b. "University–Industry Research Relations in Biotechnology" *Science.* 232: 1361–1366.

Etzkowitz, Henry. 1983. *Entrepreneurial Scientists and Entrepreneurial Universities in American Academic Science,* 21 (2–3): 198–233.

2002. *MIT and the Rise of Entrepreneurial Science.* London: Routledge.

2008. *The Triple Helix: University–Industry–Government Innovation in Action.* London: Routledge.

2013a. "Silicon Valley at Risk? Sustainability of a Global Innovation Icon." *Social Science Information* 52: 515–538.

2013b. "StartX and the Paradox of Success: Filling the Gap in Stanford's Entrepreneurial Cuture." *Social Science Information* 52: 605–627.

Etzkowitz, Henry, Gulbrandsen, Magnus, and Levitt, Janet. 2000. *Public Venture Capital.* New York: Harcourt.

Etzkowitz, Henry and Stevens, Ashley. 1995. "Inching toward Industrial Policy: The University's Role in Government Initiatives to Assist Small, Innovative Companies in the U.S." *Science Studies.* 2: 13–31.

Faulkner, Wendy and Senker, Jacqueline. 1995. *Knowledge Frontiers: Public Sector Research and Industrial Innovation in Biotechnology, Engineering Ceramics, and Parallel Computing.* Oxford University Press.

Geiger, Roger. 1986. *To Advance Knowledge: The Growth of American Research Universities, 1900–1940.* New York: Oxford University Press.

Gibbons, Michael *et al.* 1994. *The New Production of Knowledge.* Beverly Hills, CA: Sage.

Jencks, Christopher and Riesman, David. 1968. *The Academic Revolution.* New York: Doubleday.

Kaghan, William and Barnet, Gerald. 1997. "The Desktop Model of Innovation in Digital Media" In Etzkowitz, Henry and Loet Leydesdorff (eds.). *Universities and the Global Knowledge Economy: A Triple Helix of Academic–Industry–Government Relations.* London: Cassell.

Langfitt, Thomas *et al.* 1989. *Partners in the Research Enterprise.* Philadelphia: University of Pennsylvania Press.

Latour, Bruno and Woolgar, Steve. 1979. *Laboratory Life.* Beverly Hills, CA: Sage.

National Science Board. 1996. *Science and Engineering Indicators.* Washington, DC: National Science Foundation.

Powell, Walter. 1996. *Presentation to Provost's Seminar on Academic Industry Relations.* Columbia University.

Quinn, Susan. 1995. *Marie Curie: A Life.* New York: Simon and Schuster.

Shimshoni, Daniel. 1970. "The Mobile Scientist in the American Instrument Industry" *Minerva.* 8(1).

Van Looy, Bart *et al.* 2004. "Combining Entrepreneurial and Scientific Performance in Academia: Towards a Compounded and Reciprocal Matthew-Effect?" *Research Policy.* 33: 425–441.

3 University-based entrepreneurship: A synthesis of the literature

Rory P. O'Shea, Ciara Fitzgerald, Harveen Chugh, and Thomas J. Allen

Since the early 1980s, universities in developed countries have greatly increased their entrepreneurial activities, including patenting and licensing; establishing incubators, science parks, and university spin-offs; investing equity in start-ups; and assisting regional economic development. We endeavor to make the following contributions: First, we conduct a comprehensive review of the university spin-off literature. The evaluation and synopsis of the literature will identify the determinants and consequences of university spin-off activity. Second, we develop a conceptual framework containing six major research streams that have emerged: (1) studies that focus on the individual and the personality of the individual as the key determinant of whether spin-off activity occurs; (2) organizational studies that seek to explain spin-off activity in terms of university resources, incentives, and structures; (3) sociocultural development studies that explain spin-off activity in terms of culture and the rewards within the university; (4) studies that explain spin-offs in terms of external environmental influences; (5) studies that examine the development and performance of spin-offs; and (6) studies that seek to measure the economic impact of spin-off activity. Although these research domains clearly overlap considerably, we employ them as a method of classification to facilitate a discussion of the literature.

This chapter is organized in the following manner. The first section provides an overview of the existing spin-off definitions in the academic entrepreneurship literature. The second section reviews earlier research and outlines six distinct research streams we have identified in this literature. The third section builds on our review of the literature by presenting a theoretical framework for the determinants and consequences of spin-off activity.

Spin-off definition

To provide a conceptual framework, we first assess the existing definitions of spin-offs in the academic entrepreneurship literature. Roberts and Malone (1996) define spin-offs as a mechanism in which governments seek to generate economic impact from their R&D by transferring technology from the R&D function to a commercial organization. Similarly, Steffensen *et al.* (1999) and Rogers *et al.* (2001) define spin-offs based on the parent R&D organization. They include the government R&D laboratory, the university, the university research center, and private R&D organizations as examples. Smilor *et al.* (1990) and Nicolaou and Birley (2003a) take account of the human element and state a spin-off is formed by individuals who were former employees of the parent organization. Nicolaou and Birley (2003a) build further on this work and put forward a trichotomous grouping of spin-off formation. Their model looks at the type of network the academic may be embedded in prior to initiation of the spin-off. The types of network are orthodox – both the technology and the academic inventor(s) spin off from the institution; hybrid – the technology spins out from the institution but the academic inventor(s) retains a place in the university and may hold some other part time position in the company; and technology – only the technology spins off, and the academic inventor(s) maintain no connection with the new firm but may have equity. For that critical career choice, the authors also put forward the notion that the academic may exist in either of two conditions: (1) academic exodus – the inventor leaves the university to be solely with the firm – and (2) academic stasis – the inventor stays in the university and may or may not have a position in the company (Nicolaou and Birley 2003b). For the purposes of this study, we draw from the definition provided by Nicolaou and Birley (2003a). According to the authors, a university spin-off involves

- The transfer of a core technology from an academic institution to a new company
- The founding member(s) may include the inventor academic(s) who may or may not be currently affiliated with the academic institution

A review of existing research

Our review of the academic literature suggests six primary research groups or domains. The first four focus on the determinants of spin-off activity within a university context. These include (1) the attributes and the personality characteristics of academic entrepreneurs; (2) the resource endowments and capabilities of the university; (3) university structures and policies facilitating commercialization; and (4) environmental factors influencing academic entrepreneurship. The remaining two domains focus on the consequences of spin-off activity; (5) the development and performance of spin-offs and (6) studies that measure the economic impact of spin-offs on regional economies. We now present each of these in more detail, leading to the development of our conceptual framework.

(1)   Individual attributes as determinants of spin-off activity

A small but growing number of studies have highlighted the importance of individual characteristics in determining whether academic entrepreneurs will establish a spin-off or not. These studies emphasize the impact of individual abilities and dispositions on the entrepreneurial behavior of academics. Roberts's pioneering work in *Entrepreneurs in High Technology* (1991) investigated the roles that personality, motivation, and disposition play in influencing academic entrepreneurship. In particular, he compared a sample of MIT technical entrepreneurs with appropriate control groups of scientists and engineers employed at their parent incubator organizations. From his analysis, Roberts revealed MIT technical entrepreneurs to be (1) more likely to be extroverted than their rather introverted technical work colleagues; (2) more "perceiving" orientated, thus having a personality profile reflective of a Keirsey and Bates "inventor" mindset model. His study also revealed that MIT technical entrepreneurs show a moderate need for achievement and power, but demonstrate a strong need for independence, a low need for affiliation, and a drive and passion for meeting new challenges and overcoming obstacles. The R&D firm for which the MIT alumni entrepreneur has been working – "the source organization" – also influences the entrepreneurial decision in various ways. A summary of the central findings of Roberts's work is outlined later (see Table 3.1).

The common theme shared by this research is that spin-off behavior is a reflection of individual actions and therefore is largely due to the personality, ability, career choice, or willingness of the individual to engage successfully in entrepreneurial behavior.

In line with the individual characteristics of entrepreneurs, there is a strand of literature examining entrepreneurial intentions of students as encouraged in business schools in universities. One study by Souitaris *et al.* (2007) suggest that entrepreneurial education programmes augment entrepreneurial attitudes and intentions and increase the chances that students will actually attempt an entrepreneurial career at some point in their lives. As well as literature on characteristics of the

Table 3.1: *Characteristic influences on becoming a technical entrepreneur*

Family background:
'Entrepreneurial heritage' – son of self-employed father
Some influenced by achievement-oriented religious background

Education and age:
Master's degree, usually in engineering
Mid-30s age at founding

Work experience:
Decade plus of work
Development (rather than research background)
Highly productive technologist in terms of patents and papers
Challenge and satisfied by "source organization" work

Goal orientation, personality, and motivation:
"Inventor" personality
"Moderate" needs for achievement and power, low need for affiliation
Long-felt desire for own business
Heavy orientation toward independence, less concern for financial rewards

---

Source: Roberts, Edward B. 1991. *Entrepreneurs in High Technology: Lessons from MIT and Beyond.*

academic entrepreneur, there is also literature examining the phenomenon of serial entrepreneurs or "repeat commercializers." In a survey of faculty members by Hoye and Pries (2009), the findings show that 12 percent of the faculty are "repeat commercializers" and their activity accounts for 80 percent of the commercialized innovations.

(2)   *Organizational determinants of university spin-off activity*

Social scientists operating at the organizational level have adopted a different approach to the study of spin-off activity. Rather than focusing on broad social or individual forces, such researchers have centered their attention on organizational and human resource aspects of the university. Specifically, researchers have sought to establish links between spin-off activity and the level and nature of research funding, the quality of the researchers, and the presence of technology incubators and technology transfer offices.

One factor that has received attention is the level and nature of funding for R&D activities within the university. For example, Lockett and Wright (2005) found that the number of spin-off companies created from UK universities was positively associated with R&D expenditure. Blumenthal *et al.* (1996) surveyed 2,052 faculty members at 50 universities in the life sciences field and found industry-funded faculty members to be more commercially productive (patent applications and new products brought to the market) than their non-industry-funded counterparts. In a cross-sectional study of doctorate-granting research universities, Powers and McDougall (2005) found a positive and statistically significant relationship between annual university-wide R&D expenditure and spin-off activity. Similarly, Lenoir and Gianella (2006) show the extent to which funding in discovery-oriented research can potentially impact national economies. The authors explore the influence of federal funding on gene chip development and document the role of technology change in catalyzing the creation of a powerful new approach to gene research and the emergence of an entire sector in the biotech industry.

The nature and type of research engaged in by the university also seems to be important in spin-off activity. One study conducted by Shane (2004a) demonstrated that the tendency for an invention to be exploited through firm creation varies with the attributes of the age of the technical field. He is also found that radical, tacit, early stage and general purpose technology, which provide significant value to customers, are more likely than other technologies to provide the basis for spin-offs.

Faculty quality has also been cited as another factor that influences spin-off activity. Zucker et al. (1998b) linked the intellectual human capital of "star" scientists to the founding of new firms in the American biotechnology industry and to their growth and location. Stuart and Ding (2006) have more recently shown that, although it was distinguished scientists who made the transition into academic entrepreneurship, the professional gap between participants and nonparticipants in academic entrepreneurship was diminishing over time. DiGregorio and Shane (2003) also demonstrate that faculty members who develop leading edge innovations may wish to earn economic rents on valuable asymmetric information. They suggest that for reasons of credibility it may be easier for academics from top tier universities to assemble resources to create start-ups.

In recent years, the question of how universities are supporting the development of spin-offs has been attracting increased attention. For example, in a study of forty-three research institutions in five European countries, Clarysse et al. (2005) have shown that three different incubation strategies were used to manage the spin-off process. These models were the Low Selective (oriented toward maximizing the number of spin-offs created), the Supportive (oriented toward generating revenue from spin-offs), and the Incubator model (oriented toward creating financially attractive spin-outs). Davenport et al. (2002) examined spin-off strategies of industrial research centers and uncovered four different parent support strategies in the development of high-technology spin-offs.

These are (1) spin-offs by exception – unintentionally initiated by the entrepreneur where support from the parent organization may be on a contingent basis; (2) spin-offs by occasion – may be intentionally initiated by the entrepreneur where support and management for the spin-off is on a case-by-case basis; and (3) spin-offs as strategy – formed intentionally with a formal strategy and procedures in place. Degroof and Roberts (2004) also examined university spin-off policies with respect to the growth potential of spin-offs. They argue that in order for more growth-oriented ventures to emerge from research institutions located within weak entrepreneurial infrastructures, there is a need for universities to adopt a proactive highly selective and supportive model for spin-off development.

Science parks and incubation centers are recognized as supportive structures to facilitate university spin-offs. Link and Scott (2003) argue that a science park encourages an academic scientist to transition from basic to applied science. In their study, they present a direct relationship between the proximity of the science park to the university and the probability that the academic curriculum will shift from basic toward applied research. Moreover, Link and Scott (2005) introduce a discipline specific orientation as they establish that the percentage of university spin-off companies is relatively greater in science parks that have a biotechnology focus. As well as science parks, university business incubators provide start-up companies with a range of support measures including physical space within the incubator building, training and coaching, business contacts, and access to finance. University incubators have the additional advantage of drawing upon the resources available at the university, including academic support, access to research facilities, and easy access to the student pool to recruit employees. Rothaermel and Thursby (2005) argue that a university link to the sponsoring institution of the incubation center reduces the probability of new spin-out failure; however, it also delays timely graduation from the incubator. Furthermore, Rasmussen and Borch (2010) propose that a position in the university incubator augments external legitimacy for the university spin-off by showing that the project has been evaluated and has university support.

To improve university and commercial ties with industry, many universities operate a technology transfer office (TTO) as a vehicle to support the creation of spin-off companies (Hague and Oakley 2000). The advantages of TTOs have been well documented in the academic literature. The majority of literature supporting the rationale for TTOs focuses on an economic argument about the market for knowledge. The assumption is that the TTO acting on behalf of the university owning the patent has superior knowledge on how the invention may be used and by what firm (Macho-Stadler *et al.* 2007). Markman *et al.* (2005)

further develop the argument by introducing "time to market" as a variable that differentiates the role of the TTO. Markman and his colleagues' results confirm that when inventors collaborate with TTOs, technologies tend to be commercialized faster and earn higher revenues. Building on an argument for reputation as the critical success factor required to increase the efficiency of the market for knowledge, Macho-Standler *et al.* (2007) argue that TTOs are able to pool inventions across research units and "shelve" some, thereby signaling to the technology buyer a positive selection for higher-quality inventions. Debackere and Veugelers (2005) and Lerner (2005) suggest that the TTO offers a number of benefits including acting as an "honest broker" against possible conflicts of interest between commercialisation and research and teaching activities; specialisation of services, particularly in relation to IP and business development; a higher degree of financial and managerial independence which facilitates relations with third parties such as investors and patent attorneys; and, importantly, the reduction of information asymmetries in the market for scientific and technological knowledge.

However, notwithstanding the economic and social rationale for TTOs, one must be also aware of the critics whose studies contest the legitimacy of TTOs in creating and even facilitating university industry linkages. A policy paper from the Kauffman Foundation by Litan *et al.* (2007) argues that the centralization of commercialization activities at universities by a TTO leads to all the problems typically associated with monopolies. Hence they suggest either the abolition of TTOs or the implementation of competition between TTOs. Although the TTO most often has a monopoly on commercializing ideas and technology from its host institution, it has been found that faculty members circumvent the formal TTO process in many cases and choose not to disclose their ideas (Litan *et al.* 2007). Furthermore, Kenney and Patton (2009) argue that institutional arrangements can incentivize TTO officers to act as revenue maximizers for the university instead of facilitators of technology dissemination for the good of the entire society.

In light of such criticism, the National Research Council commissioned research into the effectiveness and efficiency of the university technology transfer system in the United States. The objectives of the report included investigating how technology transfer fits into the mission of the university, how TTO activities can be broadened, and how accountability to the public can be improved. The report found that IP-based technology transfer is a small fraction of the ways in which academic knowledge and discovery are moved from the university to the broader community. Other, more prevalent mechanisms include publications, conferences, consulting, and informal information exchanges. Also, the report found

Table 3.2: *Roberts and Malone's (1996) five process models*

Model	Description
1	Involves all four principal parties.
2	The roles of the technology originator and entrepreneur belong to the same individual or group, i.e., the academic entrepreneur. Therefore three key groups are involved all the way through in this model.
3	The roles of the technology originator and entrepreneur belong to the same person, and also the licensing office and venture investor roles are combined into one body; i.e., the licensing office has its own venture capital fund.
4	The licensing office and the venture investor are combined into one role, but the technologist and entrepreneur have separate roles.
5	All the four parties are individual again, similarly to model 1. This time, however, an alliance is formed between the experienced entrepreneur and the venture investor to exploit the opportunity.

that the Bayh–Dole act has not interfered directly with research and generation for its own sake (National Research Council 2010).

There have also been organizational models put forward to describe the trajectories of spin-off formation based on the individuals and processes involved. For example, Roberts and Malone (1996) put forward five alternative structural models involving four principal groups to describe the formal process by which spin-offs were formed from government-owned (R&D) organizations. The principal groups were (1) the technology originator – an individual or group of engineers/scientists that works in the organization and brings the technology to the point where it is ready to be commercialized; (2) the entrepreneur – the individual entrepreneur or entrepreneurial team that takes the technology from the technology originator and attempts to create the new venture from it; (3) the R&D organization – this is the source institution and is formally represented by the TTO; and (4) the venture investor – a venture capital organization in most cases. Different combinations of the four parties groups were involved at different stages from invention to sale or initial public offering (IPO), each constituting a different path in the creation of a spin-off. The authors provide details of the intergroup processes that occur and describe how each group is involved at different points. A brief description of the differences between the five models is given in Table 3.2.

Similarly, Radosevich (1995) puts forward two alternative models: (1) the inventor-entrepreneur – the inventor leaves the technology source so he or she may become the entrepreneur; and (2) the surrogate-entrepreneur – an external or independent entrepreneur is given rights by the technology source if the inventor does not wish or is not able to leave the technology source.

Research and public policy on academic entrepreneurship are largely based on the assumption that faculty members start businesses to commercialize inventions that have been disclosed to university administrators and have been patented. However, scholars in the technology transfer space have recently begun to challenge this paradigm. First, Litan *et al.* (2007) argue that multiple pathways for university innovation exist and can be codified to provide broader access to innovation, allow a greater volume of deal flow, support standardization, and decrease the redundancy of innovation and the cycle time for commercialization. In their view, TTOs were envisioned as gateways to facilitate the flow of innovation but have instead become bottlenecks that in many cases constrain the flow of inventions and frustrate faculty, entrepreneurs, and industry. The authors argue there needs to be more of a focus on creating incentives that will maximize social benefit from the existing investments being made in R&D and commercialization on university campuses. This challenge to the paradigm is further supported by the findings of Fini *et al.* (2010), who analyzed a sample of 11,572 professors and found that much academic entrepreneurship occurs outside the university intellectual property system. Specifically, about two-thirds of businesses started by academics are not based on disclosed and patented inventions. In the light of these calls for change, Kenney and Patton (2009) argue that the current university invention ownership model, in which universities have sole ownership of inventions, is not efficient economically or does not contribute to the enhancement of encouraging entrepreneurship and commercializing technology. The authors outline the flaws of the traditional approach, which include ineffective incentives, information asymmetries, and contradictory motivations for the university, the inventors, potential licensees, and TTOs. Such challenges in the current system can lead to misaligned incentives and critical delays in licensing. Furthermore, the authors are skeptical of the role of the TTO in the current institutional arrangements, as in their opinion, TTOs have been encouraged to become revenue maximizers rather than supporting university–industry technology transfer for societal good. The authors suggest two alternative invention commercialization models as alternatives to the traditional model. The first alternative is to vest ownership in the inventor, who could choose the commercialization path for the invention. For this privilege, the inventor would provide the university an ownership stake in any returns to the invention. This option opens up competition among TTOs, as inventors would be free to contract with their own university TTOs or any other entities that might assist in commercialization. The second alternative is to make all inventions immediately publicly available, similarly to the open source movement. This would be achieved through a requirement that all inventions be licensed nonexclusively. According to the authors, both alternatives would address the current barriers in the university–industry technology transfer process. However, a report conducted by the National Research Council challenges this viewpoint by stating that there is little evidence to suggest that faculty inventors would be more motivated to commercialize their inventions if their institutions did not provide internal support in the form of hiring professional personnel and paying or securing payment of the costs of patenting licenses. Moreover, Goldfarb and Henreksen (2003) conducted a comparative study of the US and Swedish commercialization systems and found that faculty ownership and exercise of IP is less effective in commercializing academic results.

Another form of an IP commercialization model that has been adopted rapidly across Europe is called the Easy IP Access model. Easy Access IP is the first initiative of the Easy Access Innovation partnership – a collaborative project between the University of Glasgow, Kings College London, and the University of Bristol to promote new ways of sharing IP and to adopt new approaches that make it easier for universities and industry to work together. However, the partnership is growing and now includes universities from Europe, Australia, and South Africa.[1] Through their portfolios of free IP, they provide a fast-track route for the transfer of knowledge and expertise from universities to industry, so that it can be developed for the benefit of the economy and society. In return, the universities have the opportunity to establish strong, long-term relationships with commercial partners and to fulfill their mission of disseminating knowledge and expertise to the wider community. The aim is to maximize partnerships with industry and ultimately the transfer of university knowledge for public benefit. There is an expectation that not all IP will generate a return, however, because the Easy Access IP Portfolio contains IP that is difficult to commercialize through traditional routes. A choice is made to forgo an immediate financial return in order to promote new partnerships that will benefit the universities in the long term. The rationale is that the mission of both the TTO and the university is fulfilled by releasing some of the IP free of charge, as strong, long-term relationships are developed with companies.

(3)   Institutional determinants of spin-off activity

The central tenet of this research stream is that university spin-off activity is a reflection of institutional behavior. This research suggests that universities with cultural norms that support commercialization will have

---

[1] www.easyaccessIP.org.uk.

higher levels of commercialization and higher rates of spin-off activity. For example, using a panel dataset from 1980 to 2001, O'Shea *et al.* (2005) found that university spin-off creation is a dynamic process characterized by persistence and path dependence, and that a university's prior success and experience at commercializing startups increased the likelihood of initiating successful spin-off activities in the future. A central finding of the study is that each university, as a function of its history and past success, has different resource stocks available and these resource combinations are shown to be a relevant factor in explaining interuniversity variation in spinoff activity.

In addition, George *et al.* (2006) develop a grounded and micro-level understanding of factors that influence the degree of their involvement in commercialization activities. By undertaking a two-part inductive–deductive study of 796 scientists at a large public research university, the authors find that perceptions of institutional support in terms of department norms and TTO receptiveness played a crucial role. More specifically, the authors find that the greater the extent to which institutional factors were viewed as being supportive, the more likely scientists were to be prepared to participate in technology transfer activity. Kenney and Goe (2004) also contend that "the involvement of professors in entrepreneurial activity is influenced by the social relationships and institutions in which a professor is embedded." Furthermore, in a study of a biotechnology department at Stanford, Colyvas and Powell (2007) found that two "early explorer" senior faculty members played a central role in legitimizing academic entrepreneurship activities within a biological science department at Stanford. The findings of the study concluded by stating that "it's an almost unwritten rule that you have to start a company to be a successful professor at Stanford." Djokovic and Souitaris (2008) concur with this view that "the changing role of universities towards commercialization activities combined with governmental and institutional support mechanisms is creating a fertile ground for the seeds of university spin-offs." Louis *et al.* (1989) also found that local group norms were important in predicting active involvement in commercialization.

In contrast, some cultural factors such as the "publish or perish" drive, the ambiguous relationship of researchers to money, and the "disinterested" nature of academic research to industry are seen as inhibitors of the evaluation of academic research (Ndonzuau *et al.* 2002). Thursby and Kemp (2002) found that less than half of faculty inventions with commercial potential are disclosed to the TTO. In some cases this may be because those involved do not realize the commercial potential of their ideas, but often it is due to the unwillingness to delay publication that results from the patent and licensing process (Thursby and Kemp 2002).

Goldfarb and Henrekson (2003) compare national policies in promoting the commercialization of university-generated knowledge. They compare and contrast the policies in Sweden and the United States, and find that the U.S. institutional setting is characterized by significant academic freedom to interact with industry, including significant involvement in new firms. One way the author conceptualized this notion of academic independence is through national university leave of absence policies. In the United States, there are more liberal policies, which include more liberal leave of absence and consulting privileges that generally allow academics to pursue commercial opportunities, while keeping their positions as faculty members intact. On the other hand, in Sweden, procedures for academic leave have not been adjusted to make it easier for professors to take temporary leave to organize firms. Under these circumstances, Swedish academics are more likely to confine their external involvement to consulting activities, since to proceed further may force them to make a binary decision to leave the university, and few are prepared to do that. Furthermore, Fini *et al.* (2011) discuss the policies in universities that are aimed at promoting academic entrepreneurship, such as the providing of specific contractual arrangements with faculty members, often limited by the more general rules of the academic labor market. These range, for example, from non-research-based leaves of absence to the formally recognized approach of starting a new business, the possibility of temporarily freezing the tenure clock, or appropriate recognition in individual evaluations and compensation schemes. According to the authors, such provision encourages participation in various forms of technology transfer activities, as universities can devise different micro-level policies, such as more flexible leave-of-absence schemes, pre-specified tracks for faculty who are willing to start a new business, dedicated offices to support the whole process, early-stage incubators with shared services, and subsidized facilities.

Universities that lack a culture supportive of commercialization activity may take a number of actions. For example, Stuart and Ding (2006) found strong evidence of the socially and spatially localized spread of commercial science in the United States. According to the authors, scientists are more likely to become entrepreneurs when they work in departments where colleagues had previously made the transition, particularly when the individuals who had become commercializers were prestigious scientists. Furthermore, Siegel *et al.* (2004) propose that in order to foster a climate of entrepreneurship within academic institutions, university administrators should focus on five organizational and managerial factors: (1) reward systems for university–industry technology transfer (UITT); (2) staffing practices in the TTO; (3) university policies to facilitate university technology transfer; (4) increasing the level of resources devoted to UITT; and (5) working to eliminate cultural and informational barriers that impede the UITT process. These processes, however, take time to embed into practice. For example, Kirby (2006) posits that universities need to go beyond putting short-term initiatives in place and build an entrepreneurial culture where commercialization activity is encouraged and entrepreneurial behavior runs through the whole organization.

(4)   External determinants of spin-off activity

This stream of research emphasizes the impact of broader economic factors on academics within universities. Florida and Kenney (1988) highlight the central role of the availability of venture capital in encouraging the formation of high-technology companies. However, more recent research shows that access to venture capital is the most important resource constraint faced by university spin-offs (Wright et al. 2006). In fact, early on in the spin-off process, Wright et al. (2006) found that spin-offs view venture capital as more important than internal funds. In contrast to this, their findings from venture capitalists showed they prefer to invest after the seed stage, implying a mismatch between the expectations of spin-offs and venture capitalists. Wright et al. (2004) have also suggested that the involvement of industry functioning as venture capitalists via joint venture spin-offs may facilitate the emergence of university spin-offs, as they have the necessary financial resources and commercial expertise to launch successful start-ups. Using a large database on venture-backed start-up companies, Zhang (2009) describes the characteristics of university spin-offs and investigates whether they perform differently than other firms. The findings show that venture-capital-backed university spin-offs are concentrated in the biotechnology and information technology industries. However, while the university spin-offs have a higher survival rate, they are not significantly different from other start-ups in terms of the amount of venture capital raised, the probability of completing an IPO, the probability of making a profit, or the size of employment. Knockaert et al. (2010) explored the factors explaining venture capital investment managers' attitudes to investment in academic spin-offs. The paper provides an integration of VC fund characteristics and investment managers' human capital characteristics with a dataset of 68 early-stage VC investment managers in Europe. Attitudes toward academic spin-off investment are positively affected by the presence of public sector capital and by investment managers who are more intensively involved with the entrepreneur. Specific human capital in investment managers who had worked in an academic environment is more likely associated with investment in academic spin-offs. Munari and Toschi (2011) analyze whether venture capital (VC) firms have a bias against investment in academic spin-offs and highlight intellectual property rights, the presence of academic–industrial collaborations, the scientific reputation of the parent university, and the type of business model as important factors in the academic spin-off's ability to access VC financing. A growing number of studies have recently investigated the geographic localization effects of venture capital investments. Sorenson and Stuart (2001) found that the probability that a venture capital firm will invest in a start-up decreases with the geographical distance between the headquarters of the venture capital firm and the start-up firm. In contrast, DiGregorio and Shane (2003) found no evidence that the number of venture capital investments, or the presence of university venture capital funding, is related to the amount of university spin-off activity.

According to Shane (2004b), another significant impetus in the generation of university spin-offs in the United States was the enactment of the Bayh–Dole Act, by which inventions were assigned to academic institutions rather than individual inventors. U.S. universities then became directly involved in patenting and licensing activities and set up TTOs to manage this activity (Sampat 2006), the number of which has dramatically increased since Bayh–Dole (Colyvas et al. 2002). Some European studies show that national policies that allow inventions to be assigned to academic inventors have inhibited spin-off activity (Wallmark 1997). Other researchers suggest that national policies of assigning inventions to individuals can lead to an anti-entrepreneurial attitude among faculty and university administrators who do not gain from inventors' entrepreneurial activity (Goldfarb and Henrekson 2003). However, some challenge the effect of the Bayh–Dole Act, as according to Mowery et al. (2004), "The contribution of US universities to economic growth and innovation during the 1980s and 1990s were important but no evidence suggests that these contributions were more important than those during the 1930s and 1950s." The authors argue that the effect of the Bayh–Dole Act has been exaggerated, as long prior to passage of the Bayh–Dole Act some universities were already staffed and on alert for opportunities to sell their science to industry and were executing substantial business deals. An example is Wisconsin University, which penetrated technology transfer activities in 1925, with the creation of the Wisconsin Alumni Research Foundation (WARF) to license university-held patents initially derived from the synthesis of Vitamin D. This was a historic development that resulted in the elimination of rickets, a disease of malnourishment. Over the next 80 years, WARF received over 3,000 disclosures from researchers at the university and 1,000 U.S. patents and returned 800 million dollars to the universities (Mowery *et al.* 2004). Furthermore, the recent case of *Stanford v. Roche*,[2] a legal dispute between a university and a company that had received assignment by an inventor of rights in an invention that arose as a result of the inventor's work at the company, but also benefited later from the use of federal funds at the university, raised issues with the technicalities of the Bayh–Dole Act. Stanford argued that the Bayh–Dole Act vested ownership of the invention with the university, voiding any prior agreements that the inventor might have made with the company. The ruling of the Supreme Court was clear, stating that inventions made at a university using federal funds are the property of the inventors. The Bayh–Dole Act does not require that the university own federally supported inventions, nor automatically grant the university title to such inventions. The Court also rejected the idea that mere employment is sufficient to vest title to an employee's invention in the employer. The practical consequence of the Court's decision is that it has required universities to revisit their employee assignment agreements, and include a present conveyance of rights ("I hereby assign") in order to effectively convey patent rights to the institution.

Another external determinant of spin-off activity is the Small Business Innovation Research (SBIR) and the Small Business Technology Transfer Program (STTR) programs, which are designed to encourage small business and nonprofit research institution partnerships to provide financial assistance to innovative firms during the "valley of death" stages of a company's development. The SBIR program requires the 11 federal agencies with research and development budgets that top $100 million to allocate 2.5 percent of those budgets to small businesses. The Small Business Technology Transfer Program (STTR) uses a similar approach to expand public/private sector partnerships between small businesses and nonprofit U.S. research institutions. The main difference between the SBIR and STTR programs is that the STTR program requires the company to have a partnering research institution which must be awarded a minimum of 30% of the total grant funds. Audretsch *et al.* (2002) argue that the SBIR program stimulates efforts to commercialize that would not otherwise have taken place. In particular, the findings show that a significant number of the scientists and engineers would not have become involved in the commercialization process in the absence of the SBIR Program. However, Link and Scott (2010) raise caution and argue that the SBIR is subject to entrepreneurial risk, namely the a priori uncertainty that the funded research will result in a commercialized product, process, or service. The authors argue that government acts as the entrepreneur

---

[2] Board. of Trustees of Leland Stanford Junior Univ. v. Roche Molecular Sys., Inc., 131 Supreme Court. 2188 (2011).

by leading in accepting innovative risks in circumstances where the private sector would not do the entrepreneurial action even though it would be socially beneficial through the SBIR program. For example, Lerner (1999) assessed the employment and sales growth of 1,435 firms over a ten-year period and found superior performance for the SBIR program awardees, as they grew significantly faster than matched firms over a decade. Furthermore, the SBIR recipients were in a stronger position to attract venture financing.

The knowledge infrastructure of a region is also cited as a key factor determining spin-off activity. The phenomenon of entrepreneurial universities supported by incubating technopole regions with a strong commercialization tradition, such as Kendall Square in Cambridge, Massachusetts, is well documented in the literature. Feldman and Francis (2003) argue that even though universities seem to be necessary for the development of biotech concentration, the existence of a high "knowledge base" alone might not be enough. Kenney (2000) supports this view and shows that Silicon Valley continues to be successful because all the regional infrastructure elements to create new industries exist there. According to Saxenian (1994), the entire network infrastructure of entrepreneurial managers, customers, and suppliers tends to be present in those areas. Due to the increase in the volume and recognition of university and industry linkages, new Technology and Innovation Centres have been established to bridge the gap between academic discovery and commercial exploitation. Examples of Technology Innovation Centres include the Fraunhofer-Gesellschaft Institute, where research work is oriented toward concrete applications and results. The Fraunhofer-Gesellschaft receives funding both from the public sector (approximately 40%) and through contract research earnings (roughly 60%). A UK report analyzing the application of the Fraunhofer model to create an effective Innovation ecosystem in the United Kingdom identified guiding principles for the Fraunhofer model to work effectively. These include focusing on national economic strengths and areas with strong growth possibilities; creating an effective network of powerful and influential intermediaries; and putting in place a concentration of researchers, a minimum of fifty researchers per center. Furthermore, the report stressed the need for high reputation and strong branding of the Technology Development Centre.[3] For example, Fraunhofer is the second most popular employer for German natural science graduates, fourth for ICT graduates, and seventh for engineering graduates.

---

[3] Department for Business, Innovations and Skills, The Current and Future Role of Technology and Innovation Centres in the UK. A report by Hermann Hauser, March 2010.

Singapore Biopolis is another example of a National Technology Centre. Biopolis is a biomedical R&D hub, purpose-built in 2003 to house key public and private biomedical research institutes and organizations. Parayil (2005) explored the Singapore Biopolis and identified the critical success factor in establishing a successful concept as involving the university in spin-off firms, innovation, enterprise, and entrepreneurship. Other initiatives are establishing research parks and research institutes. The author acknowledged the challenges and needs of creating and sustaining the Singapore Biopolis as creating a strong knowledge base, finding human capital, accounting for the role of civil society, and addressing intellectual property issues. Breznitz (2005) explored the role of public research institution-based industrial technology policy in Taiwan. He argues that industry has an innovation system with a division of labor between government agencies and industry, excelling in quick technology transfer and second-generation innovation, while continuously infusing the system with the most recent foreign technologies.

(5)   The development and performance of university spin-offs

In this stream of literature, we review studies on the development and performance as consequences of university spin-off activity. In a recent cohort of studies, a small number of researchers have moved to a neglected area by exploring spin-off development (Mustar *et al.* 2006) and have put forward several different phases of development that spin-offs go through. Vohora *et al.* (2004) found that the series of distinct phases that the ventures went through were (1) research; (2) opportunity framing; (3) preorganization; and (4) reorientation and sustainability. The three quite different phases in proactive spin-off processes put forward by Degroof and Roberts (2004) were (1) origination; (2) concept testing; and (3) start-up support. In their study looking at team development patterns, Vanaelst *et al.* (2006) concur with Vohora *et al.* (2004) that spin-offs must pass through the previous phase to be able to move to the next one. The phases Vanaelst *et al.* (2006) found spin-offs going through are (1) research commercialization and opportunity screening; (2) the organization-in-gestation phase; (3) proof of viability of the newly established venture; and (4) the maturity phase. In addition, Vohora *et al.* (2004) found that spin-offs face critical junctures at the end of each phase which they have to overcome before moving on to the next phase. These critical junctures were opportunity recognition, entrepreneurial commitment, threshold of credibility, and threshold of sustainability (Vohora *et al.* 2004). When spin-offs pass from one phase to the next, Druilhe and Garnsey (2004) found that they modify, refine, and develop their business model as they improve their knowledge of resources and opportunities. They are also in agreement with Vohora *et al.* (2004) that spin-off development is an iterative and nonlinear process.

A small but growing number of studies deal with the performance of academic spin-offs. According to Shane (2004a), spin-off companies are 108 times more likely than the average new firm to go public and also to create more jobs than the average new business in the United States. Furthermore, the survival rate of university spin-off companies is extremely high. Mustar (1997) found that only 16 percent of the French spin-offs he studied failed in the six-year period over which he tracked them. Dahlstrand (1997) found that only 13 percent of the spin-offs from Chalmers Institute of Technology in Sweden founded between 1960 and 1993 had failed by 1993. Furthermore, Nerkar and Shane (2003) analyze the entrepreneurial dimension of university technology transfer, based on an empirical analysis of 128 firms that were founded between 1980 and 1996 to commercialize inventions owned by MIT. Their findings suggest that new technology firms are more likely to survive if they exploit radical technologies and if they possess patents with a broad scope.

In a study of start-up teams, Ensley and Hmieleski (2005) compared the performance of university-based start-ups with that of independently started ventures and found lower performance with regard to net cash flow and revenue growth in the university-based ventures. They attributed this to the teams not being as well developed as their independent venture counterparts due to difficulty in finding the level of expertise required on the university campus, highlighting the importance of networks. Shane and Stuart (2002) offered empirical evidence of the network–performance relationship, analyzing how the social capital endowments of the founders affect the likelihood of three critical outcomes of spin-offs: attracting venture capital financing, experiencing initial public offerings (IPOs), and failure. Direct and indirect linkages to investors were found to be important as determinants of whether a business received venture funding and in reducing the likelihood of spin-off failure. Furthermore, Bruneel *et al.* (2010) explore the influence of different mechanisms in lowering barriers related to the orientation of universities and to the transactions involved in working with university partners. Drawing on a large-scale survey and public records, they examine the effects of collaboration experience, breadth of interaction, and interorganizational trust in lowering different types of barriers. The analysis shows that prior experience of collaborative research lowers orientation-related barriers and that higher levels of trust reduce both types of barriers studied. It also indicates that breadth of interaction diminishes orientation-related, but increases transaction-related barriers. Additionally, Patzelt and Shepherd (2009) draw on goal-setting theory to analyze how and why entrepreneurs perceive the usefulness of policy programs aimed at facilitating the development of academic ventures. Using a conjoint study and data on 3,136 assessments nested within 98 academic entrepreneurs, they found that access to finance offered by a policy program is key and enhances the entrepreneurs' perceived benefits of other policy measures such as providing access to nonfinancial resources (networks, business knowledge) and reducing administrative burdens, but diminishes the perceived benefits of offering tax incentives for new ventures.

(6)   The economic impact of spin-offs

University spin-offs are an important subset of start-up firms because they are an economically powerful group of high-technology companies. Among them are several billion-dollar public corporations, including Cirrus Logic, Google, Genentech, and Chiron (Shane 2004a). A small number of policy reports have looked at the impact of universities and their respective start-up companies on regional economic development. The report "Entrepreneurial Impact: The Role of MIT" (Roberts & Eesley, 2011) provides remarkable testimony to the economic impact of university sourced knowledge and technology on regional economies. According to the study, alumni founded companies that were based upon university-derived technology employed 1.7 million people and one trillion dollars in annual global revenues. The authors also reveal that more than half of those jobs were in the companies that relied primarily upon MIT technology alone. In a broader economic impact of alumni founded start-ups, Eesley and Miller (2012) estimated that Stanford alumni had founded 69,900 active organizations with combined annual revenues of 2.667 trillion ($2,667B), creating an estimated 5,387,000 jobs.

Imperial Innovations Limited Group previously moved away from merely measuring the counts of companies formed, and now considers the number of companies seed funded, where appropriate, with launch management teams. Effectively there has been a trend of moving the point of measurement away from the initial formation point and toward a point at which it is clear that the technology has been of sufficient quality to attract a management team and that the company has the financial capital to proceed. The number will be smaller than the raw number of companies formed, but is a better reflection of the metric used by technology transfer professionals as a performance indicator.

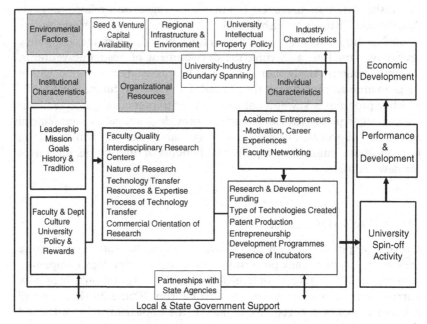

Figure 3.1: University spin-off framework.

Developing a conceptual framework for the study of spin-offs

We have identified six streams of research relating to university spin-off activity within the domain of academic entrepreneurship. We have specifically focused on research that identifies the determinants and consequences of this activity. We now seek to integrate these perspectives into a university spin-off framework. We believe this framework provides a useful organizing scheme for understanding existing literature on academic research, for explaining the determinants and consequences of spin-off activity, and for guiding future studies on this subject.

The framework (Figure 3.1) represents a conceptual integration of elements found in the academic entrepreneurship literature. It assumes a sociopsychological perspective, in that we suggest that spin-off creation varies due not only to the characteristics of individual academics but also to variation in environments and university contexts. The framework suggests that four factors (shaded in Figure 3.1) influence the rate of spin-off activity: (1) engaging in entrepreneurial activity (individual characteristics studies); (2) the attributes of universities, such as human capital, commercial resources, and institutional activities (organizational-focused studies); (3) the broader social context of the university, including the "barriers" or "deterrents" to spin-offs (institutional and cultural studies); (4) the external characteristics such as regional infrastructure that impact spin-off activity (external environment studies). We also incorporate two streams of research suggesting that the consequences of spin-off activity can be considered in terms of (5) the development and performance of spin-offs and (6) the spillover effect of spin-offs on the regional economy.

Conclusion

In this chapter, we organized the growing body of theory and research on university entrepreneurship into six different research streams. Specifically, we argued for the existence of an underlying set of individual and contextual factors that need to be recognized by universities implementing technology transfer policies. In addition, the two other primary streams of research identified (development and performance of spin-offs and the economic impact of spin-off activity) provide a parsimonious description of the outcomes of spin-off activity.

We also highlighted the role and importance of spin-off companies in economic development. Policy makers and universities are increasingly seeking to understand how higher educational institutions can best contribute to both their traditional functions and the added function of making the regional or national economy more competitive. We presented a conceptual framework that should aid researchers in completing a much-needed assessment of the impact of organizational policies, practices, and structures on university entrepreneurship. Specifically, our framework should lead to the development of organizational interventions that facilitate technology transfer and spin-off activity. The integrative framework we present suggests that university heads and policy makers can encourage and develop university entrepreneurship by using a comprehensive systems approach for the identification, protection, and commercialization of university intellectual property.

References

Association of University Technology Managers [AUTM]. 2001. *The AUTM Licensing Surveys: University Start-Up Data.* AUTM Inc., Norwalk, CT.

Audretsch, David, Link, Albert, and Scott, Jason. 2002. "Public/Private Technology Partnerships: Evaluating SBIR-Supported Research." *Research Policy* 31(1), 145–158.

Blumenthal, David, Campbell, Eric G., Causino, Nancyanne, and Louis, Karen. 1996. "Participation of Life Science Faculty in Research Relationships with Industry." *New England Journal of Medicine* 335, 1734–1739.

Breznitz, Dan. 2005. "Development, Flexibility and R & D Performance in the Taiwanese IT Industry: Capability Creation and the Effects of State–Industry Co evolution." *Industrial & Corporate Change* 14(1), 153–187.

Bruneel, Johan, D'este, Pablo, and Salter, Ammon. 2010. "Investigating the Factors that Diminish the Barriers to University–Industry Collaboration." *Research Policy* 39, 858–868.

Clarysse, Bart, Wright, Mike, Lockett, Andy, Van de Velde, Els, and Vohora, Ajay. 2005. "Spinning Out New Ventures: A Typology of Incubation Strategies from European Research Institutions." *Journal of Business Venturing* 20, 183–216.

Colyvas, Jeannette, Crow, Michael, Gelijns, Annetine, Mazzoleni, Roberto, Nelson, Richard R., Rosenberg, Nathan, and Sampat, Bhaven N. 2002. "How Do University Inventions Get into Practice?" *Management Science* 48(1), 61–72.

Colyvas, J.A., and Powell, W.W. 2007. From vulnerable to venerated: The institutionalization of academic entrepreneurship in the life sciences. *Research in the Sociology of Organizations* 25, 219–259.

Dahlstrand, Asa L. 1997. "Growth and Inventiveness in Technology-Based Spin-Off Firms." *Research Policy* 26(3), 331–344.

Davenport, Sally, Carr, Adrian, and Bibby, Dave. 2002. "Leveraging Talent: Spin-Off Strategy at Industrial Research." *R&D Management* 32(3), 241–254.

DiGregorio, Dante and Shane, Scott. 2003. "Why Do Some Universities Generate More Start-Ups than Others?" *Research Policy* 32(2), 209–227.

Degroof, Jane-Jacques and Roberts, Edward B. 2004. "Overcoming Weak Entrepreneurial Infrastructures for Academic Spin-Off Ventures." *Journal of Technology Transfer* 29(3–4), 327–354.

Djokovic, Djordje and Souitaris, Vangelis. 2008. "Spinouts from Academic Institutions: A Literature Review with Suggestions for Further Research." *Journal of Technology Transfer* 33(3), 225–247.

Druilhe, Céline and Garnsey, Elizabeth. 2004. "Do Academic Spin-Outs Differ and Does It Matter?" *Journal of Technology Transfer* 29(3–4), 269–285.

Eesley, C.E. and Miller, W.F. 2012. *Impact: Stanford University's Economic Impact via Innovation and Entrepreneurship.*

Ensley, Michael D. and Hmieleski, Keith M. 2005. "A Comparative Study of New Venture Top Management Team Composition, Dynamics and Performance between University-Based and Independent Start-Ups." *Research Policy* 34(7), 1091–1105.

Feldman, M.P. and Francis, Johanna L. 2003. "Fortune Favors the Prepared Region: The Case of Entrepreneurship and the Capitol Region Biotechnology Cluster." *European Planning Studies* 11, 765–788.

Fini, Richard, Grimaldi, Rosa, Santoni, Simone, and Sobrero, Maurizio. 2011. "Complements or Substitutes? The Role of Universities and Local Context in Supporting the Creation of Academic Spin-Offs." *Research Policy* 40(8), 1113–1127.

Fini, Richard, Lacetera, Nicola, and Shane , Scott. 2010. "Inside or Outside the IP System? Business Creation in Academia." *Research Policy* 39(8), 1060–1069.

Florida, Richard and Kenney, Martin. 1988. "Venture Capital-Financed Innovation and Technological Change in the United States." *Research Policy* 17, 119–137.

George, Gerard, Jain, Sanjay, and Maltarich, Mark. 2006. Academics or Entrepreneurs? Entrepreneurial Identity and Invention Disclosure Behavior of University Scientists. Paper presented at the University Technology Transfer and Commercialization of Research: Antecedents and Consequences Symposium, Academy of Management Conference, Atlanta, GA.

Goldfarb, Brent and Henrekson, Magnus. 2003. "Bottom-Up versus Top-Down Policies towards the Commercialization of University Intellectual Property." *Research Policy* 32, 639–658.

Hague, Donald and Oakley, Kate. 2000. Spin-Offs and Start-Ups in UK Universities. Committee of Vice-Chancellors and Principals (CVCP) Report.

Hoye, Kate and Pries, Fred. 2009. "'Repeat Commercializers' and the 'Habitual Entrepreneurs' of University–Industry Technology Transfer." *Technovation* 29, 682–689.

Kenney, Martin. 2000. *Understanding Silicon Valley: The Anatomy of an Entrepreneurial Region.* Stanford University Press, Stanford, CA.

Kenney, Martin and Goe, Richard W. 2004. "The Role of Social Embeddedness in Professorial Entrepreneurship: A Comparison of Electrical Engineering and Computer Science at UC Berkeley and Stanford." *Research Policy* 33, 691–707.

Kenney, Martin and Patton, Donald. 2009. "Reconsidering the Bayh–Dole Act and the Current University Invention Ownership Model." *Research Policy* 38, 1407–1422.

   2011. "Does Inventor Ownership Encourage University Research-Derived Entrepreneurship? A Six University Comparison." *Research Policy* 40, 1100–1112.

Kirby, David A. 2006. "Creating Entrepreneurial Universities in the UK: Applying Entrepreneurship Theory to Practice." *Journal of Technology Transfer* 31(5), 599–603.

Knockaert, Miriam, Wright, Mike, Clarysse, Bart, and Lockett, Andy. 2010. "Agency and Similarity Effects and the VC's Attitude towards Academic Spin-Out Investing." *Journal of Technology Transfer* 35(6), 567–584.

Lenoir, Tim and Giannella, Eric. 2006. Mapping the Impact of Federally Funded Extra-University Research and Development on the Emergence of Self-Sustaining Knowledge Domains: The Case of Microarray Technologies. Presented at the University Technology Transfer and Commercialization of Research: Antecedents and Consequences Symposium, Academy of Management Conference, Atlanta, GA.

Lerner, Josh. 1999. "The Government as Venture Capitalist: The Long-Run Impact of the SBIR Program." *Journal of Business Venturing* 72(3), 285–318.

Lerner, J. 2005. The university and the start-up: lessons from the past two decades, Journal of Technology Transfer 30(1/2), 49–56.

Link, Albert N. and Scott, John T. 2003. "U.S. Science Parks: The Diffusion of an Innovation and Its Effects on the Academic Missions of Universities." *International Journal of Industrial Organization* 21(9), 1323–1351.

—— 2005. "Opening the Ivory Tower's Door: An Analysis of the Determinants of the Formation of U.S. University Spin-Off Companies." *Research Policy* 34(7), 1106–1112.

—— 2010. "Government as Entrepreneur: Evaluating the Commercialization Success of SBIR Projects." *Research Policy* 39(5), 589–601.

Link, Albert N. and Siegel, Donald S. 2005. "Generating Science-Based Growth: An Econometric Analysis of the Impact of Organizational Incentives on University–Industry Technology Transfer." *European Journal of Finance* 11(3), 169–181.

Litan, Robert N., Mitchell, Lesa, and Reedy, E.J. 2007. "The University as Innovator: Bumps in the Road." *Issues in Science and Technology* 23(4), 57–66.

Lockett, Andy and Wright, Mike. 2005. "Resources, Capabilities, Risk Capital and the Creation of University Spin-Out Companies." *Research Policy* 34(7), 1043–1057.

Louis, Karen S., Blumenthal, David, Gluck, Michael E., and Stoto, Michael A. 1989. "Entrepreneurs in Academe: An Exploration of Behaviors among Life Scientists." *Administrative Science Quarterly* 34(1), 110–131.

Macho-Stadler, Ines, Perez-Castrillo, David, and Veugelers, Reinhilde. 2007. "Licensing of University Inventions: The Role of a Technology Transfer Office." *International Journal of Industrial Organization* 25(3), 483–510.

Markman, Gideon D., Gianiodis, Peter T., Phan, Phillip H., and Balkin, David B. 2005. "Innovation Speed: Transferring University Technology to Market." *Research Policy* 34, 1058–1075.

Mowery, David C., Nelson, Richard R., Sampat, Bhaven, and Ziedonis, Arvids. 2004. *Ivory Tower and Industrial Innovation: University–Industry Technology Transfer before and after the Bayh–Dole Act.* Stanford Business Books, Stanford, CA.

Munari, F. and Toschi, L. 2011. "Do Venture Capitalists have a Bias against Investment in Academic Spin-Offs? Evidence from the Micro- and Nanotechnology Sector in the UK." *Industrial and Corporate Change* 20(2), 397–432.

Mustar, Philippe. 1997. "Spin-Off Enterprises: How French Academics Create Hi-tech Companies: The Conditions for Success or Failure." *Science and Public Policy* 24(1), 37–43.

Mustar, Philippe, Renualt, Marie, Colombo, Massimo G., Piva, Evila, Fontes, Margarida, Lockett, Andy, Wright, Mike, Clarysse, Bart, and Moray, Nathalie. 2006. "Conceptualising the Heterogeneity of Research-based Spin-offs: A Multi-dimensional Taxonomy." *Research Policy* 35(2), 289–308.

National Research Council. 2010. *Managing University Intellectual Property In The Public Interest.* Washington, DC: National Research Council.

Ndonzuau, Frédéric Nlemvo, Pirnay, Fabrice, and Surlemont, Bernard. 2002. "A Stage Model of Academic Spin-Off Creation." *Technovation* 22(5), 281–289.

Nerkar, Atul and Shane, Scott. 2003. "When Do Start-Ups That Exploit Patented Academic Knowledge Survive?" *International Journal of Industrial Organization* 21(9), 1391–1410.

Nicolaou, Nicos and Birley, Sue. 2003a. "Academic Networks in a Trichotomous Categorisation of University Spinouts." *Journal of Business Venturing* 18(3), 333–359.

2003b. "Social Networks in Organizational Emergence: The University Spinout Phenomenon." *Management Science* 49(12), 1702–1725.

O'Shea, Rory P., Allen, Thomas J., Chevalier, Arnaud, and Roche, Frank. 2005. "Entrepreneurial Orientation, Technology Transfer and Spinoff Performance of U.S. Universities." *Research Policy* 34(7), 994–1009.

Parayil, Govindan. 2005. "From 'Silicon Island' to 'Biopolis of Asia': Innovation Policy and Shifting Competitive Strategy in Singapore." *California Management Review* 47(2), 50–73.

Patzelt, Holger and Shepherd, Dean A. 2009. "Strategic Entrepreneurship at Universities: Academic Entrepreneurs' Assessment of Policy Programs." *Entrepreneurship Theory and Practice* 33, 319–340.

Powers, Joshua B. and McDougall, Patricia P. 2005. "University Start-Up Formation and Technology Licensing with Firms That Go Public: A Resource-Based View of Academic Entrepreneurship." *Journal of Business Venturing* 20(3), 291–311.

Radosevich, Raymond. 1995. "A Model for Entrepreneurial Spin-Offs from Public Technology Sources." *International Journal of Technology Management* 10(7–8), 879–893.

Rasmussen, Einar and Borch, Odd Jarl. 2010. "University Capabilities in Facilitating Entrepreneurship: A Longitudinal Study of Spin-Off Ventures at Midrange Universities." *Research Policy* 39(5), 602–612.

Roberts, Edward B. 1991. *Entrepreneurs in High Technology: Lessons from MIT and Beyond.* Oxford University Press, Oxford.

Roberts, Edward B. and Malone, Denis E. 1996. "Policies and Structures for Spinning Off New Companies from Research and Development Organizations." *R&D Management* 26(1), 17–48.

Roberts, E.B. and Eesley, C.E. 2011. Entrepreneurial impact: the role of MIT – an updated report, *Foundations and Trends in Entrepreneurship*, 7, 1–149.

Rogers, Everett M., Takegami, Shiro, and Yin, Jing. 2001. "Lessons Learned about Technology Transfer." *Technovation* 21(4), 253–261.

Rothaermel, Frank T. and Thursby, Marie. 2005. "Incubator Firm Failure or Graduation?: The Role of University Linkages." *Research Policy* 34(7), 1076–1090.

Sampat, Bhaven N. 2006. "Patenting and US Academic Research in the 20th Century: The World before and after Bayh–Dole." *Research Policy* 35, 772–789.

Saxenian, AnnaLee. 1994. *Regional Advantage: Culture and Competition in Silicon Valley and Route 128.* Harvard University Press, Cambridge, MA.

Shane, Scott. 2004a. *Academic Entrepreneurship: University Spinoffs and Wealth Creation.* Edward Elgar, Cheltenham.

2004b. "Encouraging University Entrepreneurship? The Effect of the Bayh–Dole Act on Patenting in the United States." *Journal of Business Venturing* 19, 127–151.

Shane, Scott and Stuart, Toby. 2002. "Organizational Endowments and the Performance of University Start-Ups." *Management Science* 48(1), 154–170.

Siegel, Donald S., Waldman, David A., Atwater, Leanne E., and Link, Albert N. 2004. "Toward a Model of the Effective Transfer of Scientific Knowledge to Practitioners: Qualitative Evidence from the Commercialization of University Technologies." *Journal of Engineering and Technology Management* 21, 115–142.

Smilor, Raymond W., Gibson, David V., and Dietrich, Glenn B. 1990. "University Spin-Out Companies: Technology Start-ups from UT-Austin." *Journal of Business Venturing* 5(1), 63–76.

Sorenson, Olav and Stuart, Toby E. 2001. "Syndication Networks and the Spatial Distribution of Venture Capital Financing." *American Journal of Sociology* 106, 1546–1588.

Souitaris, Vangelis, Zerbinati, Stefania, and Al-Laham, Andreas. 2007. "Do Entrepreneurship Programmes Raise Entrepreneurial Intention of Science and Engineering Students? The Effect of Learning, Inspiration and Resources." *Journal of Business Venturing* 22(4), 566–592.

Steffensen, Morten, Rogers, Everett M., and Speakman, Kristen. 1999. "Spin-Offs from Research Centers at a Research University." *Journal of Business Venturing* 15(1), 93–111.

Stuart, Toby E. and Ding, Waverly W. 2006. "When Do Scientists Become Entrepreneurs? The Social Structural Antecedents of Commercial Activity in the Academic Life Sciences." *American Journal of Sociology* 112(1), 97–144.

Thursby, Jerry G. and Kemp, Sukanya. 2002. "Growth and Productive Efficiency of University Intellectual Property Licensing." *Research Policy* 31, 109–124.

Vanaelst, Iris, Clarysse, Bart, Wright, Mike, Lockett, Andy, Moray, Nathalie, and S'Jegers, Rosette. 2006. "Entrepreneurial Team Development in Academic Spinouts: An Examination of Team Heterogeneity." *Entrepreneurship Theory and Practice* 30(2), 249–271.

Vohora, Ajay, Wright, Mike, and Lockett, Andy. 2004. "Critical Junctures in the Development of University High-Tech Spinout Companies." *Research Policy* 33 (1), 147–175.

Wallmark, J. Torkel 1997. "Inventions and Patents at Universities: The Case of Chalmers University of Technology." *Technovation* 17(3), 127–139.

Wright, Mike, Vohora, Ajay, and Lockett, Andy. 2004. "The Formation of High-Tech University Spinouts: The Role of Joint Ventures and Venture Capital Investors." *Journal of Technology Transfer* 29(3–4), 287–301.

Wright, Mike, Lockett, Andy, Clarysse, Bart, and Binks, M. 2006. "University Spin-Out Companies and Venture Capital." *Research Policy* 35(4), 481–501.

Zhang, Junfu. 2009. "The Performance of University Spin-Offs: An Exploratory Analysis Using Venture Capital Data." *Journal of Technology Transfer* 34(3), 255–285.

Zucker, Lynne G., Darby, Michael R., and Brewer, Marilyn B. 1998b. "Intellectual Human Capital and the Birth of U.S. Biotechnology Enterprises." *American Economic Review* 88(1), 190–305.

4   Creating the MIT entrepreneurial ecosystem

*Elliot A. Fishman, Rory P. O'Shea,
and Thomas J. Allen*

MIT and the rise of the entrepreneurial university

Teaching and research with application to the practical world has been a guiding principle at MIT since its foundation in 1862. Beginning as a land grant university (cf. www.higher-ed.org/resources/morrill_acts.htm), MIT has a long history of partnership with the social and economic development of the state of Massachusetts. The university employs slightly over 1,000 faculty members and enrolls approximately 4,200 undergraduates and a little over 6,000 graduate and professional students. A large proportion of MIT students come there from over 100 countries outside of the United States.

MIT has been very successful in fostering entrepreneurial approaches to technology transfer and is recognized as one of the world's leading entrepreneurial universities. Ranked as one of the leading generators of spin-off activity within the United States (O'Shea 2005) over the last decade, MIT has vibrant patenting/licensing activity and recorded 706 new invention disclosures in fiscal year 2012. Many of MIT's patents are licensed or sublicensed to world-leading pharmaceutical, chemical, biotechnology, and medical device companies. According to a recent study conducted by Roberts and Eesley (2009), 25,000+ companies have been founded by MIT alumni and alumnae, creating 3.3+ million jobs and $2 trillion in annual world sales.

History – The rise of entrepreneurial science

The entrepreneurial anatomy of MIT and the culture of its faculty are partly explained by a sequence of historical events, some serendipitous and others quite deliberate, which have made it highly prolific in its spin-off activity. From its inception as a land grant college at the time of the American Civil War, MIT has had a propensity to engage with industry to a far greater extent than its Ivy League rivals. The motto on the MIT seal, "Mens et Manus" ("mind and hand"), signals the university's dedication to what founder William Barton Rogers called "the most earnest cooperation of intelligent culture with industrial pursuits" (Stratton and Mannix 2005).

MIT's connections with industry are well documented in the literature. This section draws out an important insight, however, that the way in which MIT interacts with industry has changed dramatically over time. In addition, a dynamic balance of power – revolving around intellectual property rights and research agenda – swung gradually away from MIT's original industrial sponsors (1862–1931) to Institute administrators such as Vannevar Bush and Karl Compton (1932–1939; 1946–present day), to the faculty entrepreneurs themselves. Today, spin-offs and venture capital backing have become commonplace.

A historical purview is useful to trace the development of the culture that first legitimized and ultimately encouraged technology transfer and spin-off activity. Furthermore, a historical lens also shows how path dependencies directed institutional norms to congeal into their contemporary form. History is ultimately necessary to elucidate why MIT's entrepreneurial environment is indeed multicausal. A historical narrative is further necessary to describe why MIT's culture is so difficult to replicate at different times and in different settings.

The founding of MIT (1861)

The story of MIT spin-off activity must be traced all the way back to the Institute's inception. The language and spirit of the Founding Charter drew a long arc of industrial engagement that encouraged faculty spin-off companies, though this was not within the Charter's original intent (Charter of MIT Corporation 1861). William Barton Rogers and his industrial sponsors established "a school of industrial science" that would aid "by suitable means, the advancement, development and practical application of science in connection with arts, agriculture manufactures and commerce." Perhaps signaling their pragmatic intent, they called themselves "Members of the MIT Corporation" rather than the more stuffy, academic sounding "Board of Trustees." MIT's original Corporation Members were committed to a level of cooperation between their industrial enterprises and the school's faculty that was unprecedented in higher education.

It is important to recognize that when the founders wrote, "the advancement, development and practical application of science," they were focused on MIT's benefits to established industry – not technology transfer to newly founded, spun-off ventures (the term "spin-off" did not even exist in the day). In this context, it was not surprising that the

Members of the Corporation (i.e., the Board of Trustees) recruited William Barton Rogers as the school's first president in 1862. As described in the following, he had already proven himself to be socially adept, administratively competent, and firmly situated in the scientific establishment of his time.

William Barton Rogers

Rogers, who was a geologist by training, was born into a family of physicians, scientists, and educators. His father, Patrick Kerr Rogers, and mother, Hannah (Blythe) Rogers, were immigrants from Ireland.[1] Over the course of his early career, he held professorships at the College of William and Mary (where his father once taught) and the University of Virginia. Though he published, as was expected, and gained recognition for his scientific work and geochemical innovations, he would distinguish himself in other ways.[2] By temperament and social background, Rogers was always more interested in human affairs and understanding the levers of institutional power than in mineral specimens or sedimentary deposits.

Rogers's interest in the sphere of public science was soon realized through official positions with geological surveys of New Jersey, Pennsylvania, and Virginia, where his duties were more administrative in nature than purely scientific. In these roles he traveled widely within the United States and Europe and came to know men of scientific ability and political skill. Over time his scientific curiosity, extensive travel, and comfortable social manner would generate invitations from numerous important scientific academies and societies. In the early nineteenth century these societies were gatekeepers of scientific discovery. The important scientific journals of the age were published by these scientific societies. Fellows of prestigious societies decided what experiments would be codified as new knowledge and taught to the next generation of scholars. As a fellow in multiple societies, Rogers was therefore part of a small, tightly knit elite who legitimized nineteenth-century scientific knowledge.

Rogers first demonstrated his own organizational flair in 1840 when he co-founded the Association of American Geologists and Naturalists,

---

[1] Julius Stratton (himself a later president of MIT) and Loretta Mannix (2005) point out that "Patrick Kerr Rogers, an Irish nationalist, fled Ireland for the United States in 1798 to avoid prosecution by the British authorities...[for his involvement in the nationalist uprising of that year].

[2] For further information about William Barton Rogers academic achievements, see chapter 1, Schrock, Robert R. Geology at MIT 1865–1965: A History of he First Hundred Years of Geology at Massachusetts Institute of Technology (Cambridge: MIT Press, 1977).

which became the parent organization of the American Association for the Advancement of Science (AAAS). In 1845 he was elected a fellow of the AAAS when he was just forty-one years old. By the time he was approached for MIT's top post, Rogers's curriculum vitae included memberships and fellowships in the Geological Society of London, the American Philosophical Society, the Boston Society of Natural History, the Royal Society of Northern Antiquaries (Copenhagen), and the American Academy of Arts and Sciences. By his fifty-seventh year, Rogers also held two honorary law degrees from colleges in Virginia and had speaking invitations on two continents. In the sphere of the scientific establishment, he was perfectly placed for a new role in academia.

It was a natural career progression, if not altogether planned, for Rogers to ascend to a college presidency. In 1862, a coincidental article of federal legislation known as the Morrill Act advanced his career opportunities enormously. Also known as the Land Grant Act for Universities, the Morrill Act freely awarded each American state an amount of money derived from the sale of land owned by the federal government. The amount varied by state, each state being awarded an amount based on the number of its senators and representatives in Congress. A state received money resulting from the sale of 30,000 acres for each of its senators and congressmen. This money was to be used by the state to endow institutions, to "teach agriculture, military tactics, and the mechanic arts, not to the exclusion of classical studies, so that members of the working classes might obtain a practical college education." The Morrill Act enabled a group of well-connected Boston industrialists to finally enact a plan that they conceived several years before to found (and fund) a school to train engineers in the technical arts.[3,4] The growing number of factories and mills faced a shortage of well-trained engineers, which also drove a rational self-interest behind a philanthropic initiative. To execute this plan, they were fortunate to have a man experienced in academic affairs who truly believed in the application of knowledge to practical needs, William Barton Rogers. Rogers was respected in academic circles, despite the fact that he had deviated from the firm belief in the dominance of classical education and by participating in the establishment of schools of civil engineering at the University of Virginia and at the College of William and

---

[3] In the face of heated opposition from a nearby and considerably senior neighbor, Harvard University.

[4] Following a model established by the Ecole Polytechnique and Ecole Centrale in France and by the Technische Hochschulen in Germany.

Mary.[5] Rogers was well known in the Boston area for his lectures to popular audiences on science (Stratton and Mannix 2005). His principal discipline was geology, a field strongly tied to industry at that time.

MIT's exploitation of the Morrill Act was unique. First, because this was the only federal land grant extended to a private university, and second, because MIT was the only land grant school founded by industrialists for industrialists. In other words, the Institute would develop technology and train engineers to serve the needs of established industry. MIT's technology was not initially developed for engineers to start their own companies. Neither were industrialists funding MIT labs to give science away to farmers, as at most of the agricultural land grant schools in the mid-western states. To MIT corporation members, technology was a means of improving the fortunes of privately held industrial enterprises, just like the enterprises they founded themselves. Thus, former MIT President Charles Vest only told half the story when he wrote, "The land grant movement invented a university that was committed to the economic and social development of its region. It created a university that took local needs and circumstances into account in developing its research and training programs. The land grant academic model inspired a significant element of the development of MIT as a school committed to regional development, of the Boston area in the mid-nineteenth century and New England in the mid-twentieth century" (Vest 2004).

Other land grant universities, such as the Universities of Wisconsin, Illinois, Iowa, and Kansas, and Michigan State, were, quite naturally, dedicated foremost to agricultural science, and their scientific discoveries – whether they pertained to heartier crops or fatter cows – and their discoveries were to be shared freely as a public good. Not only were they located in the farm belt, but also the constituency of these schools was largely drawn from a populist movement, not from capitalists as in the case of MIT. The agricultural schools were publicly chartered and reliably funded by the states. Because industrial involvement was not an original part of their educational model, they never experienced much in the way of tensions with industry over funding or control of a research agenda. For privately funded MIT, however, industrial linkages – and later intellectual property rights – have been a double-edged sword, from the Institute's founding right through to the 1930s.

---

[5] It is also stated that Rogers developed an idea for an MIT-like school while at UVA and went to Boston at the suggestion of his brother, a business person there, to seek support. See *MIT and the Rise of Entrepreneurial University* (2002).

Industrial linkages in the early 1900s

The gravitational field of large industry could always be sensed from the time the Institute was formally founded in 1862. The mission of MIT (or "Boston Tech," as it was known in the late 1800s) was to train engineers and perform testing (chiefly testing of industrial materials and machines). Sponsors at the turn of the twentieth century were the large New England corporations of the day. Essentially, MIT was a place where they could go to train and recruit smart engineers and outsource R&D. Furthermore, materials testing and machine building activities were often performed on behalf of specific companies, while their executives sat on MIT's board. No one considered this to be a conflict of interest. Likewise, few questioned whether a nonprofit technical institute such as MIT should set its own research agenda or follow a sponsor corporation's plan. Finally, few thought that intellectual property rights to new discoveries should reside anywhere but with the industrial patron.

Partially as a result of this industrial yoke, MIT professors were not seen as peers by faculty at nationally prominent universities. Academic colleagues at other schools, especially those at the elitist Ivy League, held MIT's direct ties to commercial interests in low regard. While MIT was teaching and perfecting methods useful to a rapidly industrializing America, other universities still viewed MIT as a high-end trade school, no matter how ingenious its faculty or socially important its discoveries (e.g., better toilet valves). Early in the twentieth century, the MIT faculty with its ambitions to perform pure research could not avoid forming an inferiority complex. While other American universities were gradually adopting the German model of research – pure and theoretical – MIT continued to rely on industrial sponsors, thus holding the school back to an earlier century.

Then in 1916, a large bequest from an anonymous donor (later revealed to be the photography tycoon George Eastman) enabled MIT to move across the Charles River to Cambridge, just down the road from Harvard. There, in former swampland, they built elegant learning halls draped in neoclassical marble. Great technological advances occurred within those walls, but given the Institute's newfound look, faculty and alumni could only wish there were more prestige behind their alma mater to match the new buildings' impressive architectural facade.

Funding crisis and the Division of Industrial Cooperation and Research (1920s)

Even after the move to Cambridge, traditions of industrial subservience remained. The school was simply undercapitalized, tuition dollars never met expenses, and they had no choice but to persist with any funding models that worked. In the same spirit as the earlier industrial testing laboratories, MIT established a new division, called the Division of Industrial Cooperation and Research (DICR),[6] which was essentially a revenue-generating scheme. Under the DICR's mandate, industrial corporations could rotate practicing engineers through MIT laboratories, which enabled the direct transfer of know-how from an academic setting to the company's shop floor. Again, MIT assumed a pragmatic approach (though in retrospect one that was not particularly savvy in a commercial sense). Not much thought was given to ownership of patent rights, so corporations regularly claimed ownership of valuable inventions. This seemed perfectly appropriate, because corporations were footing the research bills. Moreover, faculty were still discouraged from exploring risky breakthrough areas, and instead aimed their focus on applied problems of a sponsor's particular design. In return, the sponsors paid faculty salaries and laboratory expenses each year. In this context "faculty entrepreneurship" meant recruiting an industrial sponsor, and maybe drumming up some paid consulting work on the side. Though the program was initially successful, the DICR director, William Walker, became an object of ridicule to some of the more scientifically minded faculty. They saw him as a hack moving the school backward to its founding days. Corporate enrollments in the DICR program mushroomed throughout the 1920s but then fell off with the Great Depression.

The extent of sponsored research, as generated by the DICR, raised alarm bells among alumni and MIT Corporation members alike. Would their alma mater ever grow into a great research university? As technology advanced steadily, would MIT even keep up with the times if its faculty were just solving the sponsors' problems of the day? After the early success of the DICR, there was growing envy on campus and an aspiration to become a more prestigious university. The pendulum was soon to swing away from applied science toward a more theoretical approach.

Karl Taylor Compton and Vannevar Bush (1932–1945)

Under these conditions Karl Compton was inaugurated as the President of MIT in 1932. As a physicist from Princeton University, he had the right academic pedigree. He was distinguished in scientific circles, and his brother, Arthur Compton, had won the Nobel Prize for Physics in 1927. At the start of the Great Depression, Karl Compton's daunting

---

[6] The predecessor of today's Industrial Liaison program, which has been widely emulated and remains the largest of its kind in the world.

task was to distance MIT from the manipulations of industrial sponsors while maintaining earlier levels of corporate funding. At the very same time, he needed to instill a new culture of scientific rigor and discipline with complacent faculty members. Many old-timers had been accused of intellectual laziness, of not keeping up with their fields. Semiretired professors were seen by some as wasting time in labs, perfecting pedestrian industrial techniques that injured the Institute's reputation. Soon after joining MIT, Compton presented the members of the corporation with the challenge of renewing it in both size and prestige. Once assured of their backing, he repeated this mission statement with faculty and alumni.

Compton recruited new faculty from top graduate programs and focused on hiring only those with independent research potential.[7] Meanwhile, he encouraged less scientifically capable faculty to take early retirement, freeing up their slots. He found an ally in a brilliant but cantankerous Dean of Engineering named Vannevar Bush. Bush was named Vice President of the Institute and enthusiastically engaged in confrontations with recalcitrant faculty, relieving Compton of the burden of being solely responsible for the changes he envisaged. (Later Bush would achieve wartime fame as scientific director of the Office of Science, Research & Development (OSRD), which was a precursor of the National Science Foundation.)

Throughout the 1930s Compton and Bush instilled policies that placed MIT on more certain financial footing. They stimulated advanced research, embarked on fundraising and building campaigns, and raised the Institute's standing tremendously within scientific circles. Perhaps most importantly, Compton and Bush developed new government funding sources, chiefly located within the Departments of the Navy and of the Army. From World War II onward, MIT switched its primary funding model from the private sector to government sources. After the war, with the establishment of Lincoln Laboratories, this transition to military funding became a permanent state of affairs. Because books and doctoral dissertations have been written on these two men and their era at MIT, there is no need to reiterate here what is more thoroughly stated elsewhere. What does bear mentioning, however, is the establishment of MIT's patent policy during the 1930s.[8]

---

[7] Compton recruited physicists whose research had conjoint theoretical and practical import, e.g., high-voltage generators. He arranged for the transfer of intellectual property rights from Princeton to MIT, which later became the High Voltage Corporation (Etzkowitz).

[8] This theme is expounded in the doctoral dissertation of one of the authors (Fishman 1996).

Emerging patent policy and the early faculty entrepreneurs

During the 1930s MIT first established and then fine-tuned its patent policy. The original patent policy came directly from President Karl Compton's office and was signed by his own hand. Clarifications on the policy were issued both by Professor John Bunker and later by Vice President Vannevar Bush. Each man chaired MIT's Patent Committee until the eve of World War II. The Patent Committees first deliberated issues such as the ethical rationale of keeping knowledge proprietary ("to protect the public welfare"); the proper ownership of inventions and the inventors' rights to assign discoveries; the allocation of royalties and the permissibility of exclusive licenses; negotiations with government agencies; and institutional responses to uncooperative faculty entrepreneurs and the desirability of litigation against infringers. Over the course of the next eight years, MIT's early Patent Committee considered hundreds of faculty invention disclosures and devised new patent and licensing policies as they encountered novel issues. Each new deliberation established a precedent and was carefully codified for future instances of the same controversy. As a result, a thorough and consistent patent policy took shape before World War II.

By the eve of World War II, the new patent policy had been practically tested in several dozen cases. Royalties from the patents only trickled in, but now MIT had become consistent in applying for patent rights. Moreover, valuable discoveries were withheld from industry until they paid license fees, like any third party. These serendipitous developments in Institute patent policy turned out to be a chief catalyst for the emergence of faculty entrepreneurs. After World War II, MIT's patent policy enabled the Institute to obtain a substantial number of technology licenses, and in several cases, spin companies off.

But it is a mistake to automatically conclude that President Compton saw patents as a way to stimulate faculty entrepreneurship or to generate spin-offs. No companies were spun off during his tenure, and royalties from technology licenses were still just trickling in. From what can be gleaned in the archival record, Compton had condoned faculty entrepreneurship.[9] His chief concerns were about research quality and

---

[9] As Chair of the TNEC Committee, he supported firm formation from science as a cure for depression and later sold this idea to the New England Council. He and fellow MIT administrators envisioned "Research Row" along the Charles River. Compton was a proponent of ARD, the first venture capital firm, committed MIT funds and raised funds from Rice and other schools, sat on its board, and spent 10 percent of his time, according to one estimate, as an advisor to ARD and its firms. Compton may be considered one of the originators of science-based economic development in the United States.

faculty productivity and he was troubled by the constraints industrial sponsors had historically imposed on the Institute, which often impaired research quality. He wanted to reverse MIT's subordinate negotiating position with industrial sponsors. Enhancement of MIT's intellectual property rights was just one technique for acquiring research grants from industry on better terms. Once MIT Corporation could automatically assert patent rights to all of the research conducted on campus, industrial sponsors could no longer march into its laboratories and simply pluck up the valuable inventions. Someday they would have to treat the Institute as an equal.[10]

Why then do so many of the data point to increased faculty entrepreneurship during the Compton presidency? How do we explain the high correlation between a strengthened patent policy and commercial distractions of the faculty during the 1930s? The law of unintended consequences seems to have been in full force: as MIT strengthened its patent policy, faculty entrepreneurship grew too – but as an accidental effect of the new policies.[11] These new patent policies, as we have discussed, were designed to recalibrate industrial linkages. Faculty could now supplement their income by owning part of their research and selling it to the highest bidder, including the very companies that paid for their labs. Perpetually short of revenue, the Institute was open to accepting a majority share of the license fees. But it is important to note that MIT stumbled into the business of licensing technology.[12] Most contemporary articles assume otherwise, suggesting that MIT embarked on the technology transfer business with conscious intent, but the historical record shows that patent licensing was more accidental. Faculty entrepreneurs drove the process – not MIT's administration. They were especially clever and ambitious, and only revisionist histories claim that MIT's administration was skillful and strategic about commercializing early stage technology.

As faculty entrepreneurs encountered new opportunities to engage industry around intellectual property rights, the Institute's Patent Committee developed new standards for how patent licenses would be treated. A few noteworthy examples of MIT faculty entrepreneurs from the 1930s are shown in Table 4.1. We list their inventions, along with

---

[10] For further information on patent policy refer to Etzkowitz (1994).

[11] One must note that entrepreneurship preceded patent polic,y with spin-off ventures being formed from both MIT and Harvard in scientific instruments in the late nineteenth century. Raytheon and A.D. Little were other examples (Etzkowitz 2002).

[12] Although there may have been a faculty committee in process, licensing at the university was largely a bottom-up process, given that a deliberate policy was never rationalized with a business plan.

Table 4.1: *MIT patent committee*

Faculty inventor	Invention	Precedent within Patent Committee
Nicholas Milas	Activated ergesterol-antibiotic	Exclusive licensing/pharma compound
C. Hawley Cartwright	Metal deposition for optical materials	Overseeing patent agents; government negotiations
Wilmer Barrow	Microwave horns	Litigation vs. industrial infringers
Robert van de Graaf	Electrostatic generators	Equity stake in VC-backed spin-off

institutional policy precedents they established within MIT's early Patent Committee.

Post–World War II era – Spin-off companies and venture capital (1945–present day)

We now arrive at the topic that has made MIT world-renowned: spin-offs. While patent policy was established in the 1930s, with the notable exceptions of Raytheon and the Arthur D. Little Corporation, the first spin-off activity did not really occur until after World War II. The explanation for this is very simple. In the economically depressed 1930s there was very little capital of any sort available (and no such concept as institutional venture capital). It was not until after the war that Karl Compton, then Chairman of the MIT Corporation, "with a number of alumni and friends of MIT [formed American Research and Development as a venture capital firm], to move research and technological ideas forward into the market. The heads of MIT's departments of Chemical Engineering and Aeronautical Engineering served as advisors and the Treasurer of MIT served as Treasurer of ARD." Furthermore, there were few role models to emulate as the personalities and techniques for spinning off a company were not yet available on campus. Finally, there was the distraction of World War II.

Then in 1946, the High Voltage Engineering Corporation (HVEC) was created out of Robert van de Graaf's laboratory for electrostatic generators. With MIT's blessing and licensed patent rights to Van de Graaf's technology, an entrepreneur named John Trump raised start-up money from the American Research and Development Corporation. HVEC intended to build x-ray machines for the first hospitals applying radiation treatment for cancer victims. Van de Graaf generators were an efficient way to generate the necessary voltage. The HVEC venture was widely promoted and certainly known to the MIT faculty of the day. Consequently, many more faculty became curious about the function of venture capital and the possibilities of an equity windfall.

This was an early investment by American Research and Development. Quite a few other companies received start-up support from this first venture capital company. However, the big payoff did not come until ARD invested in the Digital Equipment Corporation and received a majority position in that company's stock. Digital's subsequent success sent messages in two directions: first, to potential venture capitalists who formed the strategy of broad investments, realizing that most would not provide a large return while hoping for one or a few to produce a sufficient return to cover all of the expected losses; second, to the MIT faculty, who knew then that their technology could form the basis for the formation of firms that could potentially become major successes, as Digital had demonstrated (Hsu and Kenney 2005).

In this section we have shown that from its founding days MIT cultivated close linkages with industry, but early relations with industrial sponsors did not resemble the faculty entrepreneurship of today. The ownership of laboratory discoveries, as well as the faculty's research agenda, had long been contested among vested interests. Initially, MIT faculty performed industrial testing and freely handed new discoveries to industrial sponsors. Over time, however, the balance of power changed, as evidenced through the allocation of intellectual property rights and the faculty's prerogative to select research projects for themselves. Karl Compton came to office in 1932 and quickly established a strong patent policy that was mainly enforced to strengthen negotiations with industrial sponsors. In the era before World War II, the Institute patent committee designed sophisticated patent policies and licensing strategies. Each test case before them set important precedents. Faculty entrepreneurs exploited the new policy and began inventing marketable products to enhance their own wealth, not just the share price of an industrial sponsor. As it turned out, the faculty's opportunity for personal financial gain became a strong force driving technological development and innovation.

After World War II, the MIT faculty learned how to negotiate with venture capitalists and create spin-off companies. While the first venture, the High Voltage Engineering Company, was a commercial flop, organizational learning took place. That company's spin-off experiment was eventually emulated with great success.[13] Thus, the original arc

---

[13] For example, Ionics was another early firm supported by ARD, which eventually became a Fortune 500 firm, before being sold to General Electric.

drawn by William Barton Rogers was now complete. Back in 1861 he anticipated close linkages with industry, but always in a subordinate role. What no one could predict at that time was how faculty entrepreneurship would evolve, or how Rogers's plot would take unexpected curves and eventually give the Institute the upper hand when negotiating with industry over intellectual property.

The rise of an entrepreneurial culture

Since its inception, MIT has developed a philosophy that guides thought and action as it pursues its research, educational, and entrepreneurial mission. MIT's "Mens et Manus" tradition is about connecting the rigorous scholarly pursuit of knowledge with entrepreneurial success, transferring knowledge into practice in the most effective way.[14] It is this tacit understanding about what is important to the institution serves as a compass point for today's MIT academic leaders, keeping the institution on track as it makes decisions about resource allocation and research activities (Aulet, 2008). MIT, unlike many other institutions, has been fortunate in having a clear and defined, "espoused" mission, which, from the outset, specifically focused on application in industry.[15]

However, there is another important aspect to MIT's academic culture. Faculty members are expected to support their research activities with little help from the Institute. The MIT culture rewards the "academic entrepreneur," so there is an open environment where carrying out research with a company or a new venture is not perceived in a negative way, provided it enhances the education of students and contributes to internationally visible research. There appears to be little "either/or" attitude about business sponsorship of research versus government support in its mission statement (MIT 2004). The Institute believes that its educational program can only flourish when sustained by the active participation of its faculty in research, enriched in many cases by company interaction. Although it is neither favored nor precluded, taking

---

[14] In his speech launching an Institute-wide Initiative on Innovation in October 2013, MIT President Rafael Reif stated that the purpose of the initiative was to "actively celebrate, support and intensify MIT's culture of making, (and its) faith in the creative power of mind and hand." In support of the founding mission of the university, he also stated that he wanted to launch a program that "will give students, faculty, alumni and others beyond MIT the space, skills, knowledge, tools and opportunities to design, build, test, prototype, hack, scale up and accelerate the transformation of academic ideas into practical innovations through ventures, partnerships and networks."

[15] According to Dean David Schmittlein, MIT's mission is about creating people who want to "change the world, and invent the future." MIT Sloan's mission is "to develop principled, innovative leaders who improve the world." (Dean Schmittlein talks about MIT and American innovation on *CEO Global Foresight 2014*.)

time off from an academic career to work in a company, owning a piece of a company, or developing his or her own inventions is not atypical of an MIT professor's career in the sciences and engineering. Continued and frequent examples of this activity provide strong and plentiful role models for both junior faculty and students. Once there are role models in the form of people who have exploited their ideas and done well while remaining part of the academic community, there is a snowball effect (Roberts and Eesley 2011).[16]

According to a former Director of Technology Transfer at the Whitehead Institute, a number of factors motivate MIT academics to engage in entrepreneurial activities. First, there is a quest for academics to validate their technology in the market place. Second, many academics see business as interesting and stimulating. Finally, there is a desire for the accumulation of wealth. Different people balance these three motives differently. In our interviews with academic entrepreneurs, the quest for validation of their technology came out as the strongest motivating factor. The founder of two highly successful biotech companies sums up this driver: "I wanted to see my inventions making a difference in people's lives and not just sitting idly on the research bench in the lab." This view is shared by another prolific academic entrepreneur at MIT who stated recently that his "goal has always been not just to write the scientific paper, but really push some of these ideas to the point where they will affect lives in a positive way."

Another important and necessary condition in the rise of an entrepreneurial culture at MIT is its ability to attract large financial resources to fund leading-edge science and engineering research. Having access to R&D funds has enabled MIT to develop a wealth of technology that is often world class with great commercial value. MIT may have a $700 million research operation, but former President Hockfield (2007) points out that a substantial fraction of the money supports research that is not obviously "translational," not explicitly focused on solving practical problems or responding to market needs. She argues that what has made MIT a hotbed of new insights and ideas was the government's long-term support for fundamental, pure, curiosity-driven exploration and research.

MIT has a strong record as a research-intensive institution. In the National Science Foundation FY 2009 survey of academic research and development, MIT reported research expenditures of $736,102 million,

---

[16] According to the TLO Director, "the MIT Environment is very supportive to start-up ventures. At MIT, industrial careers are respected (even in the biological sciences), and entrepreneurship is the goal of many on campus. Past successful MIT start-up ventures encourage faculty and students to take the plunge themselves and provide a group of very visible role models – a real cheerleading group."

ranking tenth among all U.S. universities.[17,18] In terms of federal funding research revenues, MIT was ranked fourth in 2009, reporting $532,235 million in research expenditure (The Center for Measuring University Performance).

As well as having a large absolute amount of funding, MIT has been successful in attracting industry funding for research. According to the National Science Foundation, MIT ranks first in industry-financed R&D expenditures among all universities and colleges without a medical school. Industry-sponsored research totaled $133 million in FY12 (includes government pass-throughs), or 20 percent of all MIT research funding. MIT's interest in attracting industry funding for research reflects its belief that such funding can improve research and education. According to Charles Vest former President of MIT: "MIT has worked hard during the last few years to develop strong and appropriate research relations with private industry for three reasons: to improve our education; to diversify our sources of financial support; and to create new pathways for contributing to the common good."[19] It has sought to attract the most accomplished faculty and students in the fields where it has built research excellence. MIT's School of Engineering was ranked first among U.S. graduate engineering schools. MIT was also ranked the world's top university in 11 of 28 disciplines ranked by QS,[20] including all five in the "engineering and technology" category: computer science, chemical engineering, civil engineering, electrical engineering, and mechanical engineering.

Expectations for continued academic achievement are high, and for the most part tenure and promotion are based on academic achievement and building an outstanding academic reputation. But according to former President Vest, what sets MIT apart from other intellectual centers is not

---

[17] Each year, the National Science Foundation (NSF) collects data from hundreds of academic institutions on expenditures for research and development in science and engineering fields and classifies them by source of funds (federal government, state and local government, industry, etc.). These data are the primary source of information on academic research and development (R&D) expenditures in the United States.

[18] All federally funded research labs (FFRLs) are excluded from these academic expenditures data. As such, the Lincoln lab R&D expenditures have not been included in the MIT R&D figures.

[19] Former MIT president Susan Hockfield supports this view by highlighting the mutually beneficial reinforcing role of working with industry. She states "forging productive links between universities and business was one of the founding principles of MIT, and this is more important than ever in today's environment" (Hockfield 2005).

[20] The Global University Rankings 2012–2013 were published by Quacquarelli Symonds, an organization specializing in education and study abroad (www.topuniversities.com). QS rankings are based on research quality, graduate employment, teaching quality, and an assessment of the global diversity of faculty and students.

that it contains extremely smart people with big ideas, but that there are so many smart people in one part of the world tailor-made to take their ideas and turn them into something real and often profitable. He states, "Our faculty's commitment to deep, fundamental research and scholarship is matched by a desire to transfer new knowledge and technologies into the world in important and beneficial ways" (Vest 2004).

Similarly to Stanford, MIT employs a system referred to as "academic steeples." Academic steeples of expertise are built by recruiting and retaining a critical mass of faculty members in a selected niche or subdiscipline. Furthermore, the teaching and research focus of MIT is in domains that are conducive to commercialization. The MIT faculty is dominated by science and engineering academics, with faculty from these areas representing over 64 percent of the population. Throughout the years, the MIT faculty have been at the forefront of research in many fields. According to Dr. for President Vest "MIT history is replete with radical thinkers . . . who have truly founded or transformed major fields of scholarship. It's faculty members have pioneered some of the foundations of brain research, and their work continues to contribute broad insights in the fields of artificial intelligence, cognitive science, linguistics, computational and systems neuroscience, and molecular and genetic neuroscience" (Vest 2004). This leading edge work in emerging technological fields has provided a foundation for a number of spin-offs to emerge.

Investing in leading-edge embryonic fields is also very important to the former President Hockfield. Her major focus was on investing in energy issues and achieving leadership in the development of transformational technologies, not only to commercialize inventions but also to solve one of the pressing needs facing the United States and the world today. This vision has resulted in the formation of the MIT Energy Initiative (MITEI), whose aim is "to help transform the global energy system to meet the needs of the future and to help build a bridge to that future by improving today's energy systems." Its core mission is to thrust the Institute to the forefront of research and development of energy sources by focusing MIT's vast resources across departments and disciplines on 10 research programs. A brief summary of the program and emerging spin-offs is provided in Table 4.2.

Organizational characteristics

MIT is an exemplar for research universities that aspire to take technology transfer seriously. A single unit or office cannot create an effective, spin-off driven, university. Fulfilling an entrepreneurial mission requires

Table 4.2: *The MIT Energy Initiative (MITEI)*

MITEI's research program	Research areas
Transformational technologies to develop alternative energy sources that can supplement and displace fossil fuels, including the economic, management, social science, and policy dimensions needed for this transformation.	• Solar • Geothermal • Wind • Wave power • Biofuels • Energy storage • Hydrogen • Superconductors • Fusion
MIT start-up examples	• BlueEnergy . . . Wind and solar systems • GreenFuel . . . Biodiesel production • Evergreen . . . Solar • Agrivida . . . Biofuel • Metabolix . . . Bioplastics • Covalent Solar . . . Solar • 1366tech . . . Solar • Sun Catalytix . . . Solar • Star Solar . . . Solar • Condon Devices . . . Synthetic Biology • Ginko Bioworks
Innovative technologies and underlying policy analysis that will improve how we produce, distribute, and consume conventional energy	• Hydrocarbon products and processing • Energy conversion alternatives • Nuclear energy • Electric power systems and policy • Heat management • Industrial energy efficiency • Carbon sequestration • Building efficiency technologies
MIT start-up examples	• Satcom . . . Electric power conversion technology • A123 Systems . . . Li-ion battery • SolidEnergy . . . Battery • 24M . . . . Spin-off from A123 • Ambri . . . Liquid metal battery • Arctic Sand . . . Power management • Luminus Devices . . . LED energy efficient • QD Vision . . . Nanocrystal display
Global systems to meet energy and environmental challenges through a multidisciplinary systems approach that integrates policy design and technology development.	• Carbon management • Buildings and urban design • Transportation and vehicle systems

Table 4.2: (cont.)

MITEI's research program	Research areas
MIT start-up examples	• Kennedy & Violich . . . Carbon-neutral homes . . . design

Tools to enable innovation, transformation and simulation of global energy systems through strategic basic research: nanotechnology, biotechnology, engineering, materials science, earth science, etc.

Source: MIT Energy Initiative website, available at http://web.mit.edu/mitei/about/index. html.

the dedicated efforts of all academics and staff. MIT's academic leaders champion improvements and teach students what the institution values and how to take full advantage of its resources. They provide start-up support and have proactive systems in place to encourage entrepreneurial thinking. A number of organizational structures and practices also facilitate commercialization of research. These include the TLO, the Martin Trust Centre for MIT Entrepreneurship, the Deshpande Center for Technological Innovation, and other entrepreneurship development programs.

MIT has one of the more active and successful TLOs, established in 1945, many years before most universities were encouraged to take similar steps by the Bayh–Dole Act. Its highly experienced industry-focused team plays a proactive role in technology transfer activities. Rather than waiting for a "technology pull" – reacting to requests for licenses from interested companies – the TLO encourages faculty to promptly disclose inventions, quickly and carefully evaluate their market value, and obtain protection of intellectual property. It also meets with venture capitalists to discuss new technologies and ongoing research at the Institute that may be appropriate for a start-up venture. This approach began at MIT at a time when such strategies were viewed as "unseemly" by some of MIT's peer institutions.

The TLO is closely attuned to the economic development mission of MIT and the entrepreneurial culture of the institution. In keeping with the university's supportive approach to faculty entrepreneurship, commercialization policies have evolved to encourage start-up activities. A central component of MIT's "pro-academic entrepreneur" start-up policy is that the TLO typically only seeks an equity stake of 5% in MIT spinoff companies. MIT does not interfere in the running and operation of the spinoff venture.

Entrepreneurship development

Over the years, MIT has seen the growth of organizations, programs, centers, courses, and awards that foster the entrepreneurial spirit on campus. The university offers many different opportunities inside and outside the classroom that complement the goals of the academic program. One of the most important is exposure to the Business Plan Competition, where students learn valuable things about themselves and gain an appreciation for other peer ideas. Other valuable learning experiences include the iTeams project, which provides students with opportunities to synthesize, integrate, and apply their knowledge. As a result, learning is deeper, more meaningful, and ultimately more useful.

MIT has supplemented a rigorous engineering curriculum with formal and experiential education in entrepreneurship, drawing on local alumnus/alumna and faculty role models. The entrepreneurship development programs, and perhaps more importantly, the underlying culture of the institution have a strong influence on students and graduates. Peers are very important in helping understand faculty performance, norms, and standards. By becoming involved with worthwhile organization such as the MIT Venture Mentoring Service, students and faculty member develop support networks that are instrumental in dealing with start-up challenges. Supporting entrepreneurial activity has long been an important part of the culture at MIT, but its role and importance have grown dramatically. This aspect of MIT's culture is fostered in a number of ways.

One of the most visible of the new programs is MIT's Deshpande Center for Technological Innovation. Founded with a $20 million grant, the Center identifies MIT researchers with promising ideas that can be developed more rapidly and effectively with a modest infusion of grant money and expert advice. Already it has awarded more than $11 million to more than ninety entrepreneurial projects, twenty-six of which have become commercial ventures (Vogel 2012). The MIT Entrepreneurship Center (now known as the Martin Trust Center for MIT Entrepreneurship), founded by Professor Ed Roberts, also plays a pivotal role in MIT's entrepreneurial activities, offering students from all parts of the Institute a wealth of resources: expert mentors, office space, classes on entrepreneurship, and networking opportunities – not only other students and faculty, but also with outside businesspeople and venture capitalists.[21] The Center aspires to be a vibrant intellectual and

---

[21] Fiona Murray serves as faculty director of the Martin Trust Center for MIT Entrepreneurship. From 1999 to 2009, Ken Morse served as the managing director of the MIT Entrepreneurship Center. Bill Aulet is the current managing director of the Center.

practical thought leader for innovation-driven entrepreneurship at MIT and worldwide. Its focus is on educating entrepreneurs who can build high-growth-potential businesses driven by real innovations.[22] From its inception, the Center, under Prof. Ed Roberts' guidance, initiated a "dual-track" faculty model that brings professors and adjunct practitioners together in the classroom so that students benefit from a broad range of perspectives and experiences. The Center supports the annual MIT $100K Entrepreneurship Competition, Innovation Teams, Accelerators, workshops, mentoring programs, and hackathons. These initiatives are designed to support MIT students by organizing resources relevant to entrepreneurship. The Center began in 1990 by offering one class, taught by an adjunct professor, but today has more than thirty courses, taught by thirty-five faculty members from all over MIT, and offers an MBA track with Sloan in entrepreneurship and innovation.[23] Student interest has skyrocketed. In 1996 only 288 students took entrepreneurship courses; now approximately 1,500 sign up for them every year. More recently, MIT launched the Founders' Skills Accelerator, which offers teams of students space inside the Trust Center to develop their companies. Each student receives a monthly $1,000 stipend, and teams can earn up to $20,000 if they hit a series of milestones aimed at turning their ideas into fully funded ventures. These milestones are self-prescribed in the areas of Customer Development, Product Development, Team, and Financial.

The educational program

In the early 1980s Dick Morse, an MIT graduate and serial entrepreneur, introduced into the curriculum of MIT's Sloan School of Management the first course aimed at preparing young entrepreneurs. Morse's course revolved around the preparation of business plans for new technology-based ventures. In addition to sharing his own experiences with the students, Morse, for the first time on a systematic basis, brought successful entrepreneurs and venture capitalists into the classroom.

The business plans were developed by interdisciplinary teams of students, comprising members from science, engineering, and management studies. The course soon became very popular, and as enrollment increased, there was a corresponding increase in the number of business plans submitted. Given the inherently competitive nature of the participants, an informal competition soon developed. At this point, some students began thinking of the possibility of a financial prize for the best plan. The award would, of course, be used as initial financing for the

---

[22] Source: Martin Trust Center for MIT Entrepreneurship Annual Report 2012/13.
[23] Ibid.

venture. Some students approached Professor Ed Roberts of the Sloan School with the idea, asking for help in raising perhaps $5,000 for the prize. Roberts, himself the founder of several companies, turned to a venture capitalist and alumnus of MIT, David Morgenthaler, who raised the ante to $10,000 and funded the first three years of the competition. Thus began the $10,000 (eventually $100,000) competition that has now been emulated by universities around the world.

To evaluate the competition, local venture capitalists were called upon to aid the faculty. This provides a "reality check" of the basic ideas and the plans for exploitation. It also began a long and very beneficial relationship between MIT and the local venture capital community. Venture capitalists now both guide and evaluate student preparation and submissions. They serve a multiplicity of roles in this portion of the educational process at no cost to MIT, functioning as teachers, sponsors, evaluators, potential employers, and investors. Venture capitalists volunteer to coach and nurture individuals and groups of students throughout the university. Several have taught full-semester, fully accredited courses for years, while others serve as guest lecturers, or help with case discussions and class exercises. Venture capitalists therefore play a vital role in MIT's strategy of educating science, engineering, and management students to engage in the formation of technology-based new ventures. One reason that the entrepreneurship program seems to work as well as it does is that the curriculum and other aspects of the academic teaching program are largely experiential in nature and highly engaging. The E-Center and the involvement of venture capitalists and experienced entrepreneurs highlight the importance MIT places on developing and enhancing students' entrepreneurial skills.

Table 4.3 (see next page) and Appendix A summarize important ways in which MIT promotes entrepreneurship on campus.

Regional ecosystem

Another factor to consider is that MIT is located in a well-capitalized region. Boston is a technological hub, where a network is there to support people who are willing to take risks, who are willing to support high-impact ventures even though there is no guarantee of success.[24] In 2010 Massachusetts received four times more venture capital as a share of gross state product than the national average,[25] and it is an important source of funding for MIT's fast-growing entrepreneurial companies. A report from PricewaterhouseCoopers and the National

---

[24] Carl Dietrich, founder of MIT's startup Terrafugia, CEO Foresight, 2014.
[25] The 2010 State New Economy Index is compiled on a annual basis by the Information Technology and Innovation Foundation (ITIF).

Table 4.3: *Entrepreneurship initiatives at MIT*

Martin Trust Center for MIT Entrepreneurship	• The Martin Trust Center for MIT Entrepreneurship builds the entrepreneurial capacity of MIT students through education, nurturing, networking, and celebration. Students and alumni use their entrepreneurship skills to found hundreds of companies each year, many using cutting-edge technologies developed in MIT labs and elsewhere. The Center is committed to fostering and developing MIT's entrepreneurial activities and interests in three primary areas: education and research, alliances, and community.
Venture Mentoring Service (VMS)	• MIT stands at the heart of a rich community of successful entrepreneurs and business people. The Venture Mentoring Service taps into this knowledge resource, supporting innovation and entrepreneurial activity throughout the MIT community by matching prospective entrepreneurs with volunteer mentors who can boost the probability of a start-up's success. • Budding entrepreneurs who apply to be VMS mentees are assigned to a team of three or four mentors who provide practical, day-to-day professional advice and coaching. The mentoring service is open to MIT faculty, students, alumni, and staff and licensees of MIT technology who reside in the Boston area.
Industrial Liaison Program	• The Office of Corporate Relations' Industrial Liaison Program (ILP) promotes MIT/industry collaboration, encouraging the flow of knowledge and resources between the Institute and innovation-driven companies for their mutual benefit. • The exchange of ideas and capabilities resulting from ILP-facilitated interactions often speeds the incorporation of new technologies into products and services – helping MIT research make its way into the marketplace and out to the global community.
Technology Licensing Office (MIT)	• The mission of the Technology Licensing Office is to enable the inventions and discoveries made at MIT to find further development in the commercial world so that the public will ultimately benefit from the breakthroughs that arise from research at the Institute. • The longstanding mission of the Technology Licensing Office is to enable inventions and discoveries to find further development in the commercial world so that the public will ultimately benefit from the breakthroughs that arise from research at the Institute. The TLO achieves this goal by patenting MIT inventions, copyrighting software, and then licensing that intellectual property to companies both large and nascent.

(*cont.*)

Table 4.3: (cont.)

Deshpande Center for Technological Innovation	• The Deshpande Center and its grants and activities are focused on increasing the impact of MIT technologies in the marketplace by bridging the divide between idea and implementation. • The Center provides grants to MIT faculty and principal investigators for research to be done in MIT laboratories. There are two types of grant available: • Ignition Grants (up to $50,000) are intended to support promising exploratory or proof-of-concept projects. • Innovation Grants are typically larger (up to $250,000) and intended to help a research project progress from an early stage to the point where it is ready to attract venture funding or commercial investment. • Deshpande Center grant recipients receive more than just money: • Volunteers from the business community, known as Catalysts, provide guidance on ensuring innovations have an impact in the marketplace. • The Deshpande Center also hosts events and programs, such as its high-profile IdeaStream Symposium, that foster entrepreneurship and build connections among innovators and the funding and business communities.
Enterprise Forum	• For over thirty years, the Enterprise Forum has been offering networking and educational programs about technology entrepreneurship. These activities are offered via the Forum's many regional chapters. Enterprise Forum programs are open to anyone interested or involved in technology entrepreneurship.
$100K Competition	• The MIT $100K encourages any MIT student with a business strategy for a marketable product or service to enter the competition. MIT's competition is the nation's premier business plan competition, teaching students how to turn their ideas into companies.
Lemelson–MIT Awards	• The Lemelson–MIT Awards honor both established and rising inventors for their ingenuity, creativity, and contribution to invention and innovation. The awards recognize the profound impact that inventors can have on economic and social well-being. The awards include the following: • The $500,000 Lemelson–MIT Prize honors outstanding midcareer inventors dedicated to improving the world through technological invention and innovation. • The $100,000 Lemelson–MIT Award for Global Innovation recognizes and supports inventors working to safeguard the well-being of our communities and planet. • The $30,000 Lemelson–MIT Student Prize honors promising young inventors studying at MIT.

Table 4.3: (cont.)

i-Teams	• A course that enables graduate students to engage in the process of bringing MIT innovations from the lab to the market. Each semester, student teams assess the commercial feasibility of scientific and engineering breakthroughs from MIT labs. The purpose of i-Teams is to develop go-to-market strategies for their research projects with guidance from faculty and volunteers from the business community.
The Legatum Center for Entrepreneurship	• The Center runs a highly competitive fellowship program for MIT students who intend to launch enterprises in low-income countries. In addition, the Center convenes an annual conference, hosts lectures, and supports teams of enterprising men and women at MIT who are passionate about starting viable businesses in the developing world.
The Monosson Prize for Entrepreneurship Mentoring	• This prize recognizes entrepreneurship mentors who have committed their time, expertise, and energy to developing future generations of successful MIT entrepreneurs. The award was established in 2005 by William Grinker '56 and his wife in memory of Adolf F. Monosson '48.
Founders' Skills Accelerator	• The MIT Founders' Skills Accelerator gives MIT student teams the opportunity to make significant progress on a start-up idea during the summer, without leaving MIT, and get money in the process. The program involves three and one-half months of business building and mentoring from seasoned entrepreneurs and professors. Importantly, the Founders' Skills Accelerator does not ask for any equity in these embryonic ventures.

Source: An MIT Inventor's Guide to Start-Ups: For Faculty and Students (Start-Up Guide).

Venture Capital Association ranked Massachusetts as the second largest state to be the recipient of venture capital investments in 2010 (see Table 4.4).

Venture capitalists help entrepreneurs identify promising innovations and assist in bringing them to the marketplace. Strong ties to the venture capital community are a key to spin-off success, according to one of MIT's most prolific academic entrepreneurs. Professor Robert Langer has founded more than 25 companies and has 811 patents, issued or pending, to his name. More than 250 companies have licensed or sublicensed Langer Lab patents. Polaris Venture Partners, a Boston venture capital firm, has invested $220 million in eighteen Langer Lab-inspired businesses.[26] According to Dr. Langer, "I also have been very happy with

---

[26] "Hatching Ideas, and Companies, by the Dozens at MIT," by Hannah Seligson (published *New York Times*, November 24, 2012; www.nytimes.com).

Table 4.4: *Venture capital investments in 2010, in $ million*

Rank	State	VC $ million
1	California	11,603
2	Massachusetts	2,472
3	New York	1,401
4	Texas	981
5	Illinois	732

Source: National Venture Capital Association (2011).

Polaris Ventures as a venture firm. I really like working with them. I work with a lot of companies and venture firms, but I have been particularly impressed with Terry McGuire of Polaris. We have had a great business relationship, and he is incredibly honest. So, if I have an idea, I will probably go to him first, and I don't want to say he will fund it every time, but he would probably fund a lot of things we do."

According to Roberts and Eesley (2009), the presence of experienced management and legal expertise in the Greater Boston region provides expertise around myriad decisions about business models, early stage financing, and patent strategy and strategic alliances that are alien to most academic scientists. Typically, MIT academics do not leave their university positions when they are involved in start-ups, preferring to partner with individuals with management expertise or to bring them in to manage the day-to-day operations of the company. For MIT students who want to start new companies, Boston's venture capitalists provide funding and guidance and introduce young scientists to experienced executives who can help them manage and nurture their promising start-ups. According to the TLO Director, "People ask me whether MIT has an incubator and I say 'yes, it's the city of Cambridge.'" This is a geography experienced in entrepreneurship. It has got a lot of experienced executives . . . , although it didn't have much 15 years ago, and a lot of indigenous venture capital. There are accountants, real estate agents, etc. . . . all used to dealing with start-ups."

Conclusion

An extraordinarily successful research university, MIT has nurtured a long-standing mission of service to its state and national interests and achieved this goal, in part, by creating a strong entrepreneurial culture and an innovative approach to technology transfer. Crucial to its success have been a large number of star faculty, in physical science, engineering, and the life sciences, all committed to generating, disseminating, and preserving knowledge, and working with others to bring this knowledge to bear on the world's great challenges. The MIT story is about proactive faculty engagement and an informal approach to commercialization, supported by a university mission that values close cooperation with industry. It is also a story about history and the leadership of key individuals – the part they played in the development of a robust entrepreneurial culture.

Finally, MIT's success needs to be understood in the context of the regional environment. Attempting to replicate the model or make recommendations to other universities based on the MIT experience may be unwise. While there are certain aspects of MIT's practice that can be applied elsewhere, there are many more that are difficult to replicate given the interrelated nature of the drivers that have fueled its entrepreneurial activity.

References

Association of University Technology Managers [AUTM]. 1980–2001. *The AUTM Licensing Surveys: University Start-up Data.* AUTM Inc., Norwalk, CT.

Aulet. 2008. How to Build a Successful Innovation Ecosystem: *Educate, Network,* and *Celebrate.* Xconomy.com June.

The Center for University Performance Research. 2002. The Top American Research Universities Report 2002. Available at http://thecenter.ufl.edu.

Charter of MIT Corporation. 1861. Acts and Resolves of the General Court Relating to the Massachusetts Institute of Technology. MIT History, MIT Institute Archives. Available at http://web.mit.edu/corporation.

Etzkowitz, Henry. 1994. "Knowledge as Property: The Massachusetts Institute of Technology and the Debate over Academic Patent Policy." *Minerva* 32(4) (Winter): 383–421.

2002. *MIT and the Rise of Entrepreneurial Science.* Routledge, New York.

Fishman, Elliot A. 1996. *MIT Patent Policy, 1932–1946: Historical Precedents in University-Industry Technology Transfer,* unpublished doctoral dissertation, University of Pennsylvania.

Hockfield, Susan. 2005. Annual Miller Lecture on Science and Ethics, presented at the MIT Program in Science, Technology, and Society, Kirsch Auditorium, Stata Center, 7 November.

2006. The University in the Global Age: A View from MIT, presented at Tsinghua University, Beijing, January 15.

2007. Universities and the Global Knowledge Economy, speech in Mumbai, 20 November.

Hsu, D. and Kenney, M. 2005. "Organizing Venture Capital: The Rise and Demise of American Research & Development Corporation, 1946–1973." *Industrial and Corporate Change* 14: 579–616.

MIT. 2004. *MIT Policies and Procedures.* MIT, Cambridge, MA.

MIT Archives. http://libraries.mit.edu/archives.

National Science Foundation [NSF]. 1991–2001. NSF Webcaspar: Your Virtual Bookshelf of Statistics on Academic Science and Engineering. Available at http://webcaspar.nsf.gov.

Roberts, E.B. and Eesley, C.E. 2011. Entrepreneurial Impact: The Role of MIT – An Updated Report. Foundations and Trends in Entrepreneurship.

Schrock, Robert R. 1977. *Geology at MIT 1865–1965: A History of the First Hundred Years of Geology at Massachusetts Institute of Technology.* Cambridge: MIT Press.

Stratton, J.A. and Mannix, L.H., completed by Alexander, P.N. 2005. *Mind and Hand: The Birth of MIT.* MIT Press, Cambridge, MA.

U.S. News & World Report. 2005. America's Best Graduate Schools, 2005 Edition.

Vest, C. 2004. *Pursuing the Endless Frontier: Essays on MIT and the Role of Research Universities.* MIT Press, Cambridge, MA.

Vogel, Chris. 2012. "How MIT Became the Most Important University in the World." *Boston Magazine* (November).

Appendix A

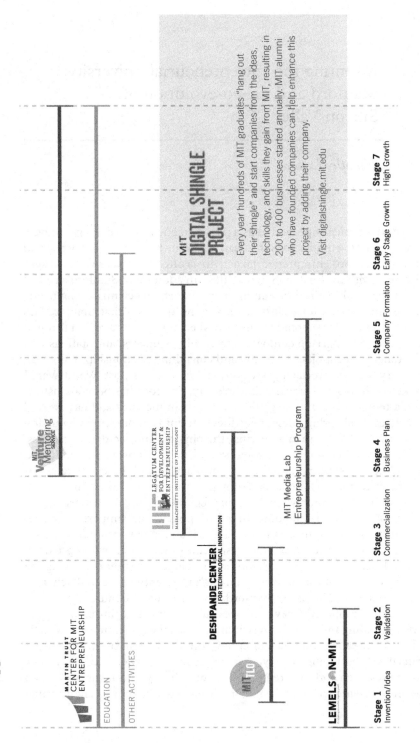

Figure 4A.1: MIT entrepreneurial ecosystem 2013.

MARTIN TRUST
CENTER FOR MIT
ENTREPRENEURSHIP

EDUCATION

OTHER ACTIVITIES

MIT
Venture
Mentoring
SERVICE

LEGATUM CENTER
FOR DEVELOPMENT &
ENTREPRENEURSHIP
MASSACHUSETTS INSTITUTE OF TECHNOLOGY

DESHPANDE CENTER FOR TECHNOLOGICAL INNOVATION

MIT
FLO

MIT Media Lab
Entrepreneurship Program

LEMELSON-MIT

MIT DIGITAL SHINGLE PROJECT

Every year hundreds of MIT graduates "hang out their shingle" and start companies from the ideas, technology, and skills they gain from MIT, resulting in 200 to 400 businesses started annually. MIT alumni who have founded companies can help enhance this project by adding their company.

Visit digitalshingle.mit.edu

Stage 1	Stage 2	Stage 3	Stage 4	Stage 5	Stage 6	Stage 7
Invention/Idea	Validation	Commercialization	Business Plan	Company Formation	Early Stage Growth	High Growth

Source: Martin Trust Center for MIT Entrepreneurship (2014).

5 Inventing the entrepreneurial university: Stanford and the co-evolution of Silicon Valley

Timothy Lenoir

Stanford is typically presented as a paradigmatic example among universities generating innovations that lead to new technology-based firms; and indeed, Stanford entrepreneurial activity is often treated as virtually synonymous with the birth of Silicon Valley. In addition to Stanford's role as an educational institution training new cohorts of scientists, engineers, and entrepreneurs for industry, there is no question that Stanford has been significant in shaping the industrial economy of the region through the creation of start-up companies by faculty, students, and staff, as well as a range of technology licensing and consulting relationships with local industry. Less appreciated, however, is that since its post–World War II makeover into a major research university, Stanford has been an institution attentive to cutting-edge developments in industry and has evolved strategies for absorbing those new directions into its core research mission in a variety of fields in engineering, the physical and biological sciences, and medicine. Despite this strong synergistic relationship with industry, though it may seem paradoxical, the primary goal of these strategies has not been to forge closer alliances with industry but rather to position Stanford more favorably for obtaining federal funding for research.

The key to understanding Stanford policies in support of entrepreneurial activity is to see them as shaped fundamentally around attracting and retaining star academic researchers capable of winning federal research grants and contracts and, in so doing, of further enhancing the research profile of the university through their entrepreneurial activities and contacts with industry. Stanford has contributed to multiple waves of innovation in Silicon Valley by successfully setting its sights on obtaining federal funding for scientific research that is at the same time industrially relevant. Creating and sustaining an entrepreneurial culture has been crucial to developing this synergistic feedback between federally supported research and research problems of industry, and it has positioned Stanford researchers to make major advances in science and engineering.

Although faculty entrepreneurial activity has taken many forms over the years at Stanford, particularly since the late 1980s, the Stanford administration has pursued a consistent and carefully monitored set of policies directed at encouraging relationships with industry primarily insofar as they enhance the research mission and profile of the research faculty. The result has been the creation of an institution that has co-evolved as a premier research university in close interactive feedback with local Silicon Valley industry. The aim of this study is to outline how these policies have evolved and provide examples of the role played by synergistic activity with industry at Stanford.

The linkage of entrepreneurship and research at Stanford was born initially out of the historical circumstance of its (initially) less-than-advantageous West Coast location and circumstances connected with its small endowment as a private institution. During the intervening years Stanford's endowment has grown, but even today at its height of $17.2 billion, Stanford's endowment is only 59 percent of Harvard's (National Association of College and University Business Officers 2012). The situation was much worse at the end of World War II, when the administration of Walter Sterling began to turn the situation around. In his 1997 state-of-the-university address, President Gerhard Casper quipped that it was an intimidating task to lead an organization that has to raise roughly 88 percent of its budget each year. This is a situation every Stanford administration has faced, and it has contributed to the invention of a university that is aggressively entrepreneurial. Faced with a severe financial crisis following World War II, Stanford administrators overcame their traditional aversion – shared by other private universities up to that time – to accepting federal funds and aggressively pursued new federal funding opportunities that became available after the war, particularly in areas related to military-sponsored research, as well as in new federal and private foundation programs targeting the transformation of American medicine.

The Terman model: Steeple building and the recipe for distinction

The basic model for the research university that Stanford has become was developed by Frederick Emmons Terman during his years as Dean of Engineering immediately following World War II. In 1945 Terman returned from his wartime position as director of the Radio Research Laboratory (RRL) at Harvard to take up new responsibilities as dean, and he came with a plan for putting Stanford's engineering school on the map as one of the premier programs in the nation. It was a plan born of his experience managing the RRL, combined with observations of the administrative structures and philosophies of Harvard and MIT. As a former student and close friend of Vannevar Bush, Terman was privy to the discussions in Bush's circle about building a postwar alliance among government, industry, and academe, the vision Bush set forth in his 1945 Report to the President entitled *Science, the Endless Frontier*. While still at the RRL, Terman began to shape a formula for success. It involved using government funding, principally Office of Naval Research (ONR) contracts, to build (1) a premier faculty in areas of electronics, which Terman was confident would be the major engineering growth area in the postwar environment; (2) a large Ph.D. program, transforming the curriculum from one focused solely on practical engineering training to one infused with physics, mathematics, and the social sciences. Terman and a handful of his close academic friends believed that the university would be the key to postwar industry. In the research triad – government, industry, university – Terman believed the postwar university was the source of key innovations. But whereas the Bush model assumed that innovative results of federally funded academic research, like all good ideas, would eventually find their way into industry through a sort of trickle-down effect, Terman felt that a more aggressive, proactive approach to leveraging academic research was necessary at an institution like Stanford that was out of the mainstream and facing financial difficulties. Terman brought three ONR contracts for work in microwave physics and engineering with him when he returned in to Stanford in 1945–1946. These resources were the beginning of a new university.

The primary resources for Terman's vision for Stanford were government grants and contracts. In contrast to some of his colleagues at Stanford, such as Board of Trustees President Donald Tressider, and even Stanford President Walter Sterling, Terman hoped to build close alliances with industry, but he did not think industry funding held the key to building a university in the postwar era. A number of efforts had been made by universities such as MIT before the war to finance research with industry funding, all with mixed results. Stanford's own experience with the klystron patent in the late 1930s was typical. The invention was made by physicist William Hansen and developed by Russell and Sigurd Varian. Licensing the patent to Sperry Gyroscope promised to supply the Hansen lab with ample funding to pursue research on other microwave devices. But the relationship proved to be unsatisfactory.

Industrial sponsors of academic research, such as Sperry, wanted control over the direction of research in the lab, and they wanted to ensure exclusivity with respect to inventions coming out of the lab. Hansen, for example, found that Sperry would not give him and his colleagues and students free rein to pursue their own research on klystrons and other microwave devices the group believed would ultimately benefit Sperry Gyroscope. Moreover, industrial sponsors only wanted to fund work directly related to their own interests. They were not necessarily interested in furthering the academic mission of the lab (or university) through funding of fellowship programs, building construction, or purchase of instruments and equipment not directly related to their own goals. While the klystron royalties were an important resource for the lab, Terman believed that government funding would be a less restrictive and substantially larger source of funding for building academic research programs. This marked a substantial change in attitude toward government sponsorship of research compared to the prewar period. Prior to the war, universities wanting to remain free and independent in their educational mission had been highly critical of and generally rejected government resources for support of research. Moreover, federal funding in support of research was not channeled toward private universities. The Manhattan Project and work at the RRL and other government labs on university campuses during the war had changed that.

Terman developed what he termed "a recipe for distinction" in building Stanford's Engineering School. The recipe contained two main ingredients. The first ingredient was to be strong in areas of mainstream interest and importance rather than in "niche" areas, even though one might be able to be the leader in esoteric areas. The second ingredient was to increase the science and engineering faculty in key areas where funding could be attracted – he called this his program for building "steeples of excellence." Terman pursued projects that he thought could be "self-financing" and would generate their own momentum of sustained growth. To accomplish this, Terman sought to get the very best talent he could. Rather than using government grants to increase salaries of faculty already on staff, Terman pursued what he termed "salary splitting." The strategy was to pay half of the salary of a new faculty member from grants and contracts. Research associates and other personnel working on sponsored projects would be entirely covered from contract funds. In addition, building expansions and equipment would be funded on contract.

Terman's goal was not just to bring money into the university. The primary goal was to build the premier research program in electronics (or other potential "steeples of excellence"). This was to be accomplished by obtaining the very best talents in the field and building a graduate program around them. Training of graduate students and the production of Ph.D.s was as important as any other component of the program. Students were to be brought into the research project as part of their graduate training. When he was asked to advise other areas on how to go about constructing their own recipe for success, during his many public discussions of these ideas in the 1960s, Terman was insistent on the centrality of the research mission of the faculty. He was scornful of going after a contract for applied research and generally rejected such contracts unless they fit into the overall mission of increasing the prowess of the research component (more on this later). He was critical, for instance, of a number of universities he advised because they went after contracts that they could fulfill with mediocre talent. Rather than simply bringing in contract dollars, Terman's goal was to get funding as a way to hire the very best talent. Additional sponsored projects would then follow on the principle that the agenda of research and development in the field was being set by the Stanford Electronics Research Lab.

If government funding provided the primary resource for Terman's program, building a connection to industry was equally critical. For Terman the key thing was to turn ideas into technology, and this required close collaboration with industry. Terman was also concerned about building an industrial base closely associated with the Stanford program. In presentations to engineering societies and various public forums, Terman repeatedly insisted that the requirements for a career in engineering had changed since before the war. Terman emphasized that engineers needed to be educated much more thoroughly in physics and advanced mathematics than previously, and he observed that technologi-cal complexity was advancing so rapidly that an undergraduate education would no longer suffice to prepare an engineer for the challenges of a career in industry. The requirements of modern industry were such that a master's degree or Ph.D. was becoming a prerequisite for many fields, particularly in the complex and rapidly changing new fields of electronics and computers. To address this problem, Terman developed Ph.D. programs with graduate fellowships funded by federal grants and contracts, and he took the innovative step of creating the so-called Honors Cooperative Program, which allowed researchers and workers at local firms to complete advanced engineering degrees at Stanford.

In this knowledge-intensive environment, Terman believed the univer-sity would play a more central role than ever in the creation of new tech-nology. He envisioned what he referred to as a "technical community of scholars" made up of local electronics firms in the Bay Area and the West Coast with research facilities near Stanford staffed by Stanford-trained engineers. It would be a dynamic community where research in Stanford labs would find its way into industry through the training of students and consulting by the faculty. Stanford-originated technologies would find their way into the electronics industry as well, providing revenues for enhancing the research program. Terman also allowed for industry to bring its own problems to the university for research, and in fact provided numerous ways for this to happen. But foremost in Terman's plan was that the university would be the center of the technical community, providing innovations, training, and guidance. He explicitly sought to limit the influence of both the government and companies in defining the problems labs such as the SEL and the Hansen Lab would investigate. Terman sought to build trust among government and industrial sponsors of research in the technical directions pursued by the research faculty. By maintaining close relationships with the needs of government and industry through consulting and training of students, the research faculty would of its own accord naturally pursue projects of benefit to the sponsors as well as advancing the research mission. Thus, instead of receiving research funds to pursue specific problems defined by a sponsor, Terman wanted both government and industry to invest funds in the research directions defined by the core faculty of the lab. Even in the case of industry funding, Terman rejected funds for specific applied industry problems in favor of funds to pursue a general research direction of interest to a company. The company funding the research would have privileged access but not exclusive rights to the research results.[1]

As plans for linking research labs with industry materialized, an additional ingredient of Terman's "recipe for distinction" emerged. The idea of using Stanford land for commercial property that would bring income to the university was already well under way by 1950 as a means for generating income to offset the ailing finances of the university. Work in the Microwave Lab under Felix Bloch had already resulted in the creation of Varian Associates by Russell Varian and Edward Ginzton. Founded in 1949, Varian Associates was the first occupant of what would become the Stanford Industrial Park.[2] Terman interested several other electronics firms in moving research facilities to the 450-acre sector of land designated for commercial development by the Board of Trustees in 1950. In 1952 the decision was taken to set aside land in this sector for the

---

[1] A number of studies, particularly those of William Stuart Leslie and Rebecca Lowen, have depicted Terman as basically selling the university to the military and industry. This picture does not stand up under close scrutiny. Terman, like nearly every other university administrator, sought government funding for academic programs as the only serious financial option for program building. Terman's own "recipe for distinction" was based explicitly on the university controlling the research agenda and being deeply involved in setting research priorities.

[2] The Stanford Industrial Park was the area of land bordering on California Avenue, Page Mill Road, El Camino Real, and a sector along the Foothill Road extension of Serra up to Arastadero Road.

Medical Center, which would move from San Francisco to the Stanford Campus in 1958.

An innovative feature of Terman's evolving program over the years was its tight coupling of teaching, research, and technology transfer through close working – particularly consulting – relationships with industry. Many examples of this successful strategy could be given, beginning with a long-term relationship with General Electric that started in 1953. GE received contracts to produce several types of microwave devices, including klystron tubes. In addition, GE was interested in the commercial development of radiological devices, particularly the medical accelerator being developed by Henry Kaplan and Edward Ginzton in the Stanford Microwave Lab. In his proposals to GE for establishing an advanced research electronics lab in the industrial park near Stanford, Terman gave a detailed exposition of Stanford's philosophy of linking research and development in electrical engineering and physics to industry.[3] The research program, Terman explained, was an outgrowth of the academic program and was closely coordinated with the instructional activities of the University, particularly in graduate training. "Initially," Terman wrote, "basic research projects are selected in the usual manner, simply on the basis of the extent to which they will add to the knowledge of the subject: but it has generally been found that practical applications of this knowledge are not long in forthcoming, and through the application of judicious assistance and planning along the way we have usually been able to produce, ultimately, not only equations and reports, but also practical devices embodying the principles involved."[4]

Research projects were taken on in fields in which some faculty member had specialized competency, an arrangement that allowed faculty to function effectively both as teachers and as research workers without undue inroads on their time. Research projects were frequently used as thesis assignments for graduate students, thus permitting Stanford to employ graduate students as members of the staff of the Electronics Research Laboratory while they were at the same time pursuing their work toward graduate degrees. A key part of the typical arrangement with research companies in the Stanford Industrial Park was that Stanford faculty, research associates, and technical personnel would provide instruction to the company researchers in the design, development, and construction of linear accelerators (or other related electronic technologies) developed at Stanford. Faculty members relevant to the company

[3] Terman to Oldenfield, 8 April 1954, Terman Papers, SC 160, Series II, Box 18, fol. 8 . . . \
TermanPapersSC160\SeriesIIBox18\fol8\Terman-Oldenfield8April1954.pdf.
[4] Ibid., p. 6.

research interests would also be appointed as Principal Associate Scientists to assist and advise the company research staff. Companies such as GE would license the Stanford patents on klystrons and medical accelerators relevant to their commercial plans[5].

An equally important aspect of Terman's vision was that the synergy between Stanford and its industrial partners was not a one-way relationship. Stanford research programs should benefit from the knowledge and expertise housed in advanced programs in industry. Consulting relationships opened some of these doors, but teaching appointments of industry scientists at Stanford, and where possible the strategic hiring of entire teams of scientists from industry, also played a role. Heading up its own teaching and research programs was viewed as a means of strengthening Stanford's research profile and ensuring it would have a cutting edge faculty defining the frontiers of new technical programs. These new "steeples of excellence" would provide the competitive edge for acquiring federal funding for new projects in the sciences and engineering. The GE agreement, one of the earliest of these joint exchanges, was typical of a pattern repeated frequently in the intervening years at Stanford. In the GE agreement, for example, provision was made for certain GE personnel to teach one three-hour course at Stanford in any academic semester without remuneration. GE staff with teaching appointments at Stanford were allowed to advise on thesis work of Stanford students.

Perhaps the most spectacular example of Terman's efforts to fertilize academic programs by absorbing advanced programs from industry is the development of the solid state physics program at Stanford. At the suggestion of his former student, David Packard, the president and cofounder of Hewlett–Packard, Terman initiated the research and teaching program in solid state electronics at Stanford. Terman and Packard had watched the field of semiconductor electronics closely since the invention of the transistor by William Shockley, John Bardeen, and Walter Brattain at the Bell Telephone Laboratories in 1947. Terman and Packard viewed solid state electronics as one of the most promising fields in electrical engineering, and they wanted the university to build a major presence in this new field. Packard and his business partner, William Hewlett, were eager to transistorize their electronic measurement instrumentation business. They were also interested in producing semiconductor devices. Hewlett and Packard deemed it in their interest to support the development of solid state at Stanford. A solid state group at the university would act as a local resource for Hewlett–Packard and other electronics firms

[5] Ibid., Exhibit A, p. 4.

on the San Francisco Peninsula. It would also train engineers in the new technology. Hewlett and Packard expected to hire some of them[6].

To build a dynamic program in solid state electronics, Terman hired John Linvill, a young engineer at the Bell Telephone Laboratories, in 1955. Linvill, an MIT Ph.D., had briefly taught on the MIT faculty before joining the technical staff of the Bell Telephone Laboratories. At Bell, he had made a name for himself by designing a new transistor-based amplifier that became widely used in local area networks. Terman liked Linvill's inventiveness and expected that his appointment would give Stanford access to the Bell Labs' technology and scientific staff.[7] Packard assisted Terman in recruiting Linvill from the Bell Labs. He actively promoted the position to Linvill. To help the university match Linvill's salary at Bell, Packard offered him a consulting arrangement with HP. Under the terms of the agreement, Linvill would give a series of lectures on transistors to HP's engineering staff. Packard also impressed upon Linvill the importance of building close relations with local electronics firms – especially those in the recently created Stanford Research Park.[8]

Terman rapidly came to appreciate that Linvill was himself a superb academic entrepreneur – a steeple of excellence. In the next fifteen years, the two men collaborated closely on building the solid state program at Stanford. At Terman's urging, Linvill "transistorized" the electrical engineering curriculum and established the Solid State Laboratory, originally as part of Terman's Stanford Electronics Lab, focused on transistor circuit research, and heavily funded by the ONR, IBM, and Texas Instruments.

A few years later, Linvill expanded the scope of the Solid State Laboratory to device physics and silicon processing. To do so, the Solid State Lab needed to acquire rare expertise in the fabrication of semiconductor devices, which could be found in only a few corporations. Fortunately, in

---

[6] Packard, David. *The H-P Way: How Bill Hewlett and I Built Our Company* (New York: HarperBusiness, 1995).

[7] As discussed in Christophe Lécuyer, "What Do Universities Really Owe Industry? The Case of Solid State Electronics at Stanford." *Minerva*, Vol. 43. No. 1, 2005: 51–71, when Terman recruited Linvill from the Bell Labs, he followed a well-established practice. Most universities and corporations eager to enter the field of solid state raided the Bell Telephone Laboratories in the 1950s and the early 1960s. Texas Instruments and Motorola hired Bell Labs physicists and chemists to build up their semiconductor business. Harvard, Berkeley, and other universities also recruited their faculty members in solid state from Bell.

[8] As discussed in Christophe Lécuyer, 2005. Frederick Terman to R. Holt, March 11, 1953, in SC160, series II, box 15, fol. 22; John Linvill, oral history interview, May 5, 1987, Tape SV5, Stanford archives and special collections; Linvill, oral history interview conducted by Christophe Lécuyer, April 25 and May 30, 2002; Gibbons, James, "John Linvill – The Model for Academic Entrepreneurship," *The CIS Newsletter*, Fall 1996. See also Leslie, *The Cold War and American Science*, 71–75.

late 1955, with Terman's urging, Shockley, the co-inventor of the transistor at the Bell Labs, moved to the San Francisco Peninsula to start his own semiconductor venture, Shockley Semiconductor Laboratory. Shockley's laboratory specialized in the making of silicon devices. The establishment of the new laboratory provided a wonderful opportunity for technology transfer – from Shockley Semiconductor to the university. Linvill and Terman asked Shockley whether they could dispatch a junior faculty member to his laboratory to work as Shockley's apprentice and learn about silicon processing. Shockley liked the idea. He needed Ph.D.s with a solid knowledge of semiconductor physics and expected that a strengthened solid state program at Stanford would supply the skilled workforce he needed. This was a critical agreement for the development of the solid state electronics program at Stanford.[9]

Linvill and Terman recruited Jim Gibbons, who had completed his Ph.D. with Linvill, to learn about silicon processing technology at Shockley. Gibbons's task was also to reproduce Shockley's lab on campus. This enterprise was funded again by the ONR.[10] Gibbons joined the Stanford faculty and the technical staff of Shockley Semiconductor in the fall of 1957. Sending Gibbons to Shockley Semiconductor was a judicious choice indeed. The firm specialized in silicon, the material that rapidly became dominant in semiconductor technology. Shockley Semiconductor was also teeming with talent. Shockley had hired an exceptional group of physicists and engineers – men such as Gordon Moore, Robert Noyce, Jean Hoerni, Jay Last, and Eugene Kleiner. These men later played a central role in the semiconductor industry in Silicon Valley. At Shockley Semiconductor, Moore, Noyce, and Kleiner introduced Gibbons to key processes in semiconductor fabrication such as crystal growing, lapping, solid state diffusion, and oxidation. Gibbons also got to know these men well. When eight staff members (Moore, Noyce, Hoerni, Kleiner, Last, Julius Blank, Victor Grinich, and Sheldon Roberts) rebelled against Shockley and left the firm to start their own venture, Fairchild Semiconductor, they asked Gibbons to join the new corporation as its ninth founder. Gibbons, who was interested in an academic career, declined the offer. This later proved to be a poor financial decision, as Fairchild

[9] See Christophe Lécuyer, 2005. In 1956, Linvill received a $13,600 grant from IBM. Texas Instruments also gave $11,625 for transistor circuit research. Terman to William Shockley, September 20, 1955, in SC160, series III, box 48, fol. 8; Linvill to R. Wallace, September 20, 1955, in SC160, series III, box 48, fol. 8; Linvill, "Excerpts from Lecture for Stanford Alumni in Los Angeles: The New Electronics of Transistors," February 15, 1956, in historical files of the Campus Report, folder: John Linvill; Linvill, "Description of Research Projects on Transistor Aplications Undertaken in Summer 1955 under Task 7," June 27, 1955, in SC160, series II, box 15, fol. 21; Gibbons, oral history interview conducted by Christophe Lécuyer, May 30, 2002.

[10] Stanford received a $35,000 grant from the ONR to set up the laboratory.

Semiconductor established itself as a major semiconductor manufacturer and made its founders quite wealthy. But Gibbons had developed ties with key players in Silicon Valley. These ties later facilitated the growth of the solid state electronics program at Stanford.[11]

Rather than following the footsteps of the "Traitorous Eight," as Shockley called his deserter research staff, by starting a new semiconductor venture, Gibbons replicated Shockley's laboratory on the Stanford campus. In March 1958, Gibbons's Stanford laboratory fabricated its first silicon device, a four-layer Shockley diode. This was a substantial achievement. Most people who had heard of Stanford's plan to build a device processing laboratory thought that its success was very unlikely. Device research and fabrication had always been the province of industry. It was also widely argued at this time that device fabrication technology was too complex for a university to master. Gibbons proved that it could be done. In this example of "reverse technology transfer," Stanford was probably the first university in the United States to fabricate silicon devices. On the basis of this achievement, the ONR increased its already sizeable grants to the Solid State Laboratory.[12] Over the next two decades, the Solid State Laboratory was the home to some of the most advanced research projects in computer engineering in the United States, including most famously the DARPA-supported VLSI (very large systems integration) project that led to the commercial development of RISC (reduced instruction set computing), which revolutionized computer chip architecture and formed the basis of MIPS, and the Geometry Engine, the basis for Silicon Graphics, and the SUN workstation, all major contributions to the dynamic firm culture of Silicon Valley.[13]

---

[11] See Christophe Lécuyer, 2005. Gibbons, "John Linvill – The Model for Academic Entrepreneurship"; Linvill, oral history interview conducted by Christophe Lécuyer, April 25 and May 30, 2002; Gibbons, oral history interview conducted by Christophe Lécuyer, May 30, 2002. For Fairchild Semiconductor, see Lécuyer, Christophe, "Fairchild Semiconductor and its Influence," in Lee, Chong-Moon, Miller, William, Hancock, Marguerite, and Rowen, Henry (eds.), *The Silicon Valley Edge: A Habitat for Innovation and Entrepreneurship* (Stanford: Stanford University Press, 2000), 158–183.

[12] See Christophe Lécuyer, 2005. Linvill, "Application for Equipment Funds for Semiconductor Device Research," February 25, 1957, in historical files of the Campus Report, folder: John Linvill; Terman to William Cooley, March 6, 1958, in SC160, series V, box 7, fol. 7; "Solid-State Devices Lab Tackles Silicon Transistors in Partnership with Industry," June 1958, in historical files of the *Campus Report*, fol.: John Linvill; Terman to Joseph McMicking, June 25, 1963, in SC160, series III, box 48, fol. 8; Gibbons, "John Linvill – The Model for Academic Entrepreneurship;" Linvill, oral history interview conducted by Christophe Lécuyer, April 25 and May 30, 2002; Gibbons, oral history interview conducted by Christophe Lécuyer, May 30, 2002.

[13] These developments are too expansive to cover in the current context. They are treated in the book-length study from which this paper is drawn.

The key components in what emerged during the 1950s as Terman's "recipe for distinction"[14] were

- Using government grants and contracts to finance "steeples of excellence"
- Salary splitting as a means to grow the faculty
- Concentration on graduate student research and production of M.S. and Ph.D. degrees
- The establishment of the Stanford Research Park as a means to create profitable exchange relations between industry and Stanford research labs, particularly in areas of electronics
- The Honors Cooperative Program as an incentive for companies to locate near Stanford and as a resource for supporting the teaching component accompanying the building of "steeples of excellence"
- Emphasis on licensing Stanford inventions and establishing faculty consulting relations as means for getting Stanford ideas into the core of industry

A number of quantitative indicators suggest the power and success of this "Terman Model." The impact of Terman's ideas on university finances and departmental growth are unmistakable.

Consider first the strategy Terman initiated of focusing on government-funded research grants and contracts as the way to grow the quality of university programs. Figure 5.1 charts Stanford research volume, degrees and faculty from 1945 to 2000. What Figure 5.1 suggests is that research volume is central to running the university, and that with Ph.D. production closely tracking research volume, Stanford is above all a research institution. Research dollars pay a very considerable portion (generally around 30%) of the bills at Stanford.

In the 1950s and 1960s the Engineering School accounted for the largest sector of government grants and contracts, and within the Engineering School, electrical engineering was the major recipient of government funding. A key objective of Terman's program was to use government funding to increase faculty and build research programs, particularly graduate programs in engineering. Indicators of the success of this enterprise are the growth of school and departmental operating budgets and the percentage of those operating budgets accounted for by outside funding – namely, from grants and contracts. as opposed to

---

[14] From the points that follow I have omitted the important "industrial affiliates programs" initiated by Terman, through which firms had access to research results and participate in conferences and workshops of special interest to their firms in exchange for an annual financial contribution to the research lab or sponsoring department.

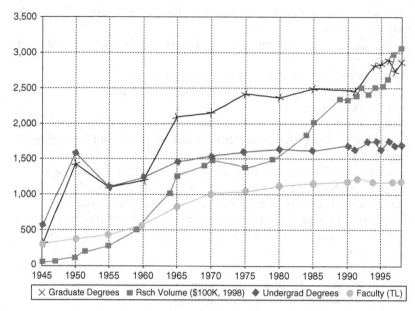

Figure 5.1: Stanford research volume, degrees, and faculty 1945–2000.
Source: Charles Kruger and Stanford University Financial Reports. Figures exclude funding for SLAC. (Stanford Linear Accelerator Center (SLAC) is one of the world's leading research laboratories in high-energy physics and synchrotron radiation, and is operated for the U.S. Department of Energy by Stanford University.)

tuition and endowment sources.[15] Certain patterns emerge from the information we do have that carry over into the post-1965 period. We present those patterns in Figures 5.2–5.4 and extrapolate to the 1950s based on sporadic data available to us for those years.

What the data indicate is that in the Engineering School roughly 60 percent of the operating budget for the entire school was financed through grants and contracts. Terman's program started in the

---

[15] It is difficult to obtain records that would permit a breakdown of department operating budgets and sources of income before 1966. In that year a change was made in the reporting of Stanford accounts in the Annual Financial Report of the university that enable us to track sources of income for individual departments. From 1950 to 1965 the practice was to simply to list the total for grants and contracts and report individual grants as line items in a general ledger rather than listing them by department and school. Hence it is difficult to extract the information we are seeking. This is not to say that data is unavailable for the period between 1950 and 1965, but Special Collections does not have a systematic and complete holding of the financial records of individual departments for those years.

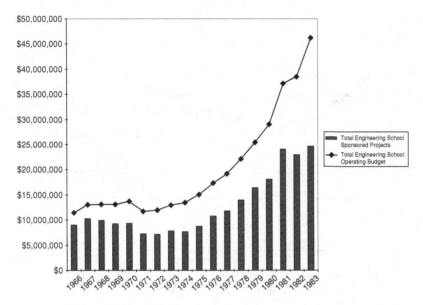

Figure 5.2: Engineering School sponsored projects compared to total Engineering School operating budget. *Source:* Stanford Annual Financial Reports.

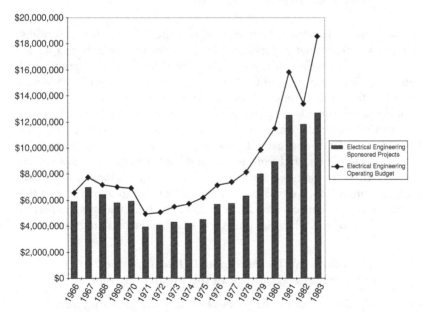

Figure 5.3: Electrical engineering sponsored projects compared to total Electrical Engineering operating budget. *Source:* Stanford Annual Financial Reports.

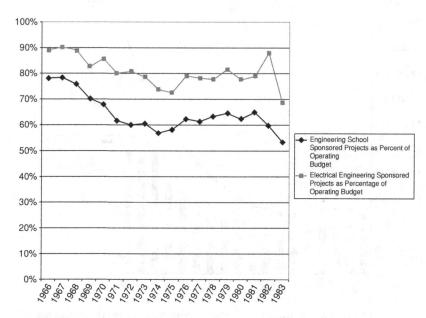

Figure 5.4: Sponsored projects as percentage of operating budget: total for School of Engineering compared with electrical engineering. *Source:* Stanford Annual Financial Reports.

Department of Electrical Engineering and the major external funding resources came to that department. Hence, it is not surprising to see an even higher percentage of the operating budget covered by grants and contracts. Reaching a high of around 90 percent in the mid-1960s and gradually falling to around 70 percent in the 1980s in the post-Vietnam period, we see roughly 80 percent of the operating budget for electrical engineering covered from grants and contracts. The sporadic data we have for the 1950s and early 1960s suggest that the percentage of the operating budget covered from grants and contracts hovered close to 90 percent. Indeed, when we shift our attention to the Hansen Labs and the Electronics Lab, we find that anywhere from 90 to 98 percent of the operating budget was covered from grants and contracts over the period we have investigated. That in a nutshell was the Terman program.

Extending the Terman model: The growth of entrepreneurial culture in the Medical School

I have argued that during his years as Dean of Engineering from 1945 to 1955, Terman developed a model for increasing the importance and prominence of the Stanford Engineering School by using government grants and contracts to expand the research and teaching program of the university. His major objective was to build a community of technical scholars – engineers with strong education at the graduate level in physics and engineering – in which close liaisons existed between university research and the advance of technology in government and industry. I have pointed to a number of elements of this program that were tightly coupled in a systematic way to realize Terman's goals. These included the building of "steeples of excellence" in key areas of electrical engineering and physics and a program of land development that facilitated linking companies with a strong interest in the directions of Stanford research to the university, with an industrial associates program (not explored in this paper) and honors cooperative program as supportive elements.[16]

Terman's model for strengthening Stanford as an engineering research center was diffused within the Medical School as well. As noted above, in the immediate post–World War II years, the financial condition of the University bordered on a crisis situation. The financial situation facing the Medical School in those years was even worse, indeed, positively desperate. The physical plant of the Medical School, located in San Francisco, was in need of renovation and expansion. The School ran a deficit of approximately $400,000 per year, which had to be financed out of University funds. In 1950, President Sterling and the Board of Trustees appointed a Committee on Future Plans of the Medical School, headed by Professor Henry Kaplan, the Director of Radiology. Kaplan's committee estimated that rebuilding the physical plant of the Medical School would cost $10–15 million. To prevent the bleeding of general funds of the University for the annual Medical School operations would require new endowment of an additional $15 million. In plant funds and endowment, the total need was estimated at $30 million. The magnitude of the sum evoked the question: Would it be wiser to modernize and add to the existing Medical School facilities in San Francisco or to build anew on an alternative site? After more than a year of study, the Board of Trustees made the decision on July 15, 1953 to move the Medical School to the main university campus.

---

[16] While Terman was widely celebrated for the transformations he brought to Stanford, his efforts were not without their critics. In particular, some advanced the criticism that the Stanford Industrial Park was exclusively occupied by electronics companies working on military contracts. A committee of the Board of Trustees urged that efforts be made to diversify the types of companies in the industrial park, and especially to seek the location of the executive offices of national professional societies in the industrial park. See Advisory Committee on Land and Building, Minutes of the Committee, 9 November 1959, Section 7. Diversification of University Support in the Land Development Program, in Terman Papers, SC 160, Sec III, Box 35, fol. 2, Land and Building Development 1959.

This was probably one of the most fortunate decisions in Stanford's history. The move of the Medical School to the main campus was accompanied by a complete revision of the medical curriculum in which more basic science was introduced. The Stanford Program, as it was called, lengthened the period of medical education from four to five years and included substantial work in basic science as well as significant exposure to laboratory training. Sterling used the attention generated by the new science-based curriculum and the move to the Stanford campus to launch a major public relations campaign and fund-raising drive for the new Medical Center. In addition to a public fund-raising drive, a key part of this effort was Sterling's lobbying effort with Congress to get the Hill–Burton Act of 1947, which supported the expansion of American medical programs, to include the financing of buildings and other capital expenses. This new Hill–Burton Act was passed in 1956. Stanford was a major beneficiary of the new federal funding. Along with a large influx of federal funds to support the new initiative, Sterling was also successful in obtaining major Ford Foundation funding to support the hiring of additional faculty for the new expanded Medical Center. Indeed, in a step signaling that the new Medical Center was heading in new directions, Sterling demanded that all heads of departments resign with the move to the main campus.[17] Two new departments were to be created in the move, the Department of Biochemistry and the Department of Genetics.

In the midst of this major transition of the Medical School, Fred Terman shifted from being Dean of Engineering to become Provost in 1955. Terman's style of encouraging entrepreneurial activity meshed well with the initiatives already reshaping the Medical School. Terman wasted no time in encouraging Medical School faculty to adopt his strategies for building programs with government funds. His advice to William Walter Greulich was typical. Greulich, concerned with the low level of Stanford salaries, wanted to increase faculty salaries by adding compensation from grant and contract funds for supporting a faculty member's normal teaching and research activity. Greulich assured Terman that he had clarified the acceptability of this notion with NIH grants officers and there seemed to be no objection. Terman, however, saw this as inappropriate: such a shift could create a bad impression with other federal granting agencies that wanted contract funds to support exclusively the work under contract. Terman wanted a consistent policy in dealing with all federal agencies. Beyond that, Terman felt it undercut the primacy of

[17] Andreopoulos, Spyros. "Stanford University Medical Center. 25 Years of Discovery." *Stanford Medicine*, Fall 1984, pp. 3–4. Also see *The Alway Years, 1957–1964*, published by the Stanford University School of Medicine, 1964.

research. As he told Greulich, permitting staff members to receive additional compensation during the academic year for work done on research contracts would "encourage (and reward) faculty to seek research contracts for the sole purpose of obtaining a substantial bonus on their salary rather than because of a desire to do the particular research involved."[18]

More importantly, Terman thought an opportunity was being missed for expanding Medical School research faculty through government funds in just the same way he had built the Department of Electrical Engineering and other parts of the Engineering School. He said to Greulich: "When in my office, you stated that teaching duties in the Medical School normally took about half the time of a faculty member, and that the other half of his time was available for research. If one could have 50 percent of this research time charged against research contracts and grants, rather than carried by the regular budget, it would free enough salary money in the Medical School budget to raise all salaries by 33 percent. If all of the research time could be charged to research contracts (which is probably an impossibility although nearly true in engineering) it would free enough salary money to double salaries.

"Since the idea of having the government or foundation pay for the services that it receives credit for would seem entirely legitimate and is certainly not immoral, I suggest this method of aiding the finances of the Medical School be taken advantage of whenever possible."

As Provost, Terman encouraged faculty to be aggressive in their pursuit of federal funding and scrupulous in accounting for the research-related costs of their work.[19] He held frequent meetings with deans and other University administrators explaining the elements of his "recipe for distinction" and his strategies for using salary-splitting and gift funds

---

[18] Terman–William Walter Greulich 1 August 1956, SC216, Box 62, fol. 8, Medical School 1956–57.

[19] See for instance Terman's memo to Dean Robert Alway, 19 January 1962, Terman Papers SC160, Series III, Box 43, fol. 1:

I understand that you and your staff have recently developed a consensus in favor of charging faculty salaries to research grants, to the extent consistent with the time devoted to such grant-supported research and with the overall funding of research, instruction, and service. I heartily approve of this policy and of its long-run contribution to the financial well-being of the school.

I would, therefore, suggest that full consideration be given to the use this year of an appropriate portion of the NIH general research support grant for faculty salaries that otherwise would be charged to university general funds.

I understand that it is NIH policy that any institutional funds which may be released by the use of the general research support grant will continue to be used for the direct costs of research or research training. I am sure that there must be substantial research and research-training related expenses in the medical school on which any recovered salary dollars could be spent within the spirit of the policy.

from corporate sponsors to expand the research faculty. The initial efforts were not easy. Terman encountered resistance from some faculty who thought federal funding should be avoided in order to remain independent, and his policies were opposed by critics concerned that the primary occupants of the Industrial Park were companies funded by military contracts. He sought to disarm such critics by seeking to attract companies in biomedical sciences into the research park. But Terman's most important strategy for building an environment that supported entrepreneurial activity was in hiring faculty with incentives similar to his own to build a powerful infrastructure to support their research programs. Perhaps the most striking success of Terman's efforts at building an entrepreneurial culture during his years as Provost was in building the new science departments of the Medical School.

Acting on the advice of Henry Kaplan, Terman's first move in expanding the new research orientation of the Medical School was hiring Arthur Kornberg.[20] Negotiations began with Kornberg in 1957. Kornberg was the Director of the Department of Microbiology at Washington University, St. Louis, where he had been since 1953 following a move from the NIH. At Washington University, Kornberg had already assembled a stellar cast of young biochemists and molecular biologists, including Paul Berg, David Hogness, Robert Lehman, Melvin Cohn, and Dale Kaiser. Kornberg and his colleagues also had an extremely impressive track record of Public Health Service grants supporting their research. Kornberg negotiated with Terman and Alway to move the entire department to Stanford beginning in 1959. This was a major coup for the new Medical School, for in the months following his initial acceptance of the Stanford offer, Kornberg received the Nobel Prize for his work on the replication of DNA. Kornberg not only moved most of his staff to Stanford but also was awarded more than $500,000 in Public Health Service grants to equip his new laboratories at Stanford.

As part of his negotiations for building biochemistry, Terman encouraged Kornberg to propose potential faculty for other departments who would complement the strengths in biochemistry, and he invited Kornberg to serve on the search committee for the chairmanship of the Chemistry Department. Kornberg immediately proposed bringing Joshua Lederberg to Stanford. Lederberg, who had been awarded the Nobel Prize in 1958, accepted the offer and left Wisconsin to form the new Genetics Department at the Stanford Medical Center in 1959. At Stanford, Lederberg wasted no time in building a program in molecular

---

[20] Kaplan threatened to leave Stanford if Alway and Terman did not succeed in getting Kornberg or someone comparable to join the effort to restructure the medical school.

medicine with matching grants of $1 million each from the Rockefeller and the Kennedy Foundations to support construction of facilities for the Kennedy Center for Molecular Medicine in 1962. Lederberg also received a $500,000 grant from NASA in support of work on planetary biology that year, a project that eventuated in the ACME[21] computing facility and then the SUMEX (Stanford University Medical Experimental) computing facility.

From their inception, the Departments of Biochemistry and Genetics have been hotbeds of innovation in the field of molecular genetics and molecular medicine, and they have been major sources of the biotech revolution in the Bay Area from the 1980s to the present. This movement has been so important that it is worth considering it a new phenomenon parallel to the Silicon Valley phenomenon, which we might call "Biotech Valley." Aggressive pursuit of federal funding and careful cultivation of relationships to industry have been key elements of the entrepreneurial strategy of both departments. Federal grant awards to the Biochemistry Department were approximately $582,000 in 1966. In 1975 they topped $1 million, and reached $2.24 million in 1982, $3 million in 1987, and $4 million in 1993. The Genetics Department enjoyed even greater success in this same time period: Federal grants to Genetics totaled approximately $740,000 in 1966, surpassing the $1 million mark to $1.75 million in 1974, $2 million in 1978, and $3 million in 1990 and due to the influx of funding from the Human Genome Initiative exceeded $6 million in 1993. In 1974 and 1975 these two departments combined accounted for 20 percent of the federal grant dollars received by the Medical School, and on the average during the period 1966–1993 these two departments have accounted annually for 6.6 percent (Biochemistry) and 7.6 percent (Genetics) of the federal grant dollars awarded to the Medical School.

The departments of radiology, biochemistry, and genetics all fit the Terman model in the style of their growth. As prime recipients of government funding, particularly from the NIH and NSF, these departments were the first medical school departments to finance their growth and operating budgets almost entirely from government grants (Figure 5.5). They also evolved important relations with industry and made extensive use of the Honors Cooperative Program in building teaching components of their programs directly linked to the emerging biotech industry. When compared with the major Engineering School departments of Electrical Engineering and Computer Science, illustrated in Figure 5.6, it is clear

---

[21] The ACME project provided time-shared real-time data acquistion and control services to research laboratories in the Stanford Medical School. The software was designed by Gio Wiederhold and its use was taught to physicians and researchers.

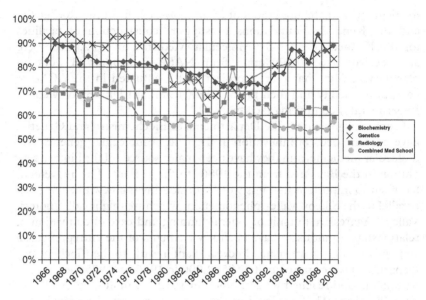

Figure 5.5: Percentage of total operating budget covered by sponsored projects for three Medical School departments. *Source:* Stanford Annual Reports.

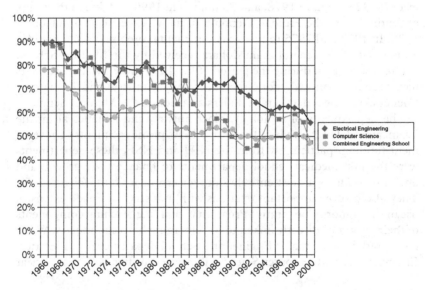

Figure 5.6: Percentage of total operating budget covered by sponsored projects for two Engineering School departments. *Source:* Stanford Annual Reports.

that very early in its formation the Terman model had made a major impact in shaping the Medical School.

Stanford and "Medical Device Valley"

The cases of semiconductors and integrated circuits illustrate how "reverse engineering" has been a standard way of energizing new research fields and disciplines in areas of engineering and the physical sciences at Stanford. With a sharp eye on the ways in which the Engineering School has encouraged entrepreneurial activity in support of building steeples of excellence, the biomedical faculty felt the Terman model translated quite nicely to the research science side of the Medical School, where departments such as Genetics and Biochemistry had established sources of federal funding within the NSF and NIH. But the model did not translate to the clinical side of the Medical School. The Stanford Clinic was oriented to medical training and patient care with little emphasis on clinical research. Clinical trials, for instance, were not a core activity. But the primary problem was the absence of an external national funding structure to support research in biomedical devices. Research in imaging and biomedical devices is multidisciplinary, and collaboration among medical, engineering, and industry groups is essential. The NIH, on the other hand, only supported peer-reviewed individual research focused on specific diseases and organ systems. Entrepreneurs among Medical School faculty in the clinical disciplines were certainly not lacking, but until the mid-1990s Stanford Medical School faculty felt that in order to pursue their innovative research in areas related to biomedical devices, they had to go outside the university. And go outside they did: during the decade of the 1990s the San Francisco Bay area emerged as the leading region for medical device development in the world. Within a 50-mile radius of Stanford more than 200 medical device companies were established, including 70 in the area of cardiovascular diseases.

The role of Stanford faculty in the formation of "Medical Device Alley" traces back to the work of Thomas Fogarty. During 1961–1962, as a surgical fellow at the University of Cincinnati, Fogarty developed the idea of the balloon catheter. Fogarty solved a number of issues that turned his prototypes into effective devices during his first year as a surgical resident at the University of Oregon Medical Center in 1963, and he connected with Edwards Laboratories, a company in Irvine, California, that would manufacture the devices. Fogarty filed a patent – the first of more than 150 patents he would eventually hold – on the first of the minimally invasive surgical devices that have revolutionized modern surgery.

The Fogarty Embolectomy Balloon Catheter (patented in 1969)[22] revolutionized surgical embolectomy procedures by transforming a long, highly invasive operation requiring multiple incisions and a lengthy hospital stay into a one-hour procedure done with a single incision under local anesthesia.

Fogarty moved to Stanford as a research fellow in cardiovascular surgery in 1969, accepted a position as instructor of cardiovascular surgery in 1970, and then joined the faculty as assistant professor of cardiovascular surgery that same year. Fogarty eventually held the position of President of the medical staff from 1977 to 1979. But Fogarty found it difficult to develop his inventions from within the clinical side of the Medical Faculty, and he left Stanford in 1980 to take the position of Director of Cardiovascular Surgery at Sequoia Hospital in Redwood City, a position he held until 1993 when he returned to Stanford as professor of surgery and director of research development in vascular and endovascular surgery. During his career at Sequoia, Fogarty continued to spin off new improved types of catheters. He also developed the endovascular aortic stent-graft for minimally invasive treatment of aneurisms and a variety of surgical clips and clamps for vascular surgery, and with Warren Hancock co-invented the Hancock tissue heart valve.

As with many inventors in a clinical medical setting, Fogarty's first inventions were developed on his kitchen table. There was no infrastructure of support at the NIH at this time for work in biomedical engineering, and not finding the sort of technical support he needed in the Stanford Medical School to pursue his inventions, Fogarty sought a more organized setting for incubating his own cardiovascular inventions and launched his own company, Fogarty Engineering, Inc., in 1980 near his home in Portola Valley, California. A fertile source of many of Fogarty's inventions over the years, the company also worked closely with other inventors and local firms in developing a range of inventions. As the principal hub of the growing biomedical device network in the Bay Area, Fogarty either founded or co-founded over thirty start-up companies in the period from 1980 to 2000. Some of these firms were founded with other Stanford faculty. Fogarty's efforts to stimulate the growth of new biomedical device firms was further facilitated in 1993 by Three Arch Partners, a venture capital firm Fogarty co-founded that specialized in funding biomedical device startups.[23]

---

[22] Fogarty TJ: USPTO 3,467,101. Balloon Catheter, September 16, 1969; Fogarty TJ: USPTO 3,435,826. Embolectomy Catheter, April 1, 1969.

[23] In 2000 Fogarty used his Lemelson–MIT Prize money to start the Fogarty Medical Foundation to reward clinicians developing innovative medical procedures and devices.

Another key contributor to developing Medical Device Alley was John B. Simpson. With a Ph.D. in immunology from the University of Texas and an M.D. from Duke, Simpson did his cardiology training in the mid-1970s at Stanford. During his training Simpson attended a series of lectures by Andreas Grüntzig, the Swiss cardiologist who was pioneering the development of balloon catheters for performing angioplasty interoperatively on coronary arteries. Inspired by this work, but unable to generate financial and moral support from either the NIH or the Stanford surgical department to spend a semester in Zurich with Grüntzig to learn his techniques for balloon angioplasty, Simpson took a leave of absence and funded his own apprenticeship with Grüntzig. Simpson was impressed with everything he learned at Grüntzig's side, but he felt that Grüntzig's system, a fixed guide catheter system that required a lot of talent and finesse to use, could be radically improved.[24] With his colleague Ed Robert, also a fellow in cardiovascular surgery at Stanford, Simpson began making catheters Silicon Valley-style in his kitchen, resulting in the invention of an alternative system using guide wires for positioning the guide catheter assembly.[25] Simpson and Robert's approach resulted in an intuitive easy-to-use system that was industrially reproducible.[26]

Following the birth of "over the wire" balloon angioplasty and the filing of the classic patents in the field, Simpson left Stanford to join Tom Fogarty at Sequoia Medical Center, where he did further training and developed more advanced techniques. With Fogarty's encouragement Simpson launched a company to develop his invention. They called it Advanced Cardiovascular Systems (ACS). Over the wire balloon angioplasty became an overnight success, one of the most successful innovations in the entire industry, and within a few years the company was worth several billion dollars.

Over the next several years the Sequoia–ACS nexus would become the central node of Medical Device Alley. There were few engineers in Silicon Valley who knew anything about catheters or other cardiovascular devices. People from all over the country came to ACS to train on the new

---

[24] For Grüntzig's system see Grüntzig A: USPTO 4,195,637 (Filed November 21, 1977). Catheter Arrangement, Method of Catheterization, and Method of Manufacturing a Dilation Element, April 1, 1980.

[25] Grüntzig A: USPTO 4,195,637. Catheter Arrangement, Method of Catheterization, and Method of Manufacturing a Dilation Element, April 1, 1980.

[26] Simpson JB, Robert EW: USPTO 4,323,071. Vascular Guiding Catheter Assembly and Vascular Dilating Catheter Assembly and a Combination Thereof and Methods of Making the Same, April 6, 1982.
    Simpson JB, Robert EW: USPTO 4,411,055. Vascular Guiding Catheter Assembly and Vascular Dilating Cather Assembly and a Combination Thereof and Method for Making the Same, October 25, 1983.

systems, and many of them were hired into the company. Some would eventually leave to start their own medical device firms. Just one of many examples was Wilfred Samson, an engineer who came out from Boston in 1982. Until he left ACS in 1994 to co-found Cardeon Corporation, Wil Samson would author more than twenty-five patents on various types of catheters and guide wire systems (after leaving ACS, Samson authored an additional twenty-three patents at Cardeon). The Cardiac Catheterization Lab that Fogarty and Simpson set up at Sequoia Medical Center was the launching pad for several other Medical Device Alley careers. Tomoaki (Tom) Hinohara, Matthew Selmon, Roger Winkle, and James Vetter are all among the Sequoia alumnae from these early years. The companies in the cardiovascular device field these individuals participated in creating included Fox Hollow, LuMend, Perclose, and Ventritex.

Paul Yock followed a similar trajectory to "Med-Tech U." After completing his medical degree at Harvard in 1979, Yock did an internship and residency in medicine at UC San Francisco. From 1982 to 1985 he was a Fellow in Cardiology at Stanford. Yock completed his training with a five-month fellowship in coronary angioplasty with Tom Fogarty and John Simpson at Sequoia Hospital in Redwood City. The period at Sequoia was incredibly fruitful. In February of 1986 Yock filed the first of (by 2004) 40 patents in interoperative cardiology, a catheter apparatus and system for intravascular two-dimensional ultrasonography. Although endoscopy had taken off in the 1980s, endoscopes were too inflexible and large to be used effectively for imaging the interior of arteries and blood vessels. Yock's ultrasonic apparatus opened the field of high-resolution intravascular imaging to assess endovascular lesions and to visually monitor the results of interventional therapy.[27] With this patent and several others in the works, Yock launched a new company, Cardiovascular Imaging Systems (CVIS). The company grew out of mentorship and financial support from his colleagues at Sequoia and "Med-Tech U." Fogarty was an investor in the startup and both Fogarty and Simpson were on the board.

The network of biomedical device companies launched by Stanford faculty in the 1980s and early 1990s was extensive. Just discussing the work of Fogarty, Simpson, Yock, and the alumnae of the Sequoia Cardiac Catheterization Lab alone provides an impressive list. From the early days of his entrepreneurial activity Tom Fogarty was the principal founder in more than a dozen Bay Area start-ups. He also was a founder of Three Arch Partners, which has provided venture capital funding for numerous

---

[27] Yock P: USPTO 4,794,931. Catheter apparatus, system and method for intravascular two-dimensional ultrasonography, January 3, 1989.

biomedical device companies. William New, another Stanford-trained engineer who had pursued a career in anesthesiology, was the founder of Nellcor, which introduced the first noninvasive system for monitoring blood oxygenation. John Simpson, the pioneer of balloon angioplasty, founded Advanced Cardiovascular Systems, which later evolved into Guidant, one of the largest cardiovascular device firms, and he was a founder in five other medical device firms, including Devices for Vascular Intervention, Perclose, and LuMend, and Fox Hollow. Simpson has also been involved as a partner in De Novo Ventures, which specializes in funding biomedical device start-ups. With Paul Yock, Simpson was involved in launching Cardiovascular Imaging Systems, which later became part of Guidant. Collectively, Stanford faculty in the Schools of Medicine and Engineering authored more than 250 medical device patents in the period from the 1970s through 2002, and they served as consultants to more than 120 medical device firms. This burgeoning industry of cardiovascular device firms in Silicon Valley – a local industry growing to $15 billion annually by 2000 – was a network created by physician–researcher–entrepreneurs who found their efforts to develop and transfer technology in university settings during the 1970s-1980s discouraged by the Medical School, which still nurtured an older-style clinical model, as well as by a national funding environment at the NIH that failed to recognize the growing confluence of biomedical engineering, imaging science, and informatics affecting all medical disciplines. These physician–entrepreneurs felt that what was needed was to bring Silicon Valley-style "Med-Tech U" back into the university. The changed climate of encouraging entrepreneurial activity in the post-Bayh–Dole era of the 1990s in the Stanford Medical School, in concert with an organized national lobbying effort to transform the funding structure of the NIH, would give them the opening they sought to reverse-engineer the system. Paul Yock was the catalyzing agent who brought all this about.

Yock's early career from 1986 to 1994 had been at UCSF. The reason Yock gives for wanting to make the move to Stanford was the more encouraging attitude at Stanford for startups and collaboration with industry. Things had changed radically since the late 1970s, and the Stanford Medical Center was now adopting a different approach than it had earlier.[28] Indeed, Fogarty had been recruited to rejoin the Stanford faculty in 1993, and John Simpson also joined the faculty as a clinical consulting professor. To promote the new approach, Paul Yock was appointed as Associate Professor and Director of the Center for

[28] Yock, P. (2004). Interview with Paul Yock. Stanford.

Research in Cardiovascular Interventions. The aim of the Center, officially founded in 1994, was to serve as a core facility for development and testing of new devices in cardiovascular medicine. The Center was to focus on early-stage concepts for new technologies, providing a clearinghouse where these ideas could be refined and tested in animal models and clinical studies.

Yock, Fogarty, Simpson, and their network of colleagues in Medical Device Alley had each emphasized from the beginnings of their own work as inventor–entrepreneurs that a key component would be close interaction with colleagues in various fields of engineering. As noted above, Fogarty had resolved the difficulties he encountered in building effective bridges outside the clinical departments by founding his own device engineering company, Fogarty Engineering. Increasingly, throughout the 1980s and early 1990s, close interaction with computer science and areas of overlap between engineering and computer science such as robotics, imaging, and sensor design had proven to be key components for stimulating the growth of the medical devices industry. But missing from Medical Device Alley was a university presence to catalyze the interactions between these areas and drive the field forward with new innovative designs by training young biomedical engineers and future inventor–entrepreneurs. While close interaction with a university environment was deemed crucial, the architects of Medical Device Alley also knew firsthand the importance of an industry presence to stimulate and accelerate device development; and they were also keenly aware of the need for integrating legal expertise in areas of intellectual property and patents with financial expertise and venture capital. What they sought, in short, was to fold the invaluable mentoring relationships with inventor–entrepreneurs, venture capitalists, and skilled medical device patent firms they associated with "Med-Tech U" into the environment of an entrepreneurial university such as Stanford.

Using the Center for Research in Cardiovascular Interventions as a base to work from, Yock and his colleagues planned several stages in a programmatic effort to address these issues. First was the construction of the Medical Device Network (MDN – soon to be renamed the Biodesign Network in 1999). The second component of the program focused on education and research by establishing a competitive innovation fellowship with courses and one-on-one mentoring of the fellows by Stanford faculty and seasoned industry experts. As a related element of this educational effort to bring "Med-Tech U" into the University, Yock launched a series of regular meetings, called "From the Innovator's Workbench," in which biomedical device inventors, venture capitalists, company founders, and lawyers were interviewed by David Cassak from

Winhover Information, Inc. The highly informative series was filmed and archived on the MDN as a resource for students and interested faculty. As a third – but future – stage, the group hoped to establish a department of biomedical engineering that would be an interschool effort between elements of the engineering and medical schools.

The Medical Device Network (MDN) was established in 1996–1997 as a working group of faculty, students, and staff at Stanford. A key aspect of the MDN was its use of the Web as a place for organizing and coordinating the activities and programs of the extended group. Since its inception, the overall goals of the MDN have been to encourage and facilitate invention, patenting, and early-stage development of medical devices within the University and to develop Stanford as an effective regional resource for education in the area of medical device design and development. In their proposals for establishing the MDN, Yock and his program coordinator Sandra Miller emphasized as the key motivation behind the MDN the real potential for stimulating new device inventions within the University if conditions were right. These conditions included (1) a focus on device development at the University as an important part of the academic mission; (2) cross-pollination between Stanford departments and between the University and industry; (3) attention to identifying potentially productive areas for invention; (4) availability of mentoring by faculty with real-world experience in device development; and (5) a convenient and user-friendly Web portal interface directly linking MDN members to patenting and licensing expertise within the Stanford Office of Technology Licensing (OTL) and other key figures in the University.

Perhaps the showpiece of the Biodesign Program that emerged from Yock's efforts was the Biodesign Innovation Fellowships and the associated Innovation Course. Yock designed this aspect of the program together with Josh Mackower, who had pioneered the strategic innovation program at Pfizer.[29] The Biodesign Innovation Fellowship and the Innovation Course were modeled on Mackower's strategic innovation program at Pfizer. Fellows were selected from candidates with either M.S.s or (usually) Ph.D.s in various engineering and medical fields and from M.D.s in surgery on the basis of their promise as emerging inventors. Many of the fellows already had some industry experience, and had started their own company, or had already developed a patentable

---

[29] Mackower was himself a prolific inventor, with over 80 patents for various medical devices in the fields of cardiology, general surgery, drug delivery, and urology. Mackower founded several medical device firms before joining Yock as Consulting Associate Professor in Medicine and co-director of the Innovation Fellowship program.

invention. The purpose of the highly multidisciplinary course of study pursued by these young inventors was to provide a year-long intensive immersion in medical device development in areas on the research frontiers of biomedical technology.

In addition to serving as a resource for stimulating research and innovation in biomedical devices across school and departmental lines, the Biodesign Program was also intended as an adjunct to the OTL. As Yock explains it, the Biodesign leadership considers itself a "plug-in module" to the Stanford OTL.[30] The OTL staff have the impossible task of staying abreast of the diverse areas of innovation at a place such as Stanford, trying to research invention disclosures and license everything from molecules to satellites with limited expertise at their disposal. With strong support from Kathy Ku, the Director of the Stanford OTL, one of the goals of the Biodesign Program was to provide expertise for evaluating inventions in the medical devices area, to assist in ways consistent with the guidelines of the OTL in marketing Stanford inventions, and to make connections for the OTL and Stanford inventors with companies in the medical device network that might have an interest in evaluating an invention. The leadership group were to serve as faculty/student advocates in the patenting and licensing process, and the senior staff of the Medical Device Network was to assist in patent searches and preparation of invention disclosures for submission to the Office of Technology and Licensing. Students or faculty with new ideas were to be matched with an appropriate MDN senior faculty member to help evaluate and develop the idea in cooperation with the appropriate Affiliate at OTL.

From biodesign to the Department of Biomedical Engineering

By the end of the academic year in 1999, all the basic components of the Biodesign Program that Yock and his colleagues had envisioned were in place, and they turned their attention toward establishing a multidisciplinary joint Medical–Engineering department of biomedical engineering. The idea of creating a biomedical engineering program at Stanford was completely natural, almost a given. Since the very early days of the move of the medical school to the Palo Alto campus, the steady stream of projects emerging out of the spontaneous collaborations among physicists, engineers, and medical school faculty had seemed to cry out for the construction of a department of biomedical engineering. But all previous

[30] Yock, P. (2004). Interview with Paul Yock. Stanford.

attempts to launch a program, going back more than thirty years, had been unsuccessful.

In the spring of 1999, Paul Yock and Thomas Andriacchi from Biomechanical Engineering and Functional Restoration formed a committee of senior faculty from the Medical School and the Engineering School to discuss the needs and opportunities for creating a new interdisciplinary effort. After several months of discussion, the group was successful in launching a new Institute for Biomedical Engineering (IBME), funded jointly for three years with $300,000 per year by the Medical School and the School of Engineering, during which time the goal was to assess prospects for creating a department of biomedical engineering joining elements of the Engineering School and the Medical School. A curricular retreat held in February 2000 and internal and external review panels evaluating the emerging program concluded that the core competencies that Stanford should build into biomedical engineering lay in the areas of biocomputation, biomaterials, biomechanics, medical devices, medical imaging, and tissue engineering.

The basic idea that emerged was to allow university-wide affinity groups to coalesce from a community of basic and clinical scientists with a shared vision for research, education, fundraising, and development of key shared resources. Encouraged by this recommendation, more than 90 faculty in the area of biodesign began meeting on a regular basis, representing interests in biomaterials, bioMEMS, biosensors, medical devices, robotics, surgical and minimally invasive techniques, tissue repair and replacement, and therapeutic delivery systems. This large group of faculty agreed that it was time to create a center to promote research and education that developed and implemented new health technologies at the emerging frontiers of engineering and the biomedical sciences – biomedical engineering. Using this same model, similar centers could be established in imaging, cell and tissue engineering, and other areas where there are significant interdisciplinary research and teaching interests. These centers could also serve as the broad bioengineering program envisioned by Dean James Plummer. The centers in aggregate would serve as a broad "institute" in bioengineering formally united under Bio-X. The four centers – Biocomputation, Biodesign, Cellular and Tissue Engineering, and Imaging – mapped directly onto four of the six theme areas that had been identified by the "global" Bio-X program.

While these discussions on how best to build the bioengineering program were taking place, two separate developments were occurring that provided additional impetus and urgency to the effort. The first was a large gift of $150 million to the university by former electrical engineering and computer graphics professor James Clark, who had left Stanford to form Silicon Graphics and then later co-founded Netscape with Marc Andreessen. Clark's gift to the university was to fund an interdisciplinary center that would leverage large-scale computing for emerging areas in biology, medicine, and engineering. The concept was that ideas and methods embodied in engineering, computer science, physics, chemistry, and other fields should be brought to bear upon important challenges in bioscience. Areas of bioscience such as molecular medicine, biosensors, and nanobiotechnology would in turn stimulate new opportunities in other fields such as robotics, and even stimulate new areas within computing itself. The Clark Center would be home to this new Bio-X program, where significant discoveries and creative inventions would be accelerated through the formation of new collaborative teams.

Concurrent with these developments in biomedical engineering and the general Bio-X initiative taking place at Stanford in the period 1999–2001, major changes were under way at the National Institutes of Health, focused on the creation of the National Institute of Biomedical Imaging and Bioengineering (NIBIB). Beginning around 1991, a widespread effort was made to expand the support of the biomedical imaging program at the NIH beyond its almost exclusive focus on cancer imaging. The limitation to cancer reinforced the view in the imaging community that a new institute was needed at the NIH to support basic research in imaging science with broad applications to a wide range of disease processes and organ systems. Advancements in biomedical engineering were also garnering headlines with promises of merging biology, medicine, and engineering to foster tissue engineering, nanoscience and nanotechnology, functional genomics, smart biomaterials, biosensors, and their applications to the prevention, diagnosis, and treatment of disease. In 1991, the American Institute for Medical and Biological Engineering (AIMBE) was created, with financial assistance from The Whitaker Foundation, to represent engineering societies on public policy issues of concern to biomedical engineering, and to engage Congress in the need for increased support for research in biomedical engineering.[31] These efforts yielded a call from Congress for a report on the state of bioengineering research at the NIH (http://becon.nih.gov/nihreport.htm) as part of the NIH Revitalization Act of 1993 (PL 103–43).

In response, an External Consultants Committee, chaired by Robert Nerem of the Georgia Institute of Technology, submitted a report in

---

[31] AIMBE (http://aimbe.org/index.htm) is an honorary society of, currently, 650 biomedical engineers who are elected to membership, 16 scientific societies representing over 32,000 engineers and scientists, 69 academic programs in biomedical engineering, and an industrial council of related manufacturers and industries.

1995 entitled "Support for Bioengineering Research" (http://becon.nih. gov/ externalreport.htm). Ron Davis, from the Stanford Biochemistry Department and one of the co-directors of the Stanford Genome Center, was on that ten-person committee. The 270 outside respondents consulted on the report included Paul Yock and members of the "Medical Device Alley" group we have been discussing. The study conducted a detailed inventory of sources and amounts of public and private funding for basic bioengineering research for the fiscal year 1993. The study determined that within the Federal government, the NIH was the largest source of support for bioengineering research. The Whitaker Foundation was the largest private nonprofit source of funding. Support for basic bioengineering research constituted approximately one-third of all Federal support for bioengineering. In contrast with other areas of NIH support, an average of 60 percent of the overall NIH extramural research budget supported basic research. Industrial support for bioengineering was at least six to ten times greater than that of the Federal government, but support for basic bioengineering research by industry was virtually nonexistent.

In 1999–2000 the NIH was the subject of more detailed study by the Center for Scientific Review, which resulted in the NIH taking several steps to address the concerns of the biomedical engineering and imaging communities. One of the problems identified was that the NIH peer review process was relatively unreceptive to non-hypothesis-driven research, which is essential to development of new technologies and tools in biomedical engineering and imaging. Although "hypothesis-driven" research could be interpreted broadly to include all the styles of research – including using knowledge to solve important problems and developing novel instrumentation to enable knowledge generation – the practice of NIH study sections had traditionally been to interpret it narrowly as the generation of new knowledge. The development of novel instrumentation in the service of new therapies frequently had to be hidden behind a screen of new knowledge generation to pass the review process.

Another related finding of these studies was that the nature of bioengineering and technology and instrumentation development research was not well understood by the biomedical research community at large. The review committees all observed that radical changes were happening in the biomedical sciences through incorporating engineering perspectives into the formulation of basic questions addressed in "hypothesis-driven research," but most biomedical scientists were not aware of the contributions engineers were making or could make. Engineers were actually embracing molecular and cellular biology in engineering and manufacturing designs in areas such as tissue engineering, drug and gene delivery, and biomimetic biomaterials, while continuing to build upon its early roots in the physical sciences (e.g., magnetic resonance, computerized tomography, ultrasound imaging, and biomechanics).

Broad changes in the NIH were needed to promote innovation and calculated risk taking. Among the changes recommended were that the NIH move away from a traditional research portfolio heavily weighted toward the individual, investigator-initiated research project, traditionally equated with hypothesis-driven research. In addition, some practices might inhibit collaboration and the participation of industry, so structures conducive to more broad-ranging collaboration were needed. The NIH's rule of crediting only one investigator per grant as principal investigator (PI), for example, was seen as a potential constraint on the willingness of some scientists to combine forces. Also deemed crucial were ways of encouraging industry's full participation at a time when closer and new forms of collaboration are considered likely to be fruitful.

The upshot of these various reviews, grass roots movements, and lobbying efforts by the bioengineering community was the generation of a clear perception of a need to consolidate the disbursed and uncoordinated dissemination of support for bioengineering through various NIH subagencies, to improve the productivity and impact of biomedical research. Establishment of NIBIB at the NIH would provide a central coordinating body, accelerate development of new technologies with clinical and research applications, and lay the foundation for a new medical information age. After two attempts to introduce Congressional bills to establish the National Institute of Biomedical Imaging and Engineering were stalled, a bill introduced by Congressman Richard Burr (R-NC) and Congresswoman Anna Eshoo (D-CA) eventually succeeded in winning approval. Anna Eshoo was from Palo Alto and represented the 14th District, home to Medical Device Alley. President Bill Clinton signed PL 106–580 establishing the National Institute of Biomedical Imaging and Engineering on December 29, 2000.[32] The NIBIB received its first budgetary allocation of $111.7 million in 2002, but at that time had not completely succeeded in drawing the disparate sources for imaging and bioengineering throughout the NIH under one roof. The budget for

---

[32] First elected to the House of Representatives in 1993, Anna Eshoo has been a strong advocate of high-tech industry. In 2005, Rep. Eshoo led House Democrats in introducing The Innovation Agenda – A Commitment to Competitiveness to Keep America #1. This comprehensive policy plan was developed in conjunction with leaders from the high technology, biotechnology, academic and venture capital communities. She was honored with the 2006 Government Leadership Award from the Semiconductor Equipment Manufacturing Industry and the 2006 Inaugural Congressional Award from the American Institute for Medical and Biological Engineering.

FY 2003 did accomplish this, however, as well as receiving a substantial increase, totaling $278.2 million.

Following closely on the heels of the establishment of the NIBIB committee, deliberations about creating a joint Medical School–Engineering School Department of Biomedical Engineering at Stanford were completed in January 2001. With the relationship to Bio-X resolved, the Department of Bioengineering was officially created as a unique joint department at Stanford between the Schools of Engineering and Medicine in June of 2002. The ten founding faculty members included Scott Delp, appointed as the Founding Chairman, and Paul Yock, M.D., named as the department Co-chair. Eight additional professors (Russ Altman, Dennis Carter, Kwabena Boahen, Greg Kovacs, Norbert Pelc, Mathew Scott, James Swartz, and Charles Taylor) from engineering and medicine formed the founding faculty. Within the first two years of founding the department these members were joined by Steven Quake, Jennifer Cochrane, Dennis Carter, Marcus Covert, and Karl Deisseroth. As a group the department received over $7 million per year in individual research awards from the NSF and NIH from 2001 to 2005, and three of the youngest members of the group (Kwabena Boahen, Steven Quake, and Karl Deisseroth) received NIH Pioneer Awards.

The senior members of the group included several superstars in the field of biomedical imaging, dynamic cardiovascular modeling and simulation, and virtual surgery. Russ Altman, for example, is a leading figure in the dynamic modeling of protein folding. Greg Kovacs is a major inventor of imaging systems and biosensor devices, including implantable biosensors, multiplexed biologic arrays, and microfluidics systems – forty-eight patents in all – and has published more than seventy-five articles, in addition to founding Cepheid in 1993, a company that develops and manufactures systems that perform genetic analysis for the clinical genetic assessment and biothreat based on microfluidic and microelectronic technologies. Other members of the founding faculty group of the Biomedical Engineering Department in 2002 were Scott Delp and Charles Taylor. Delp pioneered in the development of orthopedic surgical modeling systems and also founded MusculoGraphics, Inc., a software development firm specializing in visualization, simulation, and virtual reality technologies for medical applications. As an Assistant Professor of Research in the Department of Surgery in the Stanford Medical School, Charles Taylor pioneered the development of comprehensive systems for real-time dynamic modeling of cardiovascular systems.

These strengths in modeling and simulation were combined with the work of Stanford colleagues from several other departments. Expertise in computational biology and imaging came from Michael Levitt (chemistry), Sandy Napel (radiology), Pat Hanrahan (computer science), and faculty in robotics including Ousama Khatib (computer science) and Jean-Claude Latombe (computer science). The combined research was a key contributing factor in the departments being awarded $20 million over five years, beginning in 2004, by the NIH to lead the National Center for Physics-Based Simulation of Biological Structures (SimBioS). Recognition of the strength of the new Department of Biomedical Engineering was also responsible for the award in 2005 of the Coulter Translational Research Partnership in Biomedical Engineering, an award of $500,000 annually for five years by the Wallace H. Coulter Foundation.

Conclusion: Making research pay – The centrality of the research mission at Stanford

The formation of the Department of Bioengineering and its relationship to the Stanford Bio-X program and the Biomedical Device Network illustrate and underscore the importance of the strategies first articulated by Frederick Terman and pursued at Stanford ever since. The case studies provided here make clear just how important the notion of research – as opposed to applied science – and federal funding as an incubator of industrially relevant research are and have been to Stanford. As I have argued, the "recipe for distinction" developed by Frederick B. Terman and his colleagues in the Stanford administration in the 1950s was simple: focus on attracting and retaining the scientific and engineering talent most capable of winning federally funded research grants and contracts – steeples of excellence – and use those funds to support cutting-edge research that stimulates industrially relevant technology, which in turn reinforces the capability to do more and better research. That vision is as important today as it was fifty years ago. Since the late 1980s, federal funding for research has been steadily declining in real terms for both federally funded programs at universities and funding of R&D in industry.[33] At the same time, private funding of industrial R&D has increased significantly. For universities such as Stanford, however, in spite of its entrepreneurial faculty and close ties to industry, industrial support of research has been relatively insignificant.

The support of R&D at Stanford by different sources is illustrated in Figure 5.7 for the years 1996–2000. The chart makes it clear that Stanford raises approximately 90 percent of its research budget from federal sources. Figure 5.8 illustrates that in the year 2000, for example, nongovernment sources contributed $42 million in research funds to

---

[33] See NSF data compiled on federal funding of research and development.

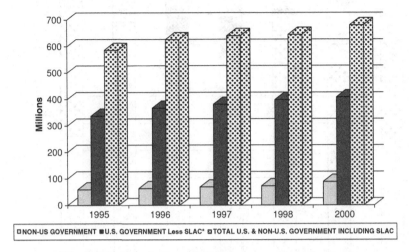

Figure 5.7: Comparison of U.S. government and other contract and grant expenditures for the years ended August 31, 1996–2000. *Source:* Stanford Annual Financial Reports.

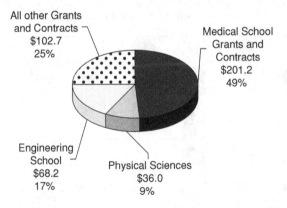

Figure 5.8: Total Stanford grants and contracts for FY 2000 in millions of dollars. *Source:* Stanford Annual Financial Reports.

Stanford in comparison with $408 million in federal funds, excluding support for SLAC. Figure 5.8 illustrates the distribution of Stanford's total grants and contracts for the year 2000 in terms of the percentages received by the Schools of Medicine, Engineering, and the Physical Sciences (included as a division within Humanities and Sciences). Figures 5.9 and 5.10, depicting the consolidated budgets of key academic

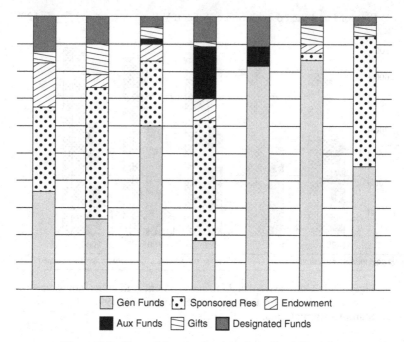

Figure 5.9: Consolidated school budgets for FY 2000: comparison of academic units. *Source:* Stanford Annual Financial Reports.

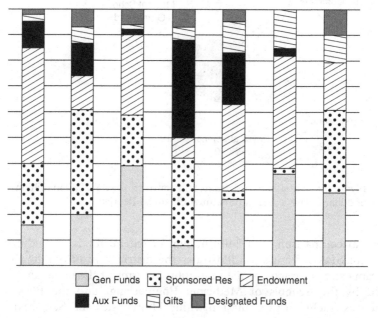

Figure 5.10: Consolidated school budgets for FY 2012: comparison of academic units. *Source:* Stanford Annual Financial Reports.

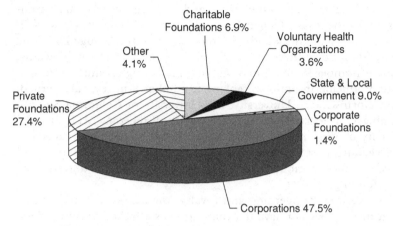

Figure 5.11: Stanford University non-U.S. government contract and grant expenditures: percentage of contribution for the year ended August 31, 2000. *Source:* Stanford Annual Financial Reports.

units in the years 2000 and more than a decade later in 2012, illustrate the importance of federal funding (in dark red) in the consolidated budgets of each of the schools: 48 percent of the total 2000–2001 budget for Engineering and 44 percent of the total budget in 2000–2001 for the Medical School. Finally, as Figure 5.11 illustrates, only 48 percent of the nongovernment funding Stanford received in 2000 (or approximately $20 million) derived from corporate sources. Thus, even in the banner years of industrial growth of R&D, a period in which corporate R&D accounts for more than 60 percent of total U.S. R&D, and in which one might expect that institutions such as Stanford would turn increasingly toward private funding sources, Stanford depended almost exclusively on federal funding for support of its research mission.

In discussing Stanford as an entrepreneurial university and the question of how and in what form Stanford encourages entrepreneurial activity among its faculty, one is inevitably drawn to consider the role of intellectual property and revenues generated by royalties and licenses on Stanford patents. Established as one of the earliest offices of technology transfer and licensing in 1966 by Neils Reimers, the Stanford Office of Technology Licensing has been one of the most successful in terms of generating revenues. During the period 1995–2000, the average annual revenues from licensing were around $40 million. That was a transitional period in Stanford's licensing portfolio because the highly lucrative Cohen–Boyer patent neared the end of its lifetime. While there were dire predictions of a turndown in revenue loss, as it turned out, Stanford's list of licensable IP was highly diversified and new licenses more than com-pensated for the loss of Cohen-Boyer. Thus in 2011, according to NSF statistics, AUTM figures, and Stanford Office of Technology Licensing reports, Stanford received $908 million in sponsored research awards, ranking it number 9, and $66.8 million in licensing revenues from 600 royalty producing inventions, ranking it number 8 in revenues earned, behind Northwestern University, the University of California System, Columbia University, New York University, Princeton, MIT, and the University of Washington. While these are substantial sums, consider-ably exceeding most top-ranked universities, they constitute only around 8 percent of the contribution to the research mission of the university by federal funding.

The large average licensing and royalty revenue is extremely attrac-tive because it does not have the commitments attached to it by federal funding, and can provide a powerful incentive for individual faculty to disclose inventions and engage in the process of technology transfer. But the money is clearly not the primary reason Stanford engages in patent-ing, licensing, and encouraging technology transfer to industry. Terman viewed these activities primarily as crucial parts of establishing long-term relationships with industry and ensuring that Stanford faculty, particu-larly in engineering, were defining the cutting-edge of new technology developments. It was important that Stanford-branded ideas, theories, and technologies got out into the marketplace. The enhanced reputa-tion for excellence resulting from these activities would make Stanford more competitive for the next generation of federally funded research, the lifeblood of the university. Relationships with industry were and have been important as a source of gifts to the university. The Hewlett–Packard gift of $400 million in 2001 and Jim Clark's gift of $150 million are just two prominent examples. But an equally significant role of managing close intellectual ties with industry has, since the days of Terman, been viewed as a crucial source for targeting new directions of research to be absorbed into the university and given a rigorous, scientific founda-tion that will lead to deeper understanding of nature as well as to new inventions.

The key to this system has been the pursuit of steeples of excellence, the identification and retention of the very best scientists and engineers working on the most important areas of research. This goal has been indistinguishable from that of encouraging entrepreneurial activity. Stan-ford President John Hennessy and Dean of Engineering Jim Plummer explained the rationale behind this policy at a day-long faculty work-shop on entrepreneurship in November 2002. Hennessy noted that in all areas of engineering, technology transfer is considered as important as publication. In many engineering disciplines and in the clinical medical disciplines, working closely with industry to translate designs, devices, and therapies into practice is one of primary means faculty have of getting their ideas accepted and further developed. In response to the question of whether he wished the university were generating more licensing, more spin-offs, and more government-sponsored research, Hennessy said, "I wish the endowment had better payout right now. First and foremost our goal has to be to attract and retain the faculty that will be the leaders in their disciplines. For many faculty being able to take their research out to the market is seen as a bonus, adding value to Stanford, and a way to make up for the horrendous housing costs. Licensing revenues have never been a 'make or break' for Stanford. The funds that are received from philanthropy are much greater than from licensing. I do think there is some merit that if you invent a great technology, you move it out to the market and see the value it provides."[34]

In his discussion with the faculty group Jim Plummer echoed many of the same sentiments: "Stanford has a long history of technology transfer. It is one of the ways that people think of us, not just around the country, but around the world. Technology transfer, however, is not just about starting a company. There are plenty of other ways that technology transfer can happen. Sometimes just publishing the results and putting them in the public domain is the right strategy; sometimes going through the OTL and licensing the technology to another company is the right strategy; and sometimes going through OTL and starting up your own company is the right strategy.

"We don't encourage our faculty to be entrepreneurs, but we don't have to, it seems to be in the air. We are supportive of entrepreneurial ideas. There is a strong connection between working on exciting state-of-the art things outside and being a better faculty member; it helps you in your teaching and research. Research on the outside may take you ways in your research that you wouldn't have gone otherwise. There is a synergy between the two. We like the feedback loop between these two."

"Let me end with a couple of conclusions. First, we are delighted when our faculty have commercial research. But that isn't, or at least I hope not, our focus. Commercial research connects our faculty to industry and that research can be defined very broadly. Faculty can do technology transfer through the OTL. They can do non-exclusive or exclusive licenses to new or established companies. These are all valuable routes."[35]

[34] Stanford Faculty Entrepreneurship Seminar: Roles, Models, and Resources, November 5, 2002, p. 9.
[35] Ibid., p. 5.

Though spoken thirty-five years after Terman retired as Dean of Engineering and Provost, the viewpoints expressed by Plummer and Hennessy in 2002 echoed the Recipe for Distinction Terman had crafted at the beginning of Silicon Valley as a strategy for co-evolving the region and the university. Today, in centers such as the newly opened Clark Center, the Photonics Research Center, the Stanford Nanotechnology Center, or in the Department of Bioengineering, patterns of entrepreneurship that draw upon federal funding to sustain the co-evolution of Silicon Valley with Stanford science and engineering are busy laying the foundations for the next wave of innovations.

6 The partnership between entrepreneurial science and entrepreneurial business: A study of integrated development at UCSD and San Diego's high-tech economy

Mary Walshok and Carolyn Lee

In the 1950s and 1960s, no one in America would have seen San Diego, California as a "center of excellence," a global player, or a "city on the move." It was a military center in a fabulously beautiful location that attracted not only tourists, but also Utopians, "health nuts," and sports enthusiasts. In the 1950s, San Diego was not as dynamic economically, culturally, or intellectually as St. Louis, Pittsburgh, or Indianapolis – cities that today look to San Diego as a model of economic transformation. However, things were happening in the region and in the state at that time that created a platform for forms of innovation and growth no one could have anticipated.

Forty years ago, regions such as Minneapolis, Philadelphia, and St. Louis already had
- world-class research universities and research centers
- capital in the form of corporate, foundation, and personal wealth
- affordable land
- business-friendly tax and public policy

Nevertheless, today, they have yet to build a critical mass of "new economy" clusters that create high wage jobs for citizens and new forms of wealth for the region. In contrast, over this same time period, the San Diego region has nurtured several thriving "new economy clusters" – biotechnology, wireless communications, and software – to complement its existing clusters of defense contracting and tourism. These clusters are anchored by the intellectual creativity of the University of California at San Diego (UCSD) and other world-class research centers such as The Scripps Research Institute (TSRI), the Salk Institute for Biological Studies (Salk), and the Sanford–Burnham Medical Research Institute. San Diego has been able to transform its economic base in response to new global imperatives. San Diego has created tens of thousands of new technology jobs including more than 100,000 new high-paying jobs in the life sciences and wireless sectors for the region to replace the 27,000 defense manufacturing jobs that disappeared in the 1990s, after the end of the Cold War. Why is this?

San Diego today has all the obvious ingredients essential to innovation and competitiveness, even though forty years ago it had none. Other than affordable land, it lacked all the other factors outlined above. There was no world-class research university, no capital for starting ventures, and until the 1980s, its regional economic development policies did not embrace technology entrepreneurship as a way to grow jobs for local citizenry. What it had, though, was a collaborative community interested in innovation and a willingness to approach economic growth through science and technology. This was enabled by a University of California-led strategy to build excellence quickly through great science, as well as a major commitment by the private sector to support the creation of a new university, and a collaborative approach by both to creating and growing a "special place," anchored, at first, by world-class research and R&D talent, and then, later on, by entrepreneurs, capital, and globally significant companies. Our case study is an effort to both document and elucidate the dynamic growth relationship between research, in particular, the formation and growth of the UCSD campus and the proximate research institutes located nearby on the Torrey Pines Mesa, and enterprise, in particular, the growth of the wireless and biotech industries, in the San Diego region. However, without the new institutional mechanisms that were created in the past two decades to encourage technology commercialization and nurture and support local enterprise creation, new high-tech-based industry clusters would never have taken root in San Diego and flourished.

Preconditions for academic entrepreneurship

To understand the economic transformation of San Diego over the last four decades, it is essential to understand five catalytic factors that were preconditions for the rise of high-tech entrepreneurship in the San Diego region. Each of these factors was necessary but each alone was not sufficient. The five factors were as follows:

(1) The role of regional land use decisions and of state infrastructure investments in the 1950s and 1960s.
(2) The focus in the early 1960s on building globally competitive basic research institutions from the ground up.
(3) The long history of a local culture of collaboration between all the relevant parties, private, public, and academic, which goes "beyond

networking" and involves shared agenda setting, shared investment, shared risk, and shared rewards. This culture of collaboration has its roots in San Diego's volatile regional economy, which has gone through several severe "boom–bust" cycles since the turn of the last century.

(4) The major commitment of time and resources by the private sector (a collection of primarily small and medium-sized enterprises, business and professional services, as well as local philanthropy), all "pooling" assets to support new and uncertain entrepreneurial ventures in 1985.

(5) A powerful "sense of place," which continues to bind people, if only for lifestyle, to the San Diego region and creates incentives for "making things work," helping new initiatives and enterprises start and succeed, through a reinvestment of personal time, connections, and cash.

1.   Regional land use decisions

In the late 1940s, following the end of World War II, San Diego's economy, which had boomed during the War Years, went into a severe postwar slump.[1,2] Civic and business leaders (particularly in the defense contracting industry) believed that the region's stability rested with a nuclear future, and for that, the region needed to attract physicists and engineers to a place that had never had a significant concentration of scientists before. In a bid to establish a new university campus, local businesses lobbied the state and city governments in the early 1950s to create a School of Advanced Science to train the engineers and scientists needed for the local defense contracting industry, in a place that had never had a research university. Roger Revelle, then Director of the Scripps Institution of Oceanography (SIO),[3] urged the University of California Regents to found a new campus of the University of California that would be the equivalent of a "public version of Caltech" on a disused military base, Camp Matthews, adjacent to land occupied by SIO on Torrey Pines Mesa. To make this plan even more attractive,

---

[1] Nancy Scott Anderson, *An Improbable Venture: A History of the University of California, San Diego* (La Jolla, CA: UCSD Press, 1993), p. 26. This work constitutes an official history of UCSD from 1900 to 1993.

[2] San Diego's population more than doubled between 1940 and 1946, increasing by 165,000. Consolidated Aircraft employed 40,000 manufacturing planes for the war effort. With the end of the war, Consolidated Aircraft lost $400 million in unfilled orders, almost overnight.

[3] For several decades prior to UCSD's founding, the Scripps Institution of Oceanography (SIO) was overseen by the University of California at Berkeley.

the local business community convinced the San Diego City Council to donate additional city lands on Torrey Pines Mesa for this new university. General Atomics, a division of General Dynamics, already had located a new research facility on city-contributed acreage nearby on Torrey Pines Mesa, bringing the first group of physicists to the region in 1955. In 1960, the mayor of San Diego lured Jonas Salk to locate his new research institute on Torrey Pines Mesa too, with the promise of city lands, donated to Salk for a dollar. And within a few years, the Scripps Clinic and Research Foundation, precursor to the present-day Scripps Research Institute (TSRI), relocated to the Torrey Pines Mesa.[4] The city of San Diego zoned additional land nearby and in adjacent Sorrento Valley for commercial development. Thus, throughout the 1950s, 1960s, and 1970s, land use decisions were made that favored the establishment of research institutions in a contiguous space on the Torrey Pines Mesa.

During this period, the civic, academic, and business leaders of the community could not have envisioned what sort of commercial and research development would ultimately result. Furthermore, at the time, there were powerful, vested interests who wanted to see these valuable large tracts of ocean view property on Torrey Pines Mesa developed for residential subdivisions. Because commercial land developers prevailed, Torrey Pines Mesa offered nearby space for young companies to be established alongside the establishment of UCSD as a world-class university. The present-day proximity of the biotech and wireless communications industries to UCSD and the other research institutions on the Torrey Pines Mesa is a direct result of these prescient decisions related to land use and zoning, made decades before the industry clusters arose.[5]

2.   *Building globally competitive research institutions from the ground up*

General Atomics, UCSD, TSRI, and Salk were all "startups" established in the 1950s and 1960s. The Sanford–Burnham Medical Research Institute was founded in 1976. Their founders all envisioned the creation of world-class institutions and leveraged private and public resources to support attracting world-class talent to San Diego. While the private

---

[4] The Scripps family has a long history of philanthropy and endowment in the San Diego region, including an early association with the founding of the Marine Biological Station in La Jolla in 1905. This has led to several major, but unrelated institutions in the San Diego region that bear the Scripps name, including SIO and Scripps Clinic and Research Foundation, a local hospital and the precursor to The Scripps Research Institute (TSRI). While SIO is now an integral part of UCSD, TSRI is not.

[5] Anderson, *An Improbable Venture*, pp. 52–65.

sector expected the University of California campus to be the source of scientists and engineers for the growing defense industry in San Diego, given the Cold War and Sputnik, the university leaders at the Scripps Institution of Oceanography, including Roger Revelle, envisioned a campus led by the new physics and biology advances of that era, including the discovery of DNA as the building block of life. Thus, UCSD, in its early days, focused on attracting senior level research talent and on building superior research facilities, not on technology commercialization or spinning off companies.

In contrast to most U.S. universities, UCSD started life as a graduate school of science and technology, focused on research in the new physics and biology of the 1960s. Undergraduates arrived later, as did the growth of UCSD as a general university encompassing arts, humanities, social sciences, and medicine, in addition to the basic and applied sciences and oceanography. The founding science faculty, recruited by Roger Revelle and others, included two Nobel Laureates and thirteen National Academy of Science members, all risk-takers, intellectual mavericks, and leaders in their fields. These academic stars were the entrepreneurial nerds of that era, before the term "nerd" came into being. In Revelle's own words, "Starting a new physics department, in a non-existent university, in a remote resort town, where [one] would be surrounded by oceanographers, was just the kind of far-out gamble that [these researchers] would be completely unable to resist."[6]

Faculty who accepted positions at UCSD brought with them funded grants, graduate students, and lab equipment. Since they were all world-class researchers with proven ability to win extramural funding for their work, UCSD shot up rapidly in the university rankings. Indeed, as Roger Revelle later said, "Attracting superstars is the cheapest way to start a research university."[7]

3. *A local culture of collaboration between academic, public, and private sectors*

The San Diego region has a long history of collaboration between the academic, public, and private sectors, going back over 100 years to the successful efforts by the Chamber of Commerce to get the U.S. Navy and the Army's Corps of Engineers to dredge San Diego harbor and make it amenable to commercial shipping.[8] The Chamber of Commerce was again involved in 1902 with other local boosters and Dr. William Ritter, a

---

[6] Ibid., p. 71.   [7] Ibid., p. 74.
[8] Abraham Shragge, "Radio and Real Estate: The US Navy's First Land Purchase in San Diego," *Journal of San Diego History*, 42(4), 240–259 (1996).

University of California zoologist from Berkeley, in creating the "Marine Biological Association of San Diego" and lobbying the University of California to create a permanent Marine Biological Station in La Jolla, the precursor of the Scripps Institution of Oceanography.[9] Half a century later, were it not for the private interests associated with the Chamber of Commerce lobbying for the founding of the university in the early 1950s following a period of economic crisis, the San Diego City Council would not have gotten involved in land use and zoning issues on the Torrey Pines Mesa that ultimately affected the location of not just UCSD, but also Scripps Research Institute, Salk Institute, and the General Atomics facility as well.

In the early 1980s, during another period of regional economic downturn and crisis, the private sector again rallied a major commitment of time and resources to engage with the university. Business and economic development leaders recognized that their repeated efforts at business attraction and their attempts to bring large research consortia (e.g., MCC and SEMATECH) to San Diego had failed. This time, it was the regional economic development corporation that led the conversation with UCSD leadership to find a solution to the regional economic malaise.[10] The result of that dialogue was the commitment by UCSD to organize a self-funded program to catalyze the development of high-tech entrepreneurs and service-based companies in the San Diego region. In 1985, UCSD CONNECT was founded by a small group of local supporters, including the San Diego Regional Economic Development Corporation, local business service providers, and successful early high-tech entrepreneurs, such as Irwin Jacobs, then the ex-CEO of Linkabit, a consulting firm that he had founded prior to founding Qualcomm,[11] and David Hale, CEO of Hybritech, San Diego's first biotech firm.

4.   *Continuous private sector commitment to engage with UCSD on supporting high-tech entrepreneurship*

The Bayh–Dole Act, which freed research institutions to transfer and commercialize research outputs, had just been passed several years prior to UCSD CONNECT's founding in 1985, so there was no history

---

[9] Abraham Shragge and Kay Dietze, "Character, Vision and Creativity: The Extraordinary Confluence of Forces That Gave Rise to the Scripps Institution of Oceanography," *Journal of San Diego History*, 49(2), 71–86 (2003).

[10] San Diego's Regional Economic Development Corporation is a private, nonprofit organization supported by approximately 150 private sector companies in partnership with San Diego and other municipal governments.

[11] Laura L. Castro, "Program Will Promote High-Tech," *San Diego Union–Tribune*, April 15, 1985.

of technology transfer at UCSD during the 1980s. Until as late as 1995, UCSD did not have a technology transfer office on campus, as these services were centrally provided by UC's system-wide Office of Technology Transfer. UCSD CONNECT was therefore a unique first partnership between the private, public, and academic communities to engage UCSD in regional development efforts. Private sector commitment to UCSD CONNECT went beyond financial support for its programs. Private sector CEOs and senior partners from local business service providers (bankers, lawyers, and accountants) gave freely of their time to mentor technology entrepreneurs starting high-tech and biotech companies. Extensive interviews with senior university leadership of that era, as well as some of CONNECT's early supporters, reveal that both university and private sector leadership learned from these early encounters how to engage with each other for mutual benefit. These early trust relationships form the basis of the extensive industrial partnerships that underlie UCSD's newest multidisciplinary research institutes, such as the California Institute for Telecommunications and Information Technology (Calit2), one of four California Institutes for Science and Innovation.[12]

5.   A powerful sense of "place" that binds all inhabitants

It is a common perception among San Diego's inhabitants that San Diego County has a physical geography that separates it from the rest of California and the United States. The Mexican border lies to the south, the Pacific Ocean lies to the west, a mountain range defines the eastern border, and a large Marine base, Camp Pendleton, separates the county from the Los Angeles/Orange County sprawl to the north. This physical isolation has defined San Diego as a "place" for nearly a century and bound its inhabitants together in a way that distinguishes San Diegans from the rest of California. Because of this seeming isolation in the southwesternmost corner of the United States, there is a powerful sense of place that binds both old established San Diegans and newly arrived transplants, if only for lifestyle, to the region. This sense of place creates common incentives among San Diegans for making things work, helping new initiatives and enterprises start and succeed, through an investment of personal time, connections, and cash.

There is a perception that everyone would be worse off if San Diegans did not collaborate for a common good. Successive generations

---

[12] Private communication with R. Rao (UCSD Director, Calit2), S. McClendon (retired General Manger of HP's San Diego facility), G. Ianuzzi (partner, Mentus Group), and J. Caulder (venture capitalist and former CEO of Mycogen and Akkadix).

of San Diegans have learned that for the region to remain vibrant, all interested parties must pool resources to support new and uncertain ventures through shared agenda setting, shared investment, shared risks, and shared rewards. Institutional mechanisms, such as CONNECT, have grown up to facilitate the creation of the trust relationships that are essential to sharing investments and pooling resources. Add to this the temperate climate and physical beauty of the region and what results is that talent and wealth stay in the region. This, in turn, forges links between the early entrepreneurs and the multiple generations of progeny companies, with time and dollars reinvested in new enterprises.

The growing concentration of wealth and reinvestment in the region is also reflected by the growth in local philanthropy. In the past thirty years, more than a billion dollars of new philanthropic funds has been established in a variety of family and regional community foundations. This new personal and corporate philanthropy has greatly benefited the UCSD campus in terms of endowed chairs, scholarship support, and multimillion-dollar gifts for facilities and capital improvements. It has facilitated the establishment of new schools such as the Graduate School of International Relations and Pacific Studies, the Jacobs School of Engineering, the Skaggs School of Pharmacy and Pharmaceutical Sciences, and the Rady School of Management. Furthermore, the other research institutes across Torrey Pines Mesa have similarly benefited from the growth in philanthropy fueled by wealth created from the phenomenal growth of San Diego's high-tech clusters.

UCSD's science and engineering resource base

From its conception in the 1950s to its founding and growth in the 1960s, UCSD's founders envisioned building a "publicly supported Caltech" or "MIT of the West." To fulfill this bold vision, UCSD's founders embarked on a deliberate strategy to attract a world-class faculty by offering them an intriguing prospect of unlimited freedom to pursue their scientific interests coupled with the opportunity to build a new university from the ground up. Indeed, on the topic of building and maintaining faculty excellence, Clark Kerr, the University of California's President (1958–1967) at the time of UCSD's founding, said, "If [faculty recruitment] is done badly and you do everything else well, you don't have a great university, but if that is done well and everything else is done badly you can still have a great university."[13]

[13] Verne Stadtman, *The University of California, 1868–1968* (New York: McGraw-Hill, 1970), pp. 277–279.

By the aggressive recruitment of academic stars from other universities with cutting-edge research interests, UCSD founders ensured the fledgling university's instant credibility, as these scientists brought with them existing funding, laboratories filled with equipment, and graduate students and other skilled personnel. In 1963, only three years after its founding, UCSD's R&D expenditures from federal sources totaled $11.084 million, ranking twenty-seventh among all U.S. universities.[14] At that point in time, UCSD had no undergraduates enrolled, and only 205 graduate students enrolled.[15] By 1972, a short decade later, UCSD's federally supported R&D funding had increased over fivefold to $57.3 million, raising the university to a fifth place ranking among all U.S. universities ($57.3 million in 1972 dollars is equivalent to $176.02 million in 2000, in real terms). A mere dozen years after its founding, UCSD had leapfrogged over other more established UC campuses such as Berkeley and UCLA in terms of federal R&D funding. Excluding a period in the late 1980s to early 1990s when growth in federal support slowed, UCSD has remained among the ten largest recipients of federal support for research activities among all U.S. universities. It continues to consistently outrank all other UC campuses. See Figures 6.1a and 6.1b.

In 2010, the latest year for which NSF statistics are available, UCSD ranked seventh, receiving $580.3 million in federal contracts and grants, and sixth by total expenditures ($943.2 million), according to the National Science Foundation. See Tables 6.1 and 6.2.[16]

Industry funding of research

For the first twenty-five years of its existence, the faculty of UCSD did not engage with industry on a systematic basis. The academic superstars and founding scientists recruited to the university in the early 1960s included Nobel Prize winner Harold Urey, other Manhattan Project physicists from the University of Chicago, and scientists from East Coast Ivy League schools. They all joined ranks with SIO's existing oceanographers such as Roger Revelle and biologists such as David Bonner. They ran their research labs with extramural funding from various federal agencies, including large contracts and grants from the Department

---

[14] William V. Consolazio, *The Dynamics of Academic Science: A Degree Profile of Academic Science and Technology and the Contributions of Federal Funds for Academic Science to Universities and Colleges*, NSF-67-6 (1967).

[15] Ibid.

[16] National Science Foundation, *WebCASPAR: Survey of R&D Expenditures at Universities and Colleges (1972–2011)*.

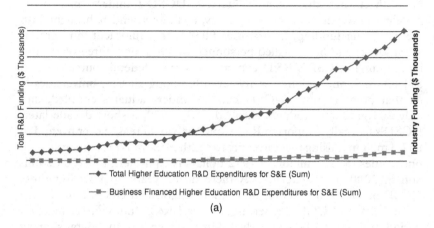

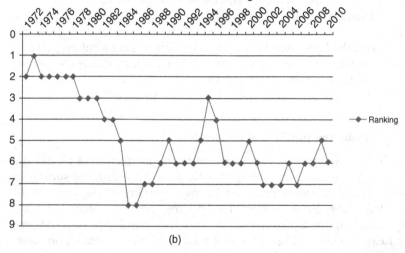

Figure 6.1: UCSD's R&D expenditures and ranking (1972–2011). *Source:* (a) National Science Foundation, WebCASPAR: Survey of R&D Expenditures at Universities and Colleges (1972–2011); (b) National Science Foundation/ Division of Science Resources Statistics, Survey of Research and Development Expenditures at Universities and Colleges.

Table 6.1: *Top twenty academic institutions*

Federally financed higher education R&D expenditures, ranked by all federal R&D expenditures, by R&D field: FY 2010 ($ in thousands)

Rank	Institution	All R&D expenditures
1	Johns Hopkins University	1,737,261
2	University of Washington	829,885
3	University of Michigan	747,778
4	University of Pennsylvania	642,180
5	University of Pittsburgh main campus	594,675
6	Stanford University	593,016
7	University of California, San Diego	580,279
8	Columbia University	572,213
9	University of North Carolina Chapel Hill	545,993
10	University of Wisconsin-Madison	545,189
11	University of California, Los Angeles	538,521
12	University of California, San Francisco	514,693
13	Duke University	514,084
14	Yale University	475,794
15	Harvard University	474,899
16	Washington University St. Louis	468,642
17	Pennsylvania State University	464,750
18	Massachusetts Institute of Technology	457,575
19	Cornell University	448,085
20	University of Minnesota	426,359

Source: National Science Foundation/National Center for Science and Engineering Statistics, Higher Education Research and Development Survey, FY 2010.

of Defense and the Office of Naval Research. While these scientists were certainly "entrepreneurial" researchers and successful in winning extramural funding from government sources, they were not focused on spinning off companies from their research discoveries, nor did they see a direct relationship between industry engagement and their research.

The few entrepreneurial faculty and students who did start companies during that era did so in isolation and without extensive assistance from UCSD itself. Irwin Jacobs, a founding professor of UCSD's Department of Applied Physics and Engineering Sciences, was a rare entrepreneur when, in 1968, he co-founded Linkabit, an advanced communications consulting firm with government and military clients, with UCLA professors Andrew Viterbi and Len Kleinrock.[17] Ultimately, Irwin Jacobs

[17] Dave Mock, *The Qualcomm Equation: How a Fledgling Telecom Company Forged a New Path to Big Profits and Market Dominance* (New York: AMACOM Books, 2005).

Table 6.2: *Top twenty academic institutions by industry-funded R&D expenditures (2010)*

Rank	Institution	All R&D expenditures	Business	% Business funding
1	Johns Hopkins University	2,004,482	67,600	3%
2	University of Michigan	1,184,445	38,739	3%
3	University of Wisconsin	1,029,295	11,594	1%
4	University of Washington	1,022,740	91,946	9%
5	Duke University	983,289	234,361	24%
6	University of California, San Diego	943,219	67,601	7%
7	University of California, Los Angeles	936,995	54,216	6%
8	University of California, San Francisco	935,509	50,979	5%
9	Stanford University	839,839	61,127	7%
10	University of Pennsylvania	836,322	39,032	5%
11	University of Pittsburgh	822,491	10,135	1%
12	Columbia University	807,235	35,548	4%
13	University of Minnesota Twin Cities	786,074	28,403	4%
14	Pennsylvania State University University Park Hershey Medical Center	770,449	64,323	8%
15	University of North Carolina Chapel Hill	755,284	26,052	3%
16	Ohio State University	755,194	120,101	16%
17	Cornell University	749,721	22,869	3%
18	Washington University St. Louis	695,974	36,777	5%
19	University of California, Berkeley	694,049	85,538	12%
20	Texas A&M University	689,624	46,754	7%

Source: National Science Foundation/National Center for Science and Engineering Statistics, Higher Education Research and Development Survey, FY 2010.

left the university in 1971 to head up Linkabit. Another early faculty entrepreneur, Ivor Royston, started Hybritech in 1978, the first biotech company in San Diego, with his lead technician Howard Birndorf. Royston would also leave the university after trying to reconcile academia with entrepreneurship.[18]

According to NSF's Survey of R&D Expenditures at Universities and Colleges, UCSD did not report industry-funded R&D until 1985. That year, UCSD received $5.99 million (3.7 percent of total R&D funding) from industry sources. In 2010, R&D funding from industry sources

---

[18] Mark P. Jones, *Biotech's Perfect Climate: The Hybritech Story*, Ph.D. dissertation in sociology, UCSD, 2005.

exceeded $67 million (7 percent of total R&D funding). See Figure 6.1a. According to NSF reports, the percentage of industry-sponsored R&D has fluctuated from a high of 7 percent to a low of 2.5 percent.

This increase in industry-funded research coincided with a change in leadership at the university. While previous UCSD chancellors did not encourage engagement with industry, Chancellor Richard Atkinson did.[19] He did not personally create industry-oriented programs, but he provided the platform of support and encouragement that enabled senior administrators and others to be innovative in reaching out to industry partners. Lea Rudee, the founding Dean of the Division of Engineering in 1981, is credited with the creation of an Industrial Affiliates Program in 1985, a modest effort by the Division of Engineering to engage with industry, including senior managers of local divisions of Hewlett Packard, Unisys, NCR, and Rohr, among others. An interview with one of the corporate founders of this Industrial Affiliates Program revealed that company executives of that era did not view sponsored research as a major focus of their corporate engagement with the university, which is why the initial percentage of industry-funded research in 1985 was low.[20]

Twenty years later, however, with $100 million in funding from the state of California, UCSD secured $200 million in industry funds toward the creation of a major multidisciplinary center of research excellence, the California Institute for Telecommunications and Information Technology (Calit2). According to Larry Smarr, Calit2's Director, Calit2's mission is "to address large-scale societal issues by bringing together multidisciplinary teams of the best minds (both on and beyond UC campuses) in a way that had been impossible earlier."[21]

While universities have traditionally focused on education and research, Calit2 extends that focus downstream to include prototype development and deployment, with industry partners, in a novel experiment to accelerate innovation and shorten the time from university research to product development and regional job creation. Calit2 is truly a new "sandbox" for those UCSD faculty and industry partners who are interested in participating in a grand experiment to invent the collaborative research environment of the future.

In recent interviews with one of Calit2's founders, this faculty member indicated that were it not for the School of Engineering's Industrial Affiliates Program, UCSD engineering faculty members would not have

---

[19] Richard Atkinson is President Emeritus of the University of California and was UCSD's chancellor between 1980 and 1995.
[20] Personal communication, S. McClendon.
[21] www.calit2.net.

built up the long-standing, close relationships with industry that made Calit2 a possibility. In 2000, a time of state budget surpluses, when the state of California challenged the University of California to create new Centers of Excellence that required leveraging state funds with industry matches, UCSD's engineering faculty was able to call on longstanding industry partners to quickly come up with the matching funds to create Calit2.[22] These close partnerships between university, government, and industry are a far cry from the isolated "Cathedral on a Bluff" that Roger Revelle envisioned for UCSD in the early 1960s.[23]

The quality of UCSD's faculty

From its founding in 1960, UCSD has concentrated on recruiting the very best scientists and scholars in the world into its faculty ranks. Today, UCSD consistently ranks in the top ten U.S. universities across a variety of surveys. It ranks tenth in the overall quality of its faculty and graduate student programs in the National Research Council Survey of Research Doctorate Programs (1995). *U.S. News and World Report* also ranks UCSD as the eighth best public university in the United States (2012). Its science and engineering departments lead in the collection of top-ranking departments including bioengineering (third), cellular and developmental biology (eighth), biochemistry (tenth), molecular biology (tenth), and neurosciences (seventh). See also Tables 6.3 and 6.4.

Other informal measures of UCSD's impact point to the world-class quality of UCSD's faculty. According to a report from Thomson Scientific (formerly ISI Science Citation), UCSD ranked as the seventh most cited institution in the world, based on its published research in science and the social sciences from 1995 to 2005. Thomson Scientific also ranked UCSD second in the nation for the most cited clinical medicine research papers, third in the nation for the most influential research in pharmacology, and fifth highest impact research institution in the nation from 1995 to 2005.[24]

In terms of faculty recruitment, UCSD has always followed the dictum that depth in strategic areas should trump comprehensiveness in all areas. By recruiting academic superstars in a particular area, UCSD could flesh out entire departments by assembling a collection of gifted junior faculty around these superstars to gain critical mass in key areas of research

---

[22] Personal communication, R. Rao.
[23] Roger Revelle, "The Multiple Functions of a Graduate School," reprint of an address delivered at The Association of Princeton Graduate Alumni, Report of the Seventh Conference, held at the Graduate College of Princeton University, Dec. 27–28, 1958.
[24] http://in-cites.com/ and www.ucsd.edu/about/.

Table 6.3: *UCSD's faculty quality rankings compared with the top twenty comprehensive universities in the United States*

Rank	University	Number of programs in top ten	Total programs	Percentage of programs in top ten
1	University of California, Berkeley	36	37	97%
2	Stanford University	32	43	74%
3	Harvard University	26	30	87%
4	Princeton University	22	29	76%
5	Massachusetts Institute of Technology	20	23	87%
6	Yale University	19	30	63%
	Cornell University	19	37	51%
8	University of Chicago	18	30	60%
9	University of Pennsylvania	15	36	42%
10	University of California, San Diego	14	29	48%
	Columbia University	14	34	41%
	University of Wisconsin–Madison	14	39	36%
	University of Michigan	14	41	34%
14	California Institute of Technology	13	19	68%
	University of California, Los Angeles	13	36	36%
16	University of Washington	11	39	28%
17	University of Illinois at Urbana–Champaign	10	37	27%
18	Johns Hopkins University	9	34	26%
19	Duke University	8	33	24%
20	University of Texas at Austin	7	37	19%

Source: National Research Council, *Research Doctorate Programs in the United States* (1995) ($N = 274$).

Table 6.4: *UCSD's faculty quality rankings in selected fields*

Field	Average rating (max = 5.00)	No. of programs	Ranking [1]
Biological sciences	4.42	7	4
Physical sciences	4.07	6	9
Engineering	3.92	4	9
Social sciences	3.78	6	12
Arts and humanities	3.37	6	19
All fields	3.93	29	10

strength. So it was that one of the founding UCSD faculty members, biologist David Bonner, targeted recruitment efforts to lure molecular biologists who were unlocking the secrets of DNA to UCSD. In the 1960s, the campus focused specifically on applied physics, with faculty advocating elimination of the word "engineering" from the name altogether. The medical school, as originally envisioned by Bonner, emphasized basic science over clinical studies to the point where critics claimed the school would only turn out basic researchers, not doctors who could practice medicine. Even the literature department was reinvented to be inclusive of all literature, instead of being divided up into separate departments by language ("English literature," "Spanish literature," etc.), as is the case at most universities. These early recruitment strategies helped to define the character of some UCSD departments for decades afterward as enclaves of "gifted group(s) of academic outlaws who saw in San Diego the chance to shed the constraints of ordinary university life."[25]

The formation of groups of researchers in interdisciplinary and multi-disciplinary areas has also been a focus since UCSD's inception. This is a direct legacy of SIO's oceanographers, whose early work in the 1920s and then contract research for the Navy during World War II relied on multiple disciplines and helped define the field of oceanography. But oceanography is not the only interdisciplinary field defined by UCSD researchers. UCSD is now world-renowned in the field of neuroscience, which, at the time of UCSD's founding, did not exist. However, UCSD's founders recruited researchers at the forefront of the intersection of physics and biology, and these UCSD faculty members helped define the field of neuroscience. Similarly, UCSD's department of cognitive science, which went on to define the field, grew out of a group of disaffected faculty with interdisciplinary interests in the departments of psychology, philosophy, and communications. Today, UCSD has as many interdisciplinary, organized research units as it does formal academic departments.[26]

None of these factors – the quality of a university's faculty, the focus on strategic recruitment to build depth in critical research areas, and the breadth of interdisciplinary research interests – necessarily yields a direct payoff in terms of prolific academic entrepreneurship and company spin-off activity. However, each of these factors represents a high degree of "entrepreneurial" science activity among the faculty. UCSD's entrepreneurial success can be measured by superior levels of research funding, national rankings of programs, citations, and the numerous honorary society memberships of its faculty. This adventurous, experimental, and risk-taking faculty culture is parallel to, and resonant with, the highly experimental, high-stakes, risk-taking culture of the entrepreneurs

---

[25] Anderson, *An Improbable Venture*, p. 85.
[26] See www.ucsd.edu for a complete listing of UCSD's schools and divisions, academic departments, and organized research units.

leading science-based companies in the San Diego region. When these two cultures, "entrepreneurial science" in the university and "entrepreneurial enterprise" in the community, are linked through concrete institutional mechanisms, one sees the phenomenal growth of companies, jobs, and wealth that constitutes San Diego's world-class innovation economy today.

UCSD's organizational characteristics that support and finance academic entrepreneurship

Fifty years ago, in the pre-Bayh–Dole era when UCSD was founded, no attention was given by the university's founders to the creation of new technology-based enterprises that would eventually occupy office and lab space on Torrey Pines Mesa. Today, there are a number of diverse academic and administrative units, staff, and resources throughout UCSD that interact with industry and are focused on technology commercialization and academic entrepreneurship. Indeed, the multiplicity of these units at UCSD can result in frequent, overlapping, and reinforcing interactions because, in UCSD's spirit of entrepreneurship, these are "bottom-up" developments with no central access point or coordination. The different components of the UCSD–industry interaction have been developed at the department level and have evolved relatively independent of each other over a twenty-year period.

TechTIPS, UCSD's technology transfer office, founded in 1995, is the largest and arguably the busiest campus technology transfer office in the University of California system. In a typical year, TechTIPS activities include[27]

- handling over 300 invention disclosures per year
- managing a portfolio of over 1,700 active inventions and 500 patents
- prosecuting over 100 new patent filings per year
- overseeing 204 licenses with a growth rate of 40 new licenses per year
- distributing millions of dollars in royalties to inventors and their departments

Until recently, TechTIPS reported to the Vice Chancellor for Resource Management and Planning, but since FY 2007, TechTIPS has been overseen by UCSD's new Vice Chancellor of Research Affairs.

In addition to TechTIPS, there are numerous other programs that also interact with industry. CONNECT, founded in 1985, was UCSD's first major program focused on innovation and entrepreneurship. Created

[27] UCSD Technology Transfer and Intellectual Property Services (UCSD TechTIPS), *Biennial Report, 2003–2004.*

through UCSD Extension, it is a regional resource working with regional entrepreneurs to support technology commercialization, in addition to helping university-based entrepreneurs and ventures get started. In 2005, CONNECT spun out of UCSD to better fulfill its mission for the San Diego high-tech community.[28] While its governance has changed, CON-NECT's location has not. Its staff still occupies the same office space and there is extensive day-to-day interaction between CONNECT and UCSD faculty, senior administrators, and UCSD Extension program staff. CONNECT's board reflects strong UCSD involvement, including a large number of UCSD deans and senior administrators.[29]

The creation of CONNECT was not an isolated incident of community engagement in the history of UC and the San Diego region. Through its public service mission as a land grant university, the University of California Extension had operated public programs in the San Diego region since 1920, decades prior to the founding of UCSD. These public programs, short courses, and workshops were particularly important during San Diego's wartime expansion, when the University of California offered college-level instruction to help allay San Diego's "[workforce] shortages of engineers, chemists, physicists and production supervisors essential to the war program."[30] As of 1966, UCSD Extension began operating as the community engagement and outreach arm of the new UCSD campus, providing a variety of innovative public programs such as CONNECT, in addition to providing continuing education and work-force training, especially in science and technology fields, for the San Diego region.[31]

Since 2000, a number of additional initiatives focused on educating entrepreneurs have developed at UCSD, including the following:

- The *von Liebig Entrepreneurism Center*, founded in 2001 with a $10 million five-year grant from the von Liebig Foundation, and housed in UCSD's Jacobs School of Engineering (JSOE), provides (a) entrepreneurship courses exclusively for undergraduate and grad-uate engineering students; (b) walk-in assistance to engineering school entrepreneurs, be they faculty, staff or students; and (c) management

---

[28] For more information about the change in CONNECT's status, see www.connect. org/press/nl2005–11–01.htm.

[29] See www.connect.org/about/board.htm for further details.

[30] Abraham Shragge, "Growing Up Together: The University of California's One Hundred-Year Partnership with the San Diego Region," *Journal of San Diego History*, 47(4), 241–259 (2001).

[31] Carolyn W.B. Lee and Mary L. Walshok, *Critical Path Analysis of California's S&T Edu-cation System: Alternative Paths to Competency Through Continuing Education & Lifelong Learning*. A report commissioned by the California Council on Science and Technology (2002).

of an active group of in-house entrepreneurs-in-residence, and also (d) runs the annual Jacobs School business plan competition. Von Liebig's Business Advisors are all unpaid business executives and angel investors who volunteer their time to mentor JSOE students and faculty on business plans based on JSOE technologies. There is funding available for grubstakes ($50–$75,000) funding of the most promising ventures. Very recently, there has been internal discussion of expanding the von Liebig Center into UCSD's Medical School.

- *Global CONNECT*, housed in UCSD Extension, provides technical and research assistance to regions around the world interested in understanding regional innovation systems and how they work. Its activities range from regional asset mapping to technical assistance in setting up CONNECT's Springboard Program, conducting workshops on the power of angel investing, and facilitating interactions and interregional partnerships between regional business accelerators from around the world. These, as well as general education programs, are provided on a contractual basis.

- The *Beyster Institute*, affiliated with the Rady School of Business, founded in 2002, runs entrepreneurship training courses for developing countries, primarily in the former Soviet Union bloc, South Asia, Africa, and the Middle East.

In addition to the specific programs named above, there are a number of industrial and/or corporate affiliate programs associated with individual schools, divisions, and departments that facilitate interactions between industry and faculty peers. See Figure 6.2.

University mission

The University of California's mission statement as a public, land-grant institution says, "The University's fundamental missions are teaching, research, and public service." Traditionally, public service has encompassed (a) agricultural extension services that assist farmers to increase their agricultural productivity, (b) delivery of health care, and (c) professional continuing education in fields such as engineering, law, and medicine. Today, the University of California's public service mission has expanded to include engagement with industry, patent/licensing activities, and the creation of spin-off enterprises, where appropriate. As one of the ten campuses of the University of California, UCSD subscribes to this vision and incorporates public service to the San Diego region, the state of California, and the nation as one of its core activities. While UCSD does not have its own unique mission statement that distinguishes

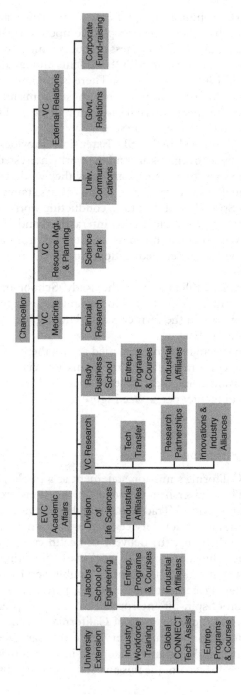

Figure 6.2: UCSD's academic and administrative units that have staff and/or programs that engage with industry and San Diego's high-tech industry clusters. *Source:* Global CONNECT, UC San Diego Extension.

the campus from the systemwide mission, there is an informal statement that "Innovation Is Our Tradition" on the campus website.[32]

UCSD's entrepreneurial faculty culture, history, and tradition

In contrast to the vast majority of colleges and universities across the United States, UCSD made a unique commitment from its inception to build a high-quality faculty and attain nationally recognized academic leadership. Roger Revelle, then Director of SIO, was a tireless champion of research excellence and carried the culture of SIO over into the planning of the new campus. These recruitment strategies were critical to the shaping of the mission and the culture of the young UCSD campus in the early 1960s and well into the 1970s. These same principles of academic excellence influence faculty recruitment today.

One of the key features of Roger Revelle's recruiting strategy for UCSD included the attraction of senior level "stars" and leveraging university and community resources to create innovative incentive packages that would motivate them to move to San Diego from more established universities on the East Coast. For instance, in the 1960s, many research universities had mandatory retirement at age sixty-five. UCSD capitalized on these rigid retirement policies and offered highly productive, respected scientists an opportunity to continue to work past the normal retirement age of sixty-five. For example, UCSD's first recruit, Nobel Prize winner Harold Urey, fell under such a rule at the University of Chicago. In addition to attracting retiring academic stars, UCSD's founders were also assertive in securing faculty positions for spouses, because this fledgling university had many, many faculty positions to fill. Many faculty spouses, such as Margaret Burbidge and Nobel Laureate Maria Mayer, were world-renowned scientists in their own rights, but had never had bona fide faculty positions until their appointments at UCSD. The other research institutions on Torrey Pines Mesa also engaged in similarly aggressive recruitment, which brought many husband–wife scientific teams to San Diego, including William and Lillian Fishman, founding scientists at the La Jolla Cancer Research Foundation, now the Sanford–Burnham Medical Research Institute.

All of these aggressive efforts at recruitment were led by a small core of founding faculty who promised opportunities for growth, funding, and above-scale salaries that were enormously attractive to a particular type of senior scientist willing to leave the secure predictability of East

---

[32] See http://ucsdnews.ucsd.edu/about/index.html.

Coast universities for UCSD, a maverick upstart campus on the West Coast. Above all, UCSD offered these "academic stars" the opportunity to surround themselves with like-minded junior faculty and establish departments and programs that were highly innovative, interdisciplinary, and collegial. In the final orchestrated dance of recruitment, these potential senior faculty recruits were led by Roger Revelle toward the highest point of UCSD's campus, then nothing but scrub brush and chaparral, where he would ask his prospective faculty, "Can't you see a great campus arising all around here?" According to N.S. Anderson's official history of UCSD, "Some saw nothing but the edge of the known world. Others were merely helpful in pointing out problems with [Revelle's plans]. Some, said Revelle, were simply able to resist our 'Siren ways....'"[33] But as for the rest, these standards of excellence, coupled with the lure of helping to build a whole new institution from scratch, netted UCSD a group of academic superstars who were also extreme risk-takers, pioneers, and highly entrepreneurial in nature. These shared cultural traits, established at UCSD's founding, were reinforced by the junior faculty, and carry through to the present day. UCSD's campus and faculty continue to have a reputation for being the most entrepreneurial in the UC system.

What is interesting about the entrepreneurial culture of TSRI, Salk, UCSD, and the now more than fifty similar research institutions that have grown up on the Torrey Pines Mesa is the extent to which individual faculty and researchers have been the advocates and shapers of this entrepreneurial research culture. Institutional leaders, such as Jonas Salk, UCSD Chancellors such as Bill McElroy, and Richard C. Atkinson, were important to these institutions, but particularly strong, credible advocates of research with the general public and key decision makers at the regional, state, and national levels. They were the public face that enabled and supported UCSD's faculty and researchers in their quest for building world-class excellence on a fast timetable. Today, the individual faculty researchers themselves are the ones who take responsibility for luring talent to the region. The new research talent they recruit continues to reinforce the entrepreneurial and pioneering mindset of the early founders. This combination of leadership at the top, justifying the value of basic research to the society, and enabling senior-level faculty and researchers to attract talent has been one of the important factors in creating the critical mass of entrepreneurial science expertise in San Diego today.[34]

---

[33] Anderson, *An Improbable Venture*, p. 73.
[34] Herb York, former UCSD Chancellor, private communication.

In the 1980s, Richard C. Atkinson was especially significant in helping the regional research institutions, especially UCSD, connect with the larger society, and industry in particular. Atkinson had come to be Chancellor of the University of California, San Diego in the early 1980s, after a distinguished career as a Professor of Psychology at Stanford University and six years as Director of the National Science Foundation. It was Atkinson who worked with Democratic Senator Birch Bayh and Republican Senator Robert Dole to craft the legislation now known as the Bayh–Dole Act, which freed institutions conducting federally funded research to patent and license the results of that work for economic and social good. Atkinson's experience at Stanford and his work in Washington, DC meant that he brought an understanding of how it would be possible to grow a great basic research institution simultaneous with making important connections to industry. In his early years at UCSD, he converted what was then a collection of applied science and engineering programs into a School of Engineering; championed a Graduate School of International Relations and Pacific Studies that had a strong economic focus; and through the Extension Division, stimulated the growth of executive education programs for high-technology industries and the formation of what has become an international model for technology commercialization, CONNECT. Throughout the 1980s, UCSD built a variety of industrial affiliate programs, as well as academic degrees that connected more directly to the needs of the burgeoning regional high-technology industry.

San Diego's location as technopole

San Diego is located at the southwesternmost tip of the United States and more than 500 miles south of Silicon Valley, where most of California's venture capital industry resides. For early entrepreneurs such as Irwin Jacobs (founder of Linkabit and Qualcomm) and Ivor Royston (founder of Hybritech, San Diego's first biotech company), there was no local venture capital available. Linkabit was bootstrapped with Navy contracts and did not enter into product development until much later in its corporate life.[35] Hybritech was originally backed by Brook Byers, of Kleiner Perkins, Caulfield and Byers, a Silicon Valley venture firm.[36]

---

[35] Dave Mock, *The Qualcomm Equation*, p. 22.
[36] See www.connect.org for Ivor Royston's remarks upon induction into CONNECT's Entrepreneur Hall of Fame, 2006.

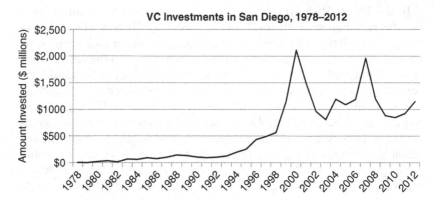

Figure 6.3: San Diego's growth in venture capital (1978–2011). *Source:* Thomson Reuters VentureXpert.

Today, San Diego has created a healthy base of capital for investment in new technology enterprises. (See Figures 6.3a and 6.3b.) The region now has the following:

- indigenous wealth with successful entrepreneurs and philanthropists that are vested in the community
- organized angel groups (e.g., Tech Coast Angels) with "tech savvy" members that reinvest in new, local ventures
- a host of local venture capital firms specializing in technology enterprises, in addition to local branches of outside venture firms

Whereas thirty years ago, regional development plans that relied on corporate attraction strategies largely failed, today multinational firms, especially pharmaceutical giants such as Pfizer, Novartis, and Johnson & Johnson, have moved large corporate research facilities to San Diego to take advantage of the concentration of biotech expertise that has amassed on Torrey Pines Mesa. These multinational firms only moved to the region after San Diego's biotech cluster had been firmly established.

With the establishment of multiple thriving industry clusters, most especially wireless and biotech, has come outside recognition of San Diego's prominence as a high-tech economy. By 2004, the Milken Institute ranked San Diego's biotech industry cluster as first in the nation, based on its R&D prominence, its availability of risk capital, and its ability to attract and keep talent to fuel local biotech company growth.[37] Similarly, Richard Florida ranked San Diego third in the United States

---

[37] Ross DeVol, Perry Wong, Junghoon Ki, Armen Bedroussian, and Rob Koepp, *America's Biotech and Life Sciences Clusters: San Diego's Position and Economic Contributions*, Milken Institute Research Report, 2004.

on his 2002 Creativity Index.[38] In 2001, the Progressive Policy Institute ranked San Diego fifth in the nation on its New Economy Index.[39]

Conclusion

In this case study, we have outlined the factors that have given rise to (a) UCSD's success as an entrepreneurial university; (b) its role as the intellectual hub of two high-tech industry clusters, wireless telecommunications and biotechnology; and (c) its continuing role as an essential resource to other emerging technology industry clusters in San Diego. A mere forty years ago, no one could have foreseen the rapid rise of high-tech as an integral part of San Diego's economy. This rapid rise to world prominence can be attributed to several factors, which, by themselves, would have not been sufficient to give rise to academic entrepreneurship and spin-off activity in the region. Together, these factors combine as a powerful force for creating the economic growth in the San Diego region today. They are as follows:

- the creation of a world-class research university by a group of committed local boosters, backed by the resources of the state of California and the University of California, a world-class public research university system
- the recruitment of a talented group of faculty, all interested in interdisciplinary research at the cutting edge, that defined UCSD as a world-class, entrepreneurial, maverick university from day one
- university leadership that recognized the importance of public service and enabled and supported senior administrators and faculty to create new institutional mechanisms to support faculty entrepreneurship and engagement with industry
- support and commitment (both time and money) from the larger entrepreneurial community that looks to the university for intellectual leadership while it contributes its business expertise to assist researchers in commercializing the fruits of their research discoveries and leading spin-off companies out of the university
- an understanding among leadership in the various sectors (public, private, and academic), that pooling of resources, sharing risks and rewards, and repeated engagement to build trust relationships, are necessary precursors to the creation of a robust regional economic "ecosystem" that benefits all parties

[38] Richard Florida, *The Rise of the Creative Class, and How It's Transforming Work, Leisure, Community and Everyday Life* (New York: Basic Books, 2002), p. 246.
[39] Robert Atkinson and Paul Gottlieb, *The Metropolitan New Economy Index: Benchmarking Economic Transformation in the Nation's Metropolitan Areas*, Progressive Policy Institute (2001).

The data presented about San Diego and UCSD demonstrate that it is the dynamic relationship between the entrepreneurial science community and an engaged business community that fuels cluster growth. Collaboration with scientists as an economic development strategy is enabled by institutional mechanisms such as CONNECT and the von Liebig Center, which support entrepreneurship and drive technology commercialization efforts and new company creation. Having a world-class research university alone is not enough. There needs to be support for enterprise creation in the local community. Mustering the political will to create the institutions and support for new business creation by itself is not enough. Regionally anchored world-class knowledge-creating institutions such as universities are critical. However, for communities such as San Diego that are fortunate enough to have both assets at hand, there is the opportunity to create the innovative companies that will anchor the as-yet-undefined industry clusters of the future.

References

Anderson, Nancy Scott *An Improbable Venture: A History of the University of California, San Diego* (La Jolla, CA: UCSD Press, 1993).

Atkinson, Robert and Gottlieb, Paul The Metropolitan New Economy Index: Benchmarking Economic Transformation in the Nation's Metropolitan Areas, Progressive Policy Institute (2001).

Castro, Laura L. "Program Will Promote High-Tech," *San Diego Union-Tribune,* April 15, 1985.

Consolazio, William V. *The Dynamics of Academic Science: A Degree Profile of Academic Science and Technology and the Contributions of Federal Funds for Academic Science to Universities and Colleges,* NSF-67–6 (Washington, DC: National Science Foundation, 1967).

DeVol, Ross, Wong, Perry, Ki, Junghoon, Bedroussian, Armen, and Koepp, Rob *America's Biotech and Life Sciences Clusters: San Diego's Position and Economic Contributions,* Milken Institute Research Report (2004).

Florida, Richard *The Rise of the Creative Class, and How It's Transforming Work, Leisure, Community and Everyday Life* (New York: Basic Books, 2002).

Goldberger, Marvin L., Maher, Brendan A., and Flattau, Pamela Ebert (eds.) *Committee for the Study of Research-Doctorate Programs in the United States, National Research Council, Research Doctorate Programs in the United States: Continuity and Change* (Washington, DC: National Academies Press, 1995).

Jones, Mark P. *Biotech's Perfect Climate: The Hybritech Story,* Ph.D. dissertation in sociology, UCSD (2005).

Lee, Carolyn W.B. and Walshok, Mary L. *Critical Path Analysis of California's S&T Education System: Alternative Paths to Competency Through Continuing Education & Lifelong Learning.* A report commissioned by the California Council on Science & Technology (2002).

Mock, Dave *The Qualcomm Equation: How a Fledgling Telecom Company Forged a New Path to Big Profits and Market Dominance* (New York: AMACOM Books, 2005).

National Science Foundation, *Federal Funds for Academic Science: 1970, NSF-72-301* (Washington, DC: National Science Foundation, 1972).

Federal Funds for Academic Science: 1969, NSF-71-7 (Washington, DC: National Science Foundation 1971).

WebCASPAR: Survey of R&D Expenditures at Universities and Colleges (1972–2011).

Revelle, Roger "The Multiple Functions of a Graduate School," reprint of an address delivered at The Association of Princeton Graduate Alumni, Report of the Seventh Conference, held at the Graduate College of Princeton University, Dec. 27–28, 1958.

Shragge, Abraham "Radio and Real Estate: The U.S. Navy's First Land Purchase in San Diego," *Journal of San Diego History*, 42(4), 240–259 (1996).

"Growing Up Together: The University of California's One Hundred-Year Partnership with the San Diego Region," *Journal of San Diego History*, 47(4), 241–276 (2001).

Shragge, Abraham and Dietze, Kay "Character, Vision and Creativity: The Extraordinary Confluence of Forces that Gave Rise to the Scripps Institution of Oceanography," *Journal of San Diego History*, 49(2), 71–86 (2003).

Stadtman, Verne *The University of California, 1868–1968* (New York: McGraw-Hill, 1970).

UCSD Technology Transfer and Intellectual Property Services (UCSD TechTIPS), *Biennial Report, 2003–2004.*

7 Knowledge for the world: A brief history of commercialization at Johns Hopkins University

Maryann Feldman, Pierre Desrochers, and Janet Bercovitz

"What are we aiming at? The encouragement of research... and the advancement of individual scholars, who by their excellence will advance the sciences they pursue, and the society where they dwell."
– Daniel Coit Gilman, First President, Johns Hopkins University, Inauguration Address Feb. 22, 1876

Six years before his death, Baltimore merchant and railroad magnate Johns Hopkins (1795–1873) organized two separate corporations, one for a hospital and another for a university, and divided $7,000,000 equally between the two in his 1870 will.[1] This gift, the largest ever made to any academic outlet at the time, gave the trustees a free hand to implement their vision of an institution primarily devoted to research and graduate training. The university opened as a graduate school for men in 1876 and the hospital welcomed its first patients in 1889. The early history of Hopkins's relationship to industry is strongly associated with its first president, Daniel Coit Gilman (1831–1908). An admirer of the German university system, which emphasized specialized training and research, Gilman sought to create an institution that would encourage graduate research and the advancement of individual scholars. As such, the new university would differ significantly from the practical teachings of land grant colleges and polytechnic schools as well as from the traditional American liberal arts college that emphasized the communication of previously held knowledge. Because of public pressure that called for the institution to play a more significant role in the local community, however,

[1] According to Samuel H. Williamson (2004), "What Is the Relative Value?" Economic History Services, available at www.eh.net/hmit/compare/, this amount would be worth approximately $120 million dollars in 2003 dollars (using the Consumer Price Index).

Gilman had to modify his original plan and include undergraduate teaching. Three professional divisions were added in later decades: medicine (1893), engineering (1912),[2] and hygiene and public health (1916).

An important feature of Hopkins was the addition in 1948 of the Applied Physics Laboratory (APL) as a permanent division of the university. The APL had been founded in 1942 under the sponsorship of the Office of Scientific Research and Development to improve the effectiveness of allied anti-aircraft shells. It can best be described as a technical resource for the Department of Defense (DOD) with a primary focus on the Navy's activities, for which it would become the largest affiliated university laboratory. Over the years, APL researchers became involved in the development of many complex projects, ranging from the development of guided missile systems to the design and construction of a navigation satellite system, the development of systems and tactics for submarines, the conduct of space science missions for NASA, and the testing and evaluation of defense systems. By design, however, few civilian or dual-use applications were pursued and the APL never shared Hopkins's philosophical commitment to the free flow of knowledge. Indeed, while the university administrators historically prohibited "closed" research in any of its academic divisions, APL was always allowed to engage in classified or secret work.

Today, Hopkins systematically ranks first among American academic institutions in terms of U.S. government research and development support (Table 7.1), although these numbers must be treated cautiously because they include APL funding, while other institutions, such as MIT, do not include the funding received by similarly affiliated laboratories. The Hopkins School of Medicine is the single largest recipient of the National Institutes of Health (NIH) research grants, while the Johns Hopkins Bloomberg School of Public Health (originally the Johns Hopkins School of Hygiene and Public Health) ranks first among public health schools in federal research support. By all of these funding measures as well as other independent quality assessments, Hopkins is one of the world's leading institutions of higher education and research.[3]

Not surprisingly, research historically conducted at Johns Hopkins led to important discoveries such as epinephrine (adrenalin) in 1897, heparin in 1916, Mercurochrome in 1919, vitamin D in 1922,

---

[2] The Hopkins engineering department opened in 1912 and acquired school status in 1919.

[3] See, for example, the various rankings of American institution of higher education by *U.S. News and World Report* and other outlets, where Johns Hopkins is typically ranked in the top fifteen overall and in the top ten for its academic reputation.

Table 7.1: *Thirty institutions reporting the largest FY 2011 R&D expenditures in all fields, by source of funds (millions of current dollars)*

Rank	Institution	All R&D	Federal government (non-ARRA)
	All institutions	65,073	36,605
1	Johns Hopkins University[a]	2,145	1,801
2	U. MI Ann Arbor	1,279	707
3	U. WA Seattle	1,149	790
4	U. WI Madison	1,112	542
5	Duke U.	1,022	511
6	U. CA San Diego	1,009	583
7	U. CA San Francisco	995	509
8	U. CA Los Angeles	982	502
9	Stanford U.	908	573
10	U. Pittsburgh main campus	899	590
11	U. PA	886	612
12	Columbia U. in the city of New York	879	564
13	U. MN Twin Cities	847	439
14	OH State U.	832	430
15	PA State U. University Park and Hershey Medical Ctr.	795	438
16	Cornell U.	782	432
17	U. NC Chapel Hill	767	494
18	U. FL	740	265
19	Washington U. St. Louis	725	414
20	MIT	724	441

[a] Johns Hopkins University includes the Applied Physics Laboratory, with $1,161 million in total R&D expenditures in FY 2011.
Notes: Because of rounding, details may not add to total. Institutions ranked are geographically separate campuses headed by a campus-level president or chancellor.
Source: National Science Foundation/National Center for Science and Engineering Statistics, Higher Education Research and Development, available at www.nsf.gov/statistics/infbrief/nsf13305/.

Dramamine in 1948, and the application of restriction enzymes to genetics in the early 1970s.[4] The university ethos and the stance of the grant-making private foundations (most prominently the Rockefeller and Carnegie Foundations) against the appropriation by a single recipient of

[4] The main innovations and breakthroughs of the Johns Hopkins Medical Institutions are documented in, among others, Harvey (1976, 1981), and Harvey *et al.* (1989) and the books and other material listed at www.med.jhu.edu/medarchives/biblio/aldidone. htm. For a more detailed list of discoveries and achievements, see www.jhu.edu/news/news_info/research.html; http://hopkins.med.jhu.edu/BasicFacts/discovery.html; www.worldcare.com/e_consultations/consortium/johns_hopkins.html.

the research that they had supported (especially in fields such as medicine and public health), however, resulted in these discoveries being placed in the public domain. The question of patenting and licensing the results of academic research has been debated on several occasions throughout the institution's history. This paper will review this history and conclude with some reflective lessons about university patenting.

The first decades: 1876–1930

Partly as a result of a dominant institutional culture that shunned private monetary gains, the opposition to private foundations, and the financial cost of effectively managing an intellectual property portfolio, most American research universities historically showed little interest in patenting. Instead, many of these institutions deferred patent-related issues to individual inventors and outside organizations, the most prominent of which was the Research Corporation[5] (Matkin 1990; Mowery et al. 2004). Hopkins was no exception, for while university administrators took little interest in the topic until the 1930s, individual researchers were not categorically prevented from patenting and commercializing the result of their research.

Saccharin: The sweetest choice in the division of innovative labor[6]

One of the first Hopkins scientists to patent the results of his research was a visiting professor, Constatin Fahlberg (1850–1910), a Russian-born (and later German) sugar expert holding a Leipzig Ph.D. After having been invited to act as an expert witness in Baltimore by a sugar importer, Fahlerg had some idle time on his hands and asked Hopkins's first chemistry professor, Ira Remsen (1846–1927), if he could work on some research of his own in Remsen's laboratory. The Hopkins scholar agreed, perhaps in part because they had similar research interests relating to

---

[5] The Research Corporation was a nonprofit organization founded in 1912 with the purpose of developing and strengthening the patents covering electrostatic precipitation technologies that were obtained by Frederick Cottrell, a faculty member at the University of California. Beginning in the 1930s, however, the Research Corporation began to manage the patenting and licensing activities of other U.S. research universities (Mowery et al. 2004).

[6] To our knowledge, the most detailed discussion of this case is to be found in Kauffman and Priebe (1978). There are several conflicting versions of the discovery of saccharin, usually (but not always) reflecting the nationality of the writer (either German or American).

the reactions of a class of coal tar derivatives.[7] Fahlberg became part of Remsen's research group. According to one version of the story, in 1878 Fahlberg overboiled a beaker in which he had put a new crystalline substance he had recently created. Later he noticed an unaccountable sweetness to his food that he traced back to this particular compound. The two researchers jointly published the discovery in three articles in the *American Chemical Journal* in 1879 and 1880 (with Remsen as lead author), and in 1879 in a German journal (with Fahlberg as lead author). Remsen, who harbored a profound dislike for private industry (Tarbell *et al.* 1980), quickly moved on to other research projects, but Fahlberg, who had previously patented other discoveries,[8] saw the potential of a low-cost sweetening agent whose production would be much more reliable than that of sugar cane. He changed the compound's name (which he had proposed with Remsen) from "benzoid sulphinide" to "saccharin,"[9] and left Hopkins in order to set up a business to produce and market his discovery. After a few years of developmental work, Fahlberg was granted U.S. and German patents on saccharin manufacture in 1884 and 1885, and from then on built his "patent war chest."[10] However, he never notified Remsen or even included him as a co-discoverer, although he referred to the jointly authored American articles in his applications.[11]

Fahlberg eventually developed an inexpensive mass production method for saccharin and moved back to Germany. After thousands of tests to prove the nontoxicity of the product, saccharin finally hit the market at the end of the century. It was initially marketed as a foodstuff for diabetics, but because of its low cost was quickly adopted by households and industries. A few years after its introduction on the market, saccharin represented 9 percent of total German sugar consumption. Soon, however, saccharin sales entered a precipitous decline triggered by

[7] Coal tar was a by-product of the destructive distillation of bituminous coal to produce coal gas.

[8] Fahlberg had been granted U.S. patents for "Improvement in processes for utilizing zinc sulphate" (1878), "Method of removing iron from ferroginous saline solutions" (1882), and "Recovery of plumbic dioxide from ferroginous solutions" (1882) (USPTO). None of these, however, seem to have led to a successful commercial product.

[9] A word derived, like the older word *saccharine* meaning sugary, from the Greek word σακχαρον (sakcharon), the Sanskrit *caccara*, and the Latin *saccharum*, meaning "sugar."

[10] Fahlberg's later patents included "Medicated benzoid sulphinide compound" (1886), "Apparatus for obtaining phosphorous trichloride," "Making pure saccharin" (1893), "Purifying saccharin" (1893), and "Making saccharin" (1896) (USPTO). Fahlberg obtained his first German patent in 1886 (Szmrecsanyi, 1997).

[11] According to the letter patent #319,082 granted in 1885, "The invention is based upon the original researches published by myself in the American Chemical Journal, Volume 1, Nos. 2 and 3, June, 1879, pages 170 to 175, and jointly by myself and Ira Remsen, in the same journal, Volume 1, No. 6, pages 426 to 438, in which a saccharine compound was first described, to which the name 'benzoic sulfinide' was given."

the lobbying activities of Central European sugar beet producers, who managed to restrict the use of saccharin to the pharmaceutical industry. Fahlberg's factory survived, however, as it was the only one that was legally allowed to produce under the ban, which lasted until World War I (Merki 1993).[12]

While Fahlberg became wealthy with the industrial development of the new sweetener, neither Remsen nor the Johns Hopkins University received, nor claimed, any royalty from this venture. In the meantime, Remsen had come to profoundly despise his former guest, a situation that is usually traced to Fahlberg's claim that the discovery was his alone, leading to Remsen's comment in a letter to English chemist William Ramsey: "Fahlberg is a scoundrel. It nauseates me to hear my name mentioned in the same breath with him" (Kauffman and Priebe 1978: 201).[13] Remsen, however, never challenged Fahlberg's patents despite an offer from Merck & Company to do so on his behalf when his university was experiencing financial difficulties at the turn of the century. As one student later recalled, "I urged Remsen to accept Merck and Company's offer to undertake the contest, but he refused, saying that he would not sully his hands with industry" (Kauffman and Priebe 1978: 202). It is worth noting that in this case, the time from invention to sustained profitability was close to twenty years. Whatever the respective merits of the case might have been, perhaps the main lesson to be derived from the saccharin episode is not so much the potential legal battle and eventual financial success of a university-based start-up firm, but rather the lengthy time lag involved in the development of a commercially successful product that required the full-time involvement of the researcher who initiated the fundamental breakthrough. This story is also notable because it is well known by undergraduates as part of the institutional history.

The Rowland Multiplex Telegraph: Academic brilliance does not connect to commerce

Throughout most of Hopkins's history, the official patent policy was essentially one that can only be described as hands-off, but an exception

---

[12] This prohibition in turn led to a booming black market in saccharin, increasingly supplied from Switzerland, one of the few European countries in which its fabrication and consumption remained legal, by firms such as Sandoz, Ciba, BASF, and Hoechst (Merki 1993). Saccharin has ever since been plagued by similar lobbying efforts by the sugar industry in many countries.

[13] According to Remsen, "The substance came to light in the course of an investigation which Fahlberg undertook at my suggestion, and carried on under my direction, and it was first described in a paper by myself and Fahlberg" (cited by Kauffman and Priebe 1978: 200).

was made in the late nineteenth century for Hopkins's first appointee in physics, Henry A. Rowland (1848–1901).[14] Rowland's academic career was a distinguished one and led to, among other honors, election to the National Academy of Sciences, the Royal Society, and the French Academy of Sciences. Despite the fact that he graduated in civil engineering in 1870 from the Rensselaer Polytechnic Institute, worked for a while as a railroad surveyor, was manually gifted, engaged in numerous experiments, and devised many instruments, Rowland was, in the early stages of his career, an unlikely candidate to seek active commercialization of his research, as he openly dedicated himself to the pursuit of "substantial reputation" rather than "filthy lucre" (Rosenberg 1990: 52). Indeed, Rowland even gained the reputation of being that period's most "insistent champion of 'pure science'" (idem: 182) and the "standard-bearer" for this cause (idem: 201). A bachelor until he was forty-two, Rowland married in 1890 and soon had three children. Around this time, he underwent a routine medical examination for an insurance policy, which revealed that he had diabetes, an incurable illness at the time, and was told that he had at most ten or fifteen years to live. As a result, his research focus changed almost overnight and he soon engaged in more applied work in telegraphy, hydroelectric power, electrical motors, and dynamos. His motives changed to accept commercial activity as he faced his own mortality. This new focus led to practical inventions, consulting activities, and the eventual grant of at least twenty-five patents.[15]

In the mid-1890s, Rowland announced the invention of an improved type of multiplex telegraph. He devoted much of the rest of his life to refining and marketing his device. In laymen's terms, his invention was a method of rapid automatic telegraphy by the use of powerful alternating currents. According to a contemporary source, his colleagues gave him vast latitude to carry out his work. Knowing that his days were numbered and working in the shadow of death, Professor Rowland devoted the last five years of his life to the perfecting of his invention. Dr. Gilman and Dr. Remsen warmly supported Professor Rowland, not only morally, but also financially. The Physical Laboratory was freely placed at his disposal during the entire course of his work in developing his invention, and he was allowed the greatest latitude as to the disposition of his own time with relation to this special work (Anonymous 1902: 540).

---

[14] For a more detailed look at Rowland's academic career, see Rosenberg (1990).

[15] Authors' count from USPTO records. Rowland was granted his first patent, "System of Electrical Distribution," in 1890 (letter patent no. 443,181). The last one, originally filed in 1897, was granted posthumously in 1903.

Rowland also benefited from the support of wealthy Baltimore businessmen, which led to the creation of the Rowland Telegraphic Company (RTC) in 1900. Incorporated in New Jersey, the company had its principal place of business in Jersey City and its plant in Baltimore. When it began operations, the company had an authorized capital stock of $500,000.00.[16] Rowland filed for a number of patents on his invention, eleven of which were granted after his death and assigned to the RTC. Despite Rowland's brilliance and the practical experience that his partners brought to the venture, the RTC story illustrates a fairly common pattern in the difficult development of an academic laboratory invention into a commercially successful product. As the company president put it in the annual report of 1907 (p. 1):

> The Rowland Telegraphic Company, seven years ago, undertook to develop a commercial machine to embody an original invention. There were no precedents to follow. The questions presented were new in mechanics and electricity; the laboratory could only afford artificial wires but not the varying conditions of the real telegraph line. We were, more than we realized, feeling our way in the beginning, but we found that Rowland had grasped . . . the real needs for a new telegraph system. This fact opened up to us the widest experimental use of telegraph wires ever accorded to a new invention. The work thus went forward with the combined advantage of laboratory and field experience. It grew upon our hands into an undertaking far greater than we had foreseen. We soon found that it was not enough to demonstrate the working principles of Professor Rowland's invention, and that only a fully commercial machine would (or could) prove the availability of the invention in commercial use; and that alone after commercial trial upon circuits of varying environment and length, and for a long enough period and thoroughly enough to show its durability and regularity and the ability of the employees to manage it.

The transition from the laboratory to the field proved especially difficult. According to the same source, it was necessary to perfect the function of each part of the machine, to standardize all the components, to make special tools and jigs, and to ensure that all similar parts were exactly alike. Furthermore, the integration of the machine into existing systems meant dealing with a diversity of telegraph wires, the complex phases of handling traffic, and difficulties changing the behavior of operators. The owners and personnel of the RTC discovered that a new invention had to be shown to be universally applicable before it was introduced at all. As the company president reported, "This elaborate work was wholly

---

[16] Approximately $10,894,257.43 in 2003 dollars using the CPI (derived from Williamson 2004).

unexpected. It led to repeated remodeling, but progressive successes always justified the continuance of our work" (idem).

The company continued to spend funds trying to develop the invention for another three years, until it had finally exhausted available resources in 1910, at which time it had $418,418 in liabilities and $283,793 in assets, of which only $28,171 were directly liquidatable (machine shop, plant, materials, and office fixtures), the rest being made up of special tools and drawings, completed machines, and patents. The company finally went into receivership on July 23, 1910. During its ten-year existence, it only managed to sell one machine to the Italian government and one to an undisclosed buyer (Anonymous 1910). Had Hopkins's authorities invested heavily in intellectual property in this case, they would have quickly found out that an elaborate patent portfolio based on brilliant science may not necessarily lead to profitability.

Silica gel

A more significant Hopkins contribution to the commercial realm resulted from the work of chemistry professor Walter A. Patrick (1888–1969) on a method of producing silica gel, a substance that had been known since at least 1640.[17] Patrick discovered that silica gel could be used effectively to adsorb vapors and poison gases in gas mask canisters. Patrick, who was working on the topic during World War I for the United States Chemical Warfare Service, then developed a more efficient process to produce a better quality output, for which he took a patent in 1919.[18] Because silica gel had many potential applications, Patrick was involved in the creation of a private company, the Silica Gel Company (SGC) of Baltimore, to which he assigned his original patent. The SGC goals were to further refine the production process of silica gel and develop new uses for both the process and the substance, which it began manufacturing in 1923. Although Patrick elected to remain at Hopkins, his involvement in the project was serious. He remained in charge of research on silica gel at the SGC and its future parent company (Grace Davison) for decades.

In its early years, the SGC licensed its process to several American corporations, such as the Climax Rubber Company, which intended to use silica gel in rubber mixtures, and the Bryant Heather Company, which intended to use it for domestic and commercial refrigeration. The

---

[17] This section is based on large part on the Walter Albert Patrick Papers, Ms. 113, Special Collection. Milton S. Eisenhower Library, The Johns Hopkins University. Available at www.library.jhu.edu/collections/specialcollections/manuscripts/msregisters/ ms113.html.

[18] "Silica Gel and Process of Making Same." USPTO patent #1,297,724 (March 18, 1919).

SGC further licensed its technology to remove impurities from gasoline and kerosene in Burma, as well as for the drying of air for use in blast furnaces in Scotland (Anonymous 1928). Among other commercial uses developed in the 1920s, silica gel was used in air conditioning, in medical applications for the adsorbing of acids and toxins, as a basis for toothpaste, and to provide relief to patients suffering from diseases such as measles, chicken pox, and ivy poisoning. To facilitate the production of silica gel, the SGC built its K-1 plant in Curtis Bay, Maryland in 1927. Despite these inroads, however, a large-scale market for silica gel failed to emerge and the SGC was unable to turn a profit. SGC was eventually purchased in 1930 by the Davison Chemical Company, a Maryland-based chemical company that had supplied the SGC with sulfuric acid on credit for years and had become its largest creditor (Hockley 1951).[19] The Davison Chemical Company was further reorganized in the early 1930s to become part of Grace Davison (GD). While the SGC ceased to have a separate corporate entity, GD instituted an extensive research program on silica gel under Patrick's guidance, which soon led to the development of new applications in air drying, refrigeration, and packaging desiccants. It was not, however, until World War II that silica gel received wide acceptance, when GD researchers used it as a basis for technologies that met three compelling wartime needs: (1) a dehydrating agent to protect military equipment from moisture damage; (2) a fluid cracking catalyst for the production of high-octane gasoline; and (3) a catalyst support for the manufacture of butadiene from alcohol, an integral part of the synthetic rubber program. As a result, production of silica gel, which had stood at a mere 78,000 pounds in 1937, had jumped to 50,000,000 pounds by 1945 (Hockley 1951). In later years, some of the main industrial uses of silica gel would include the removal of moisture from gases and liquids, the thickening of liquids, and the imparting of a dull surface to paints and synthetic films. Like saccharin, however, silica gel, a product with a wide array of potential uses, took years of development after the original laboratory breakthrough before becoming a commercially successful product.

The patent controversy: 1933–1948

Patenting became a more general concern at American universities in the early 1930s in the wake of a steady growth of industry-sponsored research and a few potentially highly lucrative discoveries and inventions (McKusick 1948). In 1933, acting under the leadership of the American

---

[19] A history of the Grace Davison company is available at www.gracedavison.com/about/history.htm.

Patent Office, the National Research Council (NRC) created a Committee on Patent Policy (CPP), which sponsored a survey of university patent policies whose report was published in the *Journal of the Patent Office Society* (Palmer 1934). The central figure of the CPP on this and later occasions was one Dr. Archie MacInnes Palmer. Probably partly as a result of Palmer's inquiry, a committee on external relations at the Hopkins School of Medicine looked at, among other things, potential conflicts of interest for faculties involved in outside activities. The report's recommendations stated that all members of the staff should be "punctilious" in informing the president of "such of their activities as involve relations to other institutions of instruction or research, or to commercial or industrial agencies, where the relations in any way involve the interest of the University."[20] A unanimous decision was made to the effect that the university should not own or control patents,[21] but its members disagreed on whether individual faculty should be allowed to or not. The same policy was simultaneously adopted by the Advisory Board of the School of Hygiene and Public Health (SHPH). It seems remarkable, however, that the stance of the Medical School and the SHPH were reached without any consultation or input on the part of the Arts and Science and the Engineering Faculty. Indeed, in later years, the Dean of the School of Medicine, Alan Mason Chesney, would simply not know what the patent policy of these other divisions of the university was, if any.[22]

Dr. Isaiah Bowman, the President of the University from 1935 to 1948, summarized very succinctly Hopkins's policy toward patents: "Our patent policy at the Johns Hopkins University is to patent nothing whatever in the field of medicine; and to permit other faculty members to patent discoveries after prior consultation with administrative officials" (Spencer 1939: 23). Here is Palmer's original report on Hopkins's general stance on patents:

---

[20] Committee on External Relations, Report to President Ames, 4/18/33. Available at the Johns Hopkins Medical Archives.

[21] According to a letter dated January 26, 1940, written by one Committee Member, Alan M. Chesney, to then JHU President Isaiah Bowman: "The reason underlying the adoption of that report were not formulated in writing at that meeting and hence do not appear in that records. According to my recollection there was not a great deal of discussion of the matter, the sentiment apparently being unanimous." Available at the Johns Hopkins Medical School Archives, folder "Patent Policy, 1930s, 1940s."

[22] As Chesney wrote on May 13, 1947 to Archie Palmer: "I regret that I cannot tell you what the policy of other divisions of the University is in regard to patents. Perhaps Mr. P. Stewart Macaulay, The Provost, could inform you on that point." Available at the Johns Hopkins Medical School Archives, folder "Patent Policy 1947–1949." Hopkins is still today generally acknowledged to be an extremely decentralized institution made up of insular cultures.

At Johns Hopkins University it is the present policy that the University should in no case own or control patents covering inventions and discoveries made in its laboratories by members of its staff, and it is considered generally undesirable that patents should be assigned to an agency controlled by the University, or in the public mind associated with the University. The attitude of the Medical Faculty of the University was expressed in a resolution of its Advisory Board which went on record in April 1933 to the effect that it was undesirable for any member of the Medical Faculty to take out a patent upon any invention or discovery that might affect the public health. The Board held further that, if in the judgment of any member of the Medical Faculty it seemed advisable to patent a particular discovery or invention affecting the public health, the circumstances in the case should be brought before the Board for review before any action was taken by the individual. (Palmer 1934: 106)[23]

The new policy was to be tested in a matter of months by a young biochemistry instructor who was later to make a name for himself, Einar Leifson.[24] In 1934, Leifson contacted Chesney concerning the possibility of taking out a patent, whether personal or in collaboration with the University, on two types of bacteria media which he had perfected:

I have recently perfected two new media for the enumeration of Bact. Coli in milk and water, and for the isolation of intestinal pathogens. One of these media is being prepared in dehydrated form by the Digestive Ferments Co. I should like to secure a patent on the manufacture and sale of this dehydrated medium. This patent would not prevent any University or Laboratory from making and using the media for themselves.[25]

Leifson, however, quickly learned that the head of the Department of Pathology where he was working, William G. MacCallum, thought it contrary to university policy for members of the staff to obtain patents on matters pertaining to public health. Disappointed with this stance, Leifson tried to justify his request in a November 9, 1934, letter to Chesney:

As you probably are aware, some years ago a committee was appointed by the American Association for the Advancement of Science to report

---

[23] Details available in the JHU's 1933 Advisory Board of the Medical Faculty Meeting, Chapter 7: Medical Patents. Available at the Johns Hopkins Medical School Archives, folder "Patent Policies 1930s, 1940s."

[24] Dr. Leifson would in later years develop media for isolation and identification of enteric bacilli, e.g., desoxychokite medium, selenite F, malonate broth, O-F basal medium, and a flagella strain.

[25] The correspondence between Leifson and JHU authorities can be found in the "Einar Leifson" folder at the Johns Hopkins Medical School Archives.

on the matter of scientific patents. The report of this committee is strongly in favor of scientific men obtaining patents.[26]

The profit motive is not the only one for seeking a patent. A patent enables the inventor to control his product to an extent which he might otherwise not be able to do. With a patent he can exercise effective control over both the price and the quality of his product. The dehydrated media on which I expect to obtain a patent will be sold with my name and recommendation on them, and for this reason I want to be able to control them both as to quality and as to price.

For the University to be justified in its opposition to such patents it would also have to be opposed to copyrights on books written by members of the Staff. There seems to be no opposition to a man collecting royalties from books he has written. Are not these books concerned with public health? Does not the copyright on a book increase the cost of the book to the profession, and was not the book produced on University time and with University facilities? If one man spends his time writing books, and another designing new apparatus and new technical methods, why should the one be allowed to profit and the other not?

As I said before, the patent which I contemplate obtaining will not in any way interfere with the free use of my media should these prove to be as valuable as they appear to be at the present time. All I want to do is to be able to control the dehydrated product which will bear my name and my approval. In addition, I should also like to make a little profit which to a man in my position is sorely needed.

Three days later, Chesney reminded the young instructor in writing of the resolution that had been passed by the Advisory Board of the Medical Faculty concerning patents, while adding that he thought that this stance on patents was "eminently correct." Chesney further added that Leifson's analogy between copyrights and patents would not stand "critical analysis." Although the archival records bear no actual evidence of this, Leifson was probably bitterly disappointed with Hopkins's stance on the matter, for in 1935 he founded a firm, Baltimore Biological Laboratory (BBL), with another young colleague, Theodore J. Carski, in order to commercialize the results of his research. The company quickly became successful enough to allow Leifson to resign his position in August 1937. In 1955, BBL was sold to Becton Dickinson for a sizeable sum.[27] In this case, the Hopkins School of Medicine anti-patent policy obviously did

---

[26] The report referred to is most certainly *The Protection by Patents of Scientific Discoveries*, Report of the Committee on Patents, Copyrights, and Trademarks, American Association for the Advancement of Science, 1934.

[27] According to the Becton Dickinson website (www.bd.com), the acquisition of BBL provided "a crucial impetus for BD to lead two fundamental changes in healthcare: the conversion to sterile disposables and the emergence of diagnostic medicine."

not prevent the transfer of a promising technology to the commercial realm through start-up creation, though it saw no financial gain.

The archival record stands mute as to whether or not Chesney ever explained his position on patents in detail to Leifson. Nonetheless, the Dean of the Medical School would write a memorandum on the topic in 1940 following an inquiry by one Miss Lape of the American Foundation Studies in Government.[28]

In the opinion of the writer the patenting of medical discoveries by persons connected with universities or research institutions is not advisable, even if the patent is taken out without any idea of private or institutional profit, but solely with a view to protect the public against either (a) an inferior medicinal product or (b) excessive charges for such a product. The reasons for this viewpoint are as follows:

1. The general adoption of the policy of patenting medical discoveries is likely to impose a limitation upon medical research and upon the free interchange of ideas between medical investigators. Individuals may well hesitate to enter a particular field of investigation or undertake a particular problem where patents are already operative, if there is a possibility of legal prosecution for infringement of patent rights.

2. Very large sums of money have been forthcoming for medical research in this country from private sources in the past. One of the principal arguments put forward for such support has been the contention that the benefits of new medical discoveries are made available to all on the same basis. If particular individuals or institutions are going to profit financially from such discoveries then the benefits will not be made available to everyone on the same basis, and one of the principal arguments for the solicitation of funds for medical research will be seriously undermined. It is not unreasonable to suppose that a diminution in the funds available for medical research might result from such a state of affairs.

3. Many medical discoveries deal with biological processes or products which are as yet poorly defined or not defined at all, speaking from the standpoint of chemistry. They often do not lend themselves to precise analysis or exact quantitative measurement and in consequence, when they form the basis of a patent, the patent right as granted may easily cover far too broad a field and give far too extensive rights. It has been said of one investigator who took out a medical patent that he patented not a process but a natural law! While this objection is not confined to medical patents alone, it applies with particular force to them.

Chesney then discussed the three main reasons usually put forward for the patenting of medical discoveries: (1) the public should be protected

---

[28] Johns Hopkins Medical Archive, Folder "Patents Policy 1930s, 1940s."

against the sale of inferior medicinal products; (2) the public should be protected against excessive prices for such products; and (3) no commercial concerns would undertake the manufacture of expensive medicinal agents unless they have a reasonable assurance of making a fair profit without the property rights conferred either by patents or by exclusive licenses to manufacture under patents. He dismissed these arguments on the following basis: (1) recent amendments made to the Food and Drug Act made possible a degree of Federal control of the quality of medicinal products which was not possible in earlier years; (2) free competition was the surest way to keep prices within limits; and (3) if a drug had real therapeutic value, there would always be someone willing to make it.[29]

The Hopkins School of Medicine stance on patents would again be reaffirmed in the aftermath of World War II, when the Committee on Patent Policy of the NRC conducted a more detailed survey on the policies, procedures, and practices of educational institutions and nonprofit research organizations in the handling of the patentable results of scientific research. In a letter dated March 3, 1949, Dr. Archie Palmer once again asked Alan Mason Chesney, by then Dean of the Hopkins Medical School, if he would be interested in participating or sending a representative to a one or two day informal conference on research and patent polices. The answer, dated from March 8, was as concise as it was negative:

> Dear Mr. Palmer:
>
> I have your letter of March 3rd and am writing to say that there has been no change in the attitude of the Faculty of the Johns Hopkins University School of Medicine in reference to patents.
>
> I do not believe that we would be interested in participating in the conference such as you describe.[30]
>
> As was pointed out earlier, Chesney does not seem to have been aware of the position of his Arts and Science colleagues on these issues. Some clues are nonetheless available as to the similar stance of the engineering faculty administration. For example, Robert Pond Sr., a young faculty member who joined the engineering school in 1947, recently told about his experience in this respect in an oral history of Hopkins:
>
> I was interested in innovation more than performance, so most of my papers are called U.S. patents. I learned to cast metal fibers, and I knew

---

[29] Chesney borrowed this argument from one Dr. Sollman, who defended this point of view in a 1939 Conference on Patents held by the American Medical Association.

[30] Letter from Alan M. Chesney to A. Palmer, March 8 1949. Available in the Johns Hopkins Medical School Archives.

it should be patentable. I went to Stewart Macaulay, the provost. I said, "How do you handle an invention?"

He said, "What did you invent?"

"I invented a way to cast metal hair."

"What do you use that for?"

"It's for radar jamming. How do I go about giving it to the university?"

He swung his chair around, looked out the window for a couple of minutes, and he said, "Pond, if you think you invented something, then it's yours."

I said, "Would you put that in writing?"

He took a piece of scratch paper and he wrote, "Anything Bob Pond invents belongs to him."

I have a lot of inventions. Now there's a man at Hopkins in charge of all the patents. But I came ahead of that. (Warren 2000: 48)

In 1948, the Hopkins Board of Trustees adopted a position on patent ownership that was, by and large, supportive of this hands-off policy:[31]

The ownership and administration of patents by the University is believed undesirable. Except for discoveries made in the course of sponsored research and those affecting the public health, members of the University staff are free to determine whether or not to apply for patents on new discoveries made in the course of University research. However, the University will expect that before making any patent application, the inventor will consult the President of the University. The resolution of the Advisory Board of the Medical Faculty adopted in April 1933, that it is undesirable for a member of that faculty to take out a patent upon any invention or discovery affecting the public health, is approved with the understanding that there may be special cases where the public interest will best be served by patent control.

Assistance to faculty who expressed a desire to obtain patents was available in the office of the University President, although in practice "the facilities of the Research Corporation or some other similar nonprofit organization may be recommended to University inventors with the expectation that satisfactory arrangements will be made directly between the inventor and such organization" (idem). Consistent with its general policy, the University made no claim to royalties derived from patents growing out of University research. It also specified that patents from government-sponsored research were to be made by its staff "as may be

---

[31] Johns Hopkins University Patent Policy adopted at meeting of the Board of Trustees, May 31, 1948. Available from the Johns Hopkins Medical School Archives, folder "Patent Policy 1947–1949" and reproduced in Palmer (1952).

necessary to obtain and assign to the government patents on discoveries made in the course of government-sponsored research in the event that the sponsor so desires." Patents from privately sponsored research were to be undertaken by the University for private sponsors under contract arrangement and university staff members were expected "to take all steps requested by the sponsor to obtain and assign to the sponsor patents on discoveries arising out of the sponsored research in accordance with the sponsoring agreement." On the other hand, the rights of publication resulting from publicly and privately sponsored research were to be protected "to the fullest extent possible, consistent with the rights of Government and the agreements with private sponsors."[32]

Patent management in the postwar period

For more than two decades after the adoption of the Board of Trustees' policy on intellectual property, individuals who were also assigned many other duties handled patent management at Hopkins and, until 1973, Hopkins's administrators referred all patent questions to a local attorney on retainer.[33] Thus the Patents and Coordinating and Advisory Committee (PCAC), whose members were reporting to the provost, handled most aspects of patent management, while individuals in other organizational units, such as the Office of Sponsored Research Administration (OSRA) and the Institute for Cooperative Research (ICR), were also sometimes involved in patenting procedures. The ICR, created in 1947 to coordinate government and industry research projects (Yoe 1989: 40),[34] handled patent management during the 1950s and 1960s, while the OSRA provided administrative and clerical services for the PCAC. The APL, in the meantime, oversaw its own patent operation. By and large, however, the approach to patents until 1973 was essentially passive, with virtually no patents being assigned to the university during this period. As will now be argued, this hands-off approach proved beneficial in light of a spectacular commercial failure that could have had disastrous consequences for the university had it taken a more proactive stance on intellectual property.

---

[32] Johns Hopkins University Patent Policy adopted at meeting of the Board of Trustees, May 31, 1948. Available at the Johns Hopkins Medical School Archives, folder "Patent Policy 1947–1949."

[33] The institutional history in this section is adapted from the Records of the Office of Patent Management, available at the Ferdinand Hamburger Archives of the Johns Hopkins University.

[34] The administrative division of ICR eventually became the precursor of the Sponsored Projects Office.

On the benefits of not patenting: The Dalkon Shield case

In the early 1960s, Hugh Davis, an obstetrician and gynecologist at the Hopkins Medical School and the director of Hopkins's Family Planning Clinic, was one of many physicians experimenting with new models of intrauterine contraceptive devices (IUDs).[35] He eventually developed a closed ring device, the "Incon Ring," and offered ownership of his invention to university administrators. While Davis's proposal was turned down, he was given the freedom to develop it on his own.[36] He then teamed up with electrical engineer and inventor Irwin Lerner and his attorney Robert E. Cohn. Lerner quickly improved on Davis's innovation by adding lateral spikes, a central membrane, and a multifilament "tail." These adaptations were intended to decrease the expulsion rate of the apparatus, increase its surface area (which Lerner and Davis believed to be an important factor in the effectiveness of an IUD), and make it easier for doctors to check its position in the uterus. The new device was labeled the "Dalkon Shield" (because it was shaped like a policeman's badge) and was patented under Lerner's name. As a result, the Dalkon Shield (DS) lost its intellectual property connection to Hopkins. Davis began testing the DS at Johns Hopkins Family Planning Clinic in 1968 and performed a study involving 640 women whose (apparently glowing) results were quickly published in the American Journal of Obstetrics and Gynecology. The partners in Lerner Laboratories formed the Dalkon Corporation that same year[37] to market their device. The device hit the market in January 1971 after A.H. Robins, a large and well-respected Richmond (VA) drug company,[38] purchased the rights to the DS from the Dalkon Corporation in June 1970 (reportedly earning Davis more than $500,000.00 in the process). Robins's researchers made several further modifications to the product, while Davis and Lerner accepted positions as consultants to the company. Davis, in the meantime, had boosted his product by appearing at a 1970 Senate hearing where he had made a strong case against oral contraceptives and further promoted his product as the "superior modern contraceptive" in both professional and

---

[35] The early history of the DS has been told, usually in dramatic terms, in many outlets. See Mintz (1985), Perry and Dawson (1985), Sobol (1991), Grant (1992), McCollum (1992), Carleton (1994), Hicks (1994), and Hawkins (1997).

[36] Personal interview with Frederick T. DeKuyper, Hopkins's legal counsel at the time, Fall 2000.

[37] The corporation was owned 55 percent by Lerner, 35 percent by Davis, and 10 percent by Cohn.

[38] Some of the best-known products of A.H. Robins are Chapstick and the cough syrup Robitussin.

lay publications.[39] Sales of the DS soon took off and it is estimated that 2.8 million units were sold in the United States between 1970 and 1974, and at least 1.7 million exported to other countries.

As the story goes, however, important health problems related to the use of the DS soon emerged. Robins removed the DS from the U.S. market in 1974 in response to a request from the Food and Drug Administration and Davis was eventually found to have been less than straightforward in reporting problems and less than honest regarding the spectacular results he had originally claimed for his device. The DS then became the center of legal battles and, by 1985, Robins had disposed of more than 9,000 claims by paying out approximately $530 million in both compensatory and punitive damages to individuals. However, the company faced an additional 5,000 cases pending in state and federal courts, at which point it filed for protection from creditors under Chapter 11 of the U.S. federal bankruptcy code. U.S. District Judge Robert R. Merhige and Bankruptcy Judge Blackwell N. Shelley then brokered an agreement under which American Home Products acquired Robins in exchange for placing about $2.3 billion in a trust for the claimants. Under the reorganization plan and a class-action settlement, also approved by the court, three trusts were created to resolve the claims of DS users, their families, and third parties. At the peak of its operations, the users' trust had a staff of almost 400, which in 10 years handled more than 400,000 claims and ultimately paid out almost $3 billion by the time it closed in April 2000, making it one of the most successful settlements for claimants of mass tort litigation.

The DS case has since been portrayed in numerous instances as "a story of corporate greed and callous disregard for the reproductive health and emotional well-being of women" (Hicks 1994: vii), while women who experienced negative side-effects and complications were typically labeled "survivors" (idem). This perspective was not limited to activists and trial lawyers. For example, on February 24, 1984, the Chief Justice for Minnesota arraigned the officers of Robins in the following terms: "You have planted in the bodies of these women instruments of death, of mutilation, of disease . . . a deadly depth charge in their wombs, ready to explode at any time" (quoted in Cox 2003). But while long on cases of "bleeding, pain, inflamed and perforated uteri, spontaneous abortions, infertility, sterility, birth defects in offspring" and "psychosocial damages" such as "strained or failed personal relationships" (Hicks 1994: vii and 2), the DS saga is rather short on actual cases of fatal illnesses

---

[39] There were more than seventy other IUDs available in the early 1970s.

directly attributable to the device.[40] Indeed, one can find reviews of the studies that were used to indict the DS that labeled these studies as "inconclusive" and gave credence to Robins's defense that blamed most of the complications experienced by women not so much on the DS, but on other factors such as promiscuity, poor hygiene, and incorrect use of the product by physicians (Kronmal *et al.* 1991; Mumford and Kessel 1992).

Whatever the merits of the DS case, and despite the fact that Hopkins was never involved in liability suits, this episode proved to be a public relations disaster for the university and, according to Hopkins legal counsel at the time, made Hopkins's administrators wary of similar ventures for a long time. While the DS case is certainly extreme by the standard of university–industry technology transfer, it is nonetheless a useful reminder that liabilities, as well as profits, are likely to accrue to academic institutions (especially wealthy ones) eager to cash in on intellectual property rights. We may ask the hypothetical question if the story would have turned out better if the university had been involved in oversight of the project.

The post-Bayh–Dole era: 1982–2000

The 1970s and early 1980s background that ultimately led to the adoption of the Bayh–Dole Act was dominated by important budgetary cuts in federal funding agencies, widespread fear of a loss of American industrial competitiveness, spectacular economic development in the vicinity of Stanford University and the Massachusetts Institute of Technology, and the Diamond v. Chakrabarty court ruling that upheld the validity of a broad patent in biotechnology and opened the door to the patenting of organisms, molecules, and research techniques emerging from this field. Patent management at Hopkins reflected this context by becoming somewhat more systematic with the appointment of a patent attorney in 1967 and with the creation of the Office of Patent Management (OPM) on November 16, 1973. Once the OPM became operational, yet another committee was established under the direction of the Provost. This University Patent Committee was responsible for policy recommendations as well as for providing technical advice to the OPM and the inventors, while the OPM had full authority to prosecute patents for the university.

---

[40] Most claimant organizations in the DS case mention the number of twenty "documented deaths" attributable to the DS, but again, the total number of women who used the DS IUD between 1971 and 1974 is generally estimated to have been around 4 million (Hicks 1994).

Following the adoption of Bayh–Dole, the Hopkins Board of Trustees approved a new Intellectual Property Policy on October 13, 1983, in an attempt to increase private sector funding, but also to try to control Hopkins's contribution to the private sector through the transfer of ideas and technologies (Schmidt 1986: 102).[41] The opening sentences of the 1992 revised version of this policy clearly indicates the extent to which the intent of Bayh–Dole was now shared by Hopkins's administration: "The Johns Hopkins University strives to support its faculty and employees in securing commercial development of intellectual and other property resulting from their research so that the benefits of that research may reach society at the earliest opportunity. This is consistent with the University's mission of developing new knowledge and facilitating the practical application of such knowledge to the benefit of the public" (Johns Hopkins University 1992). New technology transfer units were soon created in all the main divisions of the university. The first was the OTL at the Medical School (1986), which was later followed by the Office of Technology Transfer (OTT) (1995) in the other divisions of the university (including the School of Public Health) and the Office of Technology Transfer at the APL (APL-OTT) (1999).[42] The number of patents assigned to Hopkins in the meantime went up from zero in 1966 to 102 in 1999 (Figure 7.1), a year in which Hopkins filed more patent applications than all but two other major research centers (Birch and Cohn 2001). In total, 1,019 patents were assigned to the university between 1976 and February 2005.

The traditional pitfalls of university patenting and licensing, however, would soon manifest themselves, most notably the very high cost and complexity of effectively managing a patent portfolio, apparent conflicts of interest, and costly legal battles with private firms. Three short case studies illustrate these points.

---

[41] This theme seems to have been an important one in the work of the Industrial Liaison Committee, which took place in the early 1980s and set the stage for Hopkins's future approach to technology transfer (see the Annual Report of Industrial Laison Program, October 1980–October 1981, available at the Johns Hopkins Medical Archives, Box 5/R127I16, folder "Industrial Liaison, 1982"). For example, Hopkins's President, Steve Muller, pointed out that MIT was not pleased with the results of their Industrial Liaison Program, as it had resulted in many of their faculty leaving MIT and setting up "Route 128" companies with no return to MIT. From a memorandum written by David A. Blake to "The Record" on the subject of "Comments of President Muller Regarding Industrial Relations – Made at the ABMF Meeting on 12/30/80." Available at the Johns Hopkins Medical Archives, Box 5/R127I16, Folder "Industrial Liaison 1981."

[42] A divisional, as opposed to University-wide, approach to technology transfer was considered a starting point by the Industrial Liaison Committee that examined these issues in the early 1980s. See the folder "Industrial Liaison Committee (1980–1981)," Box 5/R127I16 of the Johns Hopkins Medical Archives.

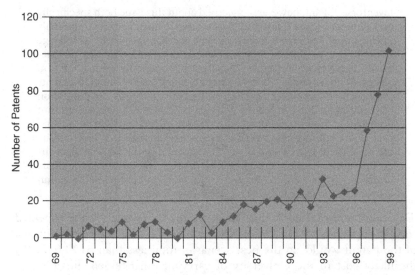

Figure 7.1: Number of patents assigned to the Johns Hopkins University, 1969–1999. *Notes:* From FY 2003 through FY 2009, total R&D expenditures and non-S&E R&D expenditures are lower-bound estimates for the national totals because (i) non-S&E R&D totals were collected only from institutions with S&E R&D, and (ii) F did not attempt to estimate nonresponse on the non-S&E expenditures item. Industry funding figures not available before 1986. Dollar amounts are in thousands. (B) UCSD's ranking among all U.S. universities and colleges, in terms of federal support for R&D activities. *Source:* Compiled from USPTO database. (A) R&D Expenditures (in nominal dollars).

The Hellige case

In 1984, Professor Richard Johns requested the Hopkins Faculty Invention Committee to discuss the topic of patent defense following the failure of Hellige, a German subsidiary of Litton Industries, to take action against two infringers of its exclusive license to practice an invention based on his and two other colleagues' research. According to Dr. Johns, Hellige's terminated its license from Hopkins, but continued to make, use, and sell the invention in spite of the patent held by the university. Dr. Johns brought the issue to the attention of John Dearden, at the time Director of University Sponsored Projects, on July 6, 1984. He followed up his apparent dissatisfaction with the conversation by writing on the same day:

> I agree that if the University decides *not* to litigate the infringements upon this patent the University should assign title back to the

inventors . . . I am, however, concerned about this issue both specifically and generally. If the University fails to litigate infringements, especially infringement by former licensees, any licensee may elect to infringe rather than to pay license fees and defend the invention against infringement. There is an aphorism, "A patent is worth only as much as you will spend to defend it." If the University will spend nothing, its patents (and licenses) are worth nothing. If the University gets the reputation of spending nothing, it will be an open invitation to infringement, not licensing . . . Your suggestion that costs of litigation might be a valid part of the indirect cost base for research is intriguing. It may well be the solution to what I saw as the fundamental problem: The vigorous defense of valid patents against infringement is a *general* obligation of the University (if it is serious about this endeavor), but expense of litigation is probably too great to be borne by a single invention.[43]

The main issues raised in this case were the following: (1) the expected royalty payments to the University from Hellige for the remaining life of the patent would, in the best scenario, total less than $100,000; (2) the likely cost to the University of carrying infringement litigation to conclusion was estimated to be at least $200,000; (3) the chance of succeeding in litigation was thought to be 50–50;[44] (4) whether or not Hopkins had an obligation to defend the intellectual property it acquired, as policy, from its faculty; (5) whether failure by the University to defend a patent might encourage additional infringements of the same and other University-held patents; and (6) whether the costs of patent defense could and should be distributed broadly within the University, or if they should be assigned to the division that would otherwise receive royalty income.[45]

The Committee agreed that that as a matter of equity and practicality, the University should normally be prepared to defend such intellectual property against infringement and that the litigation costs should be distributed broadly across the University. The Committee unanimously passed the following recommendation: "That the University takes enforcement action against the apparent infringer(s) of the University patent on Professor Johns' invention."[46] The reaction of the University

[43] Letter from Richard D. Johns to Mr. John Dearden, July 6, 1986. Available at the Johns Hopkins Medical Archives, Box 96–9, folder "DABlake – Member University Wide Invention Committee."

[44] According to David A. Blake, who was then Associate Dean for Research: "It should be noted that 50–50 is about the best odds you can get since alleged infringers usually countersue a patent holder for patent invalidity, and approximately 50 percent of U.S. patents are found invalid under such proceedings." Letter from David A. Blake to Richard S. Ross, November 26, 1984. Available at the Johns Hopkins Medical Archive, Box 96–9, Folder "DABlake – Member: University Wide Invention Committee."

[45] Faculty Invention Committee Report and Recommendation to the President, November 21, 1984. Johns Hopkins Medical Archives, folder DABlake – Member: University Wide Invention Committee," Box 96–9.

[46] Idem.

Associate Dean for Research, David A. Blake, who had been appointed to this newly created position in 1981 to oversee relationships with industry,[47] was certainly less than enthusiastic. As he wrote to Dr. Richard Ross, by then Dean of the School of Medicine:

> I have attached a copy of Dick Johns' letter to the Committee which eloquently presents the more general issue, namely, that if the University is unwilling to enforce its patents against infringers we are probably wasting our time having a patent policy and patent management system. The Committee was persuaded by Dr. Johns' points and voted unanimously to recommend to the President of the University that he initiate legal proceedings against Litton and the other infringers. One reason for bringing this to your attention is that the Patent Management Office traditionally allocates its uncovered patent legal expenses to the individual division. At this time the School of Medicine's general funds has a net negative balance related to patent activities. In the event that Dr. Muller accepts the Committee's recommendation, this negative balance could increase by at least a quarter-million dollars. Therefore, I would urge you to inform Dr. Muller that you do not wish to have the School of Medicine's general funds budget responsible for such an enormous legal cost. I should also add that I have previously told Dr. Yates [Hopkins's patent counsel] that the School of Medicine did not wish to underwrite legal costs, and recommended that patent title be returned to Dr Johns unless the University was willing to underwrite such costs.
>
> One solution might be to join other universities in establishing a patent defense fund in a manner analogous to our malpractice captive. Clearly, it would be in the best interests of all research universities to eliminate any perception in the marketplace that universities are unwilling to enforce their patents.[48]

Following this incident, it was eventually agreed upon by people involved in technology transfer operations that the School should fund the prosecution of a patent "when it is likely that an invention will be a commercial success."[49]

Spectra Pharmaceutical Services

While the Dalkon Shield case was clearly in a class of its own, other licensing agreements also proved problematic for the University. A case in point

[47] Annual Report of Industrial Liaison Program, October 1980–October 1981. Available at the Johns Hopkins Medical Archives, Box 5/R127I16, folder "Industrial Liaison 1982."

[48] Letter from David A. Blake to Richard S. Ross, November 26, 1984. Available at the Johns Hopkins Medical Archive, Box 96–9, folder "DABlake – Member: University Wide Invention Committee."

[49] Memorandum from Richard D J. Johns to Michael E. Johns, July 30, 1991. Available at the Johns Hopkins Medical Archives, box 96–7, no folder.

is another start-up from the School of Medicine, Spectra Pharmaceutical Services, which was founded in 1985 by emeritus ophthalmologist A. Edward Maumenee, a researcher whose fame was of such proportion that a six-story Hopkins building was named after him in 1982. After having observed the successful treatment with a vitamin A-based ointment (tretinoin) of a Guatemalan child whose eyes had become so sensitive to light that he could no longer leave the house, Maumenee decided to provide drugs at a price cheaper than that billed by the generic drug manufacturing companies.

While Maumenee's motives and integrity were never in doubt,[50] problems began in 1985 when one of his protégés, Scheffer C.G. Tseng,[51] published conjointly with his mentor and five other senior physicians a peer-reviewed article claiming that a vitamin A-based ointment originally developed for use on skin had achieved spectacular results in treating dry eye syndrome. Following the publication of this study, a number of Maumenee's friends pulled $3 million into the start-up, while the value of the stock per share climbed quickly from $2.00 to $8.25. Tseng and his relatives owned 530,000 shares of the stock and soon cashed in 200,000, earning more than $1 million in the process. In the meantime, a patent application was filed in 1987 by Maumenee and a collaborator, which was granted in 1989 and assigned to Spectra Pharmaceutical Services.[52] Interestingly enough, the patent made no reference to Hopkins.

Later research, however, not only failed to replicate the success of the original study, but also began uncovering a string of flaws and improprieties in the follow-up studies that Tseng was performing on hundred of patients. Although Tseng's work did not result in harm to any of his patients, it had all the appearance of a serious conflict of interest that led him to bolster his claims of success. As things turned out, the vitamin A proved viable for treating severe dry eye cases, but it did not prove successful for more than 95 percent of individuals suffering from milder forms of this condition. Meanwhile, an internal Hopkins investigation further discredited the original study. In the wake of these events, the stock value of the company crashed to $0.375 per share, a class action lawsuit was filed against Spectra's board of directors, and the company became the subject of a Congressional investigation and eventually filed for bankruptcy (Levine 1990; Turcotte Maatz 1992). According to some

---

[50] Indeed, Dr. Maumenee was strongly defended by all the faculty who know him and who were interviewed in the course of this research.

[51] Tseng, however, quickly moved on to Harvard, where he apparently had similar problems.

[52] United States patent #4,866,049, "Ophthalmic composition and method of using same." The collaborator was Richard L. Giovanoni of East Tauton, MA.

Hopkins faculty, the Spectra case caused the university personnel to think about conflict of interest more deeply than at other peer institutions. Be that as it may, not having been assigned the right to patents derived from Maumenee's research in this case probably proved, as in the Dalkon Shield fiasco, a positive thing for Hopkins.

University patenting and licensing: Lessons from Hopkins

The issues and cases discussed so far, along with more recent developments that cannot be discussed in detail because of confidentiality agreements, point to a few tentative lessons on the potential pitfalls of university patenting and licensing. Perhaps the most significant for academic institutions and their researchers are potential liability, conflicts of interest, weakening of the norms of open science, and limited revenue generation.

Potential liability

The DS saga left a profound imprint on Hopkins's technology transfer operations. The DS case is still widely invoked by current university officials who insist that licensees accept responsibility for all legal fees, settlements, and judgments arising from lawsuits, along with coverage of the university insurance policy costs. According to Hopkins's deputy general counsel, Frederick Savage, even though an increasing number of firms are contesting these provisions, Hopkins's demands are now a matter of policy that was developed at the University's highest levels based on a belief that if Hopkins had claimed ownership of the DS without sufficient liability protection, the University's general revenues, and even portions of its endowment and real-estate holdings, might have been at risk (Duffy 2002). While many administrators at other research institutions have welcomed the promise of a "big hit," it may be that a "big disaster" is probably just as likely. Thus, it is increasingly important that universities "prepare for the worst" and actively negotiate contracts that include sufficient safeguarding terms.

Conflicts of interest

Another recurring issue is the potential conflicts of interest that arise when faculty are financially tied to a particular discovery. In the early 1990s, Hopkins changed its rules so that it could accept stock instead of cash in return for rights to its patents (Birch and Cohn 2001).[53] This policy was obviously problematic in the case of large-scale studies of a product being developed by a Hopkins start-up that involved other researchers who were not only on Hopkins's payroll, but also colleagues of researchers with a financial interest in the firm. Hopkins's chief shield against bias in this case of corporate-sponsored research was disclosure, a provision that some commentators deemed insufficient (Birch and Cohn 2001).

Even more problematic is the fact that, in contrast to its chief rival, Harvard University, Hopkins's administrators did not bar scientists from conducting certain research even when they had invested in the company sponsoring the work. Instead, Hopkins's officials say they "manage" financial conflicts of interest by taking steps to discourage abuses, most notably by requiring scientists to place their stock in escrow and to disclose to patients and publications their financial ties in drug trials. While a case can be made that the researchers involved in these start-ups might have been at the pinnacle of their profession, and therefore the most qualified to conduct these tests, as some critics have pointed out – and as past Hopkins experience suggests – scientist–entrepreneurs have little incentive in this context to divulge bad news.[54]

Increasingly confronted with these issues, the School of Medicine adopted a revised policy on conflict of interests[55] in June 2002 that feature the following general principles:

1. All financial and fiduciary interests that might appear to present a conflict of interest related to research activities must be reported to and reviewed by the Committee on Conflict of Interest.
2. There is no "de minimis" level below which a financial interest is exempt from reporting.
3. The Committee on Conflict of Interest may recommend either prohibition of the proposed research activity or procedures for management of the conflict of interest.
4. It is presumed that covered parties may not participate in research projects involving human subjects while having a significant financial interest in the research project or in a financially interested company. (This presumption may not apply to projects that the institutional review board determines to meet the definition of "no more than minimal risk" to research subjects or that CCOI considers to be low risk,

---

[53] Birch and Cohn (2001) discusses the cases alluded to in this section in more detail.

[54] It is true, on the other hand, that there is also a similar pressure to produce impressive results in order to win large grants.

[55] Available at www.hopkinsmedicine.org/faculty_staff/policies/facultypolicies/conflict_interest#item1.

such as conducting studies on tissue samples.) Exceptions may be granted if an investigator provides CCOI with a compelling justification for participating in a specific research project while maintaining certain significant financial interests.

5. Covered parties are additionally responsible for complying with the requirements set forth in the School of Medicine's policy on conflict of commitment. This policy on conflict of interest is to be interpreted in a manner consistent with the policy on conflict of commitment.

The norms of open science

One of the main criticisms leveled against university patenting is that it threatens the norms of open science, and the recent history of Hopkins would seem to support this concern. In a late 1990s case for which Hopkins was criticized for being heavy-handed, a judge of the federal appellate court ruled that CellPro Inc., a Seattle-based company, had infringed on what was sometimes described as a "broad patent" garnered by Hopkins researcher Curt Civin on the use of antigens to pull stem cells from bone marrow for use in transplants. The court held that Hopkins was the first to patent the key antigen, and thus deserved the royalties. CellPro argued that it had developed a different approach and was closer to getting the technology to market first, and therefore asked the federal government to "march in" in order to let them proceed. CellPro's loss of the patent infringement case, however, ultimately caused its demise in 1998, while Hopkins's administrators came under heavy criticism in this case (Valoir 2000; Bar-Shalom and Cook-Deegan 2002).

While the CellPro case might have been beneficial to Hopkins, it was only a matter of time before researchers at the Maryland institution were themselves victims of potential infringement on patents held by others. Brickley (2002) reports that a new – and generally considered very broad – patent on disease treatments that operate through a key biological trigger, the NF-B messenger protein, was issued in June 2002 to the Massachusetts Institute of Technology, the Whitehead Institute for Biomedical Research, and Harvard University. This patent was then licensed to a biotechnology firm, Ariad Pharmaceuticals, which, within hours, launched a lawsuit against pharmaceutical giant Eli Lilly. The aggressive legal behavior of Ariad Pharmaceuticals quickly lead to widespread fears that academic involvement in prosecuting a patent that protects drugs already on the market would seriously threaten their historical exemption from such patent fights. According to William P. Tew, then Assistant Dean and Executive Director of Licensing and Business Development for the Johns Hopkins University School of Medicine: "It does present an area of concern because we don't want to blatantly flaunt the law. But the fact is, I have thousands of researchers and it would be an administrative nightmare to try to sort out what might be infringing" (Brickley 2002: 19).

Revenue generation

As is now well established, the only way an academic institution can generate significant revenues from its technology transfer activities is through a "big hit," which Hopkins has so far failed to generate. Available statistics on Hopkins's licenses in the late 1990s suggest that the majority of innovations that did get licensed brought in between $50,000 and $100,000 over the life of the patent, while the cost of filing and maintaining a patent might have ranged from $30,000 to $100,000. In fiscal year 2001, adjusted gross license income at Hopkins was reportedly $6.7 million, compared to $10.3 in FY 1999, $5.5 million in 1998, and $4.7 million in 1997, while a few million dollars were spent each year in legal fees to file and maintain patents.

The net revenues from patenting and licensing were therefore minimal when one considers that in those years support from industry was slightly below $100 million a year, while public funding was on the order of $900 million (Cavanaugh Simpson 2001; Bell 2003, National Science Foundation 2003). In other words, industrial research support at Hopkins hovered between 8 and 10 percent in those years, while patenting and licensing revenues were so minuscule that they barely left a mark on the global funding picture, as they never amounted to more than 0.5 percent of all research funding. At least partly because of this modest performance, in 2003 the licensing offices of all eight Hopkins schools were combined in the hope of handling patenting and marketing discoveries more efficiently. In a move that is somewhat reminiscent of the earlier Research Corporation, Hopkins administrators further invited at least fifteen leading medical research institutions – including the University of Michigan and the University of California, Los Angeles – to cofound a brokerage that could market and license their technologies.

To our knowledge, the employees of Hopkins's technology transfer operations never entertained any unreasonable expectations in terms of licensing revenues in the absence of a "big hit" and would have rather have had more recognition placed on their role of serving and educating faculty to the reality of technology transfer. They were nonetheless expected to run a profitable operation and, in our opinion, faced incentives to take a large number of patents to show results. The current philosophy of William P. Tew, the Director of Hopkins's recently combined Office of Licensing and Technology Development and a man with significant business experience,[56] is therefore to generate enough revenues to keep his operation in the black until a big hit materializes. As he put it: "More money is always the goal . . . but licensing technology is like going to Las Vegas . . . Most of what we do is nickel and dime stuff" (quoted by Bell 2003).

Conclusion

American universities' more proactive stance toward patenting and licensing the results of academic research in the wake of the 1980 passage of the Bayh–Dole Act came amid increased pressures to enhance their connections with (and contributions from) industry. Virtually all those with substantial research activities have since established special offices for that purpose, although one can find great diversity among approaches to patenting and technology licensing. Some universities lay claim to all research output generated in their labs, while others are more flexible in negotiating the disposition of their intellectual property. Likewise, some institutions look to their technology licensing offices to generate revenue, and others see these units as instruments for building long-term relationships with private companies as research patrons or partners. Only a small number can claim success concerning either objective (Abramson et al. 1997: 19). Furthermore, only a slim portion of new discoveries will ever draw the interest of investors, and fewer yet will bring in royalties to universities. Less often discussed, but perhaps more significant in the long run, are the potential pitfalls of a more aggressive academic stance toward patenting, for with the promise of increased revenues also comes the quasi-certitude of increased liability and restrictions of the norms of open science.

In this context, it may have been the case that Hopkins's administrators' historical lack of interest in or outright opposition to patenting and licensing academic discoveries was the most sensible one for an institution of higher education, for even though one can find cases where inventions and techniques developed in university laboratories might have proven lucrative in the short run, most of Hopkins's successful contributions to the business realm were only at an "embryonic" stage and still required several years (and often decades) of further developmental

---

[56] Tew originally joined the Hopkins School of Medicine (SOM) in the late 1970s, but left academia in the late 1970s to found Chesapeake Biological Laboratories Inc., one of Maryland's first biotech firms, where he served as CEO and chairman for two decades. He returned to Hopkins in 2000 to head Hopkins SOM's technology licensing and business development activities.

work. Of course, most of the revenues that could have been generated by a few "big hits" would have probably been wiped out if the university had somehow become liable for a commercial disaster like the Dalkon Shield.

References

Abramson, H. Norman, Encarnaçao, José, Reid, Proctor P., and Schmoch, Ulrich (eds.). 1997. *Technology Transfer Systems in the United States and Germany. Lessons and Perspectives*. Washington, DC: National Academy Press.

Anonymous. 1902. "The Rowland Multiplex Printing Telegraph System." *Electrical Age* 29(9): 540–557.

——— 1910. "The Rowland Co. Fails." *Baltimore Evening Sun*, July 24, p. 10.

——— 1928. "Water Climb Tube to Upset Chemical Fact." *Baltimore Sun*, November 16.

——— 2000. "Patent Wars." *The Economist* 355 (8165), April 8, p. 78.

Bar-Shalom, Avital and Cook-Deegan, Robert. 2002. "Patents and Innovation in Cancer Therapeutics: Lessons from CellPro." *Milbank Quarterly* 80(4): 637–676.

Basalla, George. 1988. *The Evolution of Technology*. Cambridge: Cambridge University Press.

Batzel, Victor M. 1980. "Legal Monopoly in Liberal England: The Patent Controversy in the Mid-nineteenth Century." *Business History* 22(2): 189–202.

Bell, Julie. 2003. "Hopkins Striving to Make Industry a Partner in Research: University Seeks Funding, Revenue from Discoveries." *Baltimore Sun*, September 4. Available at www.matr.net/article-7926.html.

Birch, Douglas M. and Cohn, Gary. 2001. "The Changing Creed of Hopkins Science. What Once was Heresy Is Now the Mission: A Partnership with Business to Advance Research." *Baltimore Sun*, June 25. Available at www.baltimoresun.com/news/health/bal-te.research25jun25,0,6061662.story.

Blumberg, Peter D. 1996. "From 'Publish or Perish' to 'Profit or Perish': Revenues from University Technology Transfer and the § 501 (c) (3) Tax Exemption." *University of Pennsylvania Law Review* 145(1): 89–147.

Boldrin, Michele and Levine, David K. 2001. "The Case against Intellectual Property." *American Economic Review Papers and Proceedings* 92(2): 209–212.

Bowman, Isaiah. 1939. *The Graduate School in American Democracy. Bulletin 1939*, No. 10. Washington, DC: Government Printing Office.

Brickley, Peg. 2002. "New Patent Worries Professors." *The Scientist* 16(15): 19.

Brody, William. 1999. "From Minds to Minefields: Negotiating the Demilitarized Zone Between Industry and Academia." Remarks delivered for the Biomedical Engineering Lecture Series by William R. Brody, President, the Johns Hopkins University, Tuesday, April 6. Available at www.jhu.edu/~president/speech/biomlec.html.

Bruce, Robert V. 1988. *The Launching of American Science*. Ithaca, NY: Cornell University Press.

Canadian Intellectual Property Office. 1994. *A Guide to Patents*. Ottawa: Publications Center Communications Research Branch, Industry Canada.

Carleton, Jennifer Nutt. 1994. "*Giving a Voice to the Silenced: Dalkon Shield Survivors Tell their Stories – Review of Karen Hicks' Surviving the Dalkon Shield IUD: Women vs the Pharmaceutical Industry*. New York: Teachers College Press, 1994." *Wisconsin Women's Law Journal* 9: 95–105.

Cavanaugh Simpson, Joanne. 2001. "Golden Opportunity – Or Overwhelming Obstacle?" *Johns Hopkins Magazine* 53(1): 12–22.

Chew, Pat K. 1992. "Faculty-Generated Inventions: Who Owns the Golden Eggs?" *Wisconsin Law Review* 54: 259–272.

Cohen, W., Nelson, R.R., and Walsh, J.P. 2000. "Protecting Their Intellectual Assets: Appropriability Conditions and Why US Manufacturing Firms Patent (or Not)." NBER Working Paper 7552. Cambridge, MA: National Bureau of Economic Research.

Cole, Julio H. 2001. "Patents and Copyrights: Do the Benefits Exceed the Costs?" *Journal of Libertarian Studies* 15(4): 79–105.

Cox, Michael L. 2003. "The Dalkon Shield Saga." *Journal of Family Planning and Reproductive Health Care* 29(1): 8.

DeGregori, T.R. 1985. *A Theory of Technology: Continuity and Change in Human Development*. Ames: Iowa State University Press.

Duffy, Jim. 2002. "Applying the Brakes: Waiting for Licensing Negotiations to Solve Crucial Liability Issues is a Necessary, but Frustrating, Part of Research." *Change* 6 (11), June 5. Available at www.hopkinsmedicine.org/press/Changebrakes.html.

Eisenberg, Rebecca S. 2003. "Patent Swords and Shields." *Science* 299(5609): 1018–1019.

Grant, Nicole J. 1992. *The Selling of Contraception: The Dalkon Shield Case, Sexuality, and Women's Autonomy*. Columbus: Ohio State University Press.

Gregg, Alan. 1933. "University Patents." *Science* 77(1993): 257–259.

Griliches, Zvi. 1990. "Patent Statistics as Economic Indicators: A Survey." *Journal of Economic Literature* 28: 1661–1707.

Harvey, Abner McGehee. 1976. *Adventures in Medical Research*. Baltimore: Johns Hopkins University Press.

1981. *Research and Discovery in Medicine: Contributions from Johns Hopkins*. Baltimore: Johns Hopkins University Press.

Harvey, Abner McGehee, Brieger, Gert H., Abrams Susan L., and McKusick Victor A. 1989. *A Model of Its Kind: Vol. I, A Centennial History of Medicine at Johns Hopkins University*. Baltimore: Johns Hopkins University Press.

Hawkins, Hugh. 1960. *Pioneer: A History of the Johns Hopkins University, 1874–1889*. Ithaca, NY: Cornell University Press.

Hawkins, Mary F. 1997. *Unshielded. The Human Cost of the Dalkon Shield*. Toronto: University of Toronto Press.

Henderson, Yandell. 1933. "Patents Are Ethical." *Science* 77(1996): 324–325.

Hicks, Karen M. 1994. *Surviving the Dalkon Shield IUD: Women v. the Pharmaceutical Industry*. New York: Teachers College Press.

Hockely, Chester F. 1951. *The Davison Chemical. Its Background and Contributions . . . since 1832*. Princeton, NJ: Princeton University Press.

Jaffe, Adam B. 2000. "The U.S. Patent System in Transition: Policy Innovation and the Innovation Process." *Research Policy* 29 (4–5): 531–557.

Johns Hopkins University. 1992. The Johns Hopkins Intellectual Property Policy. Available at www.jhsph.edu/Research/IPG/nsguides.htm.

Kauffman, George B. and Priebe, Paul M. 1978. "The Discovery of Saccharin: A Centennial Retrospect." *Ambix* 25(3): 191–207.

Kern, T.H. 1991a. "APL Incapable of Meeting Deadline. Neurotech Unable to Engineer the 'Damn Thing,' Suit Goes On." *Johns Hopkins News-Letter* 96(5), October 4.

———. 1991b. "APL Suffers Million-Dollar Lawsuit. Physics Lab Loses in Arbitration, Goes To Court." *Johns Hopkins New-Letter* 96(4), September 27.

Kline, Douglas J. 2004. "Patent Litigation: The Sport of Kings." *Technology Review*, April 28.

Klingaman, William K. 1993. *APL – Fifty Years of Service to the Nation. A History of the Johns Hopkins University Applied Physics Laboratory.* Laurel, MD: The Johns Hopkins University Applied Physics Laboratory.

Kronmal, Richard A., Whitney, William, and Mumford, Stephen Douglas. 1991. "The Intrauterine Device and Pelvic Inflammatory Disease: The Women's Health Study Reanalyzed." *Journal of Clinical Epidemiology* 44(2): 109–122.

Levine, Joe. 1990. "Technology Tales." *Johns Hopkins Magazine* 42(4): 14–31.

Machlup, Fritz. 1968. "Patents." In *International Encyclopedia of the Social Sciences*, vol. 11, pp. 461–472. New York: MacMillan/Free Press.

Matkin, Gary W. 1990. *Technology Transfer and the University.* New York: American Council on Education in collaboration with MacMillan.

Mazzoleni, Roberto and Nelson, Richard R. 1998a. "The Benefits and Costs of Strong Patent Protection: A Contribution to the Current Debate." *Research Policy* 27(3): 273–284.

———. 1998b. "Economic Theories about the Benefits and Costs of Patents." *Journal of Economic Issues* 32(4): 1031–1052.

McCollum, Peggy. 1992. "Dalkon Shield Claims Resolution Facility: A Contraceptive for Corporate Irresponsibility?" *Ohio State Journal on Dispute Resolution* 7(2): 351–368.

McKusick, V. 1948. "A Study of Patent Policies in Educational Institutions, Giving Specific Attention to the Massachusetts Institute of Technology." *Journal of the Franklin Institute* 245: 193–225.

Merki, Christopher Maria. 1993. *Zucker gegen Saccharine: Zur Geschichte der Kuslichen Sussstoffe.* Frankfurt: Campus Verlag.

Mintz, Morton. 1985. *At Any Cost: Corporate Greed, Women and the Dalkon Shield.* New York: Pantheon Books.

Mowery, David C., Nelson, Richard R., Sampat, Bhaven, and Ziedonis, Arvids A. 2004. *Ivory Tower and Industrial Innovation. University-Industry Technology Transfer Before and After the Bayh–Dole Act in the United States.* Stanford: Stanford Business Books.

Mumford, Stephen and Kessel, Elton. 1992. "Was the Dalkon Shield a Safe and Effective Intrauterine Device? The Conflict between Case-Control and Clinical Trial Study Findings." *Fertility and Society* 56(6): 1151–1176.

National Science Board. 2000. *Science and Engineering Indicators 2000*. Arlington, VA: National Science Foundation.

National Science Foundation. 2003. Academic Institutional Profiles 2002. Available at www.nsf.gov/statistics/profiles/data/ess_ranking.cfm

Nelson, Richard R. 2001. "Observations on the Post-Bayh–Dole Rise of Patenting at American Universities." *Journal of Technology Transfer* 26: 13–19.

2004. "The Market Economy, and the Scientific Commons." *Research Policy* 33: 455–471.

Palmer, Archie M. 1934. "University Patent Policies." *Journal of the Patent Office Society* 16(2): 96–131.

1948. *Survey of University Patent Policies*. Preliminary Report. Washington, DC: National Research Council.

1952. *University Patent Policies and Practices*. Washington, DC: National Research Council.

Perry, Susan and Dawson, Jim. 1985. *Nightmare: Women and the Dalkon Shield*. New York: MacMillan.

Petroski, Henri. 1992. *The Evolution of Useful Things*. New York: Random House.

Poirier, Jean-François. 1997. "La recherche de brevets." *Le prototype* 2(1): 3.

Rosegger, G. 1986. *The Economics of Production and Innovation. An Industrial Perspective*. Oxford: Pergamon.

Ryan, W. Carson. 1939. *Studies in Early Graduate Education. The Johns Hopkins University, Clark University, The University of Chicago*. New York: The Carnegie Foundation for the Advancement of Teaching.

Scherer, F.M. 1987. "Comment on R.E. Evenson, 'International Invention: Implications for Technology Market Analysis.'" In Z. Griliches (ed.), *R&D, Patents, and Productivity*, pp. 123–126. Chicago: University of Chicago Press/NBER.

Schmidt, John C. 1986. *Johns Hopkins. Portrait of a University*. Baltimore: The Johns Hopkins University.

Siepman, Thomas. 2004. "The Global Exportation of the U.S. Bayh–Dole Act." *University of Dayton Law Review* 30(2): 209–243.

Sobol, Richard B. 1991. *Bending the Law. The Story of the Dalkon Shield Bankruptcy*. Chicago: The University of Chicago Press.

Spencer, Richard. 1939. *University Patent Policies*. Evanston, IL: Northwestern University Law School.

Stevens, Ashley and Toneguzzo, Frances. 2004. AUTM Licensing Survey: FY 2003. A Summary. The Association of University Technology Managers.

Tarbell, D.S., Tarbell, Ann T., and Joyce, R.M. 1980. "The Students of Ira Remsen and Roger Adams." *Isis* 71(4): 620–626.

Turcotte Maatz, Claire. 1992. "University Physician–Researcher Conflicts of Interest: The Inadequacy of Current Controls and Proposed Reform." *Berkeley Technology Law Journal* 7(1)(Spring). Available at www.law.berkeley.edu/journals/btlj/articles/07_1/Maatz/html/reader.html.

Valoir, Tamsen. 2000. "Government Funded Inventions: The Bayh–Dole Act and the Hopkins v. CellPro March-in Rights Controversy." *Texas Intellectual Property Law Journal* 8(2): 211–239.

Warren, Mame. 2000. *Johns Hopkins: Knowledge for the World, 1976–2001*. Baltimore: Johns Hopkins University.
Williamson, Samuel. 2004. "What Is the Relative Value?" Economic History Services, April 2004, available at www.eh.net/hmit/compare/.
Yoe, Mary Ruth. 1989. *Engineering at the University*. Baltimore: The Johns Hopkins University.
Zacks, Rebecca. 2000. "The TR University Research Scorecard." *Technology Review*, July–August. Available at www.techreview.com/articles/july00/zacks.htm.

Appendix: CellPro – Other opinions on the case

http://lists.essential.org/pipermail/ip-health/2003-January/004094.html
http://sloanreview.mit.edu/smr/issue/2003/spring/1b/
www.dukenews.duke.edu/2002/12/cellpro.html

The CellPro case represented an important study of the pitfalls inherent in transferring a basic cancer research discovery to the marketplace. "CellPro is a cautionary tale that there is also a dark side of patenting that needs to be assessed, and current data simply do not speak to it."

The case revolved around a dispute over patent rights to a technology for isolating immature cells, called stem cells, from bone marrow. Such stem cells have the capability of maturing into a range of immune cells to reconstitute a destroyed immune system. Thus, such separation technology can be used as the basis for cancer treatments in which stem cells are used to restore a patient's bone-marrow-based immune system, which had been destroyed by radiation or chemotherapy to eliminate cancers.

In 1981, a Johns Hopkins scientist developed antibodies that could recognize such stem cells, enabling the cells to be isolated. Hopkins received a broad patent that the university believed covered any use of antibodies for such isolation. The antibody-based technology was ultimately licensed to Baxter Healthcare, which began to develop cell-separation instrumentation based on the technique.

Significantly, noted Bar-Shalom and Cook-Deegan, Johns Hopkins did not make public its licensing agreements, which is common practice and entirely permissible under the Bayh–Dole Act. This secrecy, asserted the authors, reduced the university's credibility and complicated efforts to judge the merits of the technology and of Johns Hopkins's position.

Meanwhile, researchers at the Fred Hutchinson Cancer Center in Seattle had developed a different antibody-based separation technique, which was the basis for the 1989 founding of the startup company CellPro. The company decided that it did not need to license the Johns Hopkins technology and began to develop and clinically test its own bone marrow reconstitution technique for use following chemotherapy for breast cancer.

In 1994, Johns Hopkins and the companies to which it licensed its technology filed a patent infringement suit against CellPro. CellPro ultimately lost the suit and, as a result, was driven out of business. Of significant importance, said the authors, the National Institutes of Health decided not to exercise its right of "march-in" to compel Johns Hopkins to license its technology to CellPro.

The case illustrates why federal agencies such as the NIH should shoulder more responsibility for the conduct of commercialization of technology arising from federally sponsored research. "There is no option of government non-interference," they wrote. "NIH expressed a reluctance to act against one company on behalf of another, but it did so by not marching in just as much as it would have by marching in. CellPro's survival was in its hands, whether NIH wanted it or not. NIH can wash its hands, but cannot elude responsibility for the consequences," wrote Bar-Shalom and Cook-Deegan.

The case study also shows that along with government reforms, universities must also commit to change. "The secrecy issue is not new for universities, if you look at the history of clinical research," said Cook-Deegan. "However, molecular biology and immunology did have an open science norm, but when universities began interacting with companies in those fields, the patent process imposed a cloak of secrecy, at least up to the point of filing a patent application. And such secrecy has intensified the tension in those areas of science where the norm used to be open sharing of information."

One final lesson to be learned from the CellPro case is that both academic scientists and industry could benefit from greater education on the complexities of the technology transfer process. "Scientists must understand that industry needs intellectual property protection if it is to invest in developing basic discoveries, and that complete, open sharing of information is not possible. On the other hand, the norms of secrecy that pervade business don't belong in academe."

8 From ivory tower to industrial promotion: The case of Yale University and the biotechnology cluster in New Haven

Shiri M. Breznitz

Yale University is one of the world's most highly regarded research universities. The university has a strong life sciences faculty and extensive research capabilities that are fuelling a growing biotechnology cluster. In 1993, the New Haven biotechnology cluster had only six biotechnology and pharmaceutical companies, but by 2004, it had forty-nine.[1] This chapter examines the role played by Yale University in the development of this biotechnology cluster in New Haven County, Connecticut.

The first factor we examine is how Yale made a conscious decision to invest in local economic development. This investment instigated the enormous economic transformation in New Haven and Connecticut. Yale's decision to participate in the economic development of the region had a direct effect on the creation of the biotechnology cluster. The second important factor is that the university focused on academic excellence and institutional prestige, not profit maximization. Thus, in line with its research and teaching objectives, Yale chose to invest in technology transfer and commercialization as a vital part of its institutional mission. By 2004, Yale faculty members collaborated routinely with industry; these collaborations were seen in a positive light, as part of the faculty's mission and not a distraction from their academic work. Third, the New Haven biotech industry today acknowledges and is aware of Yale's contribution to the economic growth of the region. While Yale University has been the catalyst of many of the changes in the region, it was Yale's engagement with other regional players that had such a positive impact.

The first section of this chapter provides an analysis of Yale's attitudes toward technology transfer and demonstrates that although it had the potential to create a biotechnology cluster prior to 1993, it did not do so. Although Yale was academically strong in the life sciences, it had a

---

[1] In contrast, Boston, Massachusetts, had 129 biotechnology and pharmaceutical companies in 1993.

disassociated attitude toward applicable research and before 1993 had spun out only three biotechnology companies (only one of which chose to stay in the New Haven area). The second section analyzes why Yale eventually decided to implement institutional changes. Yale's changes in policy and technology transfer resulted in a vibrant biotechnology cluster, which is described in the third section. This section also examines the impact that these changes had on the local pharmaceutical industry and on the university itself.

Before 1993

Yale University, one of the world's leading research universities, is known for its excellence in many fields, including the life sciences. However, its culture of noninvolvement in the community in general and with industry in particular created a situation in which it failed to reap the benefit from several important discoveries, such as the transgenic mouse. For many years Yale was not active in technology transfer, and by 1993 it had spun out only three biotechnology companies. This attitude of noninvolvement in industry changed between 1993 and 1996. This section examines the university finances, faculty, student enrollment, and university policies with regard to intellectual property and technology transfer, as well as regional economic development before 1993. Although Yale's resources have hardly changed over the years, its attitude toward applied research and technology transfer has created a fundamental difference in the local economy.

On the academic level, in 1994, Yale was heavily invested in the life sciences. Out of its 729 tenured faculty members, 38 percent (279) taught in the medical school, and another 5 percent (36) in the biological sciences (Office of Institutional Research 2001). According to Yale's 1995–1996 financial report, income from research grants and contracts represented 29 percent of total income, and totaled $262.2 million in fiscal year 1996.[2] Of these funds, nearly 75 percent went to support programs within the medical school and within the departments of biological and physical sciences and engineering. Of the $262.2 million, $203.6 million represented federal government funds, of which 80 percent was awarded by the National Institutes of Health (NIH).

However, Yale was not a promoter of applied research or of working with industry. In 1994, Yale spent $224,939,000 on research and development (R&D) and registered only sixteen patents. It is interesting

---

[2] Consider also Cornell University, another Ivy League university, which in 1999 had $303 million from grants and contracts, representing 21 percent of its total income, and Johns Hopkins University, which in 1996 had $497 million in revenue from research.

to compare these figures with those for MIT, which spent $374,768,000 on R&D in that year and registered ninety-nine patents (National Science Foundation 2003). While Yale spent $14,058,388 per patent, MIT spent $3,785,535 per patent. These figures show that MIT produced more patents per research dollar. Also, until 1993, compared with MIT, which had spun out thirty biotech companies at the time, Yale had spun out three companies – and only one, Alexion Pharmaceuticals, stayed in the region. These figures are broadly consistent with the reputation of Yale at that time as an institution that was only peripherally and sporadically involved with the local economy and community. As Yale's president Richard Levin noted years later, "Outsiders have long regarded the presence of Yale as one of the city's major assets, but, except for episodic engagement, the University's contributions to the community did not derive from an active, conscious strategy of urban citizenship. It is true that our students, for more than a century, have played a highly constructive role as volunteers. Even a decade ago, two thousand students volunteered regularly in schools, community centers, churches, soup kitchens, and homeless shelters, but these volunteer efforts were neither coordinated nor well supported institutionally. When I became president, in 1993, there was much to be done to transform Yale into an active, contributing institutional citizen... In prior years, however, the university had taken a relatively passive attitude toward the commercialization of its science and technology" (Yale Office of Public Affairs 2003).

With the exception of a few departments, such as pharmacology, Yale faculty members were not encouraged to work on research with practical applications before 1993. It was actually implied that such involvement would have an unfavorable result on the progress of one's academic career. As one interviewee who served on Yale's faculty during the late 1960s observed, "One of the things that depressed me was that they did not want to do any application. You could consult, but that was not a good status." Important discoveries were made at Yale during that period, but the Office of Cooperative Research had a somewhat passive view toward commercialization, and only a few discoveries were patented.[3] According to another interviewee, "There was very little applied research in biology, maybe in the medical school or pharmacology chemistry departments. In the biology department it was looked down upon. For example, we made the first transgenic mouse and [the Office of Cooperative Research] considered that not to be worthwhile in terms of invention. Yale was very

---

[3] One invention that was patented during this period and later licensed and developed by Bristol-Myers Squibb became the profitable drug Zerit, part of the AIDS drug combination treatment.

conservative for many years. Not a very active program. Yale actually lost a lot of intellectual property because of this culture. They did not patent on time."

The lack of biotech firms prior to 1993 was not due to an inhospitable environment. In fact, by 1993, Connecticut was host to five pharmaceutical companies: Pfizer, Bristol-Myers Squibb, Purdue, Bayer, and Boehringer Inglheim. Most of these companies had a major presence in the state, including research facilities; four of these companies are located in the New Haven metropolitan area. In 1995, $1.2 billion was spent on pharmaceutical R&D in Connecticut alone, representing 6 percent of the nation's total. The companies operated research-oriented facilities, staffed with scientists with a deep knowledge base in biomedicine, but interactions with researchers at Yale and other local universities were limited. None of these companies established institutional relationships with local research institutes, relying instead on opportunistic specific interactions between their investigators and individual researchers at these institutes.

In sum, the region in the period prior to 1993 and up to 1996 had a knowledge base, skilled human resources, demand for goods and services, and a supporting industry – conditions that had the potential to result in the creation and development of a biotechnology cluster. Yet by 1993 there were only six biotechnology companies in the New Haven area. These companies also represented the entire biotechnology industry in Connecticut at that time (compared with 129 in neighboring Massachusetts at the same point in time).[4] These were IBI (later bought by Eastman Kodak), Protein Sciences, Pharmacal Research, Alexion Pharmaceuticals, Neurogen Corporation, and Curagen Corporation. Only one of these companies, Alexion Pharmaceuticals, had licensed its technology from Yale University. Both Neurogen and Curagen had founders who came from Yale, but in neither case were relations with the university close. As two of the founders explain in an interview, when Neurogen was created, the goal was to secure future funding for research in the university: "Yale was inhospitable to technology spin-offs. D. Blech & Co., a VC Company, started to ask how come Yale, that has such neuroscience expertise [does not spin-off companies], and looked for the technology that built Neurogen. So John Tolman and Dorothy Gallagher left Yale for Neurogen. The first chemistry was done at Wesleyan University since Yale was not hospitable. We could not get any collaboration with Yale.

"At that time, Yale had never considered such a thing. We were called before a whole variety of committees to explain what we were doing. We

---

[4] The six companies do not include Exilexus and Genelogic, which had left previously.

asked for support, they refused. It was only after a considerable time of explaining ourselves and their making sure that we were not in some way corrupting the academic life that they in essence said: go ahead, but we'll have nothing to do with it. The only reason we wanted to do it then, at that time, was because we thought if we started a company that was successful, that would provide money back to us to put toward research, and buffer us against the winds of fortune from NIH [National Institutes of Health], where you sometimes have lots of money from grants, and other times – like now – it can be very hard to get grants. So, not to get richer, even, but just to have money coming back [to the lab]."

The process Neurogen founders went through shows that Yale faculty had to leave in order to start a company. Yale not only was passive toward applicable research and commercialization but also actively discouraged its faculty from going through such a process.

Why and how did the transition occur?

In the early 1990s, when biotechnology firms were growing steadily in a few centers in the world, New Haven was an area of old industries such as firearms, manufacturing, and insurance. Having missed the information technology (IT) boom, it was very keen on seizing the biotechnology opportunity. This section reviews Yale's reasons for investing in economic development in general and in technology transfer in particular, as well as the way in which the university chose to implement these changes, particularly through the rebuilding of the Office of Cooperative Research (OCR).

In the late 1980s and the early 1990s, while many universities in the world contributed to the development and operated within high-technology and biotechnology clusters, Yale had none. However, by 1993 the university, which was a leading institution in the life sciences, was concerned that the lack of industry and industry collaborations would harm the ability of the university to attract and retain star scientists and bright students, and thus damage university research and reputation.

According to a Yale director, "What was happening was the university was starting to become concerned that it would detract from our ability to compete, to attract the best and brightest students, the best and brightest faculty, etc., if we didn't do something about it . . . First and foremost it was all about enhancing our reputation as a university, and two things come from that. One is our ability to attract and retain the best and the brightest faculty and students, and the second is to diversify the regional economy. Those were probably the principal reasons, and we weren't against making money, but we weren't making a lot at the time. It really wasn't the principal motivator; it really was about our reputation."

In addition, the city of New Haven was not a safe place for Yale's students. The city's crime rate was higher than the U.S. national averages. This was more apparent with the shooting and death of a Yale undergraduate in 1990 (Atlas 1996). As a university within a city, Yale had to fight against local crime to ensure the safety of its students by working with the city of New Haven to revitalize the downtown area and assisting Yale employees to purchase homes in the city.[5] Specifically, a $2 million project in 1993–1994 paid for streetlights on nearly every corner of the Yale campus, an emergency campus phone system, and electronic access for every entryway on campus. As a university within a city, Yale's efforts were viewed as urban regeneration.

One important approach to revitalize the local economy was to invest in it. A possible interpretation of the decision to invest in biotechnology was that it was a way for Yale to deal with a burgeoning operating deficit that by 1993 had reached $14.8 million. However, this deficit had started in 1991 under the presidency of Benno C. Schmidt Jr., and the university had moved to reduce the deficit through budget cuts and by eliminating several departments. By 1998 the university had covered its deficit. None of the interviewees in this research either knew of, or believed, that there was any connection between the deficit and Yale's new policy of investing in applied research. In any case, building closer industry–university relations would not produce immediate income. Since the university accepted equity as part of the consideration for licensing intellectual property, the financial gains would not be realized until the company had been bought or had gone through an IPO (initial public offering) on the stock exchange.

When Richard C. Levin was appointed as the twenty-second president of Yale in 1993, concerns for recruitment of faculty and students and the need to create a secure environment for students were of uppermost importance at Yale. In line with the view of Schoenberger (1997) that moments of crisis allow room for institutional cultural change, Levin was able to implement a vast social, cultural, and economic development change in Yale. Schoenberger claims that a firm's economic growth is anchored in the cultural change of that firm. In many cases, firms choose to change their practices, social relations, and ways of thinking in order to compete better in the economic market. Thus, "different cultural trajectories create different interpretive and strategic possibilities in the

---

[5] To learn more about the four areas in which Yale made changes, see President Richard Levin's speech on page 7. In Schoenberger 1997?

face of the same technical and environmental conditions" (Schoenberger 1997, p. 221).

Levin's first speech at Yale emphasized the importance of the university's contribution to the local economy: "Our national capability in basic research was built by the far-sighted policy of public support for university-based science articulated during the Truman Administration and pursued consistently, though with varying intensity, ever since. Today, the scientific capability of American universities is the envy of the world. We neglect its support at our peril. As we seek to educate leaders and citizens for the world, as our discoveries spread enlightenment and material benefits far beyond our walls, we must remember that we have important responsibilities here at home. We contribute much to the cultural life of New Haven, to the health of its citizens and to the education of its children. But we must do more. Pragmatism alone compels this conclusion. If we are to continue to recruit students and faculty of the highest quality, New Haven must remain an attractive place in which to study, to live, and to work."

The interviewees that participated in our study overwhelmingly agreed that the catalyst of the change in Yale's attitude toward research with potential practical applications was indeed Levin's arrival in 1993. Levin, an economics professor, had a vision for Yale. He wanted Yale to be a "contributing institutional citizen" with a long-term commitment to the community (Levin 2003). By referring to Yale as a "contributing citizen," Levin was referring to a broad range of activities at the university and not solely its role as an enhancer of economic development. To pursue this vision, the university conducted an in-depth study of the activities already performed by Yale in the community and decided to invest in four areas: economic development, strengthening neighborhoods, revitalizing the downtown area, and improving the city image. Levin reflected in 2003, "The first area of focus was economic development. We had considerable faculty strength in the biomedical sciences, but no track record of encouragement or support for the transfer of technology to local businesses. The second priority was strengthening neighborhoods. Here we believed that increasing the rate of home ownership could improve the stability of neighborhoods and the commitment of residents, and that the university, with 10,000 employees, had the leverage to help. We also believed that as an educational institution, we had human resources that could assist the work of the public schools. The third area of focus was to increase the safety, appearance, and vitality of our downtown. We believed that this would greatly improve perceptions of the city and also directly benefit the university community, since we are located in the heart of downtown New Haven. Finally, we focused on the image of the city, recognizing that improvement in its physical and material conditions was not in itself enough to change perceptions of the outside world. We needed to communicate as well."

In order to support the focus on economic development, Yale reorganized the Office of Cooperative Research (OCR). The original Office of Cooperative Research, established in 1982, dealt primarily with licensing and tracking patents. There was no real attempt to create or promote technology transfer from the academic to the industrial arenas, although a notable success before the reorganization was the licensing to Bristol-Myers Squibb of the compound that became the highly successful drug Zerit. Initially, this license produced little or no income to Yale, but by 1998 it was generating royalty income of $30–$40 million annually.

In 1995, President Levin and Yale's provost, Allison Richard, persuaded Gregory Gardiner, a former Pfizer executive, to head the restructured Office of Cooperative Research.[6] Gardiner, a former member of the Yale chemistry faculty, remembered the earlier lack of enthusiasm at Yale for research with practical applications, and he was eager to help bring about change. Gardiner's expanded mission changed the function of the OCR. The duties of the OCR now include oversight for patenting and licensing activities, university inventions, and contractual relationships between faculty and industry. OCR staff work with Yale researchers to identify inventions that may ultimately become commercial products and services useful to the public. OCR staff engage in industrial partnerships to license Yale inventions. An important goal for the Yale OCR is to identify new ideas, cultivate venture funding for them, and facilitate their development into companies that become part of the New Haven economy.

Thus, the new OCR would actively promote technology transfer, new firm formation spinning out from the university, and local economic development. The former director of the OCR explained the challenges inherent in this strategy: "There were many obstacles facing Gardiner and his team. One of the biggest challenges was to communicate the new priorities and incentive structure to the Yale faculty. I was asked many times by junior faculty, 'If I get involved with new ventures through the OCR, will I still get tenure?' I told the committee [Educational Policy Committee of the Yale Corporation (the Yale trustees)] that we have to get Yale faculty to understand it is OK. At MIT, history says that this is OK, but at Yale we need a change of culture."

---

[6] Dame Allison Fettes Richard was Yale's provost from 1994 to 2002 and the University of Cambridge's Vice Chancellor from 2003 to 2010.

This quote highlights the difference between policy creation and policy diffusion. While Yale had changed its policy, its effects would not take place until the change became widespread. In order to achieve this goal of institutional cultural change, the OCR had discussions with departmental chairs and faculty to explain the institutional change and Yale's commitment to individual involvement in economic development. OCR representatives approached faculty who worked on applied research and had made important discoveries in the past. One of these faculty members recalls, "The OCR people came to professors who had records in licensing or industry interaction and asked for ideas to patent and establish companies. They came to my lab, they knew I worked in XXX and XXX. One of the compounds went to [company name]. They also recruited the management for the company. With the change, Yale has become more entrepreneurial, but we are still responsible for our research and students."

An examination of the disclosure process, the process by which a faculty member discloses his or her invention to the university, found that there was a need to change the process to prioritize the inventions that were most likely to succeed. The examination resulted in a major policy shift in which the OCR would seek out new inventions early, examine them quickly, and invest time and effort only in the strongest candidates. In addition, the upgrading of OCR practices led to the identification and recovery of more than $220,000 of unpaid royalties from several licenses. Also, recognizing that 80 percent of patents from Yale were in the biomedical field, the OCR opened a branch office in the School of Medicine with four staff members (Office of Cooperative Research 1998).

The OCR's activities were characterized by active promotion of commercialization of research on a local level, not merely passive acceptance. For example, during 1996–1997, the OCR established direct contacts with venture capital firms, since lack of funding was an issue for many of the university spin-offs. Their goal was not only to persuade venture capital firms of the relevance of university technology but also to convince them of the importance of creating new ventures in New Haven. Their hard work of seeking appropriate investors eventually paid off, and in 1998, after two years of effort, the first round of financing, from external venture capital companies, was concluded with $20 million for five companies. A Yale administrator described the environment: "We have all kinds of venture capital. One of the dirty little secrets is that although Boston thinks of itself as a major financial capital, we've got one that's even bigger. It's called Stamford/Greenwich. When there was no state income tax, all the bankers used to live in Stamford or Greenwich, not in New York City. So they all are still there, and that's where they have their finance companies."[7]

An equally important problem was the lack of appropriate infrastructure, such as laboratory space for new business ventures, as well as urban amenities to make New Haven attractive to mobile scientists and academics. In order to assist in the development, President Levin used Yale's ability to recruit top talent and in 1998 convinced Bruce Alexander, a prominent figure in urban regeneration, to join Yale's Office of New Haven and State Affairs.[8] As explained by a Yale official, "It became clear that there's no better person to kick out the economic development kind of mission that Yale would like to have than a guy like Bruce, so Rick [President Levin] convinced Bruce to take it on full time. It's one of those things where you sit around going, 'It's nice that everyone wants to do this,' but how many people are going to be able to tap a guy like Bruce Alexander to be their economic development guru? The guy who redeveloped the Harbor place in Baltimore, the guy who did South Street Seaport in Manhattan. It makes us all look smart, but it's what a university like Yale can do."

The OCR, with the Office of New Haven and State Affairs at Yale, led by Bruce Alexander, set out to build laboratory space close to Yale's scientists. Accordingly, the university attracted two developers, Winstanley Associates and Lyme Properties, LLC, both of which had experience in building labs. Winstanley bought the vacant headquarters of the telephone company on George Street, and Lyme took over the development and management of Science Park on the northern part of the campus (where the university and the city had been trying unsuccessfully for years to build a science park for years without success). At the same time, Yale invested in its properties in the downtown in order to make New Haven a safer and more enjoyable city. For example, in its Broadway street properties, Yale created a mix of local businesses and national chains – transforming the area into a vibrant shopping area and late-night gathering spot.

As a result of Yale's efforts to change its attitude to technology transfer, commercialization, and economic development, Yale created physical as

---

[7] Stamford and Greenwich are two towns in Fairfield County, Connecticut, that border New York. In the 1980s, many corporations, including financiers, moved from New York both to lower their tax bills and to be closer to the homes of their top executives, who chose to build their houses outside New York City. Thus, Connecticut has a large concentration of venture capitalists living in the New Haven metropolitan area (which includes New Haven and Fairfield counties).

[8] Yale's ability to recruit top talent is demonstrated in the recruitment of both Greg Gardiner from Pfizer and Bruce Alexander. This also confirms the notion that Yale had a choice of who to recruit and when to recruit them.

Table 8.1: *OCR activities, 1996–2000*

Activity	1996	1997	1998	1999	2000
New licenses	28	25	45	20	47
Total number of active licenses	233	190	235	244	270
License revenue	$5,007,485	$13,091,174	$33,306,248	$40,720,584	$46,121,239
Total U.S. patent applications filed	48	48	83	97	143
U.S. patents issued	13	24	24	33	32
Start-up companies formed[a]	3	1	6	3	6

[a] In total, not just in the New Haven metropolitan area, and not just biotechnology.
Note: The information provided in this table reflects all fields of technology and not just biotechnology.
Source: Office of Cooperative Research (1999–2000).

well as cultural changes. While Yale did not set cultural change toward economic development as a direct goal, it became unavoidable. While the university invested in its technology transfer office and officers, in rebuilding the downtown area, and assisting in the development of laboratory space and connections to industry, it demonstrated to faculty that the university is determined to support applied research and commercialization. This attitude change, as well as the arrival of faculty from universities that already had a tradition of working with applied research and commercialization, influenced some hesitant faculty to venture into commercialization and even entrepreneurship.

Today the OCR sees itself as a catalyst of local economic development, but hopes that in the future its involvement will not be as important. The missions of the OCR today are to benefit the community by transferring academic inventions to the public, to enhance the reputation of Yale University and its faculty, and to contribute to local economic development, while in the past the office focused solely on patenting and licensing. It took six years (1993–1998) to implement the changes at Yale and at the Office of Cooperative Research specifically. In August 1999, Greg Gardiner retired and Jonathan Soderstrom was appointed his successor as director of the OCR. As a result of the efforts by Yale in general, and the OCR in particular, twenty-one biotechnology companies have been established in the New Haven metropolitan area, and many more are in development, as described in Table 8.1.

Table 8.1 summarizes the OCR's accomplishments from 1996 through 2000. During this time licensing revenues grew from $5,007,485 in

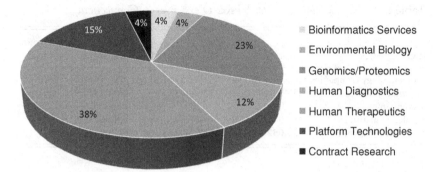

Figure 8.1: The biotechnology cluster in the New Haven metropolitan area by sector.

1996 to $46,121,239 in 2000, a growth of 821 percent. New licenses grew from twenty-eight in 1996 to forty-seven in 2000, a growth of 68 percent. The number of patents issued grew from 13 to 143, a growth of 197 percent. By 2004, Yale had sixty-one spin-offs in total, thirty-nine of which were in biotech. It is important to note that the OCR does not only build local companies. From the seventy licensing agreements put in place by the OCR in 2003, only ten were with local companies; the rest were licensed out of state and on an international level. However, while the OCR promotes the transfer of Yale's technology to industry in general, not only on a local level, Yale is strongly committed to the local economy.

The impact of Yale's economic development initiative

Yale's investment in technology transfer and the reconstruction of the OCR has resulted in direct change to the region and the university; this section reviews these changes. In 2004, the New Haven biotechnology cluster had a total of forty-nine companies, including twenty-four companies, or 49 percent, that were created with technology, ideas, or founders from Yale and with the help of the OCR. A total of twenty-one Yale spin-offs were established in New Haven between 1993 (the year Yale started to implement its changes) and 2004.

The majority of the biotechnology companies in this area are working in the human therapeutic sector. Figure 8.1 shows New Haven companies' strength in biomedicine, which reflects Yale's strength in the life sciences and the fact that 49 percent of the New Haven cluster is based on Yale University spin-offs. This includes companies that are working in more

Table 8.2: *The bioscience cluster by R&D expenses in Connecticut*

R&D expenses	Year end 2000	Year end 2001	Total growth	Percent growth
Biotechnology companies	226,154,159	277,210,873	51,056,714	23
Pharmaceutical companies	2,434,900,000	2,904,933,799	470,033,799	19
Academic institutes	391,231,208	429,893,436	38,662,228	10
Total R&D expenses	$3,052,285,367	$3,612,038,108	$559,752,741	18

Source: CURE (2003).

than one sector. The following results are based on the self-definitions of fifteen companies interviewed in the cluster.

By 2004 the cluster (biotechnology and pharmaceutical companies) employed 16,686 people directly and many more through indirect employment. Most of the biotechnology firms were small to medium-size, with less than fifty employees.

Yale's change toward technology transfer and commercialization had an impact on the state of Connecticut as a whole. Connecticut R&D expenditures in bioscience are in constant growth. The majority of the growth can be seen in the biotechnology companies. This has a direct cor-relation with the growth in total number of biotechnology companies.[9] The influence of the growth of the biotechnology industry had an impact on the existing pharmaceutical companies. In 2003, expenditures by the pharmaceutical industry in Connecticut, which dominates R&D expen-ditures in the state, accounted for more than 12 percent of all R&D dollars spent by pharmaceutical companies nationwide (Connecticut United for Excellence [CURE] 2003). This represents an extensive growth com-pared with the 6 percent spent by pharmaceutical companies in Con-necticut in 1995, as noted in Table 8.2.

Yale's contribution to the local economy is exemplified by the reaction of a local banker to a Yale professor who also founded a biotechnology company. In this case Yale's contribution can be seen in the number of employees purchasing houses in New Haven: "When I went in to get a new mortgage, I indicated some consulting income from [company name].The bank officer stopped and he said, 'You're with [company name]?' and I said, 'Yes.' He shook my hand, and he said, 'You know,

---

[9] As an illustration, we can see that the number of Yale's spin-offs in the cluster grow by 50 percent from 2000 to 2004.

Figure 8.2: New Haven biotechnology companies by location.

you have no idea how many people [from the company] have come and bought houses.' That was my first indication that 'this is how the economy works.' It [my company] has an incredible impact."

Even though Yale has been the catalyst behind the formation of many of the biotechnology companies in the cluster, it is not the leader of the cluster and does not view itself as such. From interviews with company CEOs and organization leaders, it was clear that several local organizations, including Connecticut United for Excellence (industry association) and the Connecticut Office of Bioscience, are attempting to perform this role in several ways. According to interviewees, New Haven does not function as a classic industrial district. Companies claim that one of the reasons for the inability of the cluster's companies to collaborate and communicate with each other is the divided leadership in this cluster. Biotechnology companies in New Haven grew from six in 1993 to forty-nine in 2004.[10] Even though the cluster grew significantly during that decade, it has not yet developed the communication and networking relationships among companies that are one indicator of a successful cluster.

As can be seen in Figure 8.2, the companies are spread throughout three main locations that are at least fifteen to twenty minutes (by car) away from each other, with none but the George Street facility having an unofficial area for meetings nearby (e.g., coffee shops or restaurants).[11] The lack of meeting space created a situation in which none of the smaller clusters had enough companies to create the institutional thickness needed for the networking that is seen in other clusters, in other regions where unofficial meetings and movement of employees among firms in the cluster occurs. The official opportunities for interaction occur

[10] In 2004 in New Haven there were forty-nine biotechnology companies in total, of which twenty-four were spun out of Yale. By 2004, Yale University had spun out a total of thirty-nine biotechnology companies, of which twenty-four chose to locate in New Haven.
[11] In the city of New Haven there are (1) the facility at 300 George Street and (2) the area of Science Park. Another location is (3) the town of Branford.

through Yale's seminars and conferences, as well as meetings convened by CURE and other organizations such as PricewaterhouseCoopers or Connecticut Innovations.[12] However, these meetings are known only to part of the biotechnology community and do not provide a constant and regular way of exchanging information.

The impact on the local pharmaceutical companies

The strength of the local biotech industry has changed the way the existing pharmaceutical firms interact with other players in the region. The local pharmaceutical companies have significantly changed their behavior and funding patterns, and give more weight to the local intellectual base. There are constant connections between local pharmaceutical firms and the local universities and research institutes, cultivated by Yale's OCR, CURE, and the Office of Bioscience. These connections include, but are not limited to, Yale and the University of Connecticut. Pfizer, for example, chose to utilize the local knowledge base by developing a direct relationship with Yale. Pfizer invested $35 million in a 60,000-square-foot clinical trial facility in downtown New Haven that is owned by the state of Connecticut. Additionally, Bayer initiated a scholar's program in 2003, under which a faculty member is appointed each year as a fellow who works closely with Bayer.

There are growing business relationships between local pharmaceutical firms and local biotechnology companies. Neurogen Corporation, a biotechnology company, and Pfizer began a two-year research partnership in 1998 to work on GABA neurotransmitter receptor-based drug programs for the treatment of anxiety and sleep disorders and for cognition enhancement. Bayer and Curagen Corporation collaborate on obesity and diabetes co-development, pharmacogenomics, and toxicogenomics. R&D expenditures by the pharmaceutical industry in Connecticut have doubled since 1995, and in 2003 R&D expenditures accounted for more than 12 percent of all R&D dollars spent by pharmaceutical companies nationwide (CURE 2003).[13]

The impact on Yale

The following section examines the impact of the technology transfer changes implemented by the Office of Cooperative Research on the

---

[12] Connecticut Innovations is the state's leading investor in high technology.
[13] Compared to 6 percent of all R&D expenditures in 1995.

university. First, it examines the university's finances, patenting, spin-off companies, and tenured faculty to see whether Yale's resources grew over the years and allowed the university's investment in technology transfer. The analysis confirms that Yale's resources have hardly changed over the years, and that it was the changes in attitude toward applied research and technology transfer that created the difference in the local economy. Second, the section examines how the changes made by Yale benefited and changed the university in general and the OCR in particular.

Despite the success of the OCR, total income to the university has not changed substantially between 1993 and 2002. According to Yale's 2001–2002 financial reports, income from research grants and contracts represented 28 percent of total income (the same share as in 1994), $417.6 million in fiscal 2002 (a growth of 59.2 percent from 1994). Of these funds, nearly 77 percent supported programs within the medical school and the programs of biological and physical sciences and engineering (compared with 75 percent in 1994). Of the $335 million in federal funds, 76.7 percent (compared with 80 percent in 1994) were awarded by the National Institutes of Health. A major difference in the contributions to Yale, compared with those in 1994, is that the state of Connecticut provided $83 million for research, training, and other purposes. Thus, the main difference between 1993 and 2002 is the reorganization and activity of the Office of Cooperative Research.

Examination of spin-offs and patenting finds that Yale University spun off thirty-nine biotechnology companies, twenty-four locally, compared with only three in 1993, one locally. Moreover, in 2003, Yale University registered a total of twenty-eight patents, compared with two in 1993. Furthermore, by 2000, forty-seven new licenses were issued, contributing to a royalty revenue of $46.12 million (Office of Cooperative Research 1999–2000). Figure 8.3 demonstrates the significant increase in Yale's patents between 1983 and 2003 from two to twenty-eight, an increase of 13 percent. The figure illustrates the top fifteen universities in patent growth, which were extracted from the top thirty-five universities in R&D expenditures (U.S. Patent and Trademark Office 2003).

The impact on Yale students and faculty

Yale changes have made an impact on its faculty's attitude toward applied research and working with industry. The same period saw a little change within the university toward the medical school. Between 1994 and

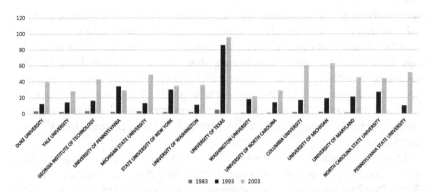

Figure 8.3: Top fifteen U.S. universities by patent growth, 1983–2003. Number of utility patents assigned annually to U.S. colleges and universities, extracted from the top thirty-five ranked by R&D expenditures in 2002. *Source:* U.S. Patent and Trademark Office (2003).

2002 there was a 22.7 percent increase in the number of tenured faculty at the medical school, compared with an 11.2 percent increase at Yale as a whole. Since 1994, student enrollment has grown by 11 percent in the medical school, compared with an increase of only 3 percent in general enrollment at Yale (Office of Institutional Research 2001). According to Yale officials, this increase in faculty at the medical school was not planned. It resulted rather from the growth in research grants and contract funding over the years. Another contributing factor was the hiring freeze in the schools of arts and sciences during the early to mid-1990s. Furthermore, in 1995, with the appointment of Michael Merson, M.D., as dean of the Yale School of Public Health, there was an increase in student enrollment in the Epidemiology and Public Health departments at the medical school.[14]

Faculty members at the Yale medical school who were interviewed explained the numerous benefits in having a local biotechnology industry. The industry–university relationships allow scientific interactions, sponsorship of students, and access to expensive equipment that is not available at Yale and expose students to industrial practices. "Now, for example, we have a company that is occupying some space in the lab . . . It is good to have them here, because you have interactions with them and transfer of expertise," said a faculty member.

[14] The School of Medicine includes the M.D., Epidemiology and Public Health, and Physician Associate programs.

While working with companies has benefits for students and research, it has no bearing on faculty responsibilities, such as teaching, in the university. A faculty member who spins off a company, or provides consulting services, cannot reduce his or her teaching or administrative load. "No. [Founding a company] didn't have any effect on my university responsibilities. In fact, the opposite occurred. [The university benefited] when getting money from the company to go on retreats, or to buy a new microscope or something," said a faculty member.

Thus, the change implemented at Yale did not change faculty responsibilities. However, the change contributed to university–industry relationships in the form of research grants and contracts, sponsorship of students, and access to industry equipment and experience.

The impact on the Office of Cooperative Research

Changes in the university did impact the OCR. In 2004, the OCR employed eighteen people, each with five to seven years' industry experience. As a private university, Yale can offer competitive salaries to senior employees recruited from industry. The employee background at the OCR had and continues to have a crucial effect on the respect and cooperation of local faculty and industry. According to a faculty member, "I do believe that [the people working at the OCR have the skill and knowledge to assess my technology]. I don't think there's any question. And I think that the communication problem has gotten much, much better. From my biased point of view, I think it's enormously improved, and that they do a very good job at Yale."

Not only does the office have the staff and expertise, it also is involved with firm creation on an unprecedented level. The office is involved in developing product scenarios, financial projections, and business strategies with the scientists. In many cases, the office is actively involved in building the company, looking for the right management and investors that will succeed in taking Yale's technology to the market. In many cases, the OCR's activity is considered extreme on the university–industry involvement scale. Even MIT, which is considered the top university in university–industry relationships, is not as involved in the creation of companies. Yale's importance in the creation of companies became clear to one of Yale's professors when he considered moving to a different university: "I went out there [to another university] and talked to the head of their tech transfer office about [the name of the company the faculty was involved with] and how [Yale contributed to the creation of the company]. He said, 'I couldn't possibly do anything like that here. We are not permitted, we don't have any resources. What Greg [Gardiner]

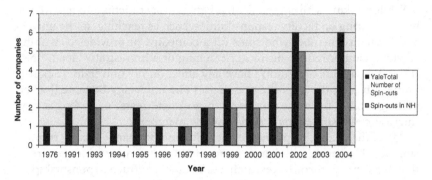

Figure 8.4: Yale University biotechnology spin-offs, 1976–2004.

is doing is unheard of.' That's another instance where I began to realize what seemed to be happening at Yale – when it's happening all around, you don't realize it, it's just happening very quickly. [In the beginning] there are no companies, all of a sudden there are a dozen, and then two dozen over a relatively short period of time."

By 2004, Yale had spun off thirty-nine biotechnology companies (see Figure 8.4), of which twenty-four, or 62 percent, chose to locate in the region. This suggests that Yale had a direct impact on the location choices made by spin-offs. The wish to stay close to the university implies that companies have a positive view of university research and resources.

Between 1993 and 2004, Yale created committees to deal with issues such as conflict of interest and the appropriate role of faculty in startups. The CCOI creates the policy on acceptable behavior and reinforces the need to pursue patenting rights while not limiting research rights; the CCR is an advisory to the OCR and the provost, and deals with new modes of teaching and learning. Thus, all intellectual property from the inventions of faculty or students belongs to Yale, and the OCR will patent the inventions. Royalties are on a sliding scale, 50/50, 60/40, 70/30, in favor of the university. The university recoups its patent expense out of royalties, if it has not recouped them otherwise.

Yale does not have pipeline agreements on research outcomes. Companies can have an option or first right to license the technology from a sponsored research project, but nothing is prenegotiated. Faculty can sit on companies' scientific advisory boards, but they cannot take full-time positions. Faculty can take full-time positions only while they are on leave of absence from Yale. "They [faculty] can be assigned to advisory boards, they can be consultants, they can do all those things, but subject to our rules on conflict of interest," explained a member of the faculty.

"The only way they can serve in a management or operative position is if they're not full-time, so they'd have to be on a leave of absence or something like that...We believe that one of our principal reasons for existence is the teaching of undergraduates; we expect all faculty members to participate in the teaching of undergraduates, and that is a firm requirement." This quote highlights the importance of teaching and research excellence at Yale. While applied research became acceptable and supported by the university, it does not have priority over teaching and research. Thus, a faculty member who wishes to have a full-time position at a spin-off company must be on a leave of absence from the university.

Conclusion

This chapter has analyzed Yale's impact on the development of the local biotechnology cluster in New Haven, Connecticut. In particular, it describes the choice Yale made as a social agent to promote economic development. The chapter follows the institutional changes Yale implemented, and evaluates the impact these changes had on the local economy and the biotechnology industry. Importantly, the Yale case explains why not all regions that have universities develop industrial clusters. Universities need to become part of the economic processes in their regions. Concerns about the lack of a biotechnology cluster and growing crime against students, which might have alienated top scientists and potential students from attending the university, were the main reason for the change at Yale. Yale found it crucial to add technology transfer and commercialization to its university objectives in order to promote the change and foster its academic prestige.

References

Atlas, S. 1996. "Yale student's killer convicted once again," *Yale Daily News.*
Connecticut United for Excellence (CURE). 2003. Economic Survey.
Levin, Richard C. 2003. Universities and Cities: The View from New Haven. Yale Office of the President, January 30, 2003. Available at www.yale.edu/opa/president/speeches/case_western_20030130.html. National Association of College and University Business Officers Endowment Study. 2006.
National Science Foundation. 2003. Table B-32, Total R&D Expenditures at universities and colleges, ranked by fiscal year 2001. Available at www.nsf.gov/statistics/nsf06329/pdf/tabb32.pdf.
Office of Cooperative Research. 1998. 1996–1998 Yale OCR annual report: From bench to bedside. Yale.
1999–2000. Report.

Office of Institutional Research. 2001. Factsheet.
Schoenberger, E. 1997. *The Cultural Crisis of the Firm.* Cambridge, MA: Blackwell.
U.S. Patent and Trademark Office. 2003. U.S. Colleges and Universities Utility Patent Grants, Calendar Years 1969–2000. Available at www.uspto.gov/web/offices/ac/ido/oeip/taf/univ/univ_toc.htm.
Yale Office of Public Affairs. 2003. President's Welcome. Available at www.yale.edu/opa/president/index.html.

9   Fostering cross-campus entrepreneurship –
     Building technology transfer within UCD to
     create a start-up environment

Colm O'Gorman and Frank W. Roche

In this chapter we discuss the emergence of commercialization activity, and specifically the TTO and ILO functions, in University College Dublin (UCD). This case emphasizes (1) how a public university has sought to encourage commercialization activity and the organizational structures developed to support commercialization; (2) how, over a period of twenty years, the TTO and ILO functions and commercialization activity evolved in the absence of what might be considered many of the university attributes, such as high levels of funded research, typically associated with high levels of commercialization; (3) how policies aimed at encouraging the commercialization of university research were embedded within a broader industrial development strategy associated with both attracting inward FDI (foreign direct investment) and developing indigenous entrepreneurial activity in emerging sectors; and (4) how a new president in a traditional public university has sought to emphasize the contribution the university makes to economic development as a means for engaging in a significant restructuring of the university and the adoption of policies that seek to maximize research activity, in particular in emerging sectors such as biotechnology and ICT, to develop external linkages with industry, and to promote commercialization.

1.   UCD: Introduction

UCD is Ireland's largest research-intensive university, located in Dublin, the capital city of Ireland. UCD considers itself among the top 1 percent of higher education institutes worldwide (UCD ranked 89 on the QS 2009 World University Rankings). UCD describes its research strengths as agri-food; culture, economy, and society; information, computation, and communications; energy and environment; and health. The university has 25,000 students, 1,000 faculty, and almost 1,800 Ph.D. students.

UCD was founded in 1854 by Cardinal John Henry Newman as the Catholic University of Ireland. Newman's vision of the "modern" university, as presented in *The Idea of a University Defined and Illustrated* (1852), included an emphasis on the diffusion of knowledge as central to the concept of the university: "[The university] is a place of teaching universal knowledge... This implies that its object is... the diffusion and extension of knowledge rather than its advancement. If the object were scientific or philosophical discovery, I do not see why a University should have students."

UCD's focus on commercialization and university–industry interactions has intensified during the past decade. In 2004, the university began a major reorganization and restructuring following the appointment of Dr. Hugh Brady, a former Professor of Harvard Medical School, as President. The reorganization of eleven faculties and over ninety departments into a smaller number of colleges and schools sought to exploit new directions in research and possibilities for increasing the research income earned by the university. UCD is currently structured into seven colleges: Agriculture, Food Science, and Veterinary Medicine; Arts and Celtic Studies; Business and Law; Engineering and Architecture; Health Sciences; Human Sciences; and Science. UCD has 944 academic staff and a further 577 research staff funded by the Irish government.

Under the direction of the new president, the university restated its ambition to be a leading research-intensive university. The refocused mission of the university reflects the importance of research as a key contributor to economic development: "the mission of UCD is to advance knowledge, pursue truth and foster learning, in an atmosphere of discovery, creativity, innovation and excellence, drawing out the best in each individual, and contributing to the social, cultural and economic life of Ireland in the wider world" (UCD Strategic Plan, Creating the Future 2005–2008). Specifically, the president recognized the role the university should play in economic development in Ireland. In the university's 2005–2008 strategic plan, the goals of UCD were stated as "the creation, preservation, interpretation and dissemination of knowledge." This first strategic plan under the direction of the new president specifically stated that "there is also an obligation to transfer and apply that knowledge for the betterment of society, whether economically, socially or culturally." The plan stated, "UCD is committed to knowledge transfer in all areas of research and scholarship" and sets specific objectives, such as to align UCD's research programs with Ireland's social, cultural, and economic objectives; to realize the full value of research programs; and to engender an entrepreneurial culture.

Listed as means to achieving these objectives were enhancing knowledge transfer through NovaUCD; initiating a knowledge management program; identifying and protecting UCD's intellectual property; training staff in knowledge transfer and entrepreneurship; and commercializing UCD's intellectual property through licensing and spin-off companies; establishing a Centre for Policy Research in support of knowledge transfer from the humanities, human sciences, and allied disciplines; establishing the Global Irish Institute as a statement of wider interest in and support of the global Irish community; continuing to forge strategic partnerships with industry, the public sector, and social and cultural organizations; and developing research services.

Dr. Hugh Brady summarized his thinking as follows: "The success of our recently established research institutes has ensured that UCD is playing a central role in shaping the Irish society and economy of tomorrow. Our prioritizing of research pre-eminence across the academic spectrum as our defining characteristic for the next decade will ensure that UCD will combine sustained academic excellence within this university with playing a key role in sustained progress and prosperity for Ireland" (Brady 2004).

This focus was re-affirmed in the current strategic plan: "This plan will establish innovation as a third, constitutive pillar of UCD's activity and identity, building on the achievements in education and research. This will simultaneously challenge our teachers and researchers to translate excellent education and research into contexts where they may be expected to have a high impact, all the while supplementing more traditional educational concerns with the development of innovative and entrepreneurial capacity amongst our students" (Strategic Plan to 2014, UCD).

2. The policy context for university commercialization activity in Ireland

The development of commercialization in UCD occurred in the context of a broader industrial policy agenda pursued by the Irish government. Ireland, and in particular Dublin, experienced rapid economic growth and development during the period from 1995 to 2008, popularly referred to as the "Celtic Tiger." In their review of explanations of the Celtic Tiger, the OECD concluded that there is no one singular "silver bullet" explanation. It is generally considered that the following factors were important: a new fiscal strategy adopted in 1987; a model of "Social Partnership" whereby the government offered tax reductions in return for wage moderation; and the Structural and Cohesion Funds that were transferred from the EU to Ireland, which accounted for 3 percent of the economy for the decade 1989–1999, and allowed investment in infrastructure and capital projects, which had been put on hold in the 1980s. These funds were spent on three areas: (1) human resource development, including the expansion of higher education; (2) physical infrastructure; and (3) production and investment aids to the private sector.

Inward FDI played an important role in Ireland's industrial development. Irish industrial policy has focused on attracting export-oriented inward FDI. While Ireland has pursued this policy successfully since the early 1960s, in the early 1990s Ireland experienced a rapid increase in inward FDI, in particular from the United States. Of the 1,004 foreign companies with facilities in Ireland, 515 (51 percent) are American, 96 (9.5 percent) are German, and 91 (9 percent) are from the United Kingdom. Of the 146,000 people employed by foreign companies, 107,000 (73 percent) work for American companies. Of the €114,000 billion sales from all foreign firms in Ireland, €110,000 billion (97 percent) is exported. Employment is in international and financial services (including software) (46 percent), medical/dental instruments and supplies (16 percent), pharmaceuticals (15 percent), computer, electronics, and optical equipment (11 percent), metals and engineering (8 percent), and miscellaneous industry (4 percent). Reviewing the effectiveness of policies aimed at attracting FDI, Murphy and Ruane (2004) argue that three factors partly explain Ireland's success at attracting inward FDI: (a) the emergence of self-sustaining clusters in area such as software, electronics, pharmaceuticals, and financial services that resulted from the targeted approach of the IDA and their efforts to build vertical linkages; (b) the extension of incentives to include internationally traded services; and (c) the emergence of a pro-FDI reputation, that reflects the consistency and pro-active nature of Irish government policies toward FDI.

In recent years, the focus of inward FDI has shifted toward higher-value activities such as R&D and HQ activities. Investments by firms such as Bristol-Myers Squibb, Citigroup, Genzyme Corporation, Pfizer Inc., and Xilinx in R&D facilities in Ireland requires access to a highly skilled workforce and often occurs in the context of explicit collaborations with Irish universities or commercial research facilities in Ireland.

In addition to a focus on FDI, industrial policy in Ireland since the 1980s has focused very selectively on supporting and encouraging indigenous firms and entrepreneurs that trade internationally. For this relatively small number of firms and entrepreneurs, generous state assistance in terms of capital grants, tax breaks, and marketing and selling support in overseas markets is available. Much of the indigenous manufacturing industry in Ireland was in decline up to the late 1980s. During the 1990s, new firms emerged in new sectors of activity, including a sizeable number of software firms focused on product development and exporting. These firms are centered around Dublin. The evolution of the software sector was an important development in Dublin, as it is associated with the subsequent emergence of a small but growing venture capital industry in Ireland.

One aspect of Irish government policy that stemmed from the desire to attract inward FDI was investment in third-level education. During the 1980s, the government recognized that inward FDI would require skilled workers, in particular those with technical skills. The policy response was to invest state and EU funds in expanding student numbers in existing universities and in the creation of new National Institutes of Higher Education that provided third-level courses that focused on science and technology, paying particular attention to the needs of industry. The focus of this investment in third-level education was on the number of graduates, and in particular, on the number of graduates in science- and technology-related disciplines.

However, such a focus on education was not in the context of a fully developed national strategy for science, technology, and innovation. There were few explicit attempts by policy makers to integrate sectoral and socioeconomic research into a STI policy until the 1990s. This reflected a general lack of research capacity and funding for research in universities, in institutes of technology, and in industry and a lack of research and technology absorption capabilities by companies and weak commercialization structures.

More recently, policy focus has shifted within the third-level education sector. In the late 1990s, the government increased research funding for universities to reflect the evolving needs of inward FDI and the policy objective of moving into higher value-added activities. These new funds, administered largely through Science Foundation Ireland (described later), are effectively the first major support for research within universities. Funding has prioritized areas of activities such as ICT and biotechnology, the key focus of industrial policy. More specifically, within the support system for indigenous industry and entrepreneurs, the universities have been identified as a potential source of entrepreneurs and innovative new firms. State development agencies began a program that supported the building of new incubators in the third-level sector and of directly supporting commercialization activity through a number of programs.

Following the start of the economic downturn, the Irish government launched its new economic policy, "Building Ireland's Smart Economy:

A Framework for Sustainable Economic Renewal," in December 2008. Specifically, this policy sets out the ambition that Ireland will be a "country where there will be a critical mass of companies – both Irish and international – at the forefront of innovation, creating the products and services of tomorrow" and "a country where entrepreneurs from anywhere in the world will want to come because it provides the best environment for the commercialization of innovative, leading-edge products and services" (Cowen 2008).

A core aspect of this new policy framework was the objective of "Building the Ideas Economy – Creating the 'Innovation Island.'" This aspect of the new framework set out specific objectives, some of which impact on the role of Higher Education Institutes. Some of the relevant objectives were as follows:

• Build on the concentration of multinational enterprises by encouraging convergence of technologies and processes and the intensification of research investment;
• Continue to expand the research and development base;
• Provide a favorable tax environment for research and development and private capital;
• Concentrate research investment and recruitment of top international research talent;
• Foster an entrepreneurial culture at the second, third, and fourth levels. The framework document also argued that the higher education sector needs a "rationalization and reconfiguration of roles," suggesting that "the challenge to the higher education sector itself is to create new possibilities through new alliances and new organizational arrangements that can advance our knowledge capacity and generate opportunity for new levels of efficiency, performance, innovation, and growth." This provides the policy context for the TCD/UCD Innovation Alliance announced in 2009 (discussed later).

However, the recent economic crisis resulted in a rapid and significant contraction in the Irish economy in 2008 and subsequent years. This has restricted the Irish government's ability to invest in higher education and to fund research at higher education institutes.

Institutional supports for research and commercialization activity

A number of new institutions were developed in the 1990s to support research and commercialization activity. Additionally, some existing state bodies such as Enterprise Ireland focused some of their resources at developing and supporting commercialization activity. Some of these initiatives and institutions are described in the following.

Advisory Council for Science, Technology, and Innovation

In 1997, the Government established the Irish Council for Science, Technology, and Innovation (ICSTI) to advise it on all aspects relating to the strategic direction of science, technology, and innovation (STI) policy. The Advisory Council for Science, Technology and Innovation (ACSTI) was established in April 2005 as a successor body to the ICSTI. ACSTI serves as the primary interface between policy makers and industry and universities and others involved in the STI arena. Its remit is to contribute to the development and delivery of a coherent and effective national strategy for STI and to provide advice to government on medium- and long-term policy for STI. Its role encompasses all aspects of STI policy, including primary, second, and third level education; scientific research, technology, and research and development in industry; prioritization of state spending in STI; and public awareness of STI issues. The ICSTI/ACSTI was one of a number of state agencies that developed the National Code of Practice for Managing Intellectual Property Arising from Publicly Funded Research (launched in 2004) and the National Code of Practice for Managing and Commercializing Intellectual Property Arising from Public–Private Collaborative Research (launched in 2005).

The Programme for Research in Third-Level Institutions

Launched in 1998, the stated objective of the Programme for Research in Third-Level Institutions (PRTLI) is to provide integrated financial support for institutional strategies, programs and infrastructure and to ensure that universities and third level educational institutions have the capacity and incentives to formulate and implement research strategies, which will give them critical mass and world level capacity in key areas of research. Since 1998, the PRTLI has awarded €1.7 billion (both government funds and private matching funds) to support both physical and human infrastructure.

Science Foundation Ireland

Science Foundation Ireland (SFI) provides awards to support scientists and engineers working in biotechnology and information and communications technology development. It emerged after an intensive study commissioned by the Irish government in 1998. Representatives from government, academia, and industry assessed industrial sectors in the Irish economy and concluded that biotechnology and information and communications technology represented "the engines of future growth in the global economy... A world class research capability in selected niches of these two enabling technologies is an essential foundation for future growth." As part of its response, the government initiated the Technology Foresight Fund, which totals more than €646 million. SFI was created in 2000 to administer this fund as a sub-board of Forfás: The National Policy and Advisory Board for Enterprise, Trade, Science, Technology, and Innovation.

In July 2000, SFI announced its first call for proposals from leading researchers. On completion of the international peer review process, SFI announced its first awards to ten outstanding researchers from Ireland, the United Kingdom and the United States. The Agreed Programme for Government, published June 2002, provided for establishing SFI as a separate legal entity and in July 2003, SFI was established on a statutory basis under the Industrial Development (Science Foundation Ireland) Act, 2003. Science Foundation Ireland (SFI) had a budget of €646 million to invest between 2000 and 2006 in academic researchers and research teams in the fields underpinning two broad areas: biotechnology and information and communications technology. This was followed with €1.4 billion for the period 2006–2013. By the end of this period, SFI was supporting approximately 3,000 researchers in Ireland's higher education institutes, led by 300 lead scientists.

Enterprise Ireland

The Irish government provides supports to entrepreneurs through a number of separate agencies and programs. Of particular importance to the emergence of knowledge-based new enterprises and university spin-offs are Enterprise Ireland's direct supports for innovative new "high-potential" start-ups and the Commercialization Fund Programme. In addition, academic spin-offs often benefit from the Employment and Investment Scheme, a tax-based incentive to encourage individuals to invest risk capital in new or established indigenous manufacturing or internationally traded service firms.

Enterprise Ireland is a government-operated business development agency. One of its duties is to support "high potential" entrepreneurship, and specifically to support the commercialization of research from third level educational institutions. Its activities include funding the development of incubators; promoting and stimulating early stage equity investments by venture funds and private business angels; supporting scientists in their commercialization activities; and providing supports such as equity investment, mentors, and export assistance to new and established firms with export aspirations in the manufacturing and internationally traded services sectors. Specifically, it supports approximately one hundred "high-potential" start-ups each year, a minority of which are new businesses originating in third-level educational institutions.

Enterprise Ireland provides a range of financial aid that supports academics and researchers to bring a new product idea or business venture from a third-level educational institution to market. Under the Commercialization Fund Programme, researchers can get between €80,000 and €150,000 to develop innovations that will ideally be ready for licensing to Irish industry or may form the basis of a new start-up. For researchers who choose to commercialize via a spin-off, there are further supports available if the spin-off is technology-based and will trade internationally.

In addition to supporting the development of incubators, Enterprise Ireland played an active role in the development of the venture capital industry in Ireland. The Irish venture capital industry emerged in Ireland in the 1990s as new technology-based firms, principally software firms, started to make their mark. In the 1990s, Enterprise Ireland has increased the flow of venture capital into new ventures by co-financing new venture capital funds. For the period 2007–2011, Enterprise Ireland invested €113 million into venture capital and seed capital funds.

3.   UCD – Resources, capabilities, and attitudes

UCD now comprises seven colleges: Agriculture, Food Science, and Veterinary Medicine; Arts and Celtic Studies; Business and Law; Engineering and Architecture; Health Sciences; Human Sciences; Science; and a number of research institutes, principal among these the UCD Conway Institute of Biomolecular and Biomedical Research.

In terms of research activity, UCD produced over two thousand peer-reviewed publications in 2011 (Table 9.1). UCD reports a doubling of publications for the period 2002 to 2011, with a 58 percent increase in impact in journals for the period 2002–2011. In terms of the research capacity and performance of staff, UCD has, in some areas, internationally recognized research experts. However, as noted previously, UCD faces many challenges in developing its research capabilities. A number of factors such as underinvestment in higher education, a lack of national funding for university research programs, and differing strategic priorities and policies within various units in the university have resulted in unequal research capacity and performance.

In absolute terms, the level of external research income generated by the university has been low. Over the past decade, there has been a significant increase in income and in proposals to raise income (Table 9.2).

Table 9.1: *UCD: Number of publications by year: 2007–2011*

	Number of publications[a]	Number of books
2007	1,355	114
2008	1.617	66
2009	1,782	73
2010	1,993	81
2011	2,054	62

[a] Peer reviewed publications in *Web of Science*.
Source: University College Dublin, Report of the President, 2011–2012.

Table 9.2: *Research awards at UCD, 2002–2011*

Year	Total value of contracts signed (€ million)	Total number of contracts awarded	Total number of proposals submitted
2002/2003	45.8	384	584
2003/2004	49.8	405	685
2004/2005	62.5	495	1,074
2005/2006	83.1	558	1,245
2006/2007	95.4	452	1,234
2007/2008	115.9	445	1,090
2008/2009	116.8	537	1,150
2009/2010	45.6	444	970
2010/2011	103.3	520	1,120
2011/2012	75.1	525	1,257

Source: UCD data. €100,000 is approximately $140,000; €200,000 is approximately $280,000; €1,000,000 is approximately $1,400,000.

Current research income (2010/2011) in UCD is approximately €103 million. To put this in context, over twenty-five years ago (1985), UCD raised approximately €4 million of external research funding, 85 percent of which was from state, EU, or other international bodies and 15 percent from industry. This increase in research income reflects the increased availability of national funding for research through Science Foundation Ireland, the increased attention and emphasis by senior management within the university on the strategic imperative of raising external research funds, and the efforts of individual academics.

Table 9.3: *Funding sources 2011/2012*

Funding source	Number of contracts	Value of contracts (€ million)
Science Foundation Ireland	60	18.6
European Commission	40	14.1
Irish Research Councils (IRCSET and IRCHSS)	99	6.1
Enterprise Ireland	85	5.1
Others	241	31.2

Source: UCD data.

The largest single source of funding is Science Foundation Ireland (Table 9.3).

There is some evidence that scientists in Ireland believe that universities are generally supportive of academic entrepreneurship and engage in external activity.[1] While no direct measure of attitudes of UCD academic staff toward commercialization is available, a survey from 1998 (part of an EU funded study of commercialization) relating to academics in Ireland, including UCD, suggests that in terms of attitudes of academics toward their host institution, 58 percent reported their university as "supportive," 33 percent as "no effect," and 10 percent as a "hindrance" (Jones Evans 1998). There was a very high level of awareness of the industrial liaison office (71 percent), and 22 percent reported having used an ILO in developing external links. A significant number, 58 percent, of all researchers and teachers (1,542 individuals) at the faculties of science, engineering, and medicine in Ireland have some form of external activity (Table 9.4). This survey suggested that the conditions for broadly defined academic entrepreneurship were favorable in that 63 percent or respondents had prior fulltime work experience in industry, while 35 percent reported having prior small business experience, 36 percent reported that immediate family members own or have owned a small business, 15 percent reported having started or owned a business, and 9 percent reported other entrepreneurial experience. In terms of direct contact with industry in the previous five years, 28 percent reported "no direct industry contact," 52 percent reported that they had approached an industrial organization, and 56 percent reported that they had been approached by an industrial organization.

---

[1] Based on a mailed questionnaire survey of all researchers and teachers (1,542 individuals) at the faculties of science, engineering, and medicine in three regions in Ireland in 1997 (a 43 percent response rate).

Table 9.4: *Commercialization activity among Irish academics (percentage of all academics that performed the activity)*

Contracted research	Undertaking specific research projects within the university system for external organizations	69 percent
Consulting	The sale of personal scientific or technological expertise to solve a specific problem	68 percent
Large-scale science projects	Obtaining large externally funded research projects, either through public grants or through industrial sources	68 percent
External teaching	Provision of short courses to nonuniversity personnel/ students and external organizations	73 percent
Testing	Provision of testing and calibration facilities to nonuniversity individuals and external organizations	40 percent
Patenting/licensing	The exploitation of patents or licenses by industry from research results	26 percent
Other		26 percent
Spin-offs	The formation of a new firm or organization to exploit the results of the university research	19 percent
Sales	Commercial selling of products developed within the university	6 percent

Source: TSER Report 1998.

4.   NovaUCD (Centre for New Ventures and Entrepreneurs): The emergence of a technology transfer office at UCD

NovaUCD (Centre for New Ventures and Entrepreneurs)[2] is involved in technology transfer through the provision of incubation space and support for academic researchers and entrepreneurs in UCD. It is organized under the Office of the Vice-President for Innovation. NovaUCD is located on a three-acre site in UCD's Belfield Innovation Park, some 4 km from the Dublin city center. Technology transfer and incubation activities were previously organized under the University Industry Programme (UIP), with two separate physical locations: the University Industry Centre and the Campus Innovation Centre (this evolution is described in the following).

In 1982, the newly formed Graduates Association of the UCD School of Engineering set itself the target of raising funds for a University Industry Centre, which would be built alongside the new engineering building that was due to be built in 1983. The Graduate Association included

---

[2] Centre for New Ventures and Entrepreneurs (NovaUCD): NovaUCD, Belfield Innovation Park, Belfield, Dublin, Ireland. Available at www.ucd.ie/innovation.

leading businessmen on its council, and it was their belief that the future of Irish industry could be greatly assisted by closer cooperation between industry and the university. They envisaged that the University Industry Centre would be the focus for interactions between industry and the university, with personnel from industry attending technical meetings, industrial exhibitions, and seminars. Approximately four hundred fifty individuals and businesses contributed to the financing of the building of the new Centre (including Ericsson, Digital, AIB, Bank of Ireland, Guinness, CRH (Cement Roadstone Holdings), and Phillips). The Centre, which was opened in 1985, comprised a 230-seat auditorium, two smaller seminar rooms, and a small exhibition area.

UCD appointed an "Industry Liaison Office" and established the University Industry Programme (UIP) in 1988. The university allocated a very modest budget, which was supplemented by a state grant that supported the establishment of ILOs in universities. At the time, such activity was not considered central to the activities of the university, with a senior university officer describing the UCD of 1988 as "anti-enterprise." The UIP operated as an autonomous unit, with its own board, and reported to the Registrar of the University. The board was chaired by a senior manager from industry (initially the Operations Manager of Guinness Group plc). The objectives set for the University Industry Programme in 1988 were as follows:

- The promotion of research and development projects with UCD in cooperation with, and funded by, Irish industry.
- The organization within UCD of a structured approach to the provision of advanced training and continuing professional education to meet the needs of Irish industry.
- Becoming the principal venue in Dublin for high-tech and industrially oriented meetings, exhibitions and conferences.
- Becoming involved in what was described as "the potentially lucrative spin-offs from research through licensing and patenting."
- Improving communications between academics and industry, including the establishment of research centers in areas such as biotechnology and robotics.

The first fulltime ILO appointed by UCD was Hugh Quigley, who remained for one year. With a grant from the Industrial Development Authority (IDA) and a university loan, incubation space comprising 3,000 square feet of office space (12 offices or units ranging in size from 150 to 380 square feet) was developed on campus. The university loan was to be repaid from the rent generated from the units. The Campus Innovation Centre (CIC) began operation in 1988/1989. The aim of the CIC was to provide an environment that facilitated the start-up and development of knowledge-based industrial enterprises utilizing the unique range of expertise and facilities on campus.

In 1988, Dr. Pat Frain was appointed Director of the newly established University Industry Programme. In 1989 he was supported by a project manager responsible for continuing professional education and an administrative staff member responsible for conference and exhibition facilities in the University Industry Centre. Frain set about attracting companies to locate in the CIC. The criteria used to identify and select companies was that they had to be new knowledge-intensive companies or spin-offs from the research and development departments of established companies wishing to develop and commercialize new innovative products and services. Firms locating in the incubator were expected to have the potential to benefit from the specialist skills and knowledge of UCD staff and the equipment, facilities, and information services available on campus.

The activities of the initial companies located at the CIC included developing test rigs for electrical connectors; researching and developing new products and processes for the recycling of waste materials; development of thermal vacuum process control equipment for use in the repair of advanced composite elements in the aviation and marine industries; a television and film production company; the genetic testing of blood and tissues from cattle and other animal species; the provision of market information services; and the provision of techno-economic consultancy services.

In June of 1989, UCD adopted a policy on college procedures relating to the establishment of campus companies. This document recommended that all spin-off companies be required to give UCD a standard 15 percent share of the equity of the company. In return, UCD would, over a three-year period, make a contribution "in kind" to the company. This "in kind" contribution would include "seed funding" (through a college department or research group or through a seed fund), rent subsidy, access to college technology and expertise, association with the UCD name, etc. It was not envisaged that UCD would make direct cash contributions to spin-off companies. These procedures were superseded by the university's IP policy. Academic spin-offs were encouraged by the IDA when in 1989 it announced a new package of support for academic entrepreneurs, allowing the involvement of academics on a part-time basis, provided they could demonstrate that there was an adequate management structure in the company. However, during the period of the 1990s, most of the companies located in the CIC were external companies attracted to the university. At one stage, of the fifteen companies located in the CIC, twelve were "external" and only three were "internal" university spin-offs. The UIP supported a small number of these companies (or spin-offs) with their own funds, in return for a share-holding. For example, in 1993, UCD formed a joint venture company, Pharmapro Ltd., with a UK firm, Proteus Molecular Design Ltd., now called Protherics plc, to develop commercial diagnostic tests and vaccines for animal diseases, including bovine tuberculosis and the then emerging disease BSE (bovine spongiform encephalopathy). The research relating to BSE was carried out in UCD by Professor Mark Rogers, a professor in zoology. His research led to the development of the TSE (transmissible spongiform encephalopathy) diagnostic technology, which was licensed to Enfer Scientific Ltd. in 1996. Enfer subsequently developed a rapid test for BSE using this technology. This licensing arrangement generated over €2 million in royalty income for UCD.

Reflecting its broad remit, industry linkages, and lack of resources, the UIP became involved in a number of activities. It started to deliver health and safety courses to industry (at the time, the relevant facul-ties within the University did not consider such activity as part of their remit). A second course in the area of sports management was also devel-oped. These initiatives were very successful, and after a number of years became profitable for the UIP. They also included a number of "firsts" for the university – for example, the first digital broadcast in Ireland and the first delivery of an education program by satellite. By 1993, contin-uing professional education programs accounted for 50 percent of UIP revenue. The UIP used these funds to support activity, including the development of the Campus Company Development Programme, and to develop patenting and licensing activity. The Campus Company Devel-opment Programme, which it had developed in conjunction with the Dublin Business Incubator Centre (BIC),[3] was a nine-month program involving one four-hour workshop each month. Participants received the support of a mentor from the BIC and other experts and were required to present their business idea/business plan at the start and at the end of the program. There was also an awards ceremony at the end of the program at which the businesses that made the most progress during the course of the program were presented with prizes.

While plans started to emerge in 1993 for developing a new purpose-built incubation center, it was not until the late 1990s that these plans were developed. The newly appointed chairman of the UIP Board, Ian Cahill, approached the then President of the University to establish what role the UIP should play during his three-year term of office. The

---

[3] A BIC is a support organization, public or private, for innovative small and medium-sized businesses and entrepreneurs.

President agreed to a review of the role of the UIP, and a committee comprising Ian Cahill, the ILO (Dr. Pat Frain), two university staff, and two external mangers from industry (from the ICT sector) was established. This committee considered the role the UIP could play, looked at international models in other universities and industry, surveyed the companies in the CIC and external companies, and surveyed academics within the university, and from this work developed a specific set of recommendations. Principal among these was that UCD should develop a clear policy on interaction with industry and the role and purpose of the UIP. Specifically, this review recommended the transfer of the profitable programs in health and safety and sports management and other multidisciplinary courses out of the UIP (and therefore the main revenue source of the UIP), in return for the allocation of a specific budget to support the UIP, including new senior posts in a number of key areas to enable the UIP to focus on supporting innovation and technology transfer.

The proposals were presented to the University's officers, who agreed to a written response. The outcome was a UIP with specified roles, each of which was to be supported by a full-time post. The roles were as follows:

- Technology transfer (identifying, protecting, and exploiting IP created in the university)
- Continuing professional development focused on innovation and technology transfer (the provision of short courses to industry and internal courses to UCD staff)
- Liaison with industry (for example, identifying specific industry-research linkages)
- Enterprise (supporting the development of entrepreneurship and campus-based ventures)

An implementation plan was developed and by October 2001 it had been implemented, with most of the new posts filled, and the health and safety courses transferred out of the UIP. In parallel with the implementation of the plan, the Director of the UIP sought to develop a new innovation and technology transfer center at the site of the 1750s Merville House. The Director (of the ILO) raised funds from Enterprise Ireland[4] and a number of external parties during the summer of 2000. The six private sector sponsors were AIB Bank, Arthur Cox, Deloitte, Ericsson, Goodbody Stockbrokers, and Xilinx who contributed 75 percent of the €10 million raised to develop the first two phases ($3,750 \text{ m}^2$) of a planned

---

[4] Enterprise Ireland is the public development agency responsible for developing indigenous industry in Ireland. This includes promoting what they term "high potential" entrepreneurship.

8,000 m^2 development. In return for this contribution, the private sector sponsors receive a small equity stake in the companies that locate in the new center. The sponsors were chosen to bring an appropriate mix of expertise and experience to the support programs offered at the new center. The balance of the €10 million was contributed by Enterprise Ireland and UCD. Additional "wet-lab" space to accommodate biotechnology start-up companies was also subsequently funded (€1 million) by Enterprise Ireland and UCD.

The new innovation and technology transfer center, named NovaUCD, emerged in a number of phases. In Phase I a new development (2,850 m^2) was added to Merville House. This phase officially opened in October 2003. Phase II, completed in September 2004, comprised the refurbishment of the main part of Merville House (900 m^2). Phase III, completed in spring 2005, comprised 340 m^2 of "wet-lab" or bio-incubation space, which can accommodate 4–6 biotechnology companies originating both on and off the campus.

In addition to developing the physical facilities, Dr. Pat Frain, Director of NovaUCD, continued the development and expansion of NovaUCD. Over the period 2004–2011, NovaUCD recorded over 300 industry partnerships; 21 new UCD spin-off companies incorporated; 370 inventions disclosed; 239 patents filed (including 125 priority patent applications); 88 license agreements concluded; over 60 start-up companies occupying incubation space at NovaUCD; over 115 new ventures supported at NovaUCD; and 101 new ventures and 170 individuals completing the UCD Campus Company Development Programme.

Over this period, under the Director, NovaUCD developed a range of services that promoted innovation and technology transfer. These included the following:
• Identifying, protecting, and exploiting intellectual property arising from UCD research
• Supporting entrepreneurs, campus companies, and other knowledge-based ventures
• Promoting a culture of innovation and entrepreneurship among researchers, staff, and students at UCD
• Promoting contract research and other forms of university–industry co-operation

Protecting and exploiting IPR

The impetus for an IP policy at UCD emerged from the University Industry Programme in the late 1980s. The ILO was aware of developments in the United States, and specifically the Bayh–Dole Act, and considered it appropriate that UCD have an IP policy. The development of an IP

Table 9.5: *IP policy in UCD*

Net income	Creators of IP	College	University/NovaUCD
Up to €100,000	75 percent	15 percent	10 percent
€100,000–€200,000	50 percent	30 percent	20 percent
€100,000–€200,000	40 percent	30 percent	30 percent
Over €1,000,000	30 percent	30 percent	40 percent

policy was a slow process, meeting with resistance from some academic staff. The then Registrar of the university engaged in a consultation process, which involved passing the proposed policy to the Deans of each of the faculties. A policy was adopted by the Governing Authority of the University in 1992. It stated that "patents are owned by the university where the university deemed that there had been significant use of university facilities." Prior to this, under common law, the university, as employer, assumed that it had ownership rights. During the 1990s, a number of developments required the university to revisit the policy. In particular, the development of research funding streams from SFI and Enterprise Ireland required that the university identify and protect IP. Under the terms and conditions of many of the funding agencies, for example, SFI and Enterprise Ireland, the University has an obligation to report inventions arising from the funded research to the funding agency in a timely manner. A draft of a new policy was developed in 1998, though because of changes in senior officers in UCD the development of the policy was delayed. This policy was adopted by the governing authority of the university in July 2006 and was formally launched by the UCD President in March 2007. This policy distributes net income from IP exploitation across the creators, the university, and the NovaUCD (Table 9.5).

NovaUCD adopted a structured approach to ensure that intellectual property was identified and captured. NovaUCD staff met with UCD researchers on a regular basis to provide advice on commercial aspects of research proposals and contracts; to monitor the progress of research projects; to remind researchers of UCD's contractual obligations to funding agencies; and to ensure that they provide appropriate assistance to the researchers at different stages of the research projects. Specific activities included the preparation of nondisclosure agreements, material transfer agreements, and research contracts; meeting contractual obligations including timely reporting of newly discovered intellectual property to relevant funding agencies; assisting researchers in identifying intellectual property and completing invention disclosure forms; due diligence on invention disclosures; undertaking searches of patent databases in association with the creators of intellectual property; and the preparation of patent filings in association with patent agents.

NovaUCD worked with researchers to identify and develop the most appropriate business model for commercialization of intellectual property. This might involve licensing to commercial partners or the creation of a spin-off company. A number of different services formed part of this process, including building market knowledge and a high level of understanding of the relevant market sectors; access to advice, diagnostic tools, and data; sourcing of licensees and marketing of inventions; negotiation and drafting of license agreements; and sourcing of finance. If NovaUCD determined that an invention could potentially be exploited, a NovaUCD technology transfer professional was assigned to the project. The technology transfer professional's role was to identify and contact prospective licensees with a nonconfidential description of the invention. A prospective licensee who wanted further information about the invention could then sign a confidentiality agreement (sometimes known as a non-disclosure agreement (NDA)) prepared by NovaUCD staff in order to review confidential information about the invention, such as a scientific manuscript, drawings, and working prototypes.

Even within this structured environment, Dr. Pat Frain noted that successfully negotiating technology transfer was still a challenge. NovaUCD's experience suggests that few unsolicited offers to transfer technology to developed larger firms are successful. For example, Dr. Pat Frain cited examples from large companies that reported that they only license a small number of the many technologies presented to them (as little as a few in every ten thousand). Frain believes that approaches to larger firms have a greater chance of success where there is a specific relationship between the firm and the university or research team working on the technology. Irish industrial policy aims to develop such relationships by encouraging industry collaboration on funded research projects. UCD is developing the Belfield Innovation Park on campus, which will seek to develop linkages between firms and researchers.

In terms of invention disclosures, Frain successfully grew the numbers. For example, in 2010, fifty-seven invention disclosures were submitted to NovaUCD, compared to fewer than fifteen in 2003. Over the period 2004–2010, 326 inventions were disclosed to NovaUCD. In terms of patent activity, twenty-eight patent applications, including fourteen priority patent applications, nine patent co-operation treaties (PCTs), and five national/regional patent applications, were filed by UCD in 2010 for IP arising from research in life sciences, engineering, and information and communication technology (Table 9.6). For the period 2004–2010,

Table 9.6: *UCD priority patent applications 2010*

Title	Patent Application	UCD School of
A new design for DSSC	A U.S. provisional patent application	Chemical and bioprocess engineering
A polymeric nanoparticle	A UK priority patent application	Agriculture, food science, and veterinary medicine with TCD
Catalyst for the release of dihydrogen from ammonia borane	A UK priority patent application	Chemistry and chemical biology
Compounds	An Irish priority patent application	Chemistry and chemical biology
Effective product recommendation using the real-time Web	A U.S. provisional patent application	Computer science and informatics
Energy monitoring system	An Irish priority and U.S. provisional patent application	Computer science and informatics
Markers of oocyte quality	A European priority patent application	Agriculture, food science, and veterinary medicine with National Maternity Hospital and Merrion Fertility Clinic
Methods of manufacturing photovoltaic electrodes	An Irish priority patent application	Electrical, electronic, and mechanical engineering
MSTN polymorphism, MSTN insertion/discovery	An Irish priority patent application	Agriculture, food science, and veterinary medicine
Nonlinear magnetophoretic separation device, system, and method	A UK priority patent application	Chemistry and chemical biology
Novel biomarkers for cardiovascular disease	An Irish priority patent application	Medicine and medical science with Heartbeat Trust and St Vincent's University Hospital
Phenotyping tumor infiltrating leukocytes	A U.S. provisional patent application	Biomolecular and biomedical science with UCSF
Plasma shutter	An Irish priority patent application	Physics
Protease anti-prion protease	An Irish and European priority patent application	Biomolecular and biomedical science

Source: NovaUCD.

UCD filed 204 patent applications, of which 107 were priority patent applications. In terms of licensing activity, UCD recorded the highest earnings from licensing income of the nine universities in Ireland.

Supports for entrepreneurs

NovaUCD provided support to staff that chose to exploit IP by forming a spin-off company. UCD's policy on intellectual property, which has the objective to "actively support the commercialization of University Intellectual Property," seeks 15 percent of the "fully diluted share capital" of campus companies. NovaUCD supported entrepreneurs, campus companies, and other knowledge-based ventures in a number of ways. The NovaUCD Campus Company Development Programme (CCDP), which commenced in 1996, was the main support program run by NovaUCD for academic entrepreneurs spinning off campus companies. The annual program, which was delivered in association with Enterprise Ireland, offered a mix of monthly workshops, mentoring, and one-to-one consultancy. It was delivered by NovaUCD staff, with support from the NovaUCD sponsors and other outside experts. It is designed to assist campus-based academic entrepreneurs in the establishment and development of knowledge-intensive enterprises by reducing the lead-in time associated with setting-up a business and providing the skills necessary to transform ideas into commercially feasible ventures. Since it started, over 156 ventures and 235 individuals have completed NovaUCD's CCDP.

Promoting a culture of innovation and entrepreneurship among researchers, staff, and students

NovaUCD introduced the NovaUCD Innovation Award in 2004 and arranged a series of events and courses to increase the awareness of related issues among UCD personnel and students. These events, which were aimed at researchers, staff, and students, covered aspects of commercialization, including intellectual property identification, protection and exploitation, commercialization, and new venture formation. Each year NovaUCD organized over 100 events aimed at increasing "awareness of intellectual property and other commercial issues and to promote a culture of entrepreneurship and innovation among researchers, students and staff." NovaUCD also delivered accredited Ph.D. modules in innovation and knowledge transfer.

NovaUCD, with the support of Dún Laoghaire-Rathdown County Enterprise Board, ran an "Entrepreneurs Live!" seminar series. These seminars were targeted at undergraduate and postgraduate students with the aim of promoting a spirit of entrepreneurship among the staff and student population across the university campus. The seminars involve well-known entrepreneurs who talk about their experiences of setting up and running their own businesses, emphasizing the highs and lows on their entrepreneurial journeys, and highlighting the lessons they learned along the way.

NovaUCD and Enterprise Ireland

NovaUCD worked closely with Enterprise Ireland in supporting technology transfer. NovaUCD was involved in a number of organizations at the national and international levels that were established to develop best practices, standards, and recognition for the knowledge transfer profession and to provide a voice for knowledge transfer at national (AURIL Ireland), United Kingdom and Ireland (Institute of Knowledge Transfer), and European (ProTon Europe) organizations.

Licensing and spin-offs from UCD/NovaUCD

By 2011, NovaUCD and its predecessor, the UIP, had assisted over 150 spin-off companies. These included the UCD spin-offs BiancaMed (medical devices), Celtic Catalysts (chiral catalysis), ChangingWorlds (intelligent mobile portal solutions), NTERA (NanoChromics displays technology), and WBT Systems (intelligent learning solutions), which have attracted over €150 million in investment.

The first recorded spin-off from UCD predates any formal supports for technology transfer. In 1966 a Professor in Engineering, Seamus Timoney, started the Timoney Technology Group, a firm that manufactured fire engines and tanks. At the time, engaging in such activity was considered as "swimming against the tide." One of UCD's most successful licenses to date relates to the development of a BSE or "mad cow disease" test, which has earned over €2 million in royalty income for UCD. As noted earlier, this test was developed following the formation of a joint venture company, Pharmapro Ltd., between a UK firm, Proteus Molecular Design Ltd., now called Protherics Plc, and UCD in 1993. Pharmapro was established to develop commercial diagnostic tests and vaccines for animal diseases including bovine tuberculosis and the then emerging disease BSE. Professor Mark Rogers, UCD School of Biology and Environmental Science, carried out the research related to BSE in UCD. His research led to the development of TSE (transmissible spongiform encephalopathy) diagnostic technology, which was licensed to a small Irish company, Enfer Scientific Ltd., in 1996. Enfer subsequently developed a rapid test for BSE using this technology. The developed BSE test, which reduced the time for a BSE diagnosis from 14 days to 3.5 hours, was validated by the Irish Government's Department of Agriculture in 1997. The test became commercially viable in 1999 when the European Commission validated it as one of three tests acceptable for use in the diagnosis of BSE in Europe. Enfer has generated significant jobs, turnover, and profits from selling diagnostic BSE test kits.

University–industry engagement

In addition to core support for spin-offs, a number of initiatives demonstrate increased industry interaction within UCD over the past decade. The university reserved a 25-acre facility in the southwest corner of the campus that houses NovaUCD for the Belfield Innovation Park. This provided a site for the National Institute for Bioprocessing Research and Training (NIBRT). In 2005 the government approved a proposal from the IDA to fund the establishment of NIBRT at UCD to the value of €72 million over seven years. NIBRT's partners include other Irish universities and institutes of technology (UCD, TCD, DCU, and IT Sligo). It is the state's first research and training facility for the biotech sector. In establishing the Institute, the government hoped it would meet a shortfall in biotechnology skills in Ireland and attract investment to create a new "biotech cluster." UCD has also been successful in attracting a number of foreign MNEs to locate research groups at the university. For example, in late 2005, Wyeth Corporation announced that its subsidiary, Wyeth Research, would establish a biotherapeutic drug discovery research facility in the UCD Conway Institute of Biomolecular and Biomedical Research. Wyeth Corporation has four existing facilities in Ireland employing over 3,000 people.

Reorganization of NovaUCD

In 2012, innovation activities were reorganized in UCD and a new office, the Office of the Vice-President for Innovation, was established. This resulted in both a reorganization of innovation activities and a renaming of NovaUCD as the Centre for New Ventures and Entrepreneurs. It became part of the new Office of the Vice-President for Innovation.

The Office of the Vice-President for Innovation was developed to "enhance the value and quality of UCD's innovation activities in order to achieve the maximum impact for the University, its partners, and for social and economic life in Ireland in the wider world." The Office of

Table 9.7: *UCD Innovation Activities*

Theme	Objective	Activities
1. Inspiring creative graduates	Support and enable initiatives to inspire creative graduates	Programs include the UCD Horizons Programme, the TCD–UCD Innovation Academy, the UCD Campus Company Development Programme, and executive education and continuing professional development programs.
2. Putting knowledge to work	Promote initiatives that provide solutions to global problems through problem-driven research	Commercializes the outputs of their research programs via technology transfer team.
3. Partnering with industry	Promote the creation and development of business partnerships including the licensing of UCD technology	NexusUCD, the Industry Partnership Centre, manages facilities and provides related support to enable industry and business to locate on campus in close proximity to the UCD research community.
4. Growing and supporting new business	Support new high-tech and knowledge-intensive companies	Centre for New Ventures and Entrepreneurs (NovaUCD).

Source: UCD.

the Vice-President for Innovation is focused on four innovation themes (Table 9.7).

5.   NovaUCD (the Centre for New Ventures and Entrepreneurs)

As part of a 2012 reorganization of innovation activity, the Centre for New Ventures and Entrepreneurs became focused on providing office space and related business support to entrepreneurs and new ventures. The Centre for New Ventures and Entrepreneurs is managed by the UCD Office of the Vice-President for Innovation, which is located at NovaUCD, and UCD's technology transfer team is part of this Office.

NovaUCD is UCD's purpose-built facility that supports new ventures and entrepreneurs. At NovaUCD, clients are offered a comprehensive business support program in addition to office space. This program comprises advice, seminars, and workshops, as well as facilitated access to the NovaUCD network of researchers, business leaders, and investors.

This highly networked environment attracts innovative entrepreneurs, experienced business partners, and staff. The NovaUCD facility contains fifty-five business incubation units (ranging in size from 12 to 85 m^2), fourteen desk spaces for individuals who are in the early stages of forming a company, and ten bio-incubation units (ranging in size from 15 to 64 m^2).

Thirty-five "knowledge-intensive" ventures were located in NovaUCD (Table 9.8). These included direct spin-offs, joint ventures between an external entrepreneur and a university faculty member, and external companies. In 2012, these thirty-five companies employed over 200 people, raised over €35 million, and collectively planned to create 300 jobs over the two-year period 2012–2014.

6. Recent developments in support structures for commercialization and university–industry interactions

Innovation alliance – UCD and TCD

A recent development in commercialization activity was the announcement of an innovation alliance between UCD and TCD. In March 2009, as a response to the economic crises and the government's call for reorganization within the third level sector, UCD and TCD set out the ambition "to develop a world-class ecosystem for innovation that will drive enterprise development and the creation of sustainable high value jobs."[5] TCD Provost Dr. John Hegarty and UCD President Dr. Hugh Brady stated that "this is a time of national crisis. Evidence shows that during recession, innovation thrives. New realities bring with them new opportunities. The Government's Smart Economy framework pinpointed the ingenuity of our people as the way forward for the country. In that context, as institutions with a relevant responsibility, we felt impelled to act and set out how we could advance the nurturing of that ingenuity."

The UCD–TCD Innovation Alliance is described by UCD as the "pivotal development in innovation". The alliance has three major components (University College Dublin 2010):

1. A joint venture in business development that will involve bringing together technology transfer and enterprise development activities. The objective set for the Alliance is the development of an enterprise corridor between TCD and UCD that will be home for up to 300 new enterprises with advanced technology centers to support indigenous industry.

---

[5] March 11, 2009, Launch of the TCD UCD Alliance.

Table 9.8: *Selected client companies*

Company name	Activity
Aonta Technologies	Provides carrier grade voice conferencing solutions to Conferencing Service Providers and Telcos
AIB Seed Capital Fund	Provides venture capital for companies at the seed and early stages of development
APC	Delivers process solutions and proprietary processing technologies for both small and large molecules
Berand Neuropharmacology	Identifies and develops novel and effective drugs for use in the treatment of brain illness
bioMerieux	Tests for clinical decisions in the areas of infectious diseases, cardiovascular emergencies, and targeted cancers
Biosensia	RapiPlex: A Rapid Inexpensive Multiplex Immunoassay platform for universal application at the point of care
Cernam	Specialist digital investigations firm with a focus on online evidence and investigation
CityHook	A service that shows and compares transport options between the airport and nearby city locations
Connectors Marketplace	A suite of professional networking tools
Credit Expo Research	System for measuring and managing credit risk
Crescent Diagnostics	Developed an osteoporosis screening tool (BQT – Bone Quality Test) that identifies the risk of osteoporosis
DOCOsoft	Document management and workflow software solutions for the global insurance and financial services markets
Enbio	CoBlast replaces the oxide layer of reactive metals with an application-specific chemically bonded and particulate-free thin surface
Equinome	Development and provision of novel genetic tests to the bloodstock industry
HeyStaks Technologies	A solution to optimize knowledge flow and deliver zero-effort collaboration in a world of Big Data
IncaPlex	Cloud development and implementation: Salesforce and Google App Engine
Innovios	Smart application of ideas to improve information flow and performance in organizations
Ionic Business Systems	Design and build content managed websites and use Web technology to create online software
Life Scientific	Bringing off-patent crop protection products to market
MuteButton	A novel technology that alleviates the symptoms of subjective tinnitus
OncoMark	Biomarker panels supporting oncology clinical decisions and drug development
Q-Validus	A provider of international certification and management services
RendezVu	Language learning technologies to provide an authentic English practice environment

Table 9.8 (cont.)

Company name	Activity
ServiceFrame	Software and services that enable the institutionalization of core governance processes
SmartBuilder Software	Software system for construction, engineering, and property management
Socowave	A commercial-grade active antenna system solution
Sportora	App connecting sports fans
Synference	Predictive analytics software
Talentevo	Employee performance management software
Tethras	App Translation Service
VideoCrisp	Cloud-based video editing software
VoucherPages.ie	Online discount voucher directory
Wattics	Software solution for energy management

Source: UCD.

2. The Innovation Academy. The Innovation Academy's mission is "the pursuit of fresh ideas and new ventures. Through the creation of a vibrant multi-disciplinary environment the Academy seeks to transform some of the brightest scholars the two institutions have to offer into energetic and resourceful entrepreneurial thinkers." The Academy straddles the existing campuses, building on areas of combined strength and individual distinctiveness in the two universities. It focuses particularly on fourth-level Ph.D. training, positioning innovation center stage in courses, facilitating student mobility between campuses, and ensuring that the breadth and depth of expertise and resources at UCD and TCD are available to Ireland's future entrepreneurs.
3. A new partnership with government and its agencies and business. This partnership aims to develop Ireland as a "thriving innovation ecosystem."

Central Technology Transfer Office

Another recent development in the management of the technology transfer functions in Irish universities is the decision by Enterprise Ireland and the Irish Universities Association to appoint a Director of the Central Technology Transfer Office (CTTO). The new director will work with Enterprise Ireland and the Directors of Technology Transfer and Vice-Presidents for Research of the seven Irish universities. The Director will work to develop systems to support industry–university engagement through activities such as standardizing IP commercialization policy, commercialization agreements, and IP systems across the universities; working to increase industry engagement with public research by acting as a central contact point for industry looking for IP opportunities from universities; and engaging with Technology Transfer Offices within the universities and monitor the performance of the TTOs.

Conclusion

UCD initiated efforts to begin supporting and encouraging commercialization as early as the mid-1980s. While such efforts may have been peripheral to the activities of most of the university's academics, they represented tangible resource commitments, such as the funding of the TTO and the development of incubation space. Building on these commitments, a strategy emerged that began to encourage commercialization by providing support for academics interested in engaging in the process. External factors, such as the Irish government's industrial development strategy of attracting inward foreign direct investment and of developing high-technology entrepreneurship, contributed to these efforts by providing resources to support the development of the TTO and the incubator on campus. The efforts of the TTO to develop commercialization led to a unique public–private partnership that funded the building of the current purpose-built incubator. In 2004, under the direction of the then newly appointed president, UCD sought to build on its underlying research infrastructure and the TTO and NovaUCD, and develop innovation as the third pillar of UCD's core mission.

References

Brady, H. 2004. Inaugural Foundation Day Address, O'Reilly Hall, Friday 4 November 2004. Speech by Dr. Hugh Brady, President, UCD: The Ideas of the University 1854–2004: Celebrating the Past.

Cowen, B. 2008. An Taoiseach (Prime Minister), Speech on Thursday, 18 December 2008.

Jones Evans, D. 1998. Universities, Technology Transfer and Spin-off Activity in Different European Regions. Targeted Socio-Economic Research Report 1042 (1998). Available at http://improving-ser.jrc.it.

Murphy, A. and Ruane, F. 2004. "Foreign Direct Investment in Ireland: An Updated Assessment." In Central Bank and Financial Services Authority Annual Report 2003, Dublin, Ireland, p. 135.

University College Dublin. 2010. Forming Global Minds, Strategic Plan to 2014, UCD, Belfield, Dublin, Ireland.

10 Stimulating academic entrepreneurship and technology transfer: A study of Kings College London commercialization strategies

Mike Wright and Igor Filatotchev

Growing attention is being devoted to the nature and processes involved in academic entrepreneurship beyond the major universities in the United States (Siegel *et al.* 2007). Lessons from the top U.S. universities may not be transferable to universities located elsewhere (Wright *et al.* 2007). This case examines the commercialization strategies adopted by Kings College London (KCL) in the United Kingdom to stimulate academic entrepreneurship and technology transfer. Information for the case is based on in-depth interviews with the head of the technology transfer office at KCL, academic entrepreneurs, and the CEOs of three spin-off companies. In addition, archival data were obtained to develop understanding of the background for technology transfer activities at KCL.

Founded in 1829, KCL is one of the oldest and largest colleges of the University of London. It has grown and developed through mergers with several institutions that have their own distinguished histories. These include the United Medical and Dental Schools of Guy's and St. Thomas' Hospitals; Chelsea College; Queen Elizabeth College; and the Institute of Psychiatry. KCL has 13,800 undergraduate students and some 5,300 postgraduates in nine academic schools. KCL is a member of the Russell Group, a coalition of the United Kingdom's major research-based universities.

We first provide background on KCL, covering its size, research quality, mission, and strategy. This is followed by an outline of the organizational structure, activities, and resources of Kings College London Enterprises (KCLE), the commercialization office of KCL. We then discuss the commercialization and spin-off process at the College and present three case synopses of spin-offs from KCL that are at different stages of their development. Finally, we discuss the regional innovation environment in terms of the availability of venture capital and government policies.

Table 10.1: *Kings College indicators*

	2002/2003	2003/2004	2004/2005
Research funding (£000)	37500.8	39391.9	42170.9
Percent	35.4	35.1	35.1
#Ph.D.s graduated	375	330	340
Research grants and contracts (£000)	93,377	99,198	101,463
Total academic staff costs (£000)	86,505	89,425	97,481

Source: HESA.

1.   Kings College London

KCL is in the top group of universities for research earnings, with income from grants and contracts of more than £101 million (2004–2005), and has an annual turnover of £364 million (Table 10.1). With respect to faculty quality, twenty-four of the College's subject areas were awarded the highest rating of 5* and 5 for research quality in the 2001 Research Assessment Exercise, which indicates that research is rated as being of international excellence. KCL's mission is "the advancement of knowledge, learning and understanding in the service of society." For the decade 2000–2010, KCL has identified ten principal strategic goals:

1. Develop and maintain a distinctive national and international profile for King's based on academic excellence and service to society.
2. Foster and recruit high-quality academic and support staff by developing their skills and talents in an environment of equal opportunity.
3. Recruit the best students on merit and potential and prepare them for work, citizenship and personal development.
4. Pursue research and scholarship at international levels of excellence in the full range of disciplines which will be represented in the College.
5. Provide research-led education and training which is responsive to the needs of individuals, business and the community.
6. Enhance the transfer of knowledge to businesses and the community to improve quality of life and promote wealth creation.
7. Create the information infrastructure necessary to support excellence in research, learning and teaching, and to ensure effective governance and management.
8. Develop and maintain the College estate to provide a high-quality work, study and residential environment which does justice to our central-London location.
9. Maintain a financial regime which ensures proper accountability, cost-effective operation and adequate reinvestment.

10. Build a cohesive policy and operational framework which adds value to the work of the Schools and ensures a consistent and effective competitive profile for the College as a whole.

The College's commercialization strategy for the period 2001–2010 sets out to address barriers to the evolution of knowledge transfer as a mainstream activity in a number of ways. First, attempts will be made to protect knowledge transfer from being crowded out by the demands of teaching, research and administration. Second, marketing and business development expertise will be strengthened at the school level. Third, the College will promote an investment planning and associated risk management culture in schools. Fourth, a greater sense of enterprise and entrepreneurial activity will be promoted at KCL. Fifth, attempts will be made to prevent the loss of spin-off companies by providing technology incubators. The College aims to be in the upper quartile of performance indicators for knowledge transfer for universities in the United Kingdom.

2.   KCL Enterprises

KCL Enterprises (KCLE) is Kings College London's (KCL) subsidiary company responsible for the business development of KCL's intellectual capital and research support. KCLE activities include the identification of new opportunities, the development of strategies for partnership, funding and/or commercialization, marketing, patenting and intellectual property protection, licensing, mentoring spin-off companies, negotiation of collaborations and contracts, and management of clinical trials agreements.

The mission of KCLE involves the maximization of income and deal flow. With respect to licensing income, the aim is to double this within three years. In terms of spin-off creation, the aim is to achieve a steady state of creating two to three spin-offs per year that will be viable with growth prospects. However, target capital gains are not specified because it is considered premature to specify expected gains from early stage ventures. KCL's senior management seeks increasing returns from technology transfer activities but recognizes that it is difficult to budget for this, as these are lumpy and unpredictable. When gains are realized, some of the university's share goes back to the initiating school, while the remainder remains in the College for strategic investment in innovative activities.

A central goal is to ensure that opportunities are developed externally and that the exchange of knowledge is facilitated. Importantly, it is recognized that spin-offs may place research back with the university. Hence, the emphasis is not on spinning off being associated with "kicking-out" the venture. KCLE has alliances with more than 100 companies in the pharmaceutical, biotechnology, and medical devices industries, including start-ups. These alliances enable industrial partners to access early stage technological developments, key opinion leaders, and a high-quality clinical trials service. KCLE seeks to partner strategically with companies that have a track record of taking products to market. Over the past decade, more than 60 technologies have been licensed. The structure of the KCLE organization is shown in Figure 10.1. The Technology Transfer Office (TTO) expertise is represented in the form of five specialist TTOs and five IP support personnel. There are a further six business development managers.

KCLE is part of the Science Enterprise Centre, Simfonec, which covers four institutions, the Royal Veterinary College, Queen Mary's College, City University, and King's College. The SEC has a core task of entrepreneurship education. This includes running courses for academics who are or who may become company directors. Simfonec was launched in March 2003 by the Department of Trade and Industry (DTI) and was created by four of London's leading universities as a collaborative Science Enterprise Centre for the exploitation and transfer of knowledge, ideas, and resources among three key sectors – academic, financial, and Small and Medium Enterprises (SMEs). Simfonec encourages the development of an entrepreneurial outlook among researchers in science and technology and orchestrates the delivery of science ideas to the commercial marketplace.

Together with collaborating universities, KCLE has entered into two partnerships with investment funds. IP Group (formerly IP2IPO) is investing £5m over five years in new KCL companies, using their experience in management and fund raising to develop these business opportunities into viable companies. KCL is also a partner in the Heptagon Fund, which is a new proof-of-concept fund for the life sciences and health care whose aim is to bridge the gap between grant funding and first-stage venture funding or commercial exploitation.

KCLE is divided into two divisions: Commercial Development and Research Support.

3.   Commercial development

Within this division are four principal activities: business development; technology transfer; company incubation; and commercial support. Each is discussed in turn.

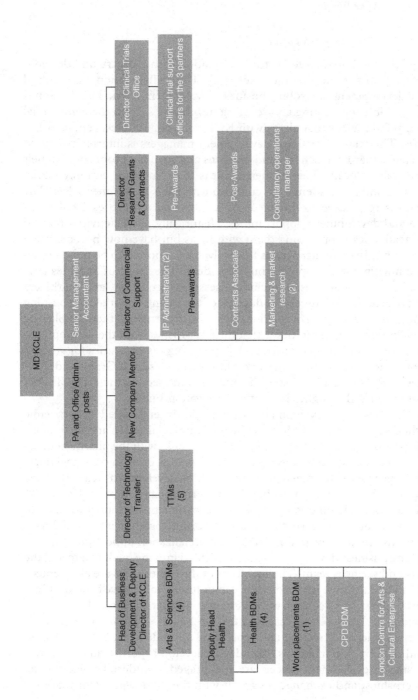

Figure 10.1: The structure of the KCLE organization.

Business development

KCLE has shifted its focus to collaboration with industry and developing spin-offs, rather than just licensing. This collaboration has involved the development of a robust business development team. The division is responsible for creating and securing new business from the commercial and public sector that aligns with KCL's research interests and capabilities. The team of business development managers is internally focused on particular KCL schools and divisions and spends a proportion of their time based locally. Part of their remit is to promote an entrepreneurial culture and get academics to come up with ideas to commercialize. The team is responsive to the needs of schools and alert to external funding and development opportunities. Historically, these activities reacted to academics approaching them with ideas but have now become more proactive. Even so, academics themselves are reported to be more proactive now in coming up with business ideas. The range of activities covered through the division include assessment, collation, and marketing of the schools' resources, production of marketing material, establishing contacts and long-term relationships with external partners, brokering collaborative opportunities with industry, assisting with the development and launch of bespoke courses, and managing opportunities for student work placements. The team works closely with Research Grants and Contracts (RG&C) and TT staff. The team is funded via the HEFCE/DTI initiative HEIF (Higher Education Innovation Fund).

The business development team is partly embedded in academic schools and works with them to shape commercialization and technology transfer decisions. For example, to increase links with the pharmaceutical industry, the business development team organizes open days, meetings, and major industry meetings. The business development team will also meet with KCL alumni to build long-term relationships and networks of advisors. The aim is for business development personnel to have an overview of an area so that they can bring together interdisciplinary expertise to identify and develop commercialization opportunities.

The business development team is divided into the health team and the arts and sciences team. The members of the health team are all scientists with Ph.D.s. Some have experience in industry, some have been postdoctoral fellows, and some have experience in other business development functions. It is seen as essential for the business development officers to have scientific training and a personal aptitude to be able to identify and develop opportunities. In order to develop expertise and networks, business development officers are encouraged to undertake placements, internships, and exchange programs with the particular sector that they are working with. For example, there is a two-way exchange with the London Development Agency. The business development officers do not have start-up or financial experience, but they do understand IP issues relevant to the commercialization of research. The arts and sciences business development team covers arts and humanities, social science, and physical science and engineering. Given its London location, arts and cultural industries provide opportunities for commercialization. For example, collaborations have been developed with the National Theatre, the National Film Theatre (NFT), Shakespeare's Globe and TATE Modern, the English National Opera, the British Museum, etc.

Technology transfer

The division is responsible for all aspects of management and commercialization of KCL's IP. It has specialist technology transfer staff dedicated to biosciences/biomedical and physical sciences and IT. Activities undertaken include working with researchers to identify new commercial opportunities, IP protection, due diligence, commercialization strategies, marketing, negotiation with potential licensees, and execution of license agreements. As well as direct out-licensing, TT staff are involved in project teams as spin-off companies are being created. TT staff also work with RG&C staff to advise on IP related to research funding. The business development team is viewed as a platform resource that feeds into the technology transfer specialists who deal with patenting, licensing, etc. As with the business development team, almost nobody in the technology transfer team has direct start-up experience.

Commercial support

This team acts as a central support group for the commercial development teams. The team will handle IP administration, IP-related agreements such as confidentiality (CDA/NDA), materials transfer (MTA), and revenue share. It will be responsible for post-deal management and tracking as well as marketing, communications, and market research.

Company incubation

An advisory body that works with academic staff to develop new spin-off opportunities and is involved with companies post-formation, providing support and links to external service providers and investors as well as acting as a conduit between the company and the College. It also provides assistance in establishing new companies on College premises.

Research support

This division comprises three principal areas: Research Grants and Contracts (RG&C), Joint Clinical Trials Office (JCTO), and KCL Consultancy.

The RG&C manages all aspects of external research funding from grant application through to management of grants once they are awarded. The team advises on costing of programs and details of awards such as particular terms and conditions. RG&C works with Finance to manage the grants post-award, including interfacing with external funders and driving down debt. The team is also involved in advice on commercial collaboration and contract research programs and negotiation of terms with external partners. Where there are IP implications, they consult with TT colleagues. The team is organized into pre- and post-awards, with individual expertise developed in funding sources, e.g., research councils, charities, commercial, EU.

The JCTO was formed to streamline commercial clinical trials and to increase income from trials. It reports to KCLE, and its management is accountable to the JCTO Board.

The KCL Consultancy is focused on boosting the level and value of ongoing consultancy activity. It provides advice on all aspects of consultancy, negotiates with the client, manages finances, provides marketing expertise, and helps develop new business for the College. The College offers indemnity protection to staff working with the Consultancy. For example, it supported a project that King's academics carried out for the UK Department of Trade and Industry on the evaluation of the UK corporate governance regulation. The results of this project were presented at the DTI Conference in January 2007 and subsequently published by the Department.

KCL Enterprises and IP Group

KCL has a partnership with the intellectual property (IP) investment company IP Group (formerly IP2IPO). IP Group's core business is the creation of value for its shareholders and partners through the commercialization of intellectual property originating from research-intensive institutions. When the Company was founded in 2001, it had a single university partnership (the University of Oxford). Today it has long-term partnerships with ten universities in total in the United Kingdom, including the Universities of Leeds, Bath, and Bristol and Queen Mary's College. As of 30 June 2006, forty-four portfolio companies had been created from these partnerships. IP Group has been highly successful in creating value for its shareholders and its partners to date. Eight of its portfolio companies have listed on the Alternative Investment Market and there has been one trade sale. In addition to this core activity of commercializing intellectual property with its partners, IP Group has three key subsidiaries – Top Technology Ventures, Modern Biosciences, and Modern Water.

Top Technology Ventures is a venture capital company that specializes in providing equity funding for UK-based early stage technology companies. *Modern Biosciences* is a specialist drug in-licensing and development company. Its objective is to operate as a channel between the life science academic research community within the United Kingdom and the pharmaceutical industry. *Modern Water* is a specialist water technologies company. Its objective is to establish and exploit a portfolio of water technologies to address the global problems of economic availability of fresh water and the treatment and disposal of wastewater. IP Group has developed a highly innovative business model based on long-term partnerships. Although all partnerships are tailored to the requirements of the university partner, IP Group offers the following benefits to its partners:

- Significant support for its partners' IP commercialization activities and, in particular, expertise in the identification of novel intellectual property with commercial potential.
- Seed capital finance for portfolio companies.
- Ongoing strategic and financial support for portfolio companies to maximize their chances of success.

4.   The commercialization and spin-off process

The early stages of formulating whether there is spin-off potential involve an organic process of assessing the opportunity and conducting IP due diligence. KCLE business development managers discuss the possibilities with academic scientists to assess their motivations and their other commitments. Whether an invention would be appropriately commercialized as a license agreement or a spin-off was usually considered to be very obvious. A central requirement was for the academic scientist to want to pursue a spin-off and to champion it. Surrogate entrepreneurs may only be used if the academic scientist is willing to be heavily involved in the spin-off. If the academic scientist is not interested in creating a spin-off, then the decision may be to license the technology. The breadth of the technology is also an important factor in the decision. Can it support a number of products or is it very narrowly focused? If it is narrow, then the technology is more likely to be licensed than to be used to create a spin-off.

If the invention is still very ill-defined, it may not be appropriate to create a company, because the technology is at a stage that is too early. KCL's proof-of-concept fund can be used to put money into a promising technology to see if it can be developed further, or to undertake commercial due diligence and market assessment. If there appears to be a prima facie case for a viable opportunity, expert advice from the IP Group is brought in to help develop the business plan. KCLE has a relationship with IP Group for the creation of spin-offs. A member of IP Group is seconded to KCLE. Following the development of a business plan, the proposal is presented to an investment panel, which involves two people from the IP Group and three from KCL (the Finance Director of KCL; the Head of KCLE; and the Vice-Principal for the research area from where the opportunity emerges). The involvement of the Vice-Principal is viewed as important in assessing how the opportunity fits with their overall strategy for the area.

KCLE uses standard agreements with scientists rather than having local school-based agreements. It has an investor reward scheme both for spin-offs and for licensing. This scheme is non-negotiable but is on a sliding scale. For licensing deals, the inventor receives all of the first £20,000 of revenue, which then decreases at higher levels of income. For spin-offs, a maximum of 40 percent of the equity is available to the academic, with 60 percent going to the College. The academic may negotiate a consultancy arrangement with the spin-off. There is no formal policy regarding the academic's involvement with the spin-off. The College provides for all academics to undertake up to thirty days per year involvement with the spin-off. However, there have been local school agreements to allow academics to spend more time with spin-offs.

KCLE seeks to identify a full management team at the time of the investment. It is emphasized that the CEO will not be an academic. However, the academic will be involved in the process of CEO recruitment. The relationship with IP Group enables suitable management to be identified through their in-house headhunters. Attempts are made to find managers with sector or niche experience. The quality of the management team, and the team generally, is considered as important as if not more important than the technology. Nevertheless, the technology has to be perceived to be robust enough to warrant creating a spin-off. The board typically only includes one founder, even though there may be a team of founders. KCLE have the right to have a College-nominated nonexecutive director on the board who will remain in post as long as he or she is perceived to be useful. The aim is to appoint external nonexecutive directors as soon as possible, either from KCLE's own network or from the IP Group's network.

KCLE incubates spin-offs on site using a distributed incubator model. Incubation involves provision of facilities, mentoring, scoping of technology, building the business plan, identifying the market, and identifying appropriate funding. The aim is to provide a tailored solution for each case. KCLE finds space for new ventures rather than having a dedicated high-profile space. Charges for space are near commercial rents, but there are no charges for mentoring and softer elements. Some of the softer elements are the more valuable. Finding space can be relatively simple, while academics can lack the nonlaboratory aspects of building a business.

Valuation of spin-offs introduces major challenges because of the specifics of the public sector context, which can create overvaluation at the initial stage, which leads in turn to difficulties in raising subsequent funding (Clarysse *et al.* 2007). With respect to valuing ventures at KCLE, there is a standard pre-agreement with IP Group. As spin-offs are very difficult to value at an early stage, this pre-agreement values all ventures at £0.5 million pre-money. This arrangement places importance on the equity split between the parties. In addition, there is an options pot amounting to around 10 percent of the equity. This element is mainly to incentivize nonexecutive directors who may enter the management team at a later date.

The TTO activity ceases to support the spin-off in terms of the right to have a KCL appointed nonexecutive director when the percentage of College ownership is diluted to a certain level. As more funds are invested and share dilution occurs, they no longer have the right to appoint a director.

5.   Spin-off activity

Since its inception in 1991, KCLE has created twenty-three spin-offs (Table 10.2). By the end of 2006, eighteen of these spin-offs were still active, two were in liquidation, and three were inactive. Total employment at the end of 2006 was 280 and total revenue for the year 2005/2006 was £8.1 million. In the 1990s, KCLE, on the average, created less than one spin-off per year. From 2000 onward, an average of 2.4 spin-offs per year have been created. Proxymogen, a spin-off company that was established by King's researchers in the neuroscience fields, achieved an IPO on the London Alternative Investment Market (AIM) in 2005, within 18 months of its creation. KCLE introduced good management and an experienced chairperson at the outset. The company had two applications for patents, but these had not been approved at the time of the IPO. Initially, the scientist who founded the company had not

Table 10.2: *King's College spin-off companies and staff start-ups*

Spin-offs	Date of incorporation	Still active or not on 01/01/2007	KCL own shares	Employees 05/06	Revenues £000s 05/06
Lidco Group Plc	31/10/1991	Yes	N	36	3,326
CeNes Pharmaceuticals Plc	03/07/1996	Yes	N	17	196
Oxford Biomedica Plc	20/09/1996	Yes	Y	69	800
Planet Biotechnology Inc.	1998	Yes	Y	10	490
MedPharm Ltd.	07/06/1999	Yes	Y	31	1,553
Insonify Ltd.	22/10/1999	In Liq	Y	0	0
Delta Dot Ltd.	13/03/2000	Yes	Y	25	220
ReNeuron (UK) Ltd.	28/09/2000	Yes	N	21	51
Qugen Therapeutics Pte Ltd.	29/11/2000	No	N	0	0
Lobal Technologies Ltd.	21/05/2001	No	N	0	0
Odontis Ltd.	31/05/2001	Yes	Y	0	0
Cerestem Ltd.	31/05/2001	No	N	0	0
Immune Regulation Ltd.	06/08/2001	Yes	Y	0	0
Brain Resource Company	28/08/2001	Yes	Y	40	741
Phytofusion Ltd.	20/03/2002	In Liq	Y	0	0
Viratis Ltd.	31/03/2003	Yes	Y	0	0
Proximagen Ltd.	26/11/2003	Yes	Y	19	606
Phonlogica Ltd.	26/02/2004	Yes	Y	1	0
Osspray Ltd.	04/02/2004	Yes	Y	2	0
IXICO Ltd.	15/12/2004	Yes	Y	9	99
Cerogenix Ltd.	14/09/2005	Yes	Y	0	0
Theragenetics	31/03/2006	Yes	Y	0	0
Simulstrat	27/07/2006	Yes	Y	0	0
Spin-off totals	23			280	8,081
		Staff start-ups			
Sensornet	14/07/1997	Yes	N	25	2200
Health Information Systems Ltd.	14/10/2002	Yes	N	8	500

considered a spin-off. Rather, the idea of the spin-off was suggested by the KCLE business development team. KCLE also discussed the idea with IP Group, who had expertise in this area. This also provided external validation for the project and helped to convince both the founder and KCLE that there was the basis for a successful company. The founder was motivated to create the spin-off as he saw it as an intellectual challenge rather than for personal gain. He also saw it as providing a legacy in terms of keeping his research team together in an applied way.

At the other end of the spectrum, KCLE have had a small number of problem cases that they have aimed to terminate because they have been resource-intensive with little possibility of any return. Hibernating a company may also not solve the problem. The general approach has been to persuade scientists that it would be more difficult to explain to peers that they had mothballed the company than to close it. They also remind the scientist of the fiduciary duties of directors. One notable problem case was the software company Insonify. While the company had good technology, it suffered because it failed to get the technology into the market quickly enough. Internal funding was initially provided by the University Challenge Fund (UCF). However, the company burnt too much in developing the technology rather than in developing it as a marketable product. A further problem was that the company did not have dedicated management, nor did it develop a suitable management team and identify a commercial partner. KCLE attempted to become involved in bringing focus to a product offering that would be attractive to customers. A major challenge was for KCLE to develop trust with the academics and to persuade them to change direction.

6.   Case study analysis

Founders and CEOs of three spin-off companies from Kings College were interviewed. These companies represent the whole spectrum of entrepreneurial firms, and they include a successful IPO (company A); a company in a run-up to the IPO (company B); and an early stage venture (company C). These interviews provided rich contextual data on the development of spin-offs that are at various stages of the firm's life cycle. The case analysis clearly indicates that young start-ups and IPO firms (generally known as "threshold" firms) have limited resource and knowledge bases that challenge their ability to survive. The transition across the stages of a venture's organizational life cycle (OLC) is seldom easy because the technological, administrative, and organizational resources that have enabled start-ups to survive become increasingly inadequate to meet the challenges of the next phase. Consequently, threshold companies must develop new capabilities as they hone and exploit their existing ones. They also have to develop effective corporate governance and control systems that make sure that the firm's resources and capabilities are managed in an effective and efficient manner. They also need to learn how to achieve a balance between growing the top line (e.g., product development, sales) and managing the bottom line (cost control, cash-flow etc.). The TTO played a critical role in helping fledging companies to define and defend intellectual property by providing legal support and introducing them to an accounting firm. More importantly, at later stages, it also helped to establish links with venture capitalists and develop an effective management team. A case study of Company A illustrates these issues.

Company A (interview with a founding director)

"When the company was set up we did not have a product, we were just a services company and lived off the profit from those services. Once the company had been formed the cost of those services doubled and we lost some of our competitiveness. Now we have £13 million in the bank we can spend some money on development programs and use the profit from services to pay our salaries. We now have an in-house financial controller who keeps control of our finances in conjunction with the chairman and CEO. When the company was formed I felt that it was all chiefs and no Indians and we needed Indians to get the work done. The work could not be done by academic staff and I had to make this point repeatedly to the chiefs. We also have external accountants and auditors as well. I now (post-IPO) feel that there is a good balance between cash burn and product development but we have had to appoint more chiefs – a project manager and a head of chemistry. Everyone is on a steep learning curve – the management team who had little understanding of small company biotech research, and the academic staff who had little commercial experience."

Stringent financial controls also need to be introduced at very early stages of a firm's life cycle. The TTO team is very aware of this problem, and it also tries to raise this awareness among the academics. The following case study illustrates this point.

Company B (interview with CEO)

"We started off running accounts like a corner-shop – by cash flow. What we do now is have a budget to work with. We have management accounts every month which is very important. We have a part-time financial controller which has been a cheap option (they can do what they need to do in one day without interfering with company business) but one that helps us to understand the business better. We did use an external accountant but the figures he returned every month meant nothing to me as he did not understand the business."

These cases also indicate that it is vital that the "threshold firm" have flexible and timely access to external resources that may fuel its chosen growth strategy or allow strategic adjustments by reverting to one or more other feasible options. Some founders can confuse their needs with those of the organization, failing to set boundaries on how they use resources. Afraid of failure, some founders may not invest sufficiently in new activities, risking the future of their organizations. Some founders may have difficulty in sharing information about firm resources and their uses with other stakeholders, depriving themselves of beneficial feedback that could improve resource use and company performance. Some of them do not recognize the potential value of good governance practices, such as presence of independent directors on the board, as Company B illustrates.

Company B (interview with CEO)

"We understand what corporate governance is so we have committees who look at certain things, e.g. health and safety and remuneration. These are not high on our list of priorities but have become more important. They are not adding value to the company; it is just a way of being seen to be acting in a proper manner, being see to be acting as a company."

Aware of these challenges, the TTO and external resource providers demand increased managerial accountability, which is often achieved by developing formal effective governance systems. A firm's governance system, per se, may not be a source of sustained competitive advantage. However, some firms are much more skilled at developing and using governance devices in ways that give them advantages over their rivals. Case analysis shows that these organizational skills may be heterogeneously distributed across spin-off firms. Implementing the appropriate governance system in a given situation may help threshold firms to realize the benefits of the resources they control through incentivizing and/or monitoring management to undertake those actions that give the firm a competitive advantage and create value for shareholders. Selecting the right mix of directors with unique and useful skills or connections can also improve the firm's competitive advantage. Knowing how to organize the board and ensure effective decision-making processes is another source of advantage. Thus, governance choices may impact both the creation of rents from the use of valuable, rare, costly to imitate, and nonsubstitutable resources and experiences among directors, and their appropriation.

Without an effective governance system, threshold firm managers may appropriate a disproportionate share of the rents that their company generates for themselves. Similarly, boards may be more effective when skilled directors have been recruited to help a firm fully realize its potential for generating economic rents, rather than the appointment of the CEO's cronies or outside directors to minimize agency conflicts between a firm and its shareholders. This suggests that there may be important differences between the structure and functioning of a board designed to minimize agency costs and another board designed to maximize a firm's rent-generating potential. The TTO normally appoints a nonexecutive director on the company's board whose role is to help academics to develop effective management and control systems, but also to make sure that the interests and objectives of King's College are met. Company C's case study illustrates these points, addressing how a company deals with gaps in the management skills and systems required to manage growth.

Company C (interview with CEO)

"We have had a shortage of certain skills/individuals. We have tried to solider on without them and then realised that we needed them. Commercial experience is vitally important, business development is also vitally important. Initially we could not afford business development but it is very important. There are ways of getting them earlier – part-time, share options etc. I would prefer to get in commercial technical people rather than rely on academics to develop strategic plans. It is important to get commercially aware people in but we have problems with the cost of that and also with getting those people to join."

The development of an entrepreneurial firm usually creates a need for different forms and functions of corporate governance. Thus, it is essential to view corporate governance as a dynamic system that may change as firms evolve over the course of their OLC. This evolution is usually accompanied by changes in the ownership structure, board composition, the degree of the founders' involvement, etc. The balance of the shareholder value protection and wealth creation roles of the governance system may change over the OLC. For example, the role boards play in obtaining and using knowledge to create value may be more important in threshold firms than in established firms competing in more mature markets. In addition, early stage equity investors may have significant impacts on the development of corporate governance in their portfolio firms, as the following case clearly illustrates.

Company A (interview with a founding director)

"Never let an academic be in charge of a company – they have no business experience – get an external CEO to be in charge. Academics know how to burn money but not conserve it. Venture capitalists were heavily involved in finding a CEO and chairman. They were also the ones who said we needed a financial controller who knew all the regulations for an IPO. We now have development plans in place after the IPO. Before that we made it up as we went along, it was dream machine type of stuff."

Boards that have directors serving on other companies' boards are usually well positioned to gain access to financial and other resources as well as valuable information about pending industry and market changes. These directors might help managers identify promising opportunities and explore how to best exploit them. The case study analysis illustrates a number of important points associated with the development of effective management teams and internal controls in university spin-off firms. It also provides evidence of the importance of the TTO in terms of developing effective governance mechanisms in young start-ups. By appointing a nonexecutive director and helping to establish links with potential executive managers and venture capitalists, the TTO plays a crucial role in terms of an early "professionalization" of an entrepreneurial firm.

7.   Innovation environment

Key sectors

KCL has focused on sectors that are central to the economy of London and southeast England, where it has built links and established partnerships. These are culture and media; financial services; IT and communications; pharmaceutical and health care; and environmental services.

Venture capital

Raising venture capital for university spin-offs raises major problems (Wright et al. 2006). In the United Kingdom, a venture capital sector developed from the late 1970s. Being based in London, KCLE has, in principle, access to a wide array of venture capital firms. However, few venture capital firms in the United Kingdom are willing to support seed stage projects. Rather, the greater emphasis of the UK venture capital market has been on later stage and management buy-out investments. Evidence from the early 1990s suggested that new high-tech firms had to meet more rigorous selection criteria than equivalent nontechnology projects. While there had been some improvement by the late 1990s, the problem still persisted (Lockett et al. 2002). Access to business angel funding has been problematical as, perhaps surprisingly, there are few financiers of this type in London. The Osspray spin-off has business angel funding, but this was not obtained at the outset.

Researchers and commercialization

UK academics are directly employed by the universities to which they are attached. They can create companies and hold equity stakes in those companies. In recent years, UK universities have devoted greater attention to asserting their rights to the ownership of IP. The provisions of the UK Patent Act 1997 state that inventions of employees who may reasonably be expected to make inventions are clearly owned by their employers, so long as this is stated in an employment contract. However, there is no formal requirement to disclose inventions. Universities are able to adopt different approaches to negotiating the relative equity stakes held by themselves and the academic.

Although the academic labor market in the United Kingdom is more flexible than in many other countries, technology transfer may still create its own tensions for university management. A particular concern is the extent to which involvement with commercial projects such as spin-off companies is valued in terms of the promotion system. In the United Kingdom, the focus of academic tenure and promotion decisions has historically been on the basis of publication (and citation) records and research funding. Similarly, the academic labor market is more fluid in terms of mobility, with academic faculty competing for posts on an individual basis.

In the United Kingdom, 167 public organizations have university status (there are 3 additional private universities). We examine government policy toward the support of academic entrepreneurship in these organizations in terms of research funding; the stimulation of entrepreneurship education, training, and support; and funding for spin-offs.

Research funding

Financing for research in public universities is funded by seven discipline-based autonomous state-funded research councils that are part of the Office for Science and Technology and the Higher Education Funding Councils (HEFCs), which finance the main operating costs of universities. The allocation of the Higher Education Funding Council for England (HEFCE) money is influenced by the (approximately) five-yearly Research Excellence Framework (REF), under which a range of discipline-based panels of peers rates the research of each university department. Falling HEFCE funding for research universities has contributed to increased fundraising from the commercial sector. In addition, major foundations and other charities finance research, in particular in the medical field.

UK policy is characterized by a systematic process involving a number of initiatives designed to increase the capability of universities to respond to the needs of business, public services, and the wider community, and to transfer knowledge. These initiatives aim to fill both the knowledge gap and the financial gap, the former by providing training and facilitating links with business and the latter by providing funding for the first stage of research commercialization.

Stimulation of entrepreneurship education, training, and support

The Science Enterprise Challenge (SEC) was launched in 1999 with the aim of establishing a network of centers in UK universities, focusing on the teaching of enterprise and entrepreneurship to science and technology students, and of encouraging the growth of new businesses by supporting start-ups, including spin-off companies based on innovative ideas developed by students and faculty within the universities. The £28.9 million SEC resulted in the creation of thirteen Science Enterprise Centres involving over sixty UK universities and higher education institutes. The majority of the Science Enterprise Centres are collaborative (three exceptions are Cambridge University, Imperial College, and Oxford University). As noted earlier, KCLE is part of the Science Enterprise Centre Simfonec, which covers four institutions, Royal Veterinary College, Queen Mary's College, City University, and King's College. The Science Enterprise Centre has a core task of entrepreneurship education. This includes running courses for academics who are or who may become company directors. These centers are essentially engaged in promoting the exploitation of IP by licensing or spin-off formation and in introducing enterprise into the curriculum. With the Science Enterprise Centres, enterprise modules are embedded in the curricula of a substantial number of science and engineering students.

The HEIF builds on the stream of funding initiated by the Higher Education Reach-out to Business and the Community fund (HEROBC). Funds are awarded to support universities and colleges in increasing their capability to respond to the needs of business, public services and the wider community, and to transfer knowledge. The HEIF focuses on encouraging proposals across the spectrum of academic activities, including the establishment and strengthening of industrial liaison offices, internal promotion of commercialization, IP expertise, incubation support, business advice, and mentoring.

Some 136 bids were submitted in July 2001 for funding up to August 2004, 89 awards were made, and a total of £80m was provided to English higher education institutions over the period 2001–2004. A second round of HEIF (HEIF 2) was allocated for the period 2004–2006, which aimed to address a key concern of the Lambert Review (2003) in relation to the need to develop technology transfer on a regional basis and to improve the recruitment and training of technology transfer staff. HEIF 2 also attempts to consolidate the Science Enterprise Challenge and University Challenge initiatives. HEIF 3 has also been launched, with up to £238 million available for the period from August 2006 to July 2008. A key element in the initiative is to allocate funds on a formula basis in order to make HEIF funding more stable and predictable. In addition, public sector research establishments that are not universities receive similar government funding through the Public Sector Research Exploitation Fund (PSRE).

Funding of university spin-offs

The UCF aims to increase the availability of early stage funding for universities. Universities that are successful in bidding for such funds establish their own seed funds with the help of University Challenge money. The seed funds are to enable academics to scope out the commercial potential of research outcomes and take the first steps toward commercializing the research. The UCF was launched in March 1998 as a £45 million seed capital fund with the government contributing £25 million and additional amounts provided by the Wellcome Trust (£18 million) and the Gatsby Charitable Foundation (£2 million). In October 2001, a further £15 million was provided. Universities were required to contribute a minimum of 25 percent of total fund value. The maximum total investment in any one project was restricted to £250,000. Funding was apportioned to fifteen successful bids in the first round, and a further five in the second one. These funds are associated with different universities (involving between two and six universities), except Imperial College and Oxford University. As noted earlier, KCLE is involved in two UCFs. KCLE is of the view that there is a need for a mixed funding approach. While it has access to UCFs, it also seeks to get real venture capital firms involved early on to emphasize the need to be business-oriented. Overall, the link with the IP Group is seen as providing a mechanism that enables funding structures to be kept simple at the start. The intention is then to develop the spin-off as fast as possible in order to obtain the upside gain, at which point the IP Group exits, to be replaced by other venture capital firms.

8.   Conclusion

This chapter has examined the case of Kings College London, one of the leading research universities in the United Kingdom. Our analysis has shown that the academic entrepreneurship activities of KCL are an integral part of the College's longer-term strategy and that there is clear university-level support for academic entrepreneurship activities. The academic entrepreneurship activities are focused on creating and developing spin-offs that have growth and wealth-creating prospects, which is feasible, given the world-class research in certain areas of the College. Given the spread of activities suitable for academic entrepreneurship and the different demands of these activities, the TTO support is distinguished by disciplinary area.

The innovation environment in the United Kingdom has provided financial and training support for academic entrepreneurship activities, which helps to alleviate the shortcomings of the private sector venture capital and business angel markets for very early stage projects. The College has developed important alliances and networks to help stimulate academic entrepreneurship and other aspects of knowledge transfer. Notably, alliances have been developed with companies in the pharmaceutical, biotechnology, and medical devices industries. A further dimension of alliances is the key partnership with the IP Group, which provides both finance and expertise to create and develop spin-offs. This collaboration has been successful in terms of enabling a number of spin-offs to be sold or floated on a stock market for significant capital gains.

References

Clarysse, B., Wright, M., Lockett, A., and Mustar, P. 2007. Academic spin-offs, formal technology transfer and capital raising. *Industrial and Corporate Change*. 16: 609–640.

Lockett, A., Murray, G., and Wright, M. 2002. Do UK venture capitalists still have a bias against investment in new technology firms. *Research Policy*. 31: 1009–1030.

Siegel, D., Veugeulers, R., and Wright, M. 2007. Commercialization of university intellectual property: A review of the literature and policy implications. *Oxford Review of Economic Policy*. 23: 640–660.

Wright, M., Lockett, A., Clarysse, B., and Binks, M. 2006. University spin-off companies and venture capital. *Research Policy*. 35(4): 481–501.

Wright, M., Clarysse, B., Mustar, P., and Lockett, A. 2007. *Academic Entrepreneurship in Europe*. Cheltenham: Edward Elgar.

11   KU Leuven: Complementing inception dynamics with incubation practices

Petra Andries, Bart Van Looy, and Koenraad Debackere

While basic research results can be channeled to industry via collaborative research schemes or licensing arrangements for patented university inventions, spinning off is the entrepreneurial route toward commercializing public research. The latter attracts a great deal of policy attention in the current wave of start-ups and new venture creation in many countries. The spin-off formation rate is often seen as a key indicator for the quality of industry–science links (OECD 2001). Within this chapter, we highlight insights obtained from experiences built up at KU Leuven with respect to the genesis and development of knowledge-intensive spin-off companies. We first focus on the context in which these insights have originated. After a short profile of KU Leuven, we highlight some key elements that contribute to the genesis of academic spin-offs. In a next step, we address the development trajectories of academic spin-offs, companies that often operate at scientific and technical frontiers. We accentuate adaptation as a phenomenon that is critical to the survival and growth of such ventures. Following this observation, we turn our attention to different modes of adaptation and we advance the notion of "simultaneous experimentation" as highly relevant during the first phases of these ventures. We argue that university incubators can influence the likelihood of survival and growth of their spin-offs through a careful and structured process of coaching, experimentation, and adaptation. This requires not only the presence of appropriate financial resources, but also the development of a subtle monitoring competence that stimulates entrepreneurs to experiment.

The genesis of spin-offs at KU Leuven

Founded in 1425, KU Leuven is the oldest and largest university in Flanders and Belgium, encompassing all academic disciplines. It has the legal status of a private institution, but receives 85 percent of its funding from the Belgian government, both in a direct and in an indirect competitive way. More than 1,450 tenured professors and 4,500 researchers are currently employed at KU Leuven, dealing with a student population of over 35,000 each year. KU Leuven's research efforts and output have increased considerably over the past decade, both quantitatively and qualitatively, thus positioning the institution at the productive end of European universities. It recorded a total of 4,673 publications in international peer-reviewed ISI-recorded scientific journals (Science Citation Index) in 2011. Over 15 percent of these publications were in journals with an impact factor in excess of four. The following domains are specific areas of excellence: biotechnology, electronics and mechanical engineering, environment, food sciences and technology, medicine and medical research, European integration, and materials sciences and technology. The spearhead expertise of the university's researchers can be seen as an important cornerstone for successful entrepreneurial activities (see in this respect also O'Shea et al. 2005).

The mission statement of KU Leuven stresses three basic activities. The university ensures the transfer of knowledge from generation to generation through its teaching activities, it performs fundamental research, and it provides services to the community by making its inventions and knowledge available to society and to companies. "As a university, it is an academic institution where research and knowledge transfer are both essential and complementary" (KU Leuven, Mission Statement, 2002). The research and knowledge transfer missions have been promoted and supported by two specialized units. The Research Coordination Office deals with basic research: designing the basic science policy of the university, allocating intrauniversity research funding, and research evaluation. The technology transfer mission deals with contract research, patents, spin-offs, and research parks and is organized via KU Leuven Research and Development (LRD). The total research expenditures of KU Leuven amounted to €345 million in 2011, of which 29 percent (€ 100 million) was derived via KU Leuven Research and Development (LRD). Of this total research budget, 45 percent supports research in exact sciences, 35 percent in biomedical sciences, and 20 percent in humanities and social sciences.

LRD was founded in 1972 to manage the industry component of the university's R&D portfolio. What started as a minor fraction of the total university R&D activity has, over the past 40 years, grown into a significant portion of the university's total R&D portfolio employing eighty-five support staff professionals. It has evolved from a specialized division toward a matrix structure, operating via a number of specialized supporting services that are closely integrated with the activities of research groups. In line with Roberts's (1991) and Thurow's (2000) insights on wealth creation through technology entrepreneurship, LRD has stimulated the exploitation of the university's research through a rich mix of mechanisms favoring entrepreneurial behavior within its many research divisions.

The fact that LRD has a history of 40 years is not unimportant. This "long" history implies that, by now, several generations of faculty and researchers have developed and built their careers alongside the presence of – and often based on – active interaction with LRD. As a consequence, the contextual impact of the historic embeddedness of LRD within the university is not to be underestimated. This historic presence is perhaps the single most important learning effect that has occurred within the university as to academic involvement in the processes of knowledge transfer for industrial and entrepreneurial innovation. It has enabled several generations of faculty and staff to become acquainted with industrial innovation, to understand its strengths and weaknesses, and to enact the benefits of academic entrepreneurship as a complement to the more traditional and established processes of industrial innovation. Hence, time and history are an integral part of the context that enables LRD to leverage the management and transfer of academic R&D at KU Leuven.

From its start onward, LRD has received a large amount of budgetary and human resource management autonomy within the university. This implies that LRD, although fully integrated into the university, manages its own budgets as well as the research personnel employed on those budgets. From an incentive point of view, creating a context with such high levels of budgetary and human resource autonomy is critical, since it allows flexibility and degrees of freedom to operate that are often lacking within the traditional university administration. It allows research groups to actively manage their laboratory space and infrastructure. To ensure this autonomy, LRD introduced the organizational concept of the research division. Researchers belonging to different departments at the university, even belonging to different faculties, can decide to join forces and to integrate the commercial–industrial component of their knowledge portfolio into a research division at LRD. As a consequence, the research division concept introduces a de facto interdisciplinary matrix structure within the university. Today, 55 divisions exist, supported by about 500 faculty members and employing about 1,600 researchers and support staff, scattered across the various faculties and departments of the university. It is obvious that not all faculties are equally represented and involved. The majority of LRD activities stems from divisions belonging to the engineering (54 percent), the biomedical (24 percent), the biosciences (9 percent), and the sciences (7 percent) faculty. The humanities and social sciences are less present, although their activities via LRD have been increasing over the last five-year period. LRD divisions enjoy complete autonomy when it comes to balancing revenue and expenses from their entrepreneurial activities. In other words, LRD divisions are entitled to accumulate financial reserves based on the benefits they generate through engaging in contract research. This is quite a unique situation, as most universities tend to centralize such profits. The decentralized modus operandi that exists within LRD therefore acts as an incentive mechanism in and of itself. LRD divisions, furthermore, are entitled to participate both intellectually and financially in the spin-off companies that they have grown and developed.

Besides the financial incentive mechanism at the level of the research division, incentives are given to individual researchers as well. Three types of incentive mechanisms exist at the individual level. First of all, researchers are entitled to salary supplements based on the net proceeds from their contract research and consultancy activities. Second, in case of lump sum and royalty payments proceeding from licensing agreements, individual researchers are entitled to receive up to 30 percent of the income generated (after expenses have been recuperated). Third, in case of spin-off creation, individual researchers can receive up to 40 percent of the intellectual property shares (i.e., the IP stock or founder shares) in exchange for the input of their know-how and goodwill. If they wish, they can also invest financially in the spin-off and will hence obtain a pro rata share in the common stock (capital shares) of the company. Finally, to ensure close contacts between LRD and the research groups, a group of innovation coordinators is established. The innovation coordinators are paid by LRD on a part-time basis (on average 20 percent of their salary) to act as a permanent liaison officer between LRD and its divisions. The rest of their time is spent as a researcher or junior faculty member within one of the LRD divisions.

This system thus implies that the university has created a matrix structure: research excellence prevails along the hierarchical lines of the faculties and their respective departments, whereas excellence in entrepreneurial and industrial innovation is rewarded along the lines of the LRD divisions. This structure, allowing for sufficient degrees of coordination between academic research and innovation, and guaranteeing sufficient autonomy to the faculty and staff engaged in entrepreneurial and industrial innovation activities, is the basis of the university's approach toward managing academic science and technology for commercial exploitation. In addition, the dual incentive mechanism can be seen as being at the core of a management process that enables the university to maintain a balance and a healthy tension between striving for scientific excellence on the one hand, and translating this excellence toward application and innovation on the other hand.

The activity profile of LRD and the genesis of spin-offs

A distinct feature of LRD is the broad scope of its activity portfolio. Over time, LRD has developed three major activity poles that underpin its role in managing academic R&D as a business. Within its matrix structure, these central activities are contract drafting and negotiations, intellectual property management, and business plan development. The first, and historically the oldest one, is the contract research pole. Over the years, LRD has grown to provide over a quarter of the university's R&D budget via contract research and strategic research activities. Through the constant development of activities within the research divisions, the contract research activities have now reached significant levels both in terms of the volume and in terms of the quality of the work performed. LRD developed and implemented the necessary processes for financial and personnel management supporting these activities. Also, the legal and intellectual property mechanisms that should underpin these activities are in place.

The second activity pole consists of managing the university's intellectual property portfolio. This activity was first formally started in 1999 (although it existed organically well before that date), with the creation of an internal intellectual property liaison office and the establishment of a network of formal collaborations with different European patent attorneys. Internal procedures and the necessary information infrastructure were created to support this activity. Finally, a patent fund was established to help research groups cover the initial costs and expenses related to their patenting needs. At the end of 2011, there was an active portfolio of 496 patent families (including both granted patents and pending applications). Given the differences between the nature and aims of academic versus industrial patent portfolios, the first criterion deployed by LRD in generating and developing the university's knowledge portfolio is "selectivity." The interest is not so much in generating a large portfolio of patents as in developing a portfolio of valuable patents. A full-time in-house staff of eight IP professionals (the majority holding Ph.D. degrees), complemented by long-term collaborations with major patent attorneys, supports this activity.

The third activity pole concerns the transfer of knowledge via the creation of spin-off companies. Notice that this activity pole is often building on the previous ones. Indeed, activities within the research divisions are often instrumental in discovering the market potential for newly developed knowledge and technology, while the development and presence of intellectual property can be an important element in the foundation process of spin-off companies.

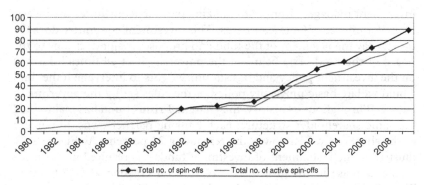

Figure 11.1: Cumulative number of spin-offs created.

In Figure 11.1 we provide an overview of the evolution of the university's spin-off portfolio. One notices a steady and at the same time modest growth during the eighties. In the nineties the adoption of legislative framework conditions in Flanders (1991; 1995) contributed to the further development of these activities. While the decree of 1991 explicated the triple mission of universities, the decree of 1995 determined the criteria that need to be fulfilled before a university can invest in spin-offs. Financial participation is only possible if the spin-off company exploits research results originating out of academic research – possibly in conjunction with other intangibles. The university can accept shares in exchange for these intangibles, but it can never own the majority of the voting rights. The university is further entitled to participate in specialized venture funds that are created to support this financial participation.

Following the development of these framework conditions, KU Leuven explicitly adopted a further strategic stance toward spin-off creation. In 1997, the university created its own seed capital fund in partnership with two major Belgian banks, the Gemma Frisius–Fund. This Fund has access to €12.5 million in seed capital to fund start-up companies that exploit university-based know-how. By the end of 2001, Gemma Frisius had invested €8.8 million in 15 spin-off companies. In July 2002, Gemma Frisius II was created with the same partners, pursuing opportunities similar to those pursued by its predecessor fund and operating according to the same investment policies and principles. Both funds initially were 10-year closed-end funds operating according to standard venture capital market principles. In 2009, it was decided to merge the two funds and turn them into a new evergreen fund. Notice that the fund management is no separate legal entity (investment company), as LRD together with two investment managers from both banking partners constitutes the investment committee of Gemma Frisius. This investment committee does the day-to-day management of the fund and proposes major decisions to the board of the fund. The board of the university is at all times informed on the investment policy and has statutory rights to intervene if the fund would violate basic university policy or the rules set by the government decree. Throughout its history, the Gemma Frisius Fund has maintained the same shareholder structure: each banking partner owns 40 percent of the shares, and LRD owns the remaining 20 percent. As Figure 11.1 illustrates, the installment of investment funds has resulted in a considerable increase in the growth rate of spin off creation at KU Leuven. This observation substantiates the initial rationale behind the creation of the fund: founding decisions have been largely inspired by the absence of local venture capital willing to invest in companies operating close to scientific and technological frontiers. Indeed, as will become apparent in the second section of this chapter, such academic spin-offs often find themselves operating within emerging industries. Given the high levels of uncertainty and unpredictability these ventures are confronted with, specific incubation processes seem to be essential to maximize their chances of survival (and consequent growth). Traditional investment companies – at least in Western European countries – tend to avoid such early stage investments and/or are less eager to become involved in incubation phases characterized by unpredictability, experimentation, and change.

To further assist the start-up entrepreneur, LRD also has access to an "Innovation & Incubation Center" that is jointly owned and operated by the university and the local regional development agency. Accommodation and managerial support for its spin-offs is provided through this center, which is located on the campus and as such promotes close proximity with university laboratories and research units. In addition, two science parks that are open to new innovative companies are present in the close vicinity of the KU Leuven. These parks house not only spin-offs of the university and other research institutions, but also R&D departments of existing companies. A third science park is still available for development, in close collaboration with the city of Leuven and the Economic Development Agency of the province.

By the end of 2012, the university had generated 103 spin-off companies, with a portfolio of 90 spin-off companies still active today. They are distributed across a wide variety of knowledge domains, ranging from mechanical and electrical engineering to bio- and life-sciences. Their product markets are as diverse as automotive, Internet security, three-dimensional modeling, rapid prototyping, stress management, and tissue engineering. When the structure of the present spin-off "deal-flow" is taken into account, it is expected to result in a steady state of three to six new spin-off creations per year for the coming five years at least. Comparing these figures on an international scale (Van Looy *et al.* 2011) clearly indicates that KU Leuven is performing above the European average in terms of spin-off creation, suggesting the adequacy of the installed incentive mechanisms and accompanying support infrastructure.

As became apparent, this relative success is driven by a multitude of enabling ingredients; scientific eminence embedded within a dual organizational setting which enables decentralized entrepreneurial initiative, and a strategic commitment at the top of the university complemented by a professional support infrastructure. At the same time, only about 10 percent of the established spin-off companies at KU Leuven have failed so far. While this could be interpreted as a spin-off formation process of too prudent a nature, the specific nature of the incubation processes deployed by LRD has undoubtedly contributed to this situation. This governance process is characterized by combining a "long view" perspective on the development process of knowledge intensive ventures with the notion of simultaneous experimentation. In the next section, we elaborate on this incubation process and we will argue that such incubation processes are essential for the governance of university spin-offs.

Governing development trajectories of spin-offs: Adaptive incubation as simultaneous experimentation

Although significant research efforts have been devoted to measuring technology entrepreneurship and to addressing the (market) conditions under which spin-off activity is the more appropriate transfer mechanism (e.g. Teece 1986; Torrisi 1998; Zucker *et al.* 1998; Arora *et al.* 2001; Klepper 2001; Shane 2002; Bartelsman *et al.* 2003; Gans and Stern 2003), these studies have not been very successful in developing a detailed understanding of the growth of technology-based new firms (Autio 2000). In addition, few studies have explicitly compared spin-offs to other start-ups, and within the spin-off population, university-based spin-offs to other types (e.g., Franco and Filston 2000; Klepper and Sleeper 2000; Nerkar and Shane 2003). New technology ventures originating at universities imply a bridging function between curiosity-driven academic research activities, on one hand, and strategy-driven corporate research, on the other. These new ventures have the potential to introduce technological disequilibria that change the rules of competition in existing industries. They allow for a multitude of experiments with often-competing "dominant designs" and "business models," only a few of which will ultimately survive. Hence, new ventures are the gene pool from which new industries may emerge in the longer run (Roberts 1991; Utterback 1994; Thurow 2000). Academic entrepreneurship in biotechnology is probably the most striking example when it comes to describing these phenomena. However, by challenging dominant designs, university-based spin-offs are in fact operating under emerging, and to a large extent unpredictable circumstances. Survival rates in such emerging sectors are extremely low (Abernathy and Utterback 1975). The question is whether university incubators could, besides spurring spin-off creation, also influence the likelihood of survival and growth of their spin-offs.

Adaptation and the survival of start-ups

One of the most pertinent questions in the field of entrepreneurship research, as suggested by Venkataraman (1997, p. 121), is "why, when and how some [entrepreneurial companies] are able to discover and exploit opportunities while others cannot or do not." Various authors have put forward that it is not the clairvoyance of the entrepreneur that determines this ability. There exists evidence that most initial selections of business models by new ventures have to be abandoned later on and that minor or major adaptations to the initial business model are inevitable. Pitt and Kannemeyer (2000) question whether many entrepreneurs are able to define the business concept correctly from the outset. To para- phrase Stoica and Schindehutte (1999: p. 1): "only in a minority of cases do entrepreneurs succeed because they define their concept correctly from the beginning, and rarely do they immediately achieve a good fit between the available opportunity and their approach to the business concept." Or as Peter Drucker (1985: p. 189) has noted, "When a new venture does succeed, more often than not it is in a market other than the one it was originally intended to serve, with products and services not quite those with which it had set out, bought in large part by cus- tomers it did not even think of when it started, and used for a host of purposes besides the ones for which the products were first designed." Existing research data confirm this. Brokaw (1991), in her update of the twenty-seven ventures that were profiled in *Inc.*'s "Anatomy of a Start- Up" series between the period of 1988 and 1990, found that by 1991, a large fraction of the surviving ventures had adapted their initial busi- ness models: "What has made or broken many of the companies we've watched . . . is . . . the ability (or inability) to recognize and react to the completely unpredictable . . . To be flexible, and not just in response to small surprises but to really big ones – like discovering you're selling to the wrong customers or selling through entirely wrong channels. Some companies even find they have to revamp from top to bottom in order to survive. They discover they're in the wrong business" (Brokaw 1991: p. 54). It thus appears that the "appropriateness" of a venture's business model determines its success, that defining an appropriate business model from the beginning is difficult, and that adaptation of the initial business model is therefore inevitable.

Technology-based businesses operating at the frontiers of science and technology will in particular have to cope with high degrees of newness (Shane and Stuart 2002). Not only is the nature and the outcome of the technical activities inherently unpredictable (Steensma *et al.* 2000), but also the market selection and commercialization processes themselves are "under development," which poses additional problems of uncertainty and ambiguity (Utterback 1987; Chesbrough and Rosenbloom 2002). Stated otherwise, in emergent markets, technological options are at best marginally understood, distribution channels and sources of supply are problematic, market needs are not clearly defined, and hence, market viability cannot be proven a priori (see Abernathy and Utterback 1975; Eisenhardt and Schoonhoven 1990; Teubal *et al.* 1991). As a consequence, ventures operating within emergent industries more often than not cannot foresee the set of all feasible business models in advance, necessitating changes to the business model over time (Andries and Debackere 2007; Gruber *et al.* 2008). And while, in general, high levels of uncertainty are known to require adaptive organizational processes (Burns and Stalker 1961; Timmons *et al.* 1990), a more profound understanding of the nature of such adaptive organizational processes within entrepreneurial ventures seems relevant for delineating appropriate governance processes, an issue we will discuss within the next section.

Modes of business model adaptation

Through case study analysis (Andries *et al.* 2013), we looked at how ventures in emerging industries develop their business models. These findings revealed the presence of two different development processes. First, we find that some ventures commit very early to one specific business model. Even though they acknowledge that the viability of this business model is uncertain, they focus on its development, thereby hoping to realize first mover advantages and to mobilize stakeholders, among which investors figure prominently. If, afterward, initial assumptions on which the choice of the particular business model was based turn out to be too optimistic or incorrect, adaptation efforts of a more radical nature become necessary. Significant efforts and investments will be needed to change the mindsets of all stakeholders and to dispose of organizational structures, ideas, and competences that have become obsolete for the development of the new business model. This may imply restructuring and laying off personnel. Moreover, it can be noticed that persuading investors to invest additionally in radical reconfigurations is often difficult, since investors might doubt whether the initial business model was wrong or whether it was poorly executed (Bhidé 1992).

Second, within some other ventures analyzed, uncertainty is not only recognized but also explicitly translated in the initial business plan and in the ventures' approach to business model development. These ventures do not commit early to one specific business model, but instead they actively experiment with various business models simultaneously. The development of a portfolio of activities can be seen as a way to spread risk and to learn about a broad range of potential business models. As a consequence, ventures enacting uncertainty opt for a project-based organization, and uncertainty is reduced with respect to a range of business models. This uncertainty reduction allows gradually narrowing down the range of options until a viable business model is found. Table 11.1 summarizes the key characteristics of both development processes.

If one accepts the presence of unpredictability as an inherent part of the life of ventures operating at scientific and technical frontiers, the simultaneous experimentation model presents itself as more relevant. However, it should be noted that the development of a portfolio of experiments is not straightforward from a resource perspective. Whereas portfolio approaches are relatively easy to deploy in R&D environments of large companies, the entrepreneurial nature of the ventures poses the challenge of reconciling liabilities of smallness with the resource implications of pursuing the exploration of a range of options. Stated otherwise, the question of which of the two models would be the more preferred becomes crucial.

Choosing between the two models

Within the first model, ventures bracket uncertainty and commit early to one specific business model. They – as well as potential investors – see this as most appropriate for obtaining a first-mover advantage. They hope or believe that it will allow the venture to achieve growth as fast as possible. Bracketing uncertainty by choosing one specific business model implies putting in place an organizational configuration aimed at the development of this business model. By developing the chosen business model, uncertainty pertaining to the underlying assumptions is reduced. This process can yield different outcomes ranging from full confirmation of initial assumptions to the complete opposite. In the latter case, change or adjustment of the business model becomes inevitable

Table 11.1: *Models of business model adaptation*

	Focused commitment	Simultaneous experimentation
Initial variety	• Commitment to one business model during the initial phase of the venture	• Multiple business models experiments conducted in parallel during the initial phase of the venture • Although experiments are related to other experiments in the portfolio, the overall portfolio displays a wide variety
Rationale	• Promise of achieving learning effects and first-mover advantages • Clarity of business model results in increased mobilizing power (toward investors and other stakeholders)	• Seen as a way to learn about a wide variety of business models and hence to address uncertainty • Learning about one option can also reduce uncertainty about other business models in the portfolio
Implications	• Implies the development of dedicated campaigns and of a specialized organizational structure, resulting in considerable expenditures • When assumptions do not become reality, change will be of a radical nature • External investors are convinced by focused business model • External investors are unwilling to finance radical change when business model turns out to be unviable	• Uncertainty reduction facilitates gradually narrowing down the range of experiments until a viable business model is found • Implies the development of a project-based organization, which becomes more elaborated and structured as the portfolio is gradually narrowed down • Implies the use of low-cost probing strategies, inclusion of business models with short-term cash-generating potential, and resource spillovers between different business models • External investors are convinced of the usefulness of a portfolio of carefully selected business model experiments; they closely monitor progress.

for the venture's survival. Given the configurational nature of organizations (Miller and Friesen 1984), significant efforts and investments are needed to change the mindsets of all stakeholders and to replace organizational structures, ideas, and competences that have become obsolete for the development of the new business model. The second model is characterized by experimentation with a set of different business models. Acknowledging that different conceivable business models are all characterized by uncertainty, the choice for translating one option into a fully elaborated resource configuration is postponed until more information becomes available with respect to a range of value propositions.

As a consequence, these entrepreneurial firms organize their activities within a first phase on a project base. Based on an analytical elaboration of these premises (Andries *et al.* 2013), it becomes feasible to examine the circumstances under which one model is more appropriate than the other.[1]

First, simultaneous experimentation becomes more interesting if first mover advantages are small. Recent research has clearly shown that first mover advantages are indeed extremely limited in emerging industries (Dowell and Swaminathan 2006). The firms that enter an emerging industry earliest have the longest life expectancy, but their advantage only lasts until the dominant design emerges. Early entrants face inertial pressures that make them less likely to accomplish and survive the transition to this dominant design (see also Abernathy and Utterback 1975). Second, simultaneous experimentation becomes more preferable if the cost of abruptly reorienting a focused, committed venture when the initial business model turns out to be unsuccessful is high. Our case studies show that, for all cases, observed reconfiguration costs are indeed relatively high. Significant efforts and investments are needed to change the mindsets of all stakeholders – including investors – and to replace organizational structures, ideas, and competences that have become obsolete for the development of the newly adopted business model.

Third, experimentation becomes more preferable if the cost difference between executing a portfolio of experiments and adopting one full implementation is low, or in other words, if low-cost probing is possible and/or synergies can be created between different experiments in the portfolio. Existing literature suggests the feasibility of deploying low-cost probing strategies. Such strategies consist of ventures using a variety of cheap experiments (including experimental products and strategic alliances) to see what types of products and services markets are more responsive to (Brown and Eisenhardt 1997). In addition, our case study findings show that it might also be beneficial to include activities with short-term cash-generating potential to support longer-term development of other activities, similarly to the recommendation of Bhidé (1992, p. 113) that "a business that is making money, elegantly or not, builds credibility in the eyes of suppliers, customers, and employees, as well as self-confidence in the entrepreneur." We also observed that ventures use the knowledge developed while exploring one option to reassess and redefine the nature of and the priorities for the activity portfolio as a whole. In short, developing a portfolio of business model experiments might inspire these

---

[1] For the mathematical elaboration of this argument, we refer to Andries *et al.* (2007).

ventures to enact spillovers, both in terms of resources and in terms of knowledge between the different activities undertaken.

Finally, a simultaneous experimentation approach is more preferable if the probability of success for a specific business is low. It is generally known that this is the case in emerging industries. Very few configurations survive competition, and the number of firms drops drastically as a dominant design emerges (Abernathy and Utterback 1975). Therefore, it appears that in emerging industries, most of the conditions tend to favor simultaneous experimentation over a focused, committed approach to business model development.

Implications: Complementing spin-off inception efforts with adaptive incubation practices

When focused commitment is compared with simultaneous experimentation, the latter becomes more interesting if first mover advantages are small, if the cost of abruptly reorienting a focused venture when the initial business model turns out to be unsuccessful is high, and if the probability of success for a specific business model is low. These conditions appear to hold especially for ventures in emerging industries. As such, these insights carry important lessons for universities engaged in the formation and support of spin off companies during the early stages of their existence.

First of all, embracing the idea of adaptation becomes critical. As illustrated, adaptation might imply that ventures develop a range of business model experiments, an idea that radically goes against the dominant investment model commonly used by outside investors pushing ventures to focus on one specific business model. As noticed by Bhidé (1992, p. 112), "investors ... prefer ventures with plausible, carefully thought-out plans to address well-defined markets. A solid plan reassures them about the competence of the entrepreneur and provides an objective yardstick for measuring progress and testing initial assumptions." However, our case studies (Andries et al. 2013) show that some investors, namely university incubators, are willing to invest in ventures that explicitly acknowledge uncertainty and that develop a portfolio of business model experiments. These investors are fully aware and supportive of the venture's intention to experiment with various business models. This results in a more flexible approach to providing and monitoring resources in the new venture. In the original business plans of these ventures, it is clearly stipulated that the industry is emerging and that various applications will be considered. The fact that ventures are able to develop a portfolio of business models and attract outside investors adds to and complements the work of Bhidé (1992), who promoted bootstrapping, i.e., launching ventures with modest personal funds as an alternative to using external capital. Bootstrapped ventures buy used instead of new equipment, rent locations on favorable terms, delay compensation to the entrepreneur, etc. (Winborg and Landström 1997, 2001; Van Auken 2005). These ventures, therefore, do not need to struggle with investors opposing radical change. However, bootstrapping poses problems in the sense that growth needs to be under strict control. If it is the case that ventures adopting a portfolio approach to business model development are able to attract outside investors, then they avoid struggles regarding radical change as well as growth limitations. The simultaneous experimentation approach, therefore, seems to offer the advantage, but not the disadvantage of bootstrapping.

Second, when investing in ventures that are active in emerging industries characterized by uncertainty, patience is crucial. Incubators (and other investors) should give such spin-offs the time and resources to experiment and adapt. In one of the cases that we studied, it took the university spin-off seven years to discover a viable business model. The company is now more than twenty years old and a world leader in its industry. Therefore, it should be clear that the assessment of the economic performance of university-based spin-offs requires extended time frames.

At the same time, being patient and open to adaptation does not mean that spin-offs can experiment and change course as frequently and as many times as they want. University incubators can play an active role in the testing of uncertain assumptions. Adaptation should be "intelligent" in the sense that it should take into account new information that becomes available in emergent markets. The ease with which new information is developed and gathered will allow entrepreneurs to test uncertain assumptions more quickly. Developing and gathering relevant new information is a disciplined activity that benefits from interaction with outside parties. Incubators should therefore mobilize networks of partners and experts to interact with the spin-off. In addition, the university incubator can be of help by forcing the entrepreneur to think carefully about alternative business models and about the consequences of adaptation and experimentation efforts in terms of required resources. As such, the university incubator can structure and monitor the adaptation effort – thereby providing guidance to the entrepreneur as well as keeping a close watch on the investment – by using discovery-driven planning tools as a decision instrument. Under discovery-driven planning, milestones involve testing of uncertain assumptions (McGrath and MacMillan 1995) instead of the financial targets traditionally used by investors. Additional investments in a specific business model experiment of the spin-off's portfolio should only be made if the assumptions tested at a certain milestone are validated. Exactly such incubation processes have been developed within LRD, especially since the creation of the Gemma Frisius Fund. Most of the supported ventures are in a very early phase of developing their business model. Funding is organized in different rounds, whereby the decision to fund depends not only on targets such as turnover, but also on whether or not the venture has been able to improve its knowledge regarding the viability of possible business models. In many cases, ventures are funded for multiple years (up to seven years in some cases) before they find a successful business model.

To conclude, entrepreneurial universities that want to foster spin-off creation face not only the challenge of adopting a strategic orientation to entrepreneurial activities, installing appropriate incentive mechanisms and an appropriate support infrastructure. Given the nature of spin-off companies operating at scientific and technological boundaries, specific incubation processes are needed as well. Indeed, we argue that university incubators can influence the likelihood of survival and growth of their spin-offs through coaching a careful and structured process of experimentation and adaptation. This requires not only the presence of appropriate financial resources and patience, but also the development of a structured monitoring competence that stimulates entrepreneurs to experiment. Ventures in emerging industries should proactively search and develop multiple business model experiments and explicitly plan for this in their business plan. Within such endeavors, planning and experimentation should not be considered as opposites.[2] In contrast, proactive planning for experimentation (i.e., combining planning and bricolage) becomes beneficial when confronted with unpredictability.

References

Abernathy, W.J. and Utterback, J.M. (1975). A dynamic model of product and process innovation. *Omega*, 3(6), 639–656.

Andries, P. and Debackere, K. (2007). Adaptation and performance in new businesses: Understanding the moderating effects of independence and industry. *Small Business Economics*, 29, 81–99.

Andries, P., Debackere, K., and Van Looy, B. (2013). Simultaneous experimentation as a learning strategy: Business model development under uncertainty. *Strategic Entrepreneurship Journal*, 7(4), 288–310.

---

[2] As in the juxtaposition of planning versus action or "bricolage" by Liao and Gartner 2006 or the effectuation/causation distinction advanced by Sarasvathy (2001).

278   Petra Andries, Bart Van Looy, and Koenraad Debackere

Andries, P., Van Looy, B., Lecocq, C., and Debackere, K. (2007). Business model development in emerging industries: Approaches of new technology-based ventures. Paper presented at the Academy of Management Conference.

Arora, A., Fosfuri, A., and Gambardella, A. (2001). *Markets for Technology: The Economics of Innovation and Corporate Strategy.* MIT Press, Cambridge, MA.

Autio, E. (2000). Growth of technology-based new firms. In D.L. Sexton and H. Landstrom (eds.), *The Blackwell Handbook of Entrepreneurship*, pp. 329–347. Blackwell, Oxford.

Bartelsman, E., Scarpetta, S., and Schivardi, F. (2003). Comparative Analysis of Firms Demographics and Survival: Micro-Level Evidence for the OECD Countries. OECD Economic Department Working Paper 348, Paris.

Bhidé, A. (1992). Bootstrap finance: The art of start-ups. *Harvard Business Review*, November–December, 109–117.

Brokaw, L. (1991). The truth about start-ups. *Inc.*, April, 52–67.

Brown, S.L. and Eisenhardt, K.M. (1997). The art of continuous change: Linking complexity theory and time-paced evolution in relentlessly shifting organizations. *Administrative Science Quarterly*, 42, 1–34.

Burns, T. and Stalker, G.M. (1961). *The Management of Innovation.* Oxford University Press, Oxford.

Chesbrough, H. and Rosenbloom, R.S. (2002). The role of the business model in capturing value from innovation: Evidence from Xerox Corporation's technology spin-off companies. *Industrial and Corporate Change*, 11(3), 529–555.

Dowell, G. and Swaminathan, A. (2006). Entry timing, exploration, and firm survival in the early U.S. bicycle industry. *Strategic Management Journal*, 27, 1159–1182.

Drucker, P.F. (1985). *Innovation and Entrepreneurship: Practice and Principles.* Harper & Row, New York.

Eisenhardt, K.M. and Schoonhoven, C. (1990). Organisational growth: Linking founding team, strategy, environment, and growth among U.S. semiconductor ventures, 1987–1988. *Administrative Science Quarterly*, 35(3), 504–529.

Franco, A.M. and Filson, D. (2000). Knowledge Diffusion through Employee Mobility. Federal Reserve Bank of Minneapolis. Staff Report 272.

Gans, J.S. and Stern, S. (2003). The product market and the market for 'ideas': Commercialization strategies for technology entrepreneurs. *Research Policy*, 32, 333–350.

Gruber, M., MacMillan, I.C., and Thompson, J.D. (2008). Look before you leap: Market opportunity identification in emerging technology firms. *Management Science*, 54(9): 1652–1665.

Klepper, S. (2001). Employee start-ups in high tech industries. *Industrial and Corporate Change*, 10(3), 639–674.

Klepper, S. and Sleeper, S. (2000). Entry by Spin-Offs. Mimeo. Carnegie Mellon University, Pittsburgh, June.

Liao, J. and Gartner, W. (2006). The effects of pre-venture plan timing and perceived environmental uncertainty on the persistence of emerging firms. *Small Business Economics*, 27(1), 23–40.

McGrath, R.G. and MacMillan, I.C. (1995). Discovery-driven planning. *Harvard Business Review*, 73(4), 44–54.

Miller, P. and Friesen, D. (1984). *Organizations: A Quantum View*. Prentice-Hall, Englewood Cliffs, NJ.

Nerkar, A. and Shane, S. (2003). When do startups that exploit patented academic knowledge survive? *International Journal of Industrial Organization*, 21, 1391–1410.

OECD. (2001). Benchmarking Industry–Science Relationships, Science, Technology and Industry Outlook 2000.

O'Shea, R.P., Allen, T.J., Chevalier, A., and Roche, F. (2005). Entrepreneurial orientation, technology transfer and spin-off performance. *Research Policy*, 34(5), 994–1009.

Pitt, L.F. and Kannemeyer, R. (2000). The role of adaptation in microenterprise development: A marketing perspective. *Journal of Developmental Entrepreneurship*, 5(2), 137–155.

Roberts, E.B. (1991). *Entrepreneurs in High Technology. Lessons from MIT and Beyond*. Oxford University Press, New York.

Sarasvathy, S.D. (2001). Causation and effectuation: Toward a theoretical shift from economic inevitability to entrepreneurial contingency. *Academy of Management Review*, 26, 2, 243–263.

Shane, S. (2002). Selling university technology: Patterns from MIT. *Management Science* 48(1), 122–137.

Shane, S. and Stuart, T. (2002). Organizational endowments and the performance of university start-ups. *Management Science*, 48(1), 154–170.

Steensma, H.K., Marino, L., Weaver, K.M., and Dickson, P.H. (2000). The influence of national culture on the formation of technology alliances by entrepreneurial firms. *Academy of Management Journal*, 43(5), 951–973.

Stoica, M. and Schindehutte, M. (1999). Understanding adaptation in small firms: Links to culture and performance. *Journal of Developmental Entrepreneurship*, 4(1), 1–18.

Teece, D.J. (1986). Profiting from technological innovation: Implications for integration, collaboration, licensing and public policy. *Research Policy* 15, 285–305.

Teubal, M., Yinnon, T., and Zuscovitch, E. (1991). Networks and market creation. *Research Policy*, 20(5), 381–392.

Thurow, L. (2000). *Creating Wealth*, Nicholas Brealey Publishing, London.

Timmons, J.A., Smollen, L.E., and Dingee, A.L.M. (1990). *New Venture Creation: Entrepreneurship in the 90's* (3rd ed.). Irwin, Homewood, IL.

Torrisi, S. (1998). *Industrial Organization and Innovation. An International Study of the Software Industry*. Edward Elgar, Cheltenham, UK.

Utterback, J.M. (1987). Innovation and industrial evolution in manufacturing industries. In B.R. Guile and H. Brooks (eds.), *Technology and Global Industry: Companies and Nations in the World Economy*, Series on Technology and Social Priorities, pp. 16–48. National Academy Press, Washington, DC.

(1994). Mastering the dynamics of innovation: How companies can seize opportunities in the face of technological change. Harvard Business School Press, Boston.

Van Auken, H.E. (2005). Differences in the usage of bootstrap financing among technology-based versus nontechnology-based firms. *Journal of Small Business Management*, 43, 93–103.

Van Looy, B., Landoni, P., Callaert, J., van Pottelsberghe, B., Sapsalis, E., and Debackere, K. (2011). Entrepreneurial effectiveness of European universities: An empirical assessment of antecedents and trade-offs. *Research Policy*, 40(4), 553–564.

Venkataraman, S. (1997). The distinctive domain of entrepreneurship research: An editor's perspective. In J. Katz and R. Brockhaus (eds.), *Advances in Entrepreneurship, Firm Emergence and Growth*, Vol. 3, pp. 119–138. JAI Press, Greenwich, CT.

Winborg, J. and Landström, H. (1997). Financial bootstrapping in small businesses – A resource-based view on small business finance. In W.D. Bygrave *et al.* (eds.), *Frontiers of Entrepreneurship Research*, pp. 471–485. Babson College, Wellesley, MA.

(2001). Financial bootstrapping in small businesses: Examining small business managers' resource acquisition behaviors. *Journal of Business Venturing*, 16, 235–254.

Zucker, L.R., Darby, M.R., and Brewer, M.B. (1998). Intellectual human capital and the birth of U.S. biotechnology enterprises. *American Economic Review*, 88(1), 290–306.

12 Toward a "global knowledge enterprise": The entrepreneurial university model of the National University of Singapore

Poh-Kam Wong, Yuen-Ping Ho, and Annette Singh

As highlighted by Wong (2006) and Wong and Singh (2011), Singapore has achieved remarkable economic growth in the past via a strategy of leveraging foreign direct investment. However, with growing competition from China and India in recent years, Singapore is rapidly moving toward a knowledge-based strategy for future growth, with increasing public policy prominence being given to the role of Singapore's universities in stimulating economic growth through industrially relevant research, technology commercialization, high-tech spin-offs, attracting foreign talents, and inculcating entrepreneurial mindsets. At the same time, increasing globalization of competition is putting pressure on public universities in Singapore to become more responsive to market forces.

As argued by Etzkowitz *et al.* (2000) and Etzkowitz (2003), universities around the world are increasingly shifting from their traditional primary role as educational providers and scientific knowledge creators to a more complex "entrepreneurial" model that incorporates the additional role of commercialization of knowledge and active contribution to the development of private enterprises in the local and regional economy. As a result, universities have become an increasingly important component of the national innovation system, and need to operate increasingly within a triple-helix nexus involving close interaction with government institutions and private industries.

This imperative for universities to shift from their traditional model to the new "entrepreneurial" model is arguably of even greater urgency in the context of the newly industrialized economies (NIEs), for four reasons. First, the universities in most NIEs are relatively younger institutions than their counterparts in the advanced, mature economies, and many are created as public institutions owned and regulated by the government. Academic faculty members are effectively state employees,

Note: This chapter draws from an earlier version written in early 2010 and published in 2011 as Wong *et al.* (2011), with substantial revision and updating of materials to early 2013.

and university administrators are usually government appointees, tasked to carry out government policies. As such, they tend to have much less autonomy than at public universities in Europe, let alone the private universities in the United States. For example, competitive differentiation among local universities is often stifled in favor of bureaucratic direction and coordination by the state.

Second, as "late-comers," these economies had traditionally placed a much stronger emphasis on absorbing and diffusing technological knowledge from the advanced countries than on indigenous innovation. Consequently, the universities in these NIEs also tend to have been tasked by their respective governments to focus strongly on their manpower development role through the assimilation of foreign technologies and knowledge, with much less emphasis on new knowledge creation through indigenous research activities.

Third, the shift toward a knowledge-based economy, rather than one based on low wages and natural resource advantages, requires a significant increase in the indigenous capabilities of local enterprises to create and commercialize new knowledge, not just use knowledge imported from advanced countries. However, many of the local private enterprises that had developed in the earlier industrialization phases still tend to be laggards, rather than leaders, in engaging in R&D and innovation activities. Consequently, compared to their more technologically advanced counterparts in the advanced economies, local industries in NIEs often have less experience, and less capability, to commercialize knowledge generated from local universities.

Last, universities in these NIEs typically operate within the environmental constraints of a relatively underdeveloped venture ecosystem where, unlike Silicon Valley (Lee *et al.* 2000), the venture capital industry is still in its infancy and focused on less risky later-stage financing. A critical mass of sophisticated business angel investors is lacking, and the dense social networks of venture professionals, mentors, and deal-making institutions (start-up law firms, serial entrepreneurs, etc.) is absent. Consequently, even if the universities were able to produce significant innovations, the underdeveloped venture ecosystem would make it difficult for such innovations to be commercialized via spin-offs.

These four factors – more rigid bureaucratic control by the state, a lower base of research and inventive outputs coming out from the university, lower demand and ability of private enterprises to commercialize university knowledge, and an underdeveloped venture ecosystem to facilitate faculty spin-offs – suggest that the preconditions for triple-helix dynamic interactions is much weaker in the NIEs than in the advanced economies. Thus, arguably, it is even more urgent for the universities in NIEs to take on an entrepreneurial role than for universities in the advanced economies, in order to compensate for these less favorable preconditions that they start from. For example, the universities in NIEs may need to be more proactive in commercializing their inventions by taking the spin-off route, rather than relying on outside private enterprises to license technologies from them, due to the weakness of the latter. Moreover, the universities may need to have more direct involvement in incubating and even seed-funding their spin-offs, due to the lack of early stage venture capital and angel investors. Similarly, universities in NIEs may need to undergo more drastic reform of their organizational structure and incentive system in order to change the culture and mindset of their staff toward knowledge commercialization.

In the context of a small NIE such as Singapore, we suggest the need for the local university system to take on an additional economic role not mentioned in Etzkowitz et al. (2000)'s model: the attraction of foreign talent. Given the small local population, Singapore needs to be able to tap top foreign talents to help staff the top echelons of specialized knowledge workers required in a knowledge economy. Just as the dynamic economic regions of Silicon Valley, London, New York City, and Boston have benefited from the influx of foreign talent, Singapore needs to do likewise to differentiate itself as the leading knowledge-economy hub in Southeast Asia. Moreover, the experience of regions such as Silicon Valley, Boston, and London strongly suggests that the competition for global talent not only works through the increasingly globalized market for qualified technical professional specialists, but also actually starts before the talent reaches the labor market – through the attraction of top students from overseas. Indeed, top universities such as Stanford, Berkeley, MIT, Cambridge, and Oxford have for decades served as magnets to attract top students from around the world, many of whom subsequently stayed to contribute to the growth of key knowledge-economy sectors in these regions – high-tech industries, creative businesses, and knowledge-intensive services. In addition, many of those who returned to their home countries often continue to build economic links with their former alma mater host regions, and indirectly contribute to the vibrancy of the latter. For example, Saxenian (2000, 2002) has documented not only the extraordinarily high level of contribution of immigrant Asian technical professionals – many of whom trained in universities in Silicon Valley itself – to entrepreneurial high-tech formation in Silicon Valley, but also the phenomenon of "brain circulation" between Hsinchu, Taiwan, Bangalore, India, and Silicon Valley. Such entrepreneurial links had major beneficial effects on the vibrancy of Silicon Valley.

In contrast to this foreign talent attraction role of Western universities, particularly leading universities in the Anglo-Saxon world, East Asian universities have traditionally been much less globalized, primarily focused on the education of the local elites. Although the use of the local language as the medium of instruction represents an obstacle to attracting foreign students, the more important reason is the lack of a political commitment to foreign talent attraction as a mission for the local university. For large East Asian economies such as Japan, China, and Korea, there may appear to be less pressing need to tap foreign talent through their universities, but for a small economy such as Singapore, this economic role is likely to be critical.

Last, but not least, although Etzkowitz *et al.* (2000) emphasize the technology commercialization role of the university in their entrepreneurial university model, we believe that the entrepreneurial university model in the context of late-industrializing economies also implies a significant emphasis on injecting a greater dimension of entrepreneurship into the contents of university education itself; i.e., not only does the university need to take on new functions, but also the nature of its core function of education needs to be reoriented as well.

The need for the university to play an active role to help foster a more entrepreneurial mindset among students is arguably more of an imperative in the context of Singapore, where the highly educated population had relatively low entrepreneurial propensity (Wong *et al.* 2005) because consistently high economic growth in the past had generated relatively full employment and bright career prospects in the corporate (mainly MNC subsidiaries) and public sectors. With stable job opportunities and steady corporate careers no longer guaranteed in the increasingly competitive global economy of the twenty-first century, universities in Singapore need to urgently reorient students' expectations of the job market and to prepare them to have a more entrepreneurial mindset.

In summary, we have theoretically expanded the entrepreneurial university model of Etzkowitz *et al.* (2000) and others to incorporate a number of additional emerging roles that the university needs to play to contribute effectively to the transition of newly industrialized economies toward knowledge-based economies. Figure 12.1 summarizes our proposed conceptual framework for defining the five key roles that an entrepreneurial university needs to play in spurring entrepreneurial development in the local economy, particularly in the context of newly industrialized nations. Three of these roles can be conceptualized as attracting resource inputs, including catalyzing the development of a vibrant venture ecosystem, while the other two roles can be defined in terms of creating entrepreneurial outputs. While many commentaries by university officials on the technology commercialization role of their universities start by lamenting that the preconditions for such activities do not exist due to the underdevelopment of their external environments, we believe

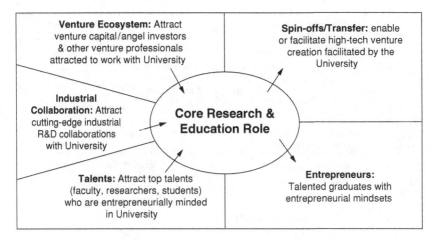

Figure 12.1: Key roles of an entrepreneurial university.

it is more constructive for the university leadership to explicitly recognize that it is part of the university's role to help create such preconditions by implementing strategic programs to attract the relevant resources. Indeed, the role of the early leaders of Stanford University, such as Frederick Terman, in stimulating the development of Silicon Valley is instructive: the creation of Stanford Research Park to attract technology companies to locate their R&D activities in the region, the focus on attracting talented faculties to the university, and the systematic cultivation of early venture capitalists and other key venture professionals/deal-makers were all integral parts of the resource attraction strategy pursued by Stanford in the formative years of Silicon Valley, when it was "newly industrializing" compared to the more advanced urban centers on the East Coast.

The five generic roles identified in Figure 12.1 are of course not independent, but interact synergistically with one another to constitute a virtuous cycle of mutual and cumulative reinforcement – e.g., by attracting talents that are already entrepreneurially minded, it is much easier for the university to produce graduates who go on to create start-ups, and the presence of a pool of successful start-up entrepreneurs will become the source of savvy business angels and venture capitalists in the future. The key challenge is to get the virtuous cycle started. The proposed framework suggests that a systematic, integrated approach that pursues all five roles may have a higher chance of success than piecemeal, isolated intervention in individual roles.

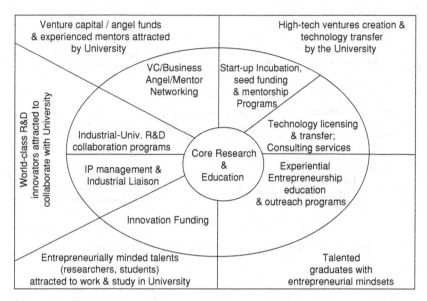

Figure 12.2: Key entrepreneurship support programs.

By using the conceptual framework outlined in Figure 12.1, we can classify into the five generic roles a wide range of university programs and activities that have been identified by the emerging literature on the entrepreneurial university model (see Figure 12.2). As is apparent from Figure 12.2, the diverse range of programs and activities are often organized under different operating units of a university, which further suggest that, in the absence of a clear strategic vision or organizational coordination framework, potential synergies may not be reaped across programs or activities. For example, entrepreneurship educational programs in many universities are confined largely to business school students, tend to be classroom-instruction-oriented rather than experiential-learning-oriented, and often do not leverage the rich technological commercialization activities taking place in the technical faculties. Similarly, in many campuses, there is very little interaction between the business faculty and the technology licensing office.

Using this conceptual framework, we now examine how the National University of Singapore (NUS), the leading university in Singapore, has sought to perform these five entrepreneurial development roles, and the extent to which synergies were being achieved through strategic visioning and organizational coordination.

Table 12.1: *Profile of the National University of Singapore (AY2011/2012)*

Indicator	AY2011/2012
Faculty members	2,196
Research staff	2,820
Undergraduate students enrolled	25,107
Graduate students enrolled	7,901
Total research funding	S$436 mil[a]
Journal articles published in SCI/SSCI (CY 2011)	4,411
Cumulative journal publications (CY 1990–2011)[b]	50,067
Cumulative US patents granted (CY1990–2011)	290

[a] External grants only.
[b] SCI/SSCI-indexed journal articles only.
Source: NUS Annual Report 2012. Thomson Reuters Web of Science, accessed through NUS Library portal, http://libportal.nus.edu.sg/frontend/index. Database of the USPTO, available at www.uspto.gov/patft/index.html.

The entrepreneurial university model of the National University of Singapore

Established in 1905, the NUS is the oldest and largest public university in Singapore, with a total student enrolment of 33,000 (three-quarters being undergraduates) and a faculty strength of over 2,000. Although there were three other local public universities in Singapore by the mid-2000s (NTU, SMU, and SIM), with a fourth (SUTD) added in 2012, these were newer and more narrow in their educational scope. Historically, the government's educational policy has emphasized public education, resulting in no large private university in Singapore, although many diploma-level private colleges and distant-learning degree programs had been allowed to operate. However, since the late 1990s, the government has actively encouraged leading overseas universities to establish branch campuses and other forms of operational presence in Singapore, with the aim of turning Singapore into a global educational hub. For example, INSEAD established a branch campus in Singapore in 2000, while James Cook University opened its branch campus in Singapore in 2003.

Table 12.1 provides a summary profile of NUS as of mid-2012. With an annual R&D budget of over S$436 million in 2012, NUS alone constituted about 5 percent of total R&D spending in Singapore that year. The total number of NUS faculty members and researchers engaged in science and technology R&D also exceeded 10 percent of total science and technology R&D personnel in Singapore in 2005. Reflecting

Table 12.2: *Ranking of NUS in the World University Rankings by the* Times Higher Education Supplement, *2010/2011–2012/2013*

	2010/2011 ranking	2011/2012 ranking	2012/2013 ranking
Overall	34	40	29
Life sciences	>50	44	33
Clinical, pre-clinical, and health	39	41	37
Physical sciences	>50	>50	39
Engineering and technology	16	19	12
Social sciences	>50	47	39
Arts and humanities	>50	38	43

Source: THE World University Rankings website. Available at www.timeshighereducation. co.uk/world-university-rankings/.

its increasing achievement in academic excellence in recent years, NUS has been ranked within or near to the top 40 in the world by the *Times Higher Education Supplement* over 2010–2012 (see Table 12.2).

Like most other public universities developed under the British Commonwealth tradition, NUS has in the past been following the traditional model of having teaching as its primary mission, with research as a secondary function (Etzkowitz *et al.* 2000). While the 1980s and 1990s saw increasing emphasis on research, mirroring the steady shift in the Singapore economy toward R&D (Wong 2006), it was not until the mid-1990s that NUS began to establish a technology licensing office. Even then, patenting activity was relatively low (only twenty-one U.S. patents granted up to 1997), and involvement of professors and students in spinning off companies was relatively rare before 2000.

Impetus for change

The major impetus for more rapid growth in technology commercialization activities came only in the late 1990s, partly precipitated by the Asian financial crisis in 1997, which caused a recession in the Singaporean economy in the following year. In response, a major economic restructuring strategy was formulated by the government (ERC 2002), where the need to accelerate the shift toward an innovation-driven, knowledge-based economy was highlighted, and the impetus for the local university to play a greater role in technology commercialization was recognized.

The external environmental impetus for change coincided with the imminent retirement of the incumbent Vice-Chancellor of NUS, thus providing an opportunity for the government to effect change at NUS at a much faster pace by bringing in an external candidate to take over the top leadership role at NUS (now retitled "President" to reflect the shift toward the U.S. university model as the global benchmark). Singapore-born and Harvard-trained, the new President, Professor C.F. Shih, came to NUS with strong credentials, having prior work experience in a leading U.S. corporation (General Electric) and a research leadership role at the helm of a major research lab in an Ivy League university (Brown University) in the United States. With the strong support of the government, he not only provided the crucial leadership to significantly accelerate the pace of change of several initiatives that were already in motion at the university, but more importantly, initiated a strategic shift of the university toward embracing an entrepreneurial university model. As is typical of visionary leaders, he did so by establishing a new strategic vision for the university that encompassed an explicit recognition of entrepreneurial development, and by creating a new organizational vehicle to spearhead change toward the new vision.

Setting strategic direction for change: The "global knowledge enterprise"

As part of his strategy to set NUS on a new direction for development, the new president articulated a new vision of the university as a "global knowledge enterprise." This vision statement signals two strategic dimensions for change: first, the need for NUS to compete in the global arena, rather than within the national economy; and second, the need to inject a more entrepreneurial dimension into NUS's research and educational activities, particularly in terms of accelerating the commercialization of the university's knowledge and producing more entrepreneurially minded graduates. The two dimensions in the new vision statement – global and enterprise – are closely intertwined, giving rise to both synergy and tensions. On one hand, since the domestic market of Singapore is small, success in knowledge commercialization requires mindsets and competences for competing globally, and hence entrepreneurial development activities must have a global orientation. On the other hand, the overall drive toward academic excellence at a global level also exerts significant constraints on what can be done in the enterprise dimension – the pursuit of enterprise activities cannot be at the expense of achieving excellence in research and education. In effect, with this vision statement, NUS aimed to level up substantially in its global competitive standing in terms of academic research and educational excellence, while at the same time differentiating itself from other academically excellent universities in the world by a special emphasis on being entrepreneurial. Politically, the vision statement reassured the academic faculties and the government of the priority that NUS would place on pursuing global academic excellence, while allowing room for new initiatives toward entrepreneurship to be explored.

A major development in the drive to become globally competitive is the shift of emphasis away from local manpower development to incorporating a twin objective of making the university a global educational hub, attracting top foreign students and faculty, in increasing competition with other leading universities in the world. In line with this globalization drive, NUS also began revising its faculty compensation policy, making it more flexible to allow the university to pay more to attract top talent, as well as to reducing pay for the underperforming faculty. Tenure and promotion policy was made much more stringent and performance-based, in line with the benchmarks of leading universities in the United States. Intake of foreign students also increased, while a larger share of local students were encouraged to go on exchange programs abroad for at least a semester to gain international experience.

To give NUS the needed institutional flexibility to become globally competitive, the Singapore government allowed NUS to become corporatized in 2006. Although public funding support remains significant, with clear strategic goals to be achieved every three to five years, NUS was given much greater autonomy in how it operated to achieve the targeted outcomes. Moreover, after corporatization, NUS was encouraged to aim high, with the government indicating that it was willing to commit higher funding if chances of achievement were realistic.

Organizational strategy: The creation and evolution of NUS Enterprise

Complementing the new vision statement, the new president created a new division in the university to spearhead the pursuit of activities to make NUS entrepreneurial. In addition, he personally hand-picked a professor from the engineering school, Professor Jacob Phang, who had been among the earliest to have started a venture to commercialize his inventions, to serve as the first CEO of the new organization. Under a broad mission to inject more of an entrepreneurial dimension into NUS education and research, the CEO was tasked to make NUS Enterprise the primary organizational vehicle for coordinating and managing all major university activities related to technology commercialization and entrepreneurship promotion within NUS. As there were already some existing units within the university that were related to that broad mission, the new CEO was asked to take these under his wing and restructure them as he saw fit, but he was otherwise given great latitude to define and

Table 12.3: *Evolution of NUS Enterprise organizational structure, 2003–2006*

Units of NUS Enterprise in 2003	(a) Core functions	(b) Revised structure since 2006
NUS Entrepreneurship Centre	* Entrepreneurship education * Outreach * Entrepreneurship and innovation Applied research and thought leadership	Expanded to include NUS Enterprise Incubator
Industry and Technology Relations Office (INTRO)	* Technology licensing and IP management * Industrial liaison	Renamed Industry Liaison Office (ILO)
NUS Consulting (NCO) NUS Extension (NEX) NUS Publishing (NPU)	* Consulting service * Continuing education * University Press	Discontinued
NUS Venture Support (NVS)	* Business incubation * Venture support services * Seed funding of NUS-related start-ups	Absorbed into NEC and renamed NUS Enterprise Incubator
NUS Overseas College (NOC)	* Overseas high-tech start-up internship cum education program	

implement new initiatives to make the university "more enterprising." To kick-start the new division, an annual operating budget equivalent to less than 1 percent of the university's overall budget was set aside for NUS Enterprise, with the understanding that the budget would not be increased over time, thus forcing the unit to be entrepreneurial in generating revenue or attracting external financial resources to fund expansion of its activities.

NUS Enterprise was set up with a broad mission, reporting directly to the president and mandated for an integrated and coordinated approach to performing the five generic roles of an entrepreneurial university. After some early experimentation, the CEO assembled and incorporated into the new NUS Enterprise all the major operating units needed to perform most of the entrepreneurial roles identified in Table 12.1. Table 12.3a shows the initial organizational structure of NUS Enterprise as of 2003, two years after the NUS Enterprise Division was formed. Basically, it comprised five existing units that were absorbed and adapted from other parts of NUS – the NUS Entrepreneurship Centre, Industry and Technology Relations Office (INTRO), NUS Consulting, NUS

Extension, and NUS Publishing. Of these, the NUS Entrepreneurship Centre was substantially expanded to undertake significantly new activities, while the IP management and technology licensing role of INTRO was also significantly expanded. In addition, the CEO created two new units – NUS Overseas College and NUS Venture Support – to initiate significantly new activities previously not performed by NUS.

While many of the functions performed by these operating units were conventional and could be found in many universities, what distinguished NUS Enterprise was (a) its effort to coordinate and create synergies across functions and (b) its entrepreneurial approach in spawning a number of new initiatives that represented significant innovations for NUS. A number of these new initiatives will be highlighted later.

Reflecting the entrepreneurial orientation of the founding CEO, the first 3–4 years of NUS Enterprise were rather fluid and fast-paced, at times even chaotic, as the organizational leadership emphasized a bias for action and getting things done rather than putting in place well-thought-out standard operating procedures and management systems. By empowering operating unit directors with strong ideas to champion them, this entrepreneurial organizational culture facilitated the rapid introduction of a number of innovative programs that were highlighted earlier. As in all entrepreneurial organizations, however, there was a tendency for too many initiatives to be started, and in some units, the long-term objectives were less well thought out, leading to a short-term focus on meeting quantitative targets.

In early 2006, the founding CEO of NUS Enterprise decided to relinquish his position so that he could devote all his time to growing the high-tech venture that he founded before he took on the NUS Enterprise CEO position. This provided an opportunity for the president to bring in a new leader from outside to help manage the transition of NUS Enterprise into a more mature and stable organization. With a strong track record in managing venture capital investment, and a prior background in running a biotech start-up, the new CEO, Dr. Lily Chan, quickly put in place a more balanced organizational development approach with a stronger emphasis on management systems. Table 12.3b summarizes the key organizational changes she instituted in 2006. Reaffirming the integrated NUS Enterprise approach, she had emphasized the need for greater coordination and cooperation among the units of NUS Enterprise by consolidating some of the separate units (e.g., Venture Support is now absorbed into NUS Entrepreneurship Centre as NUS Enterprise Incubator, and INTRO is streamlined and renamed Industry Liaison Office (ILO), while NUS Consulting was disbanded). We highlight in the following the key initiatives launched over the years by the three core divisions of NUS Enterprise – NUS Entrepreneurship Centre (NEC), NUS Overseas Colleges (NOC), and Industry Liaison Office (ILO).

Key innovative programs of NUS Enterprise

*(a) Entrepreneurship education initiatives of
NUS Entrepreneurship Centre*

NUS Entrepreneurship Centre (NEC) was established in NUS Enterprise with the aim of promoting entrepreneurial learning among the NUS community through educational programs, and of advancing knowledge in the policy and practice of technology venturing in Singapore and the region through research. The center was originally established in 1988 as a university-level center called the Centre for Management of Innovation and Technopreneurship (CMIT). In 2001, it became a division of NUS Enterprise and was renamed the NUS Entrepreneurship Centre. NEC's activities were organized into three key areas: education, entrepreneurship development, and research.

Like entrepreneurship centers established in many universities, NEC offered a wide range of educational programs, both within the classroom and extracurricular. What distinguished NEC's nonclassroom educational activities was its conscious attempts to reach beyond the campus to help evangelize and catalyze the development of the external venture ecosystem, and to turn NUS into a magnet for entrepreneurial networking activities that link the NUS community with the external venture ecosystem. As highlighted earlier, this venture ecosystem catalysis role was important because the external venture ecosystem was still relatively underdeveloped in Singapore. For example, NEC pioneered the annual national business plan competition, Startup@Singapore, in Singapore in 1999. Although the competition drew its inspiration from the MIT S$50K Competition, NEC opened the competition to the entire Singapore community rather than just to NUS students. The director of the center also helped found and chaired a business angel networking group (Business Angel Network Southeast Asia (BANSEA)) in Singapore that operated like the Band of Angels in Silicon Valley.

Another distinctive approach adopted by NEC was to launch a Technopreneurship Minor Program that was open to all NUS undergraduate students, but with a strong focus on students in science and engineering disciplines. NEC also introduced "technopreneurship" elective courses at the graduate level targeted at Master's and Ph.D. students in science and engineering who had an interest in commercializing their research. The deliberate focus on helping make technical students more business-savvy and entrepreneurially minded helped address a weakness in the existing educational programs of NUS, where students in technical disciplines had little opportunity to learn entrepreneurial skills. Interestingly, NUS Enterprise initially approached the business school in NUS to offer such courses to technical students, which declined, as it was uncertain of the sustainability of demand. Although NEC was not an academic department, through the strong championing of NUS Enterprise, NEC was granted a special academic teaching unit status by the provost to mount the courses. Through an active program of marketing that leveraged the center's various nonclassroom educational activities, NEC was able to attract a rapid increase in enrolment in its "techno-preneurship" courses from less than 200 in the first year to over 1,300 by 2005/2006. Having been shown to be viable, the minor program was transferred to the NUS Business School in 2007. NEC subsequently launched a new entrepreneurship learning program called Innovative Local Enterprise Achiever Development (iLEAD) that offers a seven-month internship opportunity in selected local high-tech start-ups for NUS undergraduates, followed by a two-week overseas study visit trip. The program was transferred to NUS Overseas Colleges (NOC) in 2010.

With new funding support from the National Research Foundation's University Innovation Fund (UIF) in 2009, the center launched several new educational initiatives to broaden its entrepreneurship education offerings. These include a new experiential learning initiative for Ph.D. students called the Extra Chapter Challenge, which offers a six-month fellowship extension to Ph.D. students who have made discoveries or inventions in their thesis research that have commercial potential. The program gives these students the opportunity to develop a commercialization plan under the supervision of a mentor with significant business experience in the industry where the inventions could be exploited. Another innovative initiative is the Innovation and Entrepreneurship Practicum grant scheme, which provides seed funding of up to S$10,000 each to students to develop their innovative ideas and validate them with prospective customers and users. A third initiative involves a collaboration with Grameen Creative Lab (GCL) to provide incubation and educational training for social innovators and entrepreneurs to launch social businesses with scalable, sustainable social impacts on socially disadvantaged groups, including low-income groups at the bottom of the pyramid.

*(b) NUS Enterprise Incubator (previously known as
NUS Venture Support)*

NUS Venture Support (NVS) was created with the explicit aim of providing targeted assistance to NUS spin-offs. Because of the relative underdevelopment of the venture ecosystem, academic entrepreneurs who wanted to spin off their own ventures faced a severe "valley of death." Thus, while the first act of NVS was to establish incubator facilities within the campus to provide NUS-related start-ups with physical infrastructural support as well as selected advisory services, it quickly recognized that this was not enough. Through the active championing of the CEO, NUS Enterprise was able to convince NUS senior management to provide an additional allocation of S$5 million (in two tranches) for NVS to establish a seed funding scheme (NUS Venture Support Fund (NVSF)) to provide very early stage seed funding of up to S$300,000 each to promising NUS spin-off companies by NUS staff, students, and alumni, with the aim of incubating them so that they can become viable candidates for external funding by venture capitalists, angel investors, or corporate investors, or until they achieve significant organic growth. Commencing in 2004, NVSF funded a total of 11 NUS start-ups by the end of 2006, out of over 40 that applied. Additionally, a separate student start-up fund known as the Fund for University Student Entrepreneurs (FUSE) was established in 2005 to provide developmental funding to new ventures started by students or recent graduates. A total of twenty-one student start-ups were funded under FUSE by the end of 2006. Co-funding for these two schemes was obtained from two public funding sources – SPRING SEEDS, which provided a 1:1 match for NVSF (capped at S$300,000), and the Entrepreneurial Talent Development Fund (ETDF) of the Standards, Productivity and Innovation Board (SPRING), which provided a 3:1 match for FUSE (capped at S$45,000 per company).

Although NVS was initially established as a separate unit from NEC, it received close advisory and management support from NEC, including the formation of the investment committee. After a new CEO came on board in 2006, NVS was merged into NEC as part of the organizational streamlining and renamed NUS Enterprise Incubator (NEI). Besides expanding the physical incubation services, NEC also initiated a mentorship program that brought experienced entrepreneurs, investors, and senior executives to campus to provide regular coaching to NUS spin-off companies. A number of new technology-specific seed funding schemes were also introduced, including one for interactive digital media and another for clean-tech. NEI has also developed a program to assist NUS professors and students in applying for various new government grant schemes that have been launched in recent years to support university technology commercialization, such as the SPRING Proof of Concept (POC) and Proof of Value (POV) grants. More recently, NEC has initiated an overseas launch-pad program to help NUS spin-offs enter key overseas markets quickly, with the first such launch pad located in Silicon Valley and the second one in Suzhou, China.

Based on its good track record in managing start-up incubation, NEC was invited in 2006 by the Brunei Economic Development Board (BEDB) to manage a start-up incubator in Brunei. In 2011, a government agency in Singapore, the Media Development Authority (MDA), also contracted NEC to manage an interactive digital media-focused incubator outside the NUS campus. Called Block 71, this new NEI-run incubator has since emerged as the single largest incubator hub in Singapore, combining space for start-ups and VCs, angel investors, and various incubation services companies.

Building on experience in incubating tech startups and seeking to jump start the development of a social entrepreneurship support ecosystem in Singapore, NEC initiated in early 2011 a program to incubate social-impact-driven start-ups by social entrepreneurs that have sustainable and scalable business models, in collaboration with the GCL. Three of the incubatees succeeded in securing funding from the normal SPRING grants meant for tech startups, while two of the incubated companies had subsequently attracted follow-on investments by impact investors, thus catalyzing the development of a fledgling impact investment community in Singapore.

(c) The NUS Overseas College program

The NUS Overseas College (NOC) program was introduced via NUS Enterprise in 2001 as a new initiative that integrated both dimensions of globalism and entrepreneurship. Conceived originally by the president, the basic concept of the NOC program was to send the brightest and most entrepreneurially minded NUS undergraduate students to five entrepreneurial hubs in the world to work as interns in high-tech start-up companies for one year, during which time they would also take courses related to entrepreneurship at partner universities in each of the regions. In essence, the NOC program represented an experiment in learning entrepreneurship by "immersion," i.e., by immersing the student as an "apprentice" in a high-tech start-up or growth enterprise in a foreign location to expose him or her to the tacit aspects of entrepreneurial practice and foreign business culture. The program was conceived as a long-term investment in grooming future entrepreneurial leaders with global mindset and network connections; as such, it was not expected that the students would start their own ventures right after graduation, but rather, to infuse in them an entrepreneurial mindset that would orient their future research toward commercial innovation, as well as influence their future career choices toward more entrepreneurial and innovative pursuits. In addition, the program also aimed to help them establish valuable lifelong social networks with the entrepreneurial communities in leading high-tech hotspots overseas, so that they would be more inclined toward, and better equipped for, working in or starting new high-tech start-ups that will have global aspirations.

The first such NOC program was launched in Silicon Valley in 2002, followed by Philadelphia in 2003, Shanghai in 2004, Stockholm in 2005, Bangalore in 2006, Beijing in 2009, and Israel in 2011. The program aimed to accommodate a total of 200 students per year. The NUS Entrepreneurship Centre worked closely with NOC to provide educational support to these overseas internship programs by helping to develop academic collaboration with the selected partner universities in the respective overseas locations (e.g., Stanford in Silicon Valley, Fudan in Shanghai, the Royal Institute of Technology (KTH) in Stockholm, and Tsinghua in Beijing), and by conducting additional entrepreneurship courses not available at those overseas locations from the partner universities, as well as providing academic supervision of internship-based student projects.

Through the organizational mechanism of NUS Enterprise, NUS was able to launch the NOC program in a relatively short time, cutting through red tape that would otherwise have hampered the program at various faculty-level committees. The strong sponsorship of the president, emphasizing that the NOC program was to be the flagship program that would give NUS high visibility in supporting entrepreneurship education, coupled with the entrepreneurial drive of the NUS Enterprise CEO, helped in speeding up the approval process. The close cooperation between NEC and NOC also helped in ensuring smooth coordination and compatibility of academic course contents between the NOC and Technopreneurship Minor Program. Despite the high cost of the program (substantial subsidies are provided by NUS to each NOC participant), the NOC program appeared to have achieved its objective of giving high visibility to the overall NUS Enterprise initiative not only in the local media, but also internationally. With an increasing number of NOC participants who have completed the program and returned to NUS full of praise and appreciation of the transformational impacts of the program on them, word-of-mouth viral marketing is beginning to spread among Singaporean student communities, thus raising the profile of NUS as an entrepreneurial university and attracting the more entrepreneurially minded high school students to want to apply to NUS. As a significant proportion of the NOC participants are foreign students from other Asian countries, this visibility is likely to spread to the student communities in these Asian countries as well. In 2011, NUS senior management invited three prominent entrepreneurship figures (the director of Entrepreneurship Centre at UC Berkeley, an entrepreneurship professor at Imperial College, and the former Chief Scientist of Israel) to serve on an independent panel to evaluate the NOC program. The panel unanimously endorsed the program and recommended its further expansion.

(d) Restructuring of technology licensing and industry liaison functions

NUS's technology transfer office was originally set up in 1992 to handle technology transfer matters as part of the Industrial and Technology Relations Office (INTRO), including the protection and licensing of NUS intellectual property (IP) and the advising of industry, faculty, and staff on matters relating to IP. However, in the initial years, the office was not perceived as being a major source of assistance by either NUS inventors or industry seeking IP for licensing, as it did not have a full complement of experienced IP professionals. A number of instances were also reported of the office making tough demands in terms of extracting licensing fees. One of the first acts of the CEO of NUS Enterprise who took over INTRO was to introduce a number of major initiatives to make the office more "inventor-friendly," with less emphasis on maximizing licensing revenue, and a stronger focus on getting greater and faster deployment of NUS technology to the marketplace, whether through licensing to existing firms or spinning off new firms. In addition, NUS Enterprise set a policy of taking equity in lieu of royalty payments, and simplifying the process of negotiation on equity valuation.

INTRO was renamed the Industry Liaison Office (ILO) in 2006 and reorganized to facilitate greater synergy between university–industry research collaboration and technology transfer facilitation. The professional staffing of the office was strengthened, and a more proactive approach was implemented to map out areas of technological strengths of the university in order to guide future innovation directions and to facilitate patent portfolio aggregation to achieve critical mass in selected technology areas. The scope of ILO was also expanded to take on the IP management role for a number of new international joint R&D programs initiated by NUS with overseas universities, including the Singapore–MIT Alliance in Research & Technology (SMART) program.

Moving beyond providing IP management services to faculty with invention disclosures and patentable technologies, ILO has in recent years become more proactive in engaging and cultivating faculty with interests in technology commercialization, including conducting training workshops to equip professors and their postdoc research fellows and doctoral students with an understanding of the technology commercialization/spin-off process and the knowledge to assess market application potentials for their inventions. Working in partnership with the NUS Entrepreneurship Centre, ILO launched in 2013 a Lean Launchpad@Singapore program for NUS professors and researchers, in collaboration with Professors Jerry Engel and Steve Blank at UC Berkeley to adapt the Lean Launchpad program that they have been running for the National Science Foundation (NSF) in the United States.

(e) Integrated organizational strategy

In summary, notwithstanding organizational changes and leadership transition, NUS had continued to emphasize the adoption of an integrated, coordinated approach to promoting entrepreneurial development through the organizational vehicle of NUS Enterprise. The strategic goals of NUS Enterprise have also been refined over time to focus on two core missions: embedding entrepreneurial learning as an integral part of an NUS education by providing experiential entrepreneurial education, and translating NUS research into innovation by providing industry partnership and entrepreneurship support. Through these two strategic thrusts, the ultimate aim of NUS Enterprise is to help NUS achieve its vision of becoming a global knowledge enterprise and playing a pivotal role in Singapore's knowledge economy. The latest organizational structure of NUS Enterprise is as shown in Appendix A.

This strategy of integrating a focus on entrepreneurship while seeking to achieve excellence in research and education has continued to receive strong support and endorsement by the new president of NUS, who took over the helm of NUS in 2008. Indeed, to further reinforce the organizational strategy of having an autonomous NUS Enterprise organization to push the entrepreneurship agenda on a university-wide basis, NUS Enterprise has been entrusted with the responsibility of bidding for, and subsequently managing, a new funding program called the University Innovation Fund (UIF) by the National Research Foundation (NRF). NUS Enterprise managed to secure a five-year (2009–2014) grant from the UIF totaling S$9 million, significantly higher than the amount awarded to the other two local universities. This grant has enabled NUS Enterprise to roll out a number of the new initiatives described earlier, as well as to significantly expand some of their existing programs, despite having a fixed operating budget allocation over the years, as mentioned earlier. NUS Enterprise further grew its income sources by taking on strategic revenue-generating assignments (such as the Brunei incubator project and an annual Entrepreneurship Summer School for students from around the world), as well as leveraging a number of government co-investment and grant schemes (such as the SPRING Incubator Development Assistance Program (IDAP), the SPRING SEEDS, POC/POV grant schemes, and the MDA iJam scheme).

Besides achieving tangible outcomes and making visible impacts from the various programs that it runs, NUS Enterprise has further enhanced its ability to attract external financial resources through its growing role and influence as a policy think tank on entrepreneurship and innovation in Singapore and the region. Over the years, the applied research arm of the NUS Entrepreneurship Centre (NEC) has conducted numerous commissioned policy research studies for various government agencies in Singapore, such as A*STAR, SPRING, and the NRF, as well as for international organizations such as the World Bank, the OECD, and the Asian Development Bank. Through such commissioned studies, as well as other channels of consultative inputs, NEC has played an instrumental role in several new public policies being launched over the years, including the SPRING SEEDS program and POC/POV grant schemes.

4.   Outcomes

Although NUS has undertaken various initiatives to embrace an entrepreneurial university model that is still in its early stages, some visible changes can already be detected, as summarized in Table 12.4. Although the number of student enrollments and faculty positions experienced only moderate expansion, a more dramatic change can be observed in the new dimensions of foreign talent attraction, entrepreneurship promotion, and technology commercialization. These are further elaborated in the following.

Patenting

The number of NUS patent applications and patents granted has visibly increased in the 2000s compared to the 1990s. The total number of

Table 12.4: *Profile of changes in NUS before and after shift to entrepreneurial university model*

Indicator	AY1996/1997	AY2011/2012
Teaching staff	1,414	2,196
of which percent foreign	39.0 percent	51.9 percent[a]
Research staff	843	2,820
of which percent foreign	70.1 percent	78.6 percent[a]
Undergraduate students enrolled	17,960	25,107
Graduate students enrolled	4,478	7,901
Graduate students as percentage of total student enrolment	20.0 percent	23.9 percent
Percentage of foreign students studying at the NUS	13 percent[b]	35.4 percent
Total research funding	N.a.	S$436 mil[c]
Journal articles published in SCI/SSCI	1,306[d]	4,411[e]
Cumulative patents granted by USPTO	19[f]	290[g]
Licensing agreements signed	8[h]	19[i]
Spin-offs	<1[h]	3[j]

[a] Percentage FY 2004–2005.
[b] Percentage of total student intake for 1997/1998.
[c] External grants only.
[d] CY1996.
[e] CY2011.
[f] Up to CY 1996.
[g] Up to CY 2011.
[h] Average 1995–1999.
[i] FY2011.
[j] Only includes spin-offs that have licensed NUS IP. Data are for CY 2011.

NUS patent applications grew from an average of less than 100 per year over 1997–2002 to more than 150 over 2003–2012. The number of U.S. patents granted also registered a distinct increase, from less than twenty per year over 1997–2002 to more than thirty per year in the period 2003–2012. With 290 USPTO-granted patents in 2011, NUS has become the seventh largest holder of Singapore-based inventions granted U.S. patents, far ahead of NTU (sixty-six patents), the second largest local university in Singapore.

Licensing

A clear increase in the intensity of technology commercialization from 2000 is also evident. As of the end of FY 2011, NUS had made 330 technology licensing agreements. Of these, around 80 percent were signed in or after 2000. The number of signed licensing agreements had also increased to over twenty per year in the period 2002–2012 from an average of less than ten per year in the period 1995–2002.

Entrepreneurial spin-offs

The results of the change in NUS policy on encouraging technology commercialization through spin-off and start-up formation after 2000 are also evident. Of the 114 spin-offs and start-ups formed between 1991 and 2011, over 95 percent were established from 2000 on. Focusing only on spin-offs, which are companies formed to commercialize NUS patented inventions (as opposed to other faculty or student start-ups that do not involve NUS-owned IP), the average spin-off formation rate of five per year in recent years is creditable, even though it is still much lower than those of some of the top American universities, such as MIT (twenty-five spin-offs in 2011) and Stanford (nine spin-offs in 2009) (AUTM STATT database, n.d.).

NUS-related spin-offs and start-ups have received significant support from NUS Enterprise, including seed funding, incubation, and exclusive licensing of IP to the founders. While some spin-offs/start-ups received only one form of support, many received multiple forms of support. For example, fifty-eight out of sixty-two companies incubated by NEI as of the end of 2011 received some form of seed funding, while fourteen out of the forty spin-offs that received exclusive NUS IP licensing also received some form of seed-funding support. Overall, more than 120 spin-off/start-up companies had received at least one form of support services from NUS Enterprise over the years up to the end of 2011. Most of the NUS spin-offs/start-ups, especially those that received seed funding from NUS Enterprise, have been assigned a specific mentor to provide coaching and advice on how to cope with various start-up challenges such as finding customers and closing sales, finding and making pitches to VCs and angel investors, and so on.

Because most of the start-ups supported by NUS Enterprise are quite recent, many are in the early stages of growth and there have been few cases of significant commercial success as yet. It is encouraging to note, however, that close to twenty of the companies supported by NUS Enterprise have significant received follow-on investment by an external investor (VC fund or angel investor) or have been acquired at a valuation generating positive returns to the early equity investors by the end of 2011. The total amount of external follow-on investments received by these companies exceeded S$25 million. In addition, NUS Enterprise assisted more than a dozen of its portfolio of start-ups to successfully bid for a number of government POC grant schemes as of the end of 2011.

Industrial research collaboration

Another avenue for translating university research into technologies with commercialization potential is through collaborative research projects with industry. The number of research collaboration agreements (RCAs) undertaken by NUS has grown substantially over the last decade, rising from an average of 36 a year over 1995–1997 to close to 150 a year over 2005–2011. The absolute number of RCAs with industry has also increased, from an annual average of sixteen over 1995–1997 to close to fifty per year over 2005–2011. Although the share of RCAs with industry has fallen over this time, it is possible that this is due to the very small numbers of RCAs in the initial period. Aside from industry, research collaboration agreements have been formed with governmental bodies, public research institutes and foreign universities. In addition to the RCAs, NUS also interacts with industry through consultancy contracts. Significant consultancy work has been undertaken by NUS faculty, averaging about 700 consultancies over 2003–2004. However, no reliable statistics are available in more recent years, due to the decentralization of such data collection to individual faculties.

Attraction of foreign talent

A marked increase in attracting foreign talent is also evident in terms of both student intake and recruitment of faculty members and researchers. Between AY1996/1997 and AY2011/2012, the proportion of foreign students more than doubled from 13 percent to over one-third. Similarly, over 1996/1997 and 2004/2005 the share of foreigners increased from 39 percent to over 50 percent among faculty members, and from 70 percent to 80 percent among researchers. While more recent data are not available, the proportions of foreign faculty and researchers may have stabilized. Based on data from the recent NOC applicant pools, foreign applications were consistently overrepresented. Similarly, data on faculty applicants for seed funding and other forms of start-up assistance from NVSF/NEI also indicates an overrepresentation of professors of foreign origins. The available evidence does suggest that NUS is indeed attracting a good share of foreign talent with entrepreneurial interest.

5.   Conclusion

In summary, our brief case analysis of how NUS has sought to implement an entrepreneurial university model strongly suggests that an integrated approach under one coordinating organizational vehicle may be a viable model for universities located in newly industrialized regions where the supply of entrepreneurial resources and the supporting venture ecosystem are underdeveloped. Not only has the pace of technology commercialization and spin-off formation activities visibly increased since the introduction of the NUS Enterprise system, but also there is evidence that the long-term effort to inculcate a more entrepreneurial mindset among NUS students is beginning to make tangible impacts. Although the shift of NUS toward an entrepreneurial university model may not have been the sole cause, the empirical evidence cited earlier is consistent with the hypothesis that an integrated approach to entrepreneurial university development, in the form of an organizational vehicle such as NUS Enterprise, may be effective in harnessing synergies across different roles. While the specific governance model adopted (e.g., the NUS Enterprise organizational design) and initiatives/programs implemented (e.g., the seed fund program and NOC programs) may be unique to the Singapore context, and may not be applicable to other contexts, the experience of NUS may nonetheless be instructive for other East Asian universities seeking to develop their own entrepreneurial university models.

Besides knowledge commercialization, our findings of a high and increasing level of recruitment of foreign students, researchers, and faculty members by NUS are also consistent with our argument that an entrepreneurial university model for universities located in small, open economies needs to incorporate the additional role of attracting foreign talent. While the level of involvement of foreigners in NUS is probably exceptional by the standards of East Asian universities, and perhaps even when compared with Anglo-Saxon universities, it does suggest that an ability to compete for talent on a global scale is likely to rank as an important feature of any entrepreneurial university model for newly industrializing economies.

Last, but not least, our case study on NUS is also suggestive of a number of critical factors for the effective implementation of an integrated organizational approach to entrepreneurial university development. These include:(1) strategic visioning and leadership at the top, backed by adequate long-term resource commitments; (2) recruiting an entrepreneurial champion to lead the change at the initial stage, and managing a leadership transition to a more institutionalized, professional organization at a later stage; and (3) establishing a number of innovative flagship programs to give the initiative high visibility.

References

Association of University Technology Managers (AUTM). N.d. Statistics Access for Tech Transfer (STATT) Database. Available at www.autm.net/source/STATT/index.cfm?section=STATT.

Economic Review Committee (ERC). 2002. Report of the Entrepreneurship and Internationalisation Subcommittee. 13 September 2002. Singapore: Ministry of Trade and Industry.

Etzkowitz, H. 2003. "Innovation in innovation: The triple helix of university–industry–government relations," *Social Science Information* 42(3): 293–337.

Etzkowitz, H., Webster, A., Gebhardt, C., and Terra, B.R.C. 2000. "The future of the university and the university of the future: Evolution of ivory tower to entrepreneurial paradigm," *Research Policy* 29(2): 313–330.

Lee, C.M., Miller, W.F., Hancock, M.G., and Rowen, H.S. 2000. *The Silicon Valley Edge: A Habitat for Innovation and Entrepreneurship.* Stanford, CA: Stanford University Press.

National University of Singapore (NUS). Various years. Annual Report. Singapore: NUS.

Saxenian, A. 2000. *Silicon Valley's New Immigrant Entrepreneurs.* San Francisco: Public Policy Institute of California.

2002. *Local and Global Networks of Immigrant Professionals in Silicon Valley.* San Francisco: Public Policy Institute of California.

Wong, P.K. 2003. "From using to creating technology: The evolution of Singapore's national innovation system and the changing role of public policy," in S. Lall and S. Urata (eds.), *Foreign Direct Investment, Technology Development and Competitiveness in East Asia*, pp. 191–238. Cheltenham, UK/Northampton, MA: Edward Elgar Publishers.

2006. "The re-making of Singapore's high tech enterprise ecosystem," in H. Rowen, M. Hancock and W. Miller (eds.), *Making IT: The Rise of Asia in High Tech*, Chap. 5, pp. 123–174. Stanford, CA: Stanford University Press.

2007. "Commercialization of university biomedical science in a rapidly changing triple-helix nexus: The case of National University of Singapore." *Journal of Technology Transfer*, 32(4): 367–395.

Wong, P.K., Ho, Y.P., and Singh, A. 2007. "Towards an entrepreneurial university model to support knowledge-based economic development: The case of the National University of Singapore," *World Development*, 35(6): 941–958.

2011. "Towards a global knowledge enterprise: The entrepreneurial university model of National University of Singapore," in P.K. Wong (ed.), *Academic Entrepreneurship in Asia: The Role and Impact of Universities in National Innovation Systems*, Chap. 7, pp. 165–198. Cheltenham, UK: Edward Elgar.

Wong, P.K., Lee, L., Ho, Y.P., and Wong, F. 2005. *Global Entrepreneurship Monitor 2004: Singapore Report.* Singapore: NUS Entrepreneurship Centre.

Wong, P.K. and Singh, A. 2011. *OECD Review of Innovation in Southeast Asia: Country Profile of Singapore.* Research report commissioned by OECD.

Appendix A

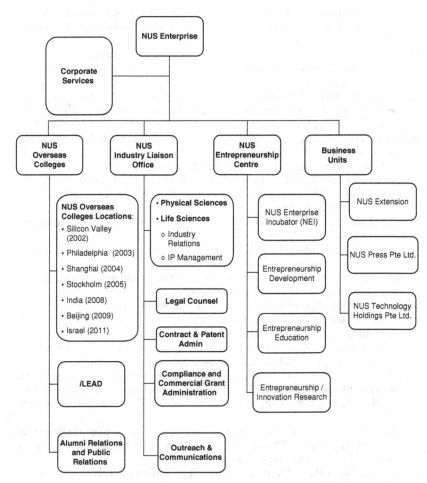

Figure 12A.1: Organization chart of NUS Enterprise as of March 2013.

13 The path to the entrepreneurial university in China: A case study of Northeastern University, China

Chunyan Zhou

Up to the end of 2012, the total assets of China's 489 universities with 3,478 university-run enterprises (UREs) had been ¥319.026 billion, of which the assets sum of the top 20 universities' UREs is ¥250 billion. Beijing University and Tsinghua University ranked first and second: around ¥100 billion[1] and over ¥70 billion (Science and Technology Development Centre in the Ministry of Education, 2013). The university is playing an increasingly important role in the economy as an entrepreneur. However, academic entrepreneurship took a noticeably different turn in China than in the United States: it is driven and run by university/research institutes administrations. Chinese universities are developing a distinctive path to the entrepreneurial university. They utilized existing technology rather than research-based inventions as the basis of firm formation. The latter is now seen as a follow-on strategy to the initial task of creating technology firms from available knowledge. Relying on their administrative, financial, and knowledge capabilities, Chinese universities redirected resources from their teaching and research budgets to establish firms, university-run enterprises (UREs). Concepts such as science parks, incubators, high-tech industrial development zones, and technology transfer expanded the new mission of the university to grow the economy in the late 1980s. These imported innovation mechanisms were utilized in a different way than in their country of origin. In China, they became the basis of a Communist Party-led, government-pulled, and university-based economic development strategy. Recent developments includes a variety of university technology transfer departments working between the university and industry. For instance, Zhejiang University established a special department, the "local liaison department." to link the school to local industry and government. Many others have a "Science and Technology Industrial Development Department" that

---

[1] ¥100 billion is approximately equivalent to US$16 billion.

is charged with administrating their UREs and developing relations with the local industry sector.

Academic institutions in China played a much more direct role in firm formation than is typical of U.S. universities. Indeed, Chinese universities have created large-scale and high-tech UREs that belong to a part of their organizational structure, run by their administration. Although university–industry collaborations in China can be traced back to the 1950s and even earlier, science and technology (S&T) enterprises created with university resources only began to appear in the early 1980s. Industry was heretofore expected to be the prime mover in technology-based firm formation. In an important document, "Solution on Implementing the Outline of Science and Technology Program," enterprises were encouraged to take the lead in technological innovation, with the expectation that the university would assist them. When this strategy did not produce results, government encouraged universities, through a combination of incentives and budget cuts, to substitute for industry in creating firms from a large repository of knowledge about advanced, if not leading-edge technology, which resided in the university. Thus, university entrepreneurial activities were increasingly encouraged. Nevertheless, the university with entrepreneurial activities may not necessarily be an entrepreneurial university based upon research results and spillover of internally generated knowledge (Zhou and Peng, 2008). In contrast to the examples of entrepreneurial universities in the United States, China's university is seeking a workable path to serve economic growth and social development. This chapter discusses the distinctive Chinese path to the entrepreneurial university through a case study of Northeastern University (NEU), a leading academic institution in a region traditionally dominated by heavy industry. *Chinese Entrepreneurs*, a well-known magazine in the country, published an Internationalization Index of Chinese Enterprises and 2012 Top 50 China Emerging Multinationals, in which the Neusoft Group ranked twelfth.

1.   The Chinese entrepreneurial university model in contrast to its counterpart in the United States

According to case studies of MIT and Stanford University (Etzkowitz 2002; 2008), New England as a "brown field" region had a declining industrial foundation in the 1930s, whereas the Bay Area, around Palo Alto, was a green field site, largely lacking an industrial base. However, the economic development in both areas was driven by entrepreneurial universities – MIT and Stanford University – through knowledge-based academic entrepreneurship and university technology transfer/licensing.

Entrepreneurial universities and industrial firms have been playing the main melody of economic and social development in the areas together.

An entrepreneurial university cannot only be defined as a university that encourages entrepreneurship and develops entrepreneurial ideas. It strives not only to continually participate in society's technological innovation, but also to bring such innovation to bear on society's needs. In general, entrepreneurial university prototypes shows four primary characteristics:

- Top-level human resources are hired; first-class research achievement and advanced facilities are invested in scientific and technological research or knowledge produced.
- Entrepreneurship activities are widely accepted and supported on/off campus.
- Organizational mechanisms for research application are in place to interface between the university and industry, e.g., a Technology Transfer Office (TTO) or an Office of Technology Licensing (OTL).
- Members of the university use their research results in labs to form quasi-firms and then firms, which help finance the university's research and other activities.

Many other U.S. universities have succeeded in developing these characteristics. In addition, successful university-originated start-ups often act as angels to newly emerging firms, providing a source of venture capital (Etzkowitz and Pique 2005). However, Chinese universities are far less likely to possess these characteristics, even though technology transfer is attracting greater attention, national centers of technology transfer have now been established in six universities, and some have even set up international centers of technology transfer to help introduce technology from other countries.

From 1949, when the "Peoples Republic of China" was born, to 1978, in which China started a reform and openness strategy, the Chinese university was influenced by the former Soviet Union and mainly engaged in teaching programs. Research was carried on by research institutes, usually pointed at national (military/defense) goals, separated from university and industry. Since the first National Conference of Science and Technology, held in 1978, the university has enhanced research and engaged in regional economic growth. The second National Science and Technology Conference (2006) indicated that industry must become the main actor in innovation and that the university should contribute to innovation. Nevertheless, industry has lagged as the university has become a prime mover in establishing new technology-based firms, UREs, within the university.

Historically, Chinese UREs have undergone four stages.[2] In the first stage, from 1983 to 1988, most UREs were based on the faculty's technological expertise and developed slowly due to the influence of the political, economic, and ideological system of the time. The second or organized collectivization stage was from 1988 to 1993, when there were two outstanding landmarks. One was the rapid development in 1986 of Founder Electronic Co. under the leadership of Xuan Wang (1937–2006), known as "the contemporary Bi Sheng"[3] for inventing a Chinese laser typesetting system and financed by Peking University. The other was the rise of NEU Science Park along with the entrepreneurial initiatives of Professor Jiren Liu, who successfully initiated a URE, NEU–Alpine, now known as Neusoft. The third stage, from 1994 to 1999, is a development period in which entrepreneurial activities became widespread. Since NEU Science Park was successful, other universities followed suit and set up on their own. In 1999, the Central Committee of the Communist Party of China and State Council enacted a resolution to enhance technological innovation and achieve greater industrialization. It legislated for UREs and emphasized the support of university science parks. Moreover, the Ministry of Education and Ministry of Science and Technology jointly determined that twenty-two National Science Parks should be established, beginning in 2001.

Government policies, measures, and laws play a critical role in the national innovation system of China. Since the 1980s, policy has promoted the development of science and technology, knowledge industrialization, and high-tech industry. However, the policies sometimes lack stability and continuity. Policies and laws in the United States aim at guidance and prevention, whereas in China they are used as tools to control or remedy. Every official who has taken an important action is typically trying to create new ideas to put forward in order to demonstrate political achievement. This leads to less consistent policies and is a commonplace phenomenon. Since government plays the most important role in regional innovation, the instability and absence of foresight in policy and law produces a serious inhibiting effect. In the "government-pulled" model (Zhou, 2008, 2012), government can call on a university to participate in innovation any time and anywhere. To pull innovation out of universities, the Chinese government is both the innovative organizer and its main investor. On occasion, this strategy has subjected universities to

---

[2] Although Tsinghua University established the first technological URE of China, Tsinghua Technology Service Company, on early February 1 of 1980, universities widely started to build their UREs from 1983.

[3] Bi Sheng (970–1051): the inventor of movable type printing in ancient China.

significant financial risk. To redress the problem, government has taken steps, since 2001, to make UREs independent by moving them into separate legal business entities, although universities retain ownership. Although these "firms" are not "spin-offs" in the U.S. sense, the intention is that UREs will become "public" independent entities through IPOs on the stock exchange in the future.

Therefore, Chinese entrepreneurial university characteristics are as follows:

- must be party-led and government-pulled
- owns UREs (wholly owned or joint venture)
- pursues academic entrepreneurship based on advanced research on the campus, but the technologies may be self-developed on campus or not – imported partly or completely
- accepts academic entrepreneurship completely as a university mission – in ideology and practice

2.   Co-development of NEU and industries in Liaoning Province

Liaoning regional development follows the government-pulled model. The model has made it easier to achieve large-scale innovation projects and to reorganize regional innovation resources and fill the gaps that are necessary for innovation in a region, forming a consensus in regional innovation. It has also helped to artificially foster university–industry links, protect the university's interest in entrepreneurship by policies, and build an innovation platform within the region. The disadvantages are as follows: University–industry joint innovations tend to be "shows" rather than real commercial ventures. Personnel, equipment, and funds are all provided by the state. Another danger is that the university and industry might lose the flexibility to deal with problems in the innovation process and the two parties might rely excessively on government, resulting in passivity and inertia. They need government funding to "pull" them forward.

In August 1950, NEU was renamed "Northeastern Institute of Engineering" by the then Northeast Administration Committee and became one of the 64 key universities of the country. This experience gave the campus the advantage in engineering disciplines. However, on March 8, 1993, it was renamed Northeastern University and in September 1998, NEU was affiliated by the Ministry of Education (MOE) and jointly developed by MOE, Liaoning Province, and Shenyang City government, resulting in its strong service mission for local industry development. NEU and Liaoning industries are co-developing through interactions.

2.1   Founding and development of NEU

In 1922, Yongjiang Wang (then Governor of Fengtian Province, now Liaoning Province, renamed by General Xueliang Zhang, son of General Zuolin Zhang as then overlord of the Northeast of China) and Yinchang Xie (then Director of Fengtian Education Department) appealed to Zuolin Zhang, the head of the Northeastern Army, to establish a university as part of a strategy to build a strong Northeast China. NEU was founded on April 26, 1923. Its founding President was Governor Yongjiang Wang, who set out NEU's educational mission to integrate theory and practice. At the very beginning, the university established its own factory to provide students with practical work experience. In August of 1928, Marshal Chang Hsueh-liang, Zuolin Zhang's son, became president of NEU. He encouraged research and "exploring profound problems and training professional talents." In 1953, the university administration made a decision to strengthen scientific and technological research. With a neighboring institution as partner, the Institute of Computer Technology of the Chinese Academy of Sciences, NEU developed China's first computer in 1958.

In the early 1950s, President Shuliang Jin initiated a university–industry cooperation model on the basis of the reciprocal principle of "needs and consensus." In fact, since the 1950s, the university was requested to meet local industrial needs. Its disciplines and specialties reflect heavy industries in the area that revolve around mining, machine tools, and metal smelting. However, after reform and the opening up of China, a huge "industrial gap" appeared during the 1980s and early 1990s. Traditional industries withered away as new industries began to appear. Failing companies looked to the government to save them, and indeed, the Liaoning Provincial government attempted to help existing industries by linking them to universities.

NEU, as one of the leading universities in the area, had to help industry to overcome this difficult period. There were two dilemmas for the university: (1) investment was insufficient and (2) thousands of research results by faculty and students were left unexplored. The university badly needed money and the opportunity for knowledge application at the same time as industry was starved of new technologies and ideas. The need and the ability to meet that need were perfect partners. Even before 1988, when the Science Park was founded, NEU–industry collaboration had achieved distinct results. Collaboration took four forms: consulting for enterprises; working together to resolve difficult problems; joint ventures to form new companies; and training technology workers for new enterprises.

The year 1988 was a vital turning point at NEU. Young Jiren Liu, China's first Ph.D. in applied computer science, established his quasi-firm, a research center, with two other founders after he came back from one year of study in the American National Institute of Standards and Technology (NIST). This is a vey beginning of professors moving away from serving existing businesses and beginning to create their own entrepreneurial ventures. The university administration decided to expand its entrepreneurship activities, creating the Science and Technology Development Zone of Nanhu, including the Science Park of NEU and Sanhao Street of Science and Technology. The Science Park provided not only an ideal ground for university–industry collaboration, but also an arena for raising funds through entrepreneurship. In the 1980s, UREs were primarily low-tech, traditional service enterprises such as guest houses, small factories, and presses. Since the early 1990s, they have become a mixture of low- and high-tech, traditional and modern, joint and independent enterprises, in the service, marketing and production industries.

2.2   NEU's role in the higher education cluster of Liaoning Province

There are 14 regional-level cities and 14 county-level cities in Liaoning Province, and a population of 40.67 million. In the 1950s, Liaoning was an old industrial area producing the first furnace steel, the first large-scale transformer of electricity, the first jet plane, and the first 10,000-ton ship designed by the Chinese. However, in the 1980s, the region was not involved in new technology. Even now, heavy chemical engineering products still make up to 75 percent of production output. Most industries are traditional low-tech, such as textiles, mining, machine tools, and iron and steel smelting. From the point of view of economic growth, it represents high investment, high consumption of resources, and high pollution, but low output and low efficiency. In 2004, its GNP was 1/20 of the country total, but energy consumption was almost 1/10 of the total. Basically, Liaoning Province had a large population and traditional heavy industry, but was not strong in science and technology.

China's reform agenda has put pressure on Liaoning to reform state enterprises and determine the future direction for its industries. It has to revitalize existing industries and create new ones. Liaoning has to innovate in the face of major challenges: (1) The R&D expenditure as a percentage of GDP ranged from 0.8–1.6 percent from 2000 to 2010 (Jing Zhang 2012). In 2012, it touched 1.98%. In more developed parts of the world it has been 3–5%. For example, Sweden, Finland and Israel

Table 13.1: *Liaoning science and technology workers*

	2005	2006	2007	2010
Number of S&T practitioners	186,000	188,000	191,000	219,000
Number of scientists and engineers	123,000	129,000	136,000	148,000

Source: Liaoning Statistical Yearbook 2011.

achieved 3.37%, 3.78%, and 4.35% respectively in 2011 (World Bank, 2013). The R&D/Sales ratios of most well-known companies worldwide are about 10%; for example, Ericsson and Huawei in Shenzhen have recorded 23% and 14.4% results.[4] (2) The economic benefits of science and technology are still very low; only around 20 percent of research results make a contribution to productivity every year. Few of China's high-tech products exporting come from Liaoning, compared to 40 percent in Gunagdong Province in 2006.[5]

Nevertheless, Liaoning has particular advantages. For example, it had sufficient S&T practitioners (Table 13.1) and 76 higher education institutions (HEIs), 1,202 science and technology R&D institutes, 23 university science parks, and three national and four provincial Advanced and High-tech Development Zones. According to the 2009 Liaoning Statistical Yearbook in HEIs' Research, in 2009 there were 57 higher education institutions and 37,135 scientists and engineers that participate in S&T activities. The total research project number reached 14,217, among them 2,124 at the national level. Total funding was ¥3,239 billon.

Every advanced and high-tech area has its official incubators. In early 2006, there were 1,150 firms taking advantage of them. In addition, there are 34 nongovernment incubators with a further 652 firms (Science and Technology Department of Liaoning Province, 2006). However, the local government looks to enterprises to achieve technological innovation, but asks university and research institutes to work with them. Government supports university–industry links directly through policies and laws and indirectly through initiatives such as science and technology development zones. A great transition took place in Liaoning and throughout China: a shift toward knowledge-based industries through technological innovation in which universities play an increasing role.

---

[4] Liaoning Province as an old industrial base is pushed to independent innovation "crossroads" (2006.02.21), *Liaoning Daily*. Available at http://chinaneast.xinhuanet.com/2006-02/21/content_6282143.htm. Cited on Feb. 3, 2014.
[5] Ibid.

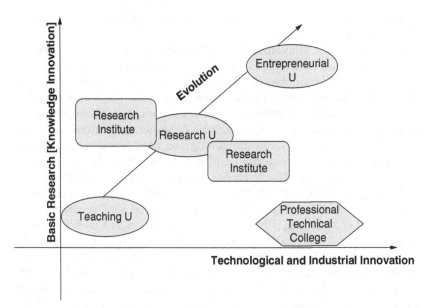

Figure 13.1: The Higher Education Cluster in Liaoning regional innovation.

There are many factors that determine entrepreneurship success at NEU, such as cultural tradition, practice base, the needs of local industry, academic research that can be capitalized, the government's ability to lead and organize, and the emergence of top-class entrepreneurs, as well as organizational mechanisms and policies that facilitate university technology transfer. In fact, technology transfer through an entrepreneurial approach is a process of new knowledge spillover and practical application. Entrepreneurial professors in universities actually are "transmission agents" for scientific and technology information. The existence of such agents is essential for university entrepreneurship to succeed.

There are 40 universities and 36 professional colleges in Liaoning Province. Each of these HEIs has its own characteristics and status, e.g., professional colleges and teaching or research universities. These HEIs constitute the higher education cluster of Liaoning Province (Figure 13.1).

Most higher education institutions are concentrated in Shenyang and Dalian, forming both a convergent and divergent distribution. Northeastern University and Dalian University of Technology are the two leading universities. They are respectively located in Shenyang (north) and Dalian (south). Since Shenyang is the capital city of Liaoning

Province, NEU has strategic significance in regional innovation and development.

NEU has built a foundation for the IT industry of Liaoning Province. Government had identified IT as a "mainstay industry" due to its uses in renewing existing industries as well as creating new ones. As one of the leading universities in the province, NEU thus plays an important role in the formation of regional industries and technological innovation. It is currently focusing on manufacturing technology, automation engineering, engineering of environmental protection, refinement of chemical engineering, nanomaterials, and green energy, as well as modern agriculture technology. It actively organizes internal resources to address technological difficulties and supports incubation and commercialization by relevant research groups of results from national S&T projects.

Up to May 2011, NEU has 2,401 faculty and 24,514 undergraduate students; 5,613 postgraduate students and 3,069 Ph.D. candidates. In addition, it has 65 bachelor specialties, 173 disciplines that can train postgraduate students, and three training stations for professional degrees: MBA, MPA, and Master of Engineering; 84 disciplines that may award Ph.D.s; 14 postdoctoral stations; 3 national key labs; 1 state environment protection key laboratory of eco-industry; four national engineering (technology) research centers and 6 MOE key labs; 6 MOE engineering (technology) research centers; and 1 state–local joint engineering laboratory.[6] On the other hand, NEU inherits its tradition of collaboration with industries and commitment to knowledge-based firm formation. Therefore, NEU is capable of being one of the HEIs in transition between the research and entrepreneurial university, trying to develop an entrepreneurial model in China and contributing to the region.

2.3   NEU Science Park

Relying on its dominant disciplines, NEU strives to develop its high-tech firms, forming one of its main managerial characteristics. In 1990, the University established the first STP of China, becoming one of the first national university science parks. The Park was identified as a national high-tech entrepreneurship center in 2006. It is located at NEU in the central city of the Northeast Area, Shenyang of Liaoning Province. The region has been home to traditional industries, such as textiles, steelmaking, machine tools, and mining, since the 1950s. Therefore, the university focused on engineering education matched to those needs before the 1990s. Since then, the focus has switched to automation, computing, and

---

[6] See Northeastern University of China at http://baike.baidu.com/view/2482.htm#6.

Table 13.2: *Time when enterprises entered the incubator*

	1993	1996	1997	1998	1999	2000	2001	2002	2003	2004	2008	2011
Incubating enterprises	1	2	2	3	3	8	3	14	32	112	106	
Accumulated number of graduated enterprises	1	1	2	4	5	7	15	22	24	25	26	36

Source: Data in 2008 from www.zggxkj.com.cn/?module=show&id=18; data in 2011 from www.stdaily.com/kjrb/content/2011–05/06/content_302403.htm (cited on March 12, 2013); others are from the author collected from www.neu.edu.cn (cited in 2006).

IT engineering. Given access to the resources of the Institute of Computer Technology of the Chinese Academy of Sciences and the research foundation that produced the first computer of China, NEU identified the IT industry as the target for developing UREs. As a result, it founded Neusoft in 1988, which became known as "China's Microsoft."

NEU Science Park has three components: a scientific park, an entrepreneurial park, and an industry park. The scientific park is a virtual area made up of stress labs, engineering centers, and research institutes. It supports technology transfer and high-tech firm formation. The entrepreneurial park incubates new high-tech firms, transferring research results and training entrepreneurial talents. The industry park hosts enterprises that have graduated from entrepreneurial development zones all over the country, including the one in Shenyang. They are both developers and disseminators of technological innovation. As of 2005, the Park had 450 companies, among them, 110 high and new technology firms. Its incubator focuses on IT, new materials, advanced equipment, and light mechanical and electrical integration. See Table 13.2.

NEU Science Park, owns 35,000 m² space for incubating new firms. The park also works as an entrepreneurial park and industrial park. It has three subparks: NEU Software Park (in Shenyang), Neusoft Software Park (in Dalian), and NEU Sujiatun Science Park. As the NEU technology transfer center was identified as a national model institution for technology transfer in 2009, the university has completed a platform for academic entrepreneurship and technology transfer.

2.4   NEU Science & Technology Industry (Group) Co., Ltd.

Established in August 2005, the NEU Science & Technology Industry Co. Ltd., invested in by NEU, is a wholly state-owned limited liability company, approved by State-owned Assets Supervision and the Administration Commission of the State Council (SASAC) and the Ministry of Education (MOE). With ¥500 million, it is classified as a corporate legal entity in self-management, self-financing, self-development, and self-restraint. Its tasks include the following: under the leadership of NEU administration, on behalf of the school, exercise the rights of the investor, perform the functions of the investor, and operate the enterprise legally; increase the value of the university in high-technology radiation and social service, and improve application of scientific and technological achievements through small and medium-sized high-tech enterprise incubation; continue to foster innovation and entrepreneurship; and fulfill the interaction between industrial development in the region and the University.

NEU Science & Technology Industry Co. Ltd. has fostered a number of enterprises such as Neusoft, a leading group of regional IT industrial clusters.[7] Since the academic entrepreneurship strategy was adopted, NEU has continuously invested around ¥30 billion in its enterprises. In 2010, the annual income of the NEU Science & Technology Industry Co. Ltd reached ¥6.52 billion. For the end of 2010, its total assets had reached ¥11.95 billion (Science and Technology Development Centre in the Ministry of Education, 2012). NEU Science & Technology Industry Co. Ltd. also manages the NEU Science Park, incubating high-tech firms. In 2006, it had ten joint ventures and twenty-three wholly owned subenterprises. However, the number changes all the time. It has on line fourteen wholly owned enterprises and fourteen joint ventures (six Sino–foreign among them), involving computer and software, digital medical, automation and instrumentation, equipment manufacturing, metallurgy new materials, energy saving, and environmental protection and integrated services. See Figure 13.2.

3.   UREs and the development of NEU

Since 2000, UREs have entered their fourth or normative stage. In 2001, starting from Tsinghua University and Peking University, government mandated that universities separate from UREs through establishing university "Enterprises Group Co., Ltd." to reduce the risk that universities may be involved in financial dilemmas, through bankruptcy of a firm or liability for product flaws.

In general, NEU UREs have undergone three stages. The first one is "making a reservoir to foster fish." The university sets up an internal

[7] Official website of NEU Science & Technology Industry Co. Ltd. http://www.neucy.cn.

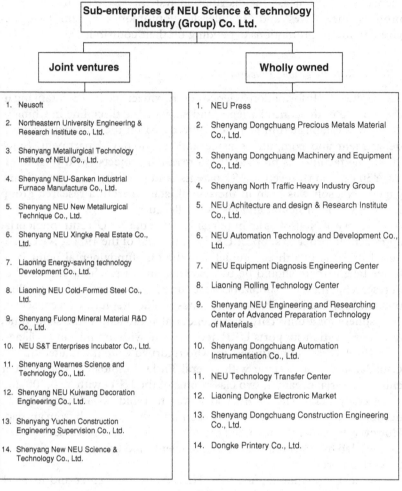

Figure 13.2: Subenterprises of NEU Science & Technology Industry (Group) Co. Ltd. *Source:* www.neucy.cn/attachcom.php; cited March 2013.

fund of about ¥1 million annually to encourage fundamental research. It does not take any fee within the first three years of its UREs. The second stage is "incubating and flying a kite." The university held that since there are different criteria in academy and industry, UREs should not operate like academic institutions. It developed the policy of "three unleashes": (1) unleash the hiring system; let URE hire employees by themselves; (2) unleash the distribution system; let UREs distribute the profit by themselves; and (3) unleash the promotion system; let UREs give employees promotions depending on their contributions.

3.1   Rapidly growing Neusoft

The College of Information Science and Engineering of NEU, ranking in the top two in the control science and engineering discipline in China in 2012, was established in October 1996 based on the automatic control department and computer science and technology department. Since 2000, the faculty has finished 1,738 research projects (with total funding ¥304 million), received 181 patents, and published 9,544 academic papers. Neusoft was born in the school, started from a research group led by a young professor and his two colleagues.[8]

The story of Neusoft is an important part of the NEU's entrepreneurial approach. In order to support UREs, at the end of the 1980s, NEU proposed its "one-two-three" guidelines; the one fundamental point is to foster talent; there should be two centers, one in teaching and another in research; and there should be three functions: dissemination, production, and application of knowledge. These guidelines formed a consensus atmosphere for a university entrepreneurial approach. At the same time, its administration supports URE development with funding and policies.

In 1989, three young professors who returned from the United States, Canada, and Japan, along with several Ph.D. candidates, started their entrepreneurial dream in two classrooms of the NEU with ¥30,000 and three computers. The original idea was to build an advanced lab in network and software technology to continue their research from abroad. However, financial problems led them to consider getting the seed capital for their lab by providing knowledge to clients and using clients' facilities to work on projects.

The next year they founded the NEU Software Center and in 1991 they organized the joint venture NEU–Alpine with the Alpine company of Japan. Two years later, it became a joint stock company. On June 18, 1996, Shenyang Neu–Alpine Software Co. became the first professional software enterprise to be marketed on the Shanghai Stock Exchange. In 1998, it was renamed Neusoft Group Co., a joint venture with Shanghai Baosteel Group Corporation. Such measures ensured multiple sources of investment for Neusoft to innovate and develop. Within four years, NEU was selecting the best senior students in the NEU computer department and giving them special training to work for Neusoft.

[8] For the Neusoft case study, please see Chunyan Zhou (2012).

The main founder of and President of Neusoft, Jiren Liu (born in 1955), is a successful entrepreneur and one of the Vice-Presidents of NEU, the Director of the National Engineering Research Center of Computer Software, and the representative for China at the APEC Business Advisory Council. He graduated from NEU with a Bachelor's, Master's, and Ph.D. in computer software and worked for the university from 1982 as a faculty member. Under his leadership Neusoft has grown in value from $250,000 to $556 million. In 2005, its sales income reached ¥2.7 billon (approximately $310 million). It has developed from the original three cofounders to over 8,000 employees, and from two to over ten thousand stockholders.

Neusoft has three main divisions: software and services, medical treatment systems, and IT education and training. It integrates research, design, development, production, marketing, training, and service of software products. At present, it consists of eight regional headquarters and forty branch institutions and has established affiliates in the United States and Japan. The primary branches include Neusoft Software Park Industrial Development Co., Neusoft Medical System Co., and Neusoft Joint Stock Co. In this way, Neusoft operates as a business rather than as an academic institution. Since Neusoft was listed on the Shanghai Stock Exchange, the NEU only possesses 20 percent of the stock shares.

3.2   Support from the NEU administration and local government

On the NEU campus, since 2001, there have been 8,469 research projects supported by government agencies and industrial firms; 659 patents have been achieved; and some research results were transferred to industry or became the base for building UREs.[9] The NEU is building a new type of industrial park to encourage UREs to expand and move to industry. Its Science Park aims at technology transfer from the university, whereas the new industry park aims at following international advanced science and technology to facilitate economic development. It will concentrate on attracting multinational corporations to locate their R&D institutions in the park. The industry park, expected to be located on a new campus, will provide more opportunities and space for a university–entrepreneurial approach. The new campus is located on the south bank of the Hun River, with a beautiful natural environment. According to the present president, Professor Jicheng He, the campus will serve two functions. The first is to build the second NEU Science Park to incubate more high-tech firms. The other is to combine NEU's network and software school

[9] See http://baike.baidu.com/view/2482.htm#6, cited on February 3, 2014.

into the new campus to provide necessary technologies for Liaoning industry.

Another important factor is a change in the criteria of academic assessment. The university administration has made market results a criterion for academic promotion and assessment of technological results. In the past, the number of publications, various rewards, and invention patents decided the academic level of a professor. China can afford allowing some scholars to focus on theoretical issues, but it must encourage more faculty and students to work on application-oriented research. For example, research is being carried out for the Shanghai Baosteel Group Corporation "to achieve grain refinement in the rolling of new-generation steel materials," and a "production process of clean steel," developed by the NEU faculty, has increased sales income for the Fushun Steel Corporation. These achievements are all considered as factors for faculty to be promoted.

3.3   *University–Enterprise Cooperation Committee of NEU*

The NEU, led by the former Ministry of Metallurgy and subsequently by the Ministry of Education before September of 1998, started to be managed by the Department of Education, Liaoning Province, and Shenyang City together in 2001. The decentralization further ignited the university's local economic service mission at the same time as government played a growing role in building university–industry linkage. The best example is the University–Enterprise Cooperation Committee of the NEU, which was established on November 2, 1991. It consists of the Economic and Trade Committee of Liaoning Province Government, the Educational Department of Liaoning Province Government, the NEU, and thirty-five of the largest state enterprises in Liaoning Province.

Government thus becomes a "regional innovation organizer," playing the role of a leading institution of university–industry cooperation and innovation. According to the relevant rules, first the NEU must publish its newest research achievement to the membership enterprises, and transfer technology to them as a priority. Second, in the selection of research problems and training talents, it should consider the needs of membership enterprises. Enterprises, in turn, should issue their technology needs and problems to the NEU to resolve. Within the first year of the Committee's life, over 500 university–industry contracts were signed, worth ¥270 million, creating an economic value of ¥2 billion.

The University–Enterprise Cooperation Committee of the NEU aims at strengthening university–industry linkage. The Committee commissioned relevant Liaoning departments to organize an annual conference to summarize existing linkages. Participants include relevant NEU leaders and experts, the principals of administration and technology in given enterprises, and the directors of science and technology in each city government of Liaoning Province. Government supports university and industry through making financial resources available to them, including those from the Ministry of Science and Technology, the Ministry of Education, the China Academy, and the China NSF. The university is expected to serve local innovation in three ways: providing entrepreneurship education; helping industry resolve problems or jointly establishing R&D centers; and supporting UREs, especially from the research in its labs. Industry is encouraged to rely on university research to renew existing or achieve new technological innovations and products. The provincial government also tries to build a platform for enterprises to access universities, as well as organizing some innovation projects by itself.

3.4   Direct return from UREs to NEU

Most successful UREs bring returns to the university. The contribution of UREs to NEU basically embodies three aspects:

- They expand the influence of NEU. For example, in the 1990s, many in China did not know of NEU, but they knew of NEU–Alpine. They recognized the university through the marketing company, for it was the first software company on the Shanghai Stock Exchange. Its high profile helped attract many excellent software experts to work in NEU Science Park or its UREs.
- Many employees in UREs also work for the university as faculty. They have "double identities." Even the President, Jiren Liu, is still a professor and vice president of NEU. He takes on training Ph.D. candidates as well as normal teaching and research. In this way, he can give students some practical problems from relevant industry, so that teaching and research activities become realistic and meaningful.
- UREs accumulate educational investment for further development of the university. UREs have used their capital to improve faculty living conditions, set up scholarships, and explore new research fields.

Moreover, UREs are also developing a more educational function as they become involved in jointly built professional colleges, such as the Neusoft Institute of Information, Sino-Dutch Biomedical, the Information Engineering School of NEU, and the Software School of NEU. As we know, many large-scale companies in the world have established their own "corporate institutes," for example, HP Business School, Siemens Management Institute, and Ericsson China Institute, as well as some

Table 13.3: *Situation of Neusoft Institute of Information*

Location	Dalian	Nanhai	Chengdu	Total
Year established	2000	2002	2002	
Land area (m^2)	585,000	400,000	1,000,000	1,985, 000
Number of students	14,000 +	around 7,000	5,000+	26,000+

Source: The author collected the data from www.neusoft.com/cn/services/1098/.

Chinese corporation institutes, such as Kingdee, Haier, Lenovo, and Konka.

UREs' educational activities are run as joint ventures with the mother university. Their reputations strengthen each other. Working together with NEU, Neusoft has built the Neusoft Institute of Information in three cities of China: Dalian, Nanhai, and Chengdu (see Table 13.3) These institutes use NEU's resources and reputation, but conversely raise NEU's reputation and its faculty's income. Neusoft's Research Institute will continuously contribute to the new NEU Academy.

4.   Conclusion

4.1   The difference between UREs and spin-offs

The triple helix theory emphasizes the optimum role of university–industry–government cooperation in innovation (Etzkowitz 2003). The model in China is quite different from the one in the United States. On one hand, neither the university nor industry is strong enough to become the organizer of regional innovation. On the other hand, the power relations among the university, industry, and government suggest that only government can become the organizer. Thus, government typically pulls the other two spheres to achieve regional innovation. In addition, government guidance influences industrial firms predominantly, including those that have been changed to private ownership.

The premise of a government-pulled triple helix is that government's organizational role in organizing national/regional innovation is absolutely important and decisive. In a "government-pulled triple helix," government initiates and controls significant projects through science and innovation policies and measures. All or most research universities, key research institutes, and large-scale enterprises are affiliated with (central or local) government; therefore, the active role is played primarily by government administrative power. Thus, government policies and resolutions regulate the performance evaluation of innovation – government

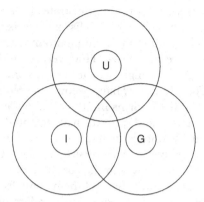

Figure 13.3: Revised triple helix.

organizes the primary innovation agents, such as high-tech industrial development zones (including Science Parks and incubators), markets for technology and intellectual property, and science and technology information networks.

A triple-helix field concept, in which each institutional sphere has an internal core and external field space, is proposed in order to understand the difference between UREs and spin-offs (Zhou 2001). The core allows the spheres to keep independence, and interaction between spheres takes place in the outside space (Figure 13.3). The triple-helix field gives rise to the dynamics of interaction among helices. The key to achieving an ideal triple helix of regional innovation is to create three relatively independent and balanced helices through analyzing the weak factors in a region and filling in the gaps. The roles of the university and industry in China have serious deficiencies, especially that of industry. In this case, government has to impel the university to become an important source of high-tech industry development. Sometimes, various levels of government also participate directly in economic activities.

How can a government that regulates and supervises the market deal with its own firms? Can universities resolve the tension among teaching, research, and creating/running enterprises? These problems arise from the core area, rather than the outer space. An institutional sphere may lose its distinct character. If each helix cannot keep its own specific status, it is very difficult for the spheres to interact in the external field space, since the confusion of functions or statuses inevitably results in a disordered system. However, the primary system of China is state-owned: it takes it for granted that UREs as state-university-owned enterprises enter the industry sphere.

The differences between UREs and spin-offs illustrate these issues. Most spin-offs are essentially high-tech. But UREs are a mixture of low-tech and high-tech, traditional and modern, joint and independent, production (marketing) and service industries. However, many UREs are among the leaders in the Chinese high-tech industry; e.g., Tongfang, Wangxin, Neusoft, and Founder. They have become the No. 3, 12, 15, and 25 in the China Top-100 S&T Firms in 2002, and many more are expected in the future. Also, UREs and spin-offs have essential differences in ownership, arising from the ambiguity of the university sphere in the triple-helix field. Most UREs are part of a university structure. Unlike spin-offs in the United States, UREs are within the core area of the university, rather than the external field space. Both of them come from the mother university's research, but spin-offs become independent of their origin and part of industry. UREs essentially "belong" to the university.

A third important difference is the part the government plays. The Chinese government's role in UREs is considerably stronger than the relationship the U.S. government has with spin-offs. In fact, the UREs that have come out of the activities of universities are among the government's outstanding achievements. Ownership or affiliated relationships are an umbilical cord that makes the ties between UREs, the university, and government inevitably connected. This umbilical cord benefits both the university and its UREs. The URE–university–government relationship constitutes the very ground of the "government-pulled model" for regional innovation in China. Summing up, spin-offs have jumped to the outside of the university core but UREs have not.

4.2   The path to an entrepreneurial university in China

Neusoft has played an important part in the evolution that has seen the NEU emerge as an entrepreneurial university, "pulled" by government policies and "pushed" by industrial needs, co-evolving with regional development. The role of the university in a society is generally determined not only by economic logic, but also by a "social contract" concerning the division of labor. A "conventional social contract" prescribes that the university is an institution for education and the production of knowledge. In addition, the university should be a nonprofit enterprise for the common welfare. However, UREs have made them richer and richer. A number of professors in China, once poor, are driving a growing number of UREs to contribute to the economy. According to the Science and Technology Centre in the Ministry of Education, S&T UREs generated ¥ 6.234 billion in 2004, 79.73 percent of the total amount, and an increase of ¥1.821 billion (41.26 percent) in 2003. In addition, these S&T enterprises paid ¥3.848 billion in tax to the government (Science and Technology Development Center 2005). In 2009, Beijing Peking University gained total profit ¥2.66 billion (Science and Technology Development Center 2010). And up to the end of 2012, the total assets of the University's UREs have reached ¥100 billion (Science and Technology Development Center 2013).

From the NEU's evolution, we learnt that the "steeples of excellence" strategy is good for a university, even one with limited research resources and funds for entrepreneurship. The entrepreneurial university has emerged in China under difficult conditions, during a period of industrial decline with limited government resources. Nevertheless, it has made a significant contribution to national industrial and academic development that may provide a model for other developing countries. The Neusoft story illustrates that a university may use research in which it holds a comparative advantage as an entrepreneurial breakthrough point to drive other disciplines and fields. Tsinghua University has strengths in multiple disciplines, but the NEU's computer science discipline makes it the national leader. Entrepreneurship and discipline development have mutually supported each other and advanced together.

NEU's UREs are in transition from "university-owned and -run" to "university-owned but firm-run" and then to public or even multinational enterprises in which the university retains only a modest part of the stock. Put differently, UREs are undergoing an evolution from core areas to external field space, becoming spin-offs. Neusoft is a typical example of URE transformation, from campus company to an independent firm. The university will benefit from each enterprise that it founds and continually contribute to industry, not only through university–industry collaboration but also through firm formation.

The Chinese entrepreneurial university will persist as a distinctive model that entrepreneurial universities in other countries can follow by investing in their own UREs, not only contributing spin-off firms.[10]

References

Etzkowitz, Henry (2002). *MIT and the Rise of the Entrepreneurial University*. Routledge, p. 18.

Etzkowitz, Henry (2003). Innovation in innovation: The triple helix of university–industry–government relations. *Social Science Information* 42(3), 293–338.

[10] Stanford University has announced an investment program in spin-off form the student-government-originated StartX accelerator initiative. See Henry Etzkowitz, StartX and the Paradox of Success: Filling Gaps in Stanford's Entrepreneurial Culture. *Social Science Information*, December 2013, Vol. 52, pp. 605–627.

Etzkowitz, Henry (2008). *The Triple Helix, University–Industry–Government Innovation in Action*, Routledge.

Etzkowitz, Henry and Pique, Josep (2005). Silicon Valley in Transition from Network to Gravitation Field. Presented at the International Association Science Park Conference in Helsinki, 2005.

Etzkowitz, Henry and Zhou, Chunyan (2008). Introduction to Special Issue Building the entrepreneurial university: A global perspective. *Science and Public Policy* 35(9), 627–635.

Jing Zhang (ed.-in-chief) (2012). *Liaoning Statistical Yearbook 2011*. Shenyang, China: Bureau of Statistics of Liaoning Provinces.

Liaoning Daily. Liaoning Province as an old industrial base is pushed to independent innovation "crossroads" (2006.02.21). Available at http://chinaeast. xinhuanet.com/2006-02/21/content_6282143.htm. Cited on February 3, 2014.

Science and Technology Development Center (2004). *Statistical Analysis Report of National University-Run Industry*. Ministry of Education of the People's Republic of China. Available at www.cutech.edu.cn/. Cited on February 3, 2014.

Science and Technology Development Centre in the Ministry of Education (2010). *China Statistical Report of Universities Industry 2009*. Beijing: Ministry of Education of the People's Republic of China.

Science and Technology Development Centre in the Ministry of Education (2012). *China Statistical Report of Universities Industry 2010*. Beijing: Ministry of Education of the People's Republic of China. Available at http:// www.cutech.edu.cn/cn/kjcy/xbcytj/A011106index_1.htm.

Science and Technology Development Centre in the Ministry of Education (2013). *China Statistical Report of Universities Industry 2012*. Beijing: Ministry of Education of the People's Republic of China.

Science and Technology Department of Liaoning Province (2006). Strengthening macro policy guidance to improve the capability in independent innovation. Available at www.most.gov.cn/ztzl/qgkjdh/qgkjdhjyjl/200601/ t20060104_27625.htm. Cited on February 3, 2014.

World Bank (2013). Research and development expenditure (% of GDP). Available at http://data.worldbank.org/indicator/GB.XPD.RSDV.GD.ZS/ countries?order=wbapi_data_value_2011+wbapi_data_value+wbapi_data_ value-last&sort=as.

Zhou, Chunyan (2001). Science and Technology Field. *Science of Science and Management of S&T*, 22, 13–15.

Zhou, Chunyan (2002). *Transforming from Science to Technology: The Scientific Basis of the Technological Era*. Shenyang: Northeastern University Press.

Zhou, Chunyan (2008). Emergence of the entrepreneurial university in evolution of the triple helix: The case of Northeastern University in China. *Journal of Technology Management in China*, 3(1), 109–126.

Zhou, Chunyan and and Peng, Xumei (2008). The entrepreneurial university in China: Nonlinear paths. *Science and Public Policy* 35(9), 637–646.

Zhou, Chunyan (2012). From a university-run enterprise to a leading group of regional IT industrial clusters: In a perspective of an academia–government–industry triple helix. In Claudio Petti (ed.), *Technological Entrepreneurship in China: How Does It Work?* Chap. 4. Cheltenham, UK and Northampton, MA: Edward Elgar Publishing.

14 Public research organizations as a base for high-tech entrepreneurship in Europe: The case of IMEC and INRIA

Philippe Mustar, Mirjam Knockaert, and Bart Clarysse

The extant literature has addressed the issue of spin-off firm creation from universities or from firms with R&D activities, but much less attention has been devoted to the role of another important factor in the knowledge production process: public research organizations (PROs). This is surprising. In many European countries and in the United States, PROs play an important role in the fundamental and applied research landscape. Examples of these PROs are the CNRS in France and the Max Planck Gesellschaft in Germany. Even though the latter were created in order to carry out fundamental research (often financed with public money), the majority of PROs were created in order to handle topics of general interest or in order to support government policy (Larédo and Mustar 2001; Mustar and Larédo 2002). Since the 1980s, the PROs have, like the universities, been subject to significant transformations. Cox *et al.* (2001) identified a number of challenges these organizations face: (1) the new relationships with other actors in the innovation system, including a convergence with universities; (2) the challenge of commercializing their research, including a trade-off between the provision of knowledge to existing firms and starting new commercial ventures; and (3) the development of adequate systems to measure and evaluate the processes and effects of research.

A large European project, called Eurolabs, provided insight into the importance of public and semipublic research centers. It analyzed 557 of the 769 research centers that exist in Europe (Eurolabs 2002). These centers employed over 100,000 qualified scientists and their aggregate annual budget was over 25 billion euros in 1999. The study confirms that a large proportion of research budgets is spent by PROs, accounting for about 14 percent of the gross domestic expenditure on R&D (GERD) for the EU15 at the end of the 1990s (European Commission 2003). EURAB (2005) indicates that these Research and Technology Centres account for about 40 percent of publicly funded R&D in the EU 15. Larédo and

Mustar (2004) show that in large parts of continental Europe the traditionally close association between universities and fundamental research
on the one hand, and between government laboratories and applied
research on the other, no longer holds. We now face different institutions
that cover the whole spectrum of research activities. Therefore, a study
on spin-offs from European universities should by definition also disclose
information about spin-offs from the so-called research institutes.

Both for universities and for public research institutes, spin-offs have
become an increasingly important vehicle of commercialization (Mustar
1994, 1997). In Belgium, and more specifically Flanders, the government has explicitly included the creation of spin-offs as a determinant
of the future financing from government. Since the public research labs
focus their research efforts on very particular domains, they are often
very important sources of technological progress and spin off research-
based start-ups more easily than universities, which have to spread their
research efforts over a large number of technology domains.

To better understand the spin-off process, in this chapter, we analyze
two top-level PROs in Europe, INRIA in France and IMEC in Belgium.
First, we position the PRO in the research landscape of each country.
Second, we describe IMEC and INRIA and position these institutes in
the regional PRO landscape. In the third part, we analyze the spin-off
policies of both research institutes. Subsequently, the results of these
policies are discussed.

1.   Overview of the research landscape in
Belgium and France

In France, in 2003, 191,629 full-time equivalents (FTEs) were employed
as researchers in universities, PROs, and the private sector. About half
of the researchers were employed by the public sector (universities and
PROs), and a considerable proportion of these researchers worked at
PROs (22.8 percent). In Belgium in 2003, 30,916 researchers were
employed by both public and private sector. Even though the proportion of researchers working at PROs is less than that in France, they
still account for over 7 percent of the total research population in this
country (see Table 14.1). Furthermore, the actual number of researchers
employed by the PROs in Belgium will be significantly higher than the
figures in Table14.1, since the researchers on payroll at the PROs that
work at the associated universities are calculated as university researchers
and not as PRO researchers. This, however, is not the case for all PROs.
If we analyze the largest three PROs, namely IMEC, VIB, and VITO,
we find that VITO has no researchers on its payroll who are counted as

332   *Philippe Mustar, Mirjam Knockaert, and Bart Clarysse*

Table 14.1: *Importance of PROs in France and Belgium*

	France		Belgium	
	Number of researchers (FTEs)	Percentage in the research population	Number of researchers (FTEs)	Percentage in the research population
University and higher education	47,383	24.7 percent	12,389	40.1 percent
Public research organizations	43,600[a]	22.8 percent	2,285[b]	7.4 percent
Private companies	100,646	52.5 percent	16,242	52.5 percent
Total	191,629	100 percent	30,916	100 percent

Sources: Indicateurs de sciences et de technologie, 2006, Economica, Paris and OSTC, Belgium.

[a] The 11,664 researchers from the CNRS are included in the PRO sector even if they are working in universities in mixed laboratories. The not-for-profit organizations are also included.

[b] Of which 1,194 are in Flemish PROs.

university researchers. In contrast to VITO, IMEC and VIB are set up as "interuniversity research labs," which means that their research is also embedded within the parent universities. Of the 745 researchers on the IMEC payroll, about 60 are counted as university researchers, since they physically work at universities. Even though this number is still marginal in the case of IMEC, in the case of VIB it is substantial, with approximately 389 researchers on the VIB payroll who are counted as university researchers. VIB is a virtual research organization, whereas IMEC has a separate campus. Although there are many arguments to favor a separate campus, politically this remains a difficult view to defend, as it always includes choosing a city for location. This city is usually one of the home cities of the supporting universities. IMEC could do it because it needed a very expensive clean room to foster the research. This is not something that could be built in three different universities. VIB did not have these required upfront investments, so it became a virtual institute with only its headquarters co-located on the campus.

2.   The case of IMEC and INRIA

IMEC is the largest Belgian PRO, with respect to both the number of researchers and the research budget. INRIA is dedicated to fundamental and applied research in information and communication science and technology. It is one of the major participants in the development of the

ICT field in France. For each country these institutes are very important producers of knowledge and technology.

IMEC (Inter University Micro Electronics Centre), Belgium

IMEC, the Inter University Micro Electronics Centre (Leuven, Belgium), was set up following a program developed by the Flemish government in the field of microelectronics. Targeted at strengthening the microelectronics industry in Flanders (Belgium), it included the establishment of a laboratory for advanced research in microelectronics (IMEC), the establishment of a semiconductor foundry, and the organization of a training program (later INVOMEC and MTC). IMEC was founded in 1984 as a nonprofit organization. Today, it is Europe's leading independent research center in the field of microelectronics and nanotechnology, enabling design methods and technologies for ICT systems. The research organization has evolved significantly in its technology transfer policies over the years and has set up twenty-seven research-based spin-offs.

The current budget of the research institute amounts to 227 million euros. More than half of this research happens with international industrial partners and about 20 percent with Flemish industrial partners. The remaining 16 percent of the total budget comes as a subsidy from the Flemish government. IMEC generates the remaining 10 percent from projects for the European Community, the European Space Agency, and other government contracts. The number of staff amounts to 946 people on the payroll and 543 nonpayroll collaborators (2006). In total, its staff consists of fifty-one different nationalities.

INRIA, France

INRIA was set up by the French government in January 1967 as a precursor to the important role that computer science was anticipated to play in the coming decades. The institute was named IRIA (Institut de Recherche en Informatique et en Automatique – Research Institute for Computer Science and Control Theory). At the end of 1979, the institute decided to focus on its research and technology transfer mission and became the French National Institute for Research in Computer Science and Control (INRIA). It was placed under the dual authority of the Ministry of Research and the Ministry of Industry. Since the 1980s, INRIA has experienced constant growth. New research units have been founded in different French regions. Today, INRIA has six research sites in French territory: Rocquencourt (near Paris), Rennes (West of France), Sophia

Antipolis (South), Lorraine (East), Rhône-Alpes (Center East), and one unit organized around three sites: Saclay, Bordeaux, and Lille. In 1995, INRIA was chosen as the European pilot of the international consortium W3C, launched in 1994, in parallel with MIT for the United States. In January 2007, INRIA, Microsoft Corporation, and Microsoft Research Laboratory, Cambridge, founded the Microsoft Research–INRIA Joint Centre. The Centre's objective is to pursue fundamental long-term research in formal methods, software security, and the application of computer science research to science. Within its mission of fundamental and applied research, INRIA is also dedicated to technology transfer in this field of information and communication science and technology. This last mission takes different forms: training, diffusion of technical information, expertise, participation in international programs, research partnerships with industry, and, last but not least, creation of new ventures. About eighty companies have been founded since 1984.

INRIA has an annual budget of 160 million euros, 20 percent of which comes from its own research contracts and development products. In 2006, INRIA has a workforce of 3,700 with 2,900 scientists (including 1,000 doctoral candidates who work on theses as part of INRIA research projects). On this workforce of 3,700, 1,500 are on the INRIA payroll. These include 570 researchers, 300 hundred Ph.D.s, 200 postdocs, 190 personal assistants, and 250 technical and other staff (Table 14A.1 in the Appendix gives a view of this hybridization between INRIA and its partners).

A majority of the scientists working at INRIA are from INRIA's partner organizations, such as CNRS, universities, and leading engineering schools (see Table 14A.1 in Appendix 1). All these people work on 138 joint research projects. Often, the spin-offs from INRIA and their licenses are a result of these research projects. INRIA tries to combine scientific excellence and technology transfer. In 2006, INRIA had 730 active research contracts (80 percent of the contracts are with private sector partners) and nearly 3,000 scientific publications (plus 230 active patents numbered and 80 software licenses deposited with the Agence pour la Protection des Programmes). Like IMEC, INRIA is strongly internationalized: More than 30 percent of the researchers hired during the past years were of foreign origin.

In Table 14.2, we summarize the key indicators for both institutes.

3.   Positioning IMEC and INRIA in the European research scene

IMEC and INRIA are considered to be important research institutes in the European environment. Indeed, they employ a significant number of

Table 14.2: *Key indicators of IMEC and INRIA*

	IMEC	INRIA
Date of establishment	1984	1967
Mission	To perform R&D, ahead of industrial needs by three to ten years, in microelectronics, nanotechnology, and design methods and technologies for ICT systems	To perform fundamental and applied research in information and communication science and technology
Number of researchers (excluding Ph.D. researchers)	745[a]	570 (on payroll); 1,800 (including scientists from partner organizations)
Number of staff on the payroll	94	1,500
Number of nonpayroll staff	543	1,500
Research budget (million euro)	227[b]	160
Percentage of revenues generated from external sources	84 percent	20 percent
Number of spin-offs established since founding	27	82

[a] 1 January 2006.
[b] 2006.

researchers, as the following figures show. Table 14.3 takes into account only those PROs that have over 450 FTEs employed, and excludes public agencies.

Table 14.3 includes only the EPST, EPIC, and foundations with more than 500 workforce. The public agencies are not taken into account.

It shows that INRIA is among the mid-size PROs in France, with CNRS, CEA, and INRA employing the most people. Given that all PROs in France employ 43,600 researchers in total, and INRIA employs 1,800 researchers, we can conclude that INRIA is a research institute of significant size.

Table 14.4 below positions INRIA as a research institute compared to other PROs and some of the French universities. Université Pierre et Marie Curie Paris 6 is considered the largest French university, characterized by a very strong proportion of researchers compared with the other French universities. The three other universities can be considered the common "more typical" French university.

Table 14.3: *Overview of the largest French PROs (2006)*

Name	Number of FTEs employed	Full name	Domain
CEMAGREF[a]	900	Centre de machinisme agricole du génie rural des eaux et des forêts	Agricultural machinery, water, and forestry
CNRS[a]	26,080	Centre national de la recherche scientifique	Scientific research
INRA[a]	8,848	Institut national de recherche agronomique	Agricultural research
INRETS[a]	450	Institut national de recherche sur les transports et leur sécurité	Transport and safety research
INRIA[a]	3,500	Institut national de recherche en informatique et en automatique	Informatics, artificial intelligence
INSERM[a]	6,620	Institut national de la santé et de la recherche médicale	Health, medical research
IRD[a]	2,200	Institut français de recherche scientifique pour le développement et la coopération	Development research
LCPC[a]	535	Laboratoire central des ponts et chaussées	Roads and bridges
BRGM[b]	850	Bureau de recherches géologique et miniéres	Mining, geology
CEA[b]	14,937	Commissariat l'énergie atomique	Nuclear energy, materials, microelectronics
CIRAD[b]	800	Centre de coopération internationale en recherche agronomique pour le développement	Agricultural research for development
CNES[b]	2,500	Centre national d'études spatiales	Space research and space activities
CSTB[b]	750	Centre scientifique et technique du bâtiment	Building research
IFP[b]	1,700	Institut français du pétrole	Energy, environment
IFREMER[b]	1,385	Institut français pour l'exploitation de la mer	Marine and fisheries research
INERIS[b]	551	Institut national de l'environnement industriel et des risques	Environmental safety
ONERA[b]	2,000	Office national d'études et de recherches aérospatiales	Aerospace research

Table 14.3: (cont.)

Name	Number of FTEs employed	Full name	Domain
CURIE[c]	2,000	Institut Curie	Treatment and research against cancer
PASTEUR[c]	2,500	Institut Pasteur	Health and medical research

Note: The figures appearing in this table are orders of magnitude. In some PROs Ph.D. students or external people are included; in the majority they are not.

Source: "Principaux organismes de recherche," Edition 2006, Ministère délégué à l'enseignement supérieur et à la recherche, Paris, 70 pp.

[a] EPST (établissements publics à caractère scientifique et technique/public scientific and technological establishments): staff are civil servants.

[b] EPIC (établissements publics à caractère industriel et commercial/public establishments with an industrial and commercial status): these state-owned organizations are engaged in economic activities and staff are not civil servants.

[c] Private foundations, not for profit.

Table 14.4: *Overview of PROs and universities in France*

	Number of students	Number of researchers	Number of ongoing Ph.D. theses	Ph.D.s delivered per year
INRIA	–	570 on payroll (but a total of 1,800)	1000	250[a]
INRA	–	8,900	1,600	400[a]
CEA	–	15,000	1,000	250[a]
Université Pierre et Marie Curie Paris 6(1)	30,000	4,000	2,800[a]	700
Université Nice Sophia Antipolis	24,900	1,408	1,448	208
Université Louis Pasteur Strasbourg	18,000	1,600	1,200	260
Université des Sciences et technologies de Lille	20,000	1,447	1,061	169

Source: Annual reports and estimation from the available website information (2005).

[a] Estimates. These Ph.D.s are prepared in these OPRs or in the framework of research projects of these institutes (but only the universities can deliver the Ph.D. diploma, so these Ph.D. students have at least an administrative link with a university).

[**] the number of researchers working in these OPRs and Universities can be higher, if we take into account people from universities working in OPRs and people of other OPRs (CNRS, INSERM . . .) working in mix labs in universities.

Again, it is clear that from a research perspective, INRIA plays an important role in comparison to the number of researchers working in other PROs and at universities.

Although PROs are less important with respect to the research force compared to universities in Belgium, Table 14.5 shows the importance of IMEC as a research institute in the regional (Flemish) landscape.

In Flanders, there are four research organizations (VIB, IMEC, VITO, and IBBT) and six universities (KU Leuven, Ugent, VUB, UA, LUC, and KUB). For the purpose of this study, we only focus on the largest PROs with observable experience in formal technology transfer activities. IMEC accounts for the highest percentage of researchers compared to the other PROs, namely VIB and VITO. Another indication of the importance of IMEC is provided by the doctoral research at the different institutes. Even though PROs in Belgium are not allowed to grant doctoral degrees, most PROs are intensively involved with doctoral research and open their knowledge base and infrastructure to these researchers. For instance, of the 1,004 IMEC researchers, 212 were Ph.D. students. Taking into account that in Belgium during 2005, 3,593 people were enrolled as doctoral students, this indicates that about 6 percent of all doctoral students carry out their doctoral research at IMEC or in close collaboration with IMEC. If we considered only the domain of microelectronics, the proportion of research that is carried out in collaboration with IMEC would be very significant.

4.   **Spin-off models at IMEC and INRIA:**
       Strategy and results

IMEC

In contrast to the mission of the universities, IMEC targets at realizing research that has applications in industry. Only a minority (20 percent) of the research budget of the research institute comes from the Flemish government, in contrast to most of the universities in the region. Since its founding in 1984, IMEC has had to rely to a large extent on external resources. In 2005, more than half of the total research budget, €102 million, came from contract research with industry. This €83 million was raised by the four largest Flemish universities. The relatively low amount of financing that is provided to the research institute by public sources translates into a very specific strategy toward industry in general. This large amount of contract research is accompanied by patents and spin-offs. The technology transfer policy at IMEC focuses

Table 14.5: *Overview of PROs and universities in Flanders*

	Full name	Domain		Number of students (2004) (1)	Number of researchers, including Ph.D. students (2004) (1)	Number of employees on payroll (2005) (2)	Number of Ph.D.s obtained in 2005 (3)
IMEC	Inter University Micro Electronics Centre	Micro-electronics	PRO	—	1,004	920[*]	—
VIB	Flemish Institute for Biotechnology	Biotechnology	PRO	—	547	389[a]	—
VITO	Flemish Institute for Technological Research	Energy, environment, and materials	PRO	—	146	419[a]	—
KU Leuven	Catholic University Leuven		University	29,164	4,376	8,017[b]	427
Ugent	University of Ghent		University	26,149	4,062	6,400[b]	347
VUB	Free University Brussels		University	9,229	975	2,545[b]	118
UA	University of Antwerp		University	8,293	14,28	3,400[b]	100

Sources: (1) Annual reports; (2) annual reports and interviews with personnel departments; (3) annual reports and website information.
[a] FTEs.
[b] Numbers.

on the diffusion of research results to society and, at the same time, generation of commercial income.

IMEC has built up an attractive IP portfolio that guarantees a solid position on the current and future markets. In 2005, IMEC handed in ninety patent applications and forty-four patents were filed. In 2004, fifty-one patents were granted, which is significantly more than the thirty-one patents that were granted to the four largest Flemish universities.

Given that IMEC has, to a large extent, run its operations in a self-sustainable way, it has followed an active technology transfer policy with clear patenting, licensing, and spin-off strategies. With respect to the spin-off policy, it has evolved to a centrally led technology "pull model" with strong incubation facilities and support and links with the venture capital industry. Moray and Clarysse (2005) identify three generations of science-based entrepreneurial firms at IMEC. These "generations" are conceptualized based on their level and source of capital at time of founding, the maturity of the technology at that time, and the human capital of the founding team.

The first generation of start-ups runs up to 1995. During this period, IMEC only brought in (a limited amount of) cash. The main source of finance for spin-offs was incumbent firms. Most of the seven start-ups in this period had at least a working alpha prototype at the time of founding, and only a limited number of IMEC researchers made the step from the research institute to the start-up (on average 1.5 FTEs). During these early years (1992–1993), business development was organized in its most generic form. Two persons, the heads of IMEC's business development division, managed the commercialization of research through setting up ventures.

During the early nineties, IMEC made some major changes in the organization of its business development activities. IMEC increasingly transferred technology from the research center to the spin-offs, even though this was not done in a systematic way. Of the eight companies started up between 1996 and 1998, three received both technology transfer and money transfer from IMEC, whereas in the other five only capital contribution was made. During this period, a separate "incubation" cell was established. This cell moved a couple of times in the organizational structure of IMEC, showing that IMEC went through an important learning phase in the second half of the nineties as to where to position these "spin-off activities." The Incubation and Industrialization (I&I) Department has, since its inception in 1996–1997, professionalized its activities from an organizational and methodological perspective.

From 1999 onward, a third generation of IMEC science-based entrepreneurial firms emerges. All but one of the established companies received a transfer of technology from IMEC and were established with a less mature technology at the time of founding compared to the previous stages. Moray and Clarysse (2005) describe how the starting configuration of the companies that emerged from IMEC over this period had changed a lot, with the companies starting up with a significantly larger number of employees and a technology that still needed more time to reach an alpha prototype. As a result, they needed more coaching and incubation support before they could start up.

Spin-off process   Even though IMEC's technology transfer office only employs about eight people, the total number of people involved in technology transfer is estimated at forty-five, taking into account people from other departments who get involved. Spin-off projects are managed as follows: First, there is operational support to develop the business plan. At the onset of the incubation phase, the project leader of I&I passes the incubation plan on to his colleagues from the enterprise cell within the financial department. This cell supports the project from a "corporate" perspective, covering juridical/IP matters as well as accounting and fiscal issues. Second, the project gets some strategic support. Although during this stage there is not a board of directors, the researcher–entrepreneurs are coached in the development of the company's business model by a steering committee. This committee meets monthly and consists of the VP and the Project Leader of I&I, the VP of the Financial Department, the VP of Business Development, and (one of) the inventors/researcher–entrepreneurs.

The incubation phase usually takes twelve to eighteen months and should result in a venture capital investment in the "incubation company." It is also at this time that the intellectual property is formally transferred to the spin-off and that the incubation costs are discounted. The enterprise cell follows up on the company after external capitalization and provides feedback to the VP of the Financial Department.

Typically, at the beginning, the spin-off receives nonexclusive licenses for all technologies they potentially need throughout incubation. After the incubation phase, ideally when a first injection of external capital takes place (VC, BA, corporate, etc.), exclusive licensing agreements would be negotiated for technologies specific to advancing the spin-off at this stage.

Financing new ventures   In the early years, the main financial partners for the science-based entrepreneurial firms were large corporate firms. Also, IMEC – and the universities from the associated labs – brought in a part of the capital. During the mid-nineties, venture capital in Europe had become a more legitimate source of funding for start-ups and, in 1997, a venture capital fund called IT Partners, which would target the semiconductor industry, was set up. By setting up this IMEC-"friendly" venture capital fund, IMEC wanted to consider only those projects requiring capital in the range of €750,000–1,000,000.

In 1999–2000, IMEC decided to launch an incubation fund because of the increasing difficulty in securing venture capital for the early-stage, high-potential projects that had not yet made a working prototype or drafted a long-term business plan. IMEC's incubation fund was established in October 2001 with €5 million to stimulate new possible spin-off initiatives by providing the necessary (pre)seed capital to prepare prototype products and early market introductions during the incubation period. The fund only considers project proposals based on IMEC technology. Proposals must include a first feasibility analysis of the idea, work plan, and required budget. Once a project is approved by the fund, budget is released for setting up a company to realize the project, work out an extensive business plan, and attract the needed skills. Then the start-up is expected to attract venture capital to realize its goals. Under the terms of the fund, it may provide up to 60 percent of the required capital. Up to 1999 the cost of the incubation phase was completely incurred by IMEC. It fully carried the risk. After that, the costs associated with the incubation phase (i.e., the physical infrastructure and administrative support) are discounted to the firm when a first-round external investment takes place.

In March 2006, a new investment fund, Capital-E, was established. This fund is closely linked to IMEC and has a capital of €35.5 million. This includes the capital that was raised through the Arkimedes initiative of the Flemish government (€15 million euro). Capital-E aims at investing in seed and early stage initiatives in micro- and nanoelectronics. The fund is open to investments in other than IMEC spin-offs in Flanders and Western Europe.

INRIA

INRIA is mainly financed by public sources and focuses on realizing knowledge returns to society. The technology transfer policy is therefore focused on diffusion and dissemination of knowledge generated within the research institute, and less on realization of financial returns than is the case at IMEC. As with IMEC, the spin-off policy of INRIA has evolved over time.

In the first phase, from 1984 till 1997, INRIA encouraged the creation of spin-off companies, but without a precise strategy. In 1984, INRIA created the first spin-off, called Simulog, which has become active in the domain of digital simulation. Between 1984 and 1986, another six companies were established. In none of the cases was INRIA involved as a shareholder. The first time that INRIA was involved as a shareholder was with the founding of Ilog. INRIA invested money in the start-up, even though this was not the standard policy and prompted some opposition within the Institute. Today, Ilog is INRIA's success story. It is listed on Nasdaq and Euronext and has 800 employees and offices in eight countries. INRIA invested €120,000 Euro in the spin-off, and realized a multiple of twenty on the company's shares. INRIA earned more than €2 million on the shares, even though realizing returns from participation has never been the main objective. Between 1988 and 1990, INRIA spun off a further twelve companies and took shares in three of them. From 1990 onward, the number of spin-offs decreased due to a slowdown in the economy, which hit the IT sector particularly hard.

In the second phase, from 1998 until now, INRIA developed a more active policy toward spin-off companies. INRIA-Transfert was established. INRIA-Transfert is a wholly owned subsidiary of INRIA with €13.2 million of share capital. Its main objective is to identify and support the best innovative IT start-up companies from the institute or from outside the institute. INRIA-Transfert is interested in projects where the technology is related to INRIA's expertise. In collaboration with private and public partners, INRIA-Transfert participated in the creation of I-Source Gestion, which is a seed fund for investing in companies in the field of information and communication technology, whether or not they are based on INRIA technology.

Between 1998 and 2006, fifty spin-offs were created based on INRIA's research. The INRIA's spin-off definition is a broad one: it takes into account all the firms created from INRIA's research results with or without a licensing agreement between the new firms and the Institute. In contrast, IMEC (Vanhelleputte and Reid 2004) has a clear IP strategy, which implies that each spin-off that is started should have a license agreement with the parent institute. However, this does not mean that the definition is fundamentally different between the two institutes. As both public research institutes do not have students, they do not include student-based start-ups in their definitions. The sharp increase in the yearly number of spin-offs compared to the previous period can be explained by the new Law on Innovation and Research that was inaugurated in July 1999 and that facilitated the creation of companies by researchers and academics. Only in a limited number of cases is INRIA a shareholder in the spin-offs. Very often, INRIA provides an exclusive license to the spin-off company.

Spin-off process   INRIA-Transfert guides teams of entrepreneurs who are in the process of setting up high-tech IT companies through the start-up process. These teams can be part of the research organization or can come from outside. INRIA-Transfert coaches entrepreneurs/researchers on eleven levels: team and organization; quality of execution; technical product development; proved client benefits; competitive advantage; entry barriers; market size; strategic and product marketing; strategic marketing; economic efficiency; resources; and financial strategy. To coach teams on these levels, INRIA-Transfert has brought together a network of top-level operational experts (large companies, investors, and technology experts). The coaching process takes between six and twenty-four months.

The INRIA IPR (intellectual property rights) policy is based on the fact that the institute has to reconcile knowledge dissemination to the wider public, on one hand, and protection of developed knowledge, on the other. Therefore, since 1998, INRIA has given exclusive licenses to spin-offs for a limited number of years (two to three). In return, the research institute receives a small amount of money. After this period, the spin-off has a buy option set at a fixed price and a small number of stock options (1 to 3 percent). The sales price for transfer of technology is typically between €100,000 and €500,000. This type of technology transfer is considered a valuable asset to the company by investors.

Financing new ventures   In 1999, INRIA-Transfert created I-Source Gestion in close partnership with two major French financial institutions: AXA Private Equity (the AXA Group is an important global player financial protection business) and CDC Entreprises (Caisse des Dépôts – CDC – is a state-owned financial institution that performs public-interest missions). INRIA-Transfert is one of the major subscribers to each of the five funds managed by I-Source Gestion, gathering more than €150 million for early stage companies.

I-Source Gestion is an early stage venture capital firm, focusing on information and communication technologies. It invests in a first round in early stage companies (either just created or up to three years of existence) and in the subsequent financing rounds if required. The funds are managed by an independent senior investment team with a background in the industry, in finance, and in entrepreneurship. I-Source Gestion has built a partner network including research laboratories and their

Table 14.6: *Number of spin-offs at INRIA and IMEC in 2006*

	IMEC	INRIA
Number of spin-offs established since founding	27	82

incubators, institutional and private investors, and world-class high-tech companies such as Alcatel.

5.   Results of IMEC and INRIA spin-off policies

An important difference between the research institutes is their dependence on public resources. Whereas IMEC is, to a large extent, self-sustainable in its activities, and strives for self-sustainability, the funds of INRIA are mostly provided by government. In this section, we analyze to what extent the differences with respect to commercial orientation and self-sustainability translate into different results with respect to the number of spin-offs established and their nature.

Number of spin-offs

INRIA's first spin-off was established in 1984; for IMEC it was in 1986. The number of spin-offs per researcher (as shown in Table 14.6) is quite similar for both institutes: whereas IMEC has 745 researchers, INRIA has 1,800 scientists (including 570 paid by INRIA and researchers from other institutions working on INRIA projects). In IMEC, on the average, one spin-off is created per twenty-seven researchers; in INRIA, it is one spin-off per twenty-one researchers. Interestingly, however, IMEC invests much more resources in supporting spin-offs than INRIA does. Whereas the extended TTO workforce (including people involved in the spin-off process from the different departments) at IMEC consists of forty-five people, INRIA only has three people involved in spinning off ventures (but twenty involved in the "direction of transfer and innovation"). This indicates that, even though the rate of spin-off creation is similar in the two institutes, the effort spent in the pre-spin-off process is significantly higher for the IMEC spin-offs than for the INRIA spin-offs. This reflects in part the IP process, which plays a more significant part at IMEC. IMEC clearly sees the spin-offs as an alternative to licensing out the technology and wants to make sure that IP is valued at start-up. This means that its start-ups, by definition, are IP-based and highly valued

Table 14.7: *Overview of capitalization of IMEC and INRIA spin-offs (in euros) in 2006*

	IMEC	INRIA
Number of spin-offs established since founding	27	82
Total capital raised by all spin-offs	120,656,880	36,472,000
Median capital per spin-off	932,500	60,000
Median capital raised/employee	88,685	9,498

companies. In contrast, INRIA does not make this emphasis, so venture capital at start-up is not a clear necessity.

Capitalization

The twenty-seven companies that spun off from IMEC since 1984 have, so far, raised over €120 million of capital, compared to the eighty-two spin-offs from INRIA which have raised €36.5 million (see Table 14.7). The median capital that was raised by IMEC spin-offs is close to €1 million, compared to €60,000 raised by INRIA spin-offs. Similar results are obtained from comparing the median capital raised per employee. This indicates that, even though both institutes are active in similar fields, the types of spin-offs that originate from the research institutes are different in nature. IMEC spins off ventures to fulfill its mission to disseminate knowledge, and to provide a return on investment to help reach its self-sustainability goal. It clearly creates more exit-oriented spin-offs that are created either with some kind of (non-) exclusive license agreement or with a direct transfer of one or more patents. The spin-off further develops the technology and builds a platform with multiple possible applications. As a result, the capitalization at start-ups is very high and is raised through venture capital input. Most of the time, IMEC takes shares in the spin-offs, either in return for transfer of technology or in return for capital. INRIA, which is mainly concerned with a mission of dissemination of knowledge and technology, is seldom a shareholder in the spin-off companies, or only takes a symbolic share in the spin-off. Gaining income through realization of surplus value on spin-off participation is not an objective as such, given the great extent to which the institute is financed by government. The main focus is on disseminating knowledge, and transfer of technology to spin-offs is seen as one of the potential ways of dissemination. Given the importance that INRIA attaches to dissemination and provision of sufficient return

Table 14.8: *Overview of employment generated by IMEC and INRIA spin-offs in 2006*

	IMEC	INRIA
Number of spin-offs established since founding	27	82
Total employment generated by spin-offs	504	1,356
Median employment per spin-off	7	7.5

to society on capital provided by government, we analyze the impact of spin-offs on employment generation for both institutes.

Employment

A number of data sources were used to determine employment creation. For IMEC data we relied on the Belfirst database, which holds information on the company's annual accounts. Data was checked with interview and website information. Employment creation was calculated as the absolute number of employees that the spin-off had, either at the time of the interview (2003–2005) or on December 31, 2005. In the case where a spin-off was acquired, employment at the time of the acquisition was taken into account. In total, reliable information on employment could be retrieved for twenty-three of IMEC's spin-offs. Five of these spin-offs had gone bankrupt, and one was not liquidated yet, but had ceased its operations. In total, the twenty-three spin-offs have generated positions for 504 full-time employees (FTEs). Of course, we have to take into account that most of the spin-offs are relatively young companies, which might only realize growth later on in their life cycle.

For INRIA data, we relied on the national database Infogreffe, the Amadeus database, and website information. Of the 82 spin-offs, 44 still exist as independent companies, 17 were liquidated, 14 others merged with other companies, and 7 were acquired. In total, information was retrieved on 40 spin-off companies that had created 1,356 new jobs, mainly in France (because of the difficulties of accountancy we do not take into account the jobs created by the 21 merger or acquisition cases). See Table 14.8.

It is obvious that a relatively small number of spin-offs account for the highest degree of employment generation. With respect to the IMEC spin-offs, Photovoltech has grown at a pace of twenty FTEs over the last four years, whereas Coware has followed the same pace over the last six years. Acunia/Smartmove had grown at an annual employment generation rate of 16.7 FTEs at the time the company was acquired, the end of 2002. With respect to the INRIA spin-offs, it was Dolphin Integration, Esterel Technologies, Kelkoo, and Ilog that were the major success stories when it came to employment generation. Ilog, for instance, employed 800 people at the end of 2006.

The analysis clearly shows that even though the capitalization of IMEC spin-offs is significantly higher than that of INRIA spin-offs, there is no significant difference with respect to employment generation. Again, we can relate this to the specific policy of INRIA, which aims at providing sufficient societal returns for the public money invested in the research institute. It also indicates that a high capitalization of the spin-offs might indicate an exit criterion but does not necessarily signal large employment growth. IMEC has, to a much larger extent, followed an exit strategy for the investments it makes in spin-off companies, given that realization of surplus value on participations is one way of reaching self-sustainability. From a societal perspective, it is completely unclear whether public venture capital toward spin-offs contributes to the employment these spin-offs create or not. Comparison of the IMEC and the INRIA data seems to suggest that they do not really differ in terms of employment growth. This does not mean that they do not differ in terms of value realized for the investor. Therefore, in a final section, we analyze which spin-offs from the research institute have contributed the most to income generation.

Valuation

Research coming out of research institutes is typically in an early stage of development, and spin-offs are often set up with incomplete teams and with no, or few, first commercial contracts. Taking into account the early stage of development at the time of start-up, investments in these spin-offs can be classified as seed or early stage investments in venture capital (VC) terms. Many researchers have shown that in this stage of investment it is hard to realize positive returns on investment, and that there is an imbalance between the risk that is involved with these investments and the return (Murray, 1998). In this section, we analyze the extent to which IMEC or INRIA have realized surplus values on the participations they took in spin-off companies.

Interestingly, such information is not available from INRIA. INRIA only seldom participates in spin-off companies and often these participations are rather small. Besides, realizing a return as a VC fund is not a goal as such, and therefore there is little follow-up on participation in spin-offs. For instance, INRIA had a small amount of stock options in Kelkoo. This was a spin-off created in 1999 and became one of the success stories of the institute. The company was acquired by Yahoo in 2004 for €435 million, and INRIA exerted its stock options at this time. INRIA did have shares in another success company, namely Ilog, and realized a surplus value of over €2 million on the sales of the shares. This money was used to finance the I-Source fund, which is now, among others, financially supporting spin-offs from INRIA.

IMEC has taken a quite different approach to participating in spin-off companies. Since 1984, three companies were established with support of IMEC, but IMEC did not invest in the companies, nor had part of the shares of the companies. Two cases were spin-ins rather than spin-offs. In thirteen cases, technology was transferred from IMEC to the spin-off. Up to today, seven companies have realized a trade sale. From the point of view of IMEC, five trade sales were successful ones, meaning that a multiple above one was realized. In the other two cases, IMEC sold its shares below historic value. Five companies went bankrupt. The other companies are still in the portfolio of IMEC, and are either booked at historic value or have experienced a value decrease in accounting terms (four companies).

For the analysis of surplus value realized, we only selected those investments that had been exited, which means in practice that the spin-offs either had realized a trade sale or had been liquidated/went bankrupt. The advantage of this approach is that the life cycle of the companies can be reconstructed and that the exit value of the investments by the spin-off institute can be objectively measured, in comparison to internal rate of return (IRR) estimates before exit, which seem to be overvalued (Dittman et al. 2004).

Based on the information received on the exit value realized, we identified successful and failed spin-offs from the financial point of view of the research institute. In case a multiple of more than one was realized (meaning that at least the investment was recuperated), we identify the investment as successful. In case a multiple of less than one was realized, we identify the investment as a failure, since the research institute was unable to recuperate the money invested upon exit. We only integrate into the analysis those spin-off investments that have already been exited. Five spin-off investments can be considered successful ones. Six other investments are considered failures, given that the companies went bankrupt or were sold or liquidated at a multiple below one (see Figure 14.1).

The average multiple realized by IMEC on its spin-off investments amounts to 5.8, which means that the research institute on average received close to 6 times the money invested per company. The median multiple is, however, 0.88, indicating that outliers are accounting for most of the surplus value realized.

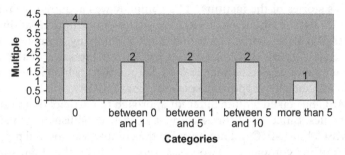

Figure 14.1: Overview of financial multiples realized by IMEC on spin-off investments n = 11.

IMEC has realized an annual return of 22.69 percent on its investments in spin-offs, which is high compared to what is generally expected as a good return on investment for early-stage funds. However, as is often the case in early-stage investing, this ROI is mainly to be attributed to one star investment, which is overcompensating for the fact that other investments were unsuccessful. In the case of IMEC, most of the return is to be attributed to one spin-off on which IMEC realized a multiple of 48.5. Without this successful trade sale, the annual ROI is only 7 percent. In total, IMEC has realized a surplus value of €12.25 million Euro on spin-off investments since the origination of the first spin-off. Even this is a considerable amount of money, and is high compared to the returns and surplus values realized by the venture capital industry on this type of early-stage investment. This amount remains small, however, compared to the budget that IMEC has at its disposal on a yearly basis.

6.   Conclusion

Public research institutes are extremely important in Europe (Senker *et al.* 1999). Often they regroup the disperse research efforts that are undertaken at universities and create a critical mass of research investments in focused technological domains. Budget constraints for universities often do not allow them to concentrate on one particular technological domain. The public research institutes solve this gap. However, it is a misunderstanding that all the researchers in these public research institutes work in an isolated way at these institutes. On the contrary, many of them remain located at the campuses of the universities. In this way, the public research institutes are, to a certain extent, virtual institutes that finance research groups at the universities, besides hosting these research groups at a particular physical location. In contrast to universities, which have in Europe, at least to a certain extent, a primary focus on teaching and research, the public research institutes have a primary focus on technological research and commercialization. The blurry boundary between research institutes and universities is situated in the domain of academic research. Both universities and research institutes perform academic research.

Although there are major similarities between the Belgian and French public research institutes, IMEC and INRIA, there also exist fundamental differences. The most important difference lies in the missions of the two institutes. Completely in line with the French perception of the role of the public sector, INRIA has a purely societal objective. It trains Ph.D.s and views spin-offs as vehicles that bring technology to the market. Spin-offs are expected to create new activities and employment, not so much to provide income to INRIA. The results are quite in line with the mission. INRIA is the parent institute of a large number of relatively small spin-offs. They start up with a low level of capital, even the minimum capital, but they create on the average as many jobs as the IMEC spin-offs.

In contrast to INRIA, IMEC has a clear objective of realizing income through spinning off companies. The start-ups around IMEC result from a very careful policy. IMEC makes a rational choice between spinning off companies or not. Only in the cases where they evaluate that the creation of a spin-off is a better way to transfer the technology will the institute pursue that path. The result is that relatively few spin-offs originate from IMEC. Only twenty-four have been spun off, in contrast to the eighty-four that have originated from INRIA. IMEC only wants to create ventures that have a real chance of experiencing a successful trade sale. But the results are very remarkable. IMEC has realized over 22 percent IRR on its spin-offs so far and this on a yearly basis. However, the investments have been quite high, the rate of return is realized on a very small number of spin-offs, which means that the associated risks have been quite high as well, and the result in gross employment is less than in the INRIA case.

From a societal point of view, the IMEC approach requires a lot of capital and is quite beneficial for commercializing research to the private market, but is ineffective if total employment creation is the objective. Hence, governments should be extremely careful and clear when expectations toward spin-offs are developed and when spin-off policies are designed.

References

Cox, D., Gummett, P., and Barker, K. (eds.) (2001). *Government Laboratories: Transition and Transformation* (Amsterdam: IOS Press).

Crow, M. and Bozeman, B. (1998). *Limited by Design: R&D Laboratories in the U.S. National Innovation System* (New York: Columbia University Press).

Dittmann, I., Maug, E., and Kemper, J. (2004). How fundamental are fundamental values? Valuation methods and their impact on the performance of German venture capitalists, *European Financial Management* 10(4): 609–638.

Eurab (2005), Research and Technology Organisations (RTOs) and ERA, European Research Advisory Board Final Report, EURAB 05.037, December.

Eurolabs (2002). *The Public Research System in Europe: A Comparative Analysis of Public, Semi-public and Recently Privatised Research Centres* (Manchester: PREST, The University of Manchester).

European Commission (2003). Third European Report of S&T Indicators, Brussels, p. 67.

Larédo, P. and Mustar, P. (eds.) (2001). *Research and Innovation Policies in the New Global Economy: An International Comparative Analysis* (Cheltenham: Edward Elgar).

(2004). Public sector research: A growing role in innovation systems, *Minerva* 42: 11–27.

Moray, N. and Clarysse, B. (2005). Institutional change and resource endowments to science-based entrepreneurial firms, *Research Policy* 34(7): 1010–1027.

Mustar, P. (1994). Organisations, technologies et marchés en création: La genèse des PME high tech, *Revue d'économie industrielle* 67(1): 156–174.

(1997). How French academics create hi-tech companies: The conditions for success or failure, *Science and Public Policy* 24 (1): 37–44.

Mustar, P. and Larédo, P. (2002). Innovation and research policy in France (1980–2000) or the disappearance of the Colbertist state, *Research Policy* 31(1): 55–72.

Senker, J. *et al.* (1999). European Comparison of Public Research Systems, SPRU, University of Brighton.

Vanhelleputte, J. and Reid, A. (2004). The paradox: Can attaining global research excellence be compatible with regional technology development? *R&D Management* 34(1): 33–44.

Wright, M., Clarysse, B., Mustar, P., Lockett A. (2007). *Academic Entrepreneurship in Europe*, Edward Elgar, Cheltenham, UK/Brookfield, VT.

Appendix A

Table 14A.1: *INRIA staff by category and affiliation in 2006*

	Assistant	Researcher	Professor	PhD	PostDoc	Trainee	Technical	Visitor	Other	Total
INRIA	187	541	7	326	197	75	277	10	46	1,666
CNRS	18	113		28	11		22	1	4	197
French public research institution	1	47	8	100	14	12	6	2	5	195
French educational institution (school, university)	14	45	613	682	40	196	19	17	12	1,638
Foreign educational institution or organization		22	27	80	26	105	2	202	1	465
Private organization or firm		12	3	74	4		5	4	3	105
Other		3	2	32	9	2	6	16	19	89
Total	220	783	660	1,322	301	390	337	252	90	4,355

Source: http://ralyx.inria.fr/2006/staff-count-affiliation.html#.

Notes: Staff description: Assistant: personal assistant, Researcher: full time scientist, Professor: university staff, Trainee: all interns (master students, etc.), Technical: research engineers, software engineers. Some staff may be counted twice when they belong to several teams.

15 Conclusion: Strategies for enhancement of academic entrepreneurship

Rory P. O'Shea and Thomas J. Allen

Given the increasing need for research and technology discoveries from academic institutions to be transferred more swiftly into the marketplace, universities are playing an increasingly important role in theories of regional economic development (Shane 2004; Cunningham and Harney 2006; Slaughter and Rhoades 2004). Several such theories view the university as an institution that generates knowledge, encourages the diffusion of new ideas on which innovation is based, and creates skilled personnel and entrepreneurs. However, these theories do not provide a constructive generalized explanation for the ways universities can contribute to their local economies (Breznitz *et al.* 2008). As a consequence, university heads, policy makers, and technology transfer administrators seek explanations of the dynamic factors that contribute to the emergence of a successful entrepreneurial university. They want to know how to increase spin-off activity. Research over the last decade is only beginning to address the critical need for technology commercialization programs that promote university-based entrepreneurship on campus, and thereby increase spin-off rates.[1]

The purpose of this volume is to build upon this existing work by exploring the dynamics underlying the domain of academic entrepreneurship and the factors that influence its development. To achieve this aim, we have compiled a number of studies of universities that have been generally successful in stimulating academic entrepreneurship and the creation of new firms. These studies analyze how a university defines itself as part of a region, as well as through what activities, if any, university commercialization strategies affect spin-off activity in the

---

[1] Rothaermael *et al.* (2007) present a detailed analysis and synthesis of the stream of research on university entrepreneurship, now encompassing 173 academic articles published worldwide in a number of refereed scholarly journals between 1981 and 2005. The authors define university entrepreneurship broadly, to include any published research pertaining to entrepreneurial activities in which a university could be involved, including, but not limited to, patenting, licensing, creating new firms, facilitating technology transfer through incubators and science parks, and facilitating regional economic development.

354

context of their regional environment. An understanding of these different actions and their outcomes can provide a much needed explanation for how specific economic results can be achieved, allowing for feasible local economic predictions and appropriate expectations for universities. From the beginning, it was the intention of this research to take an inductive approach – first to gather the information, and then to develop a normative model that would incorporate the variety of factors that emerged from the field. The spin-off performance module, presented in this chapter, has been constructed by reviewing the literature and analyzing the studies presented in this volume. By providing historical examples of what has worked, we hope to stimulate thought and action on the part of the many universities and policy-makers who would like to transition toward more entrepreneurially focused universities.

From our analysis, it is important for policy makers and university leadership to realize that two important caveats need to be considered in the design of an effective spin-off program. First, because spin-off programs may take years or even decades to generate a positive return on investment, it is important to recognize that building successful technology commercialization programs is a long-term effort, which requires sustained commitment and financial resources. As a result of historical factors, infrastructural deficits, or cultural conditions, effects of transformation efforts at academic institutions do not occur instantaneously, but instead must be seen as a process that take many years or even decades. For example, MIT could be said to have begun working in this direction in the nineteenth century and certainly no later than 1945. UC San Diego and Yale took less time, but nevertheless, even their efforts are thirty to forty years old. In addition, anyone familiar with the high-clustering literature realizes that clusters in Silicon Valley and the Route 128 complex near Boston did not suddenly emerge, nor did they appear spontaneously or randomly without a large amount of planning and "positive loop of production interactions" and preparation (Roberts 1991; Bresnahan et al. 2004). Our findings from this volume show that there are no quick or easy solutions to the issue of creating start-ups at universities. Nor is there any substitute for institutional commitment in promoting university start-ups. Crucial to success is an enduring commitment on the part of faculty, students, staff, and alumni to support entrepreneurial behavior, wherever enacted.

Second, it can be seen from the studies that the success of spin-off programs is related to the institutional arrangements that enable knowledge transfer and innovation to emerge. It is very apparent in reading through the chapters in this volume that there are many different technology commercialization strategies that universities can pursue in order to contribute to regional economic development.[2] In our volume we find that universities in our study enacted many different strategies to enhance policies, practices, and a campus climate supporting spin-off success. It should also be noted that some universities' approach to providing support and guidance to entrepreneurial activities was contingent on the entrepreneurial context of institution. For example, MIT has traditionally adopted low support–low selectivity policies given its location in an entrepreneurially developed cluster. In contrast, Yale, KU Leuven, and the National University of Singapore (NUS), which have an underdeveloped regional venture ecosystem, have taken a more proactive role in fostering a more entrepreneurial mindset among students and faculty developing commercial partnerships and providing formal incubation capabilities to their spin-off projects.

It is also important to recognize that the problem of university spin-offs cannot be understood in isolation from external factors. The development of entrepreneurially based universities requires considerable planning and outside help in addition to a university's internal efforts. In some instances, government involvement with innovative efforts is deep. The extreme example is Northeastern University in China, where a very rigid economic and governmental structure exists to promote university-industry cooperation and innovation at a regional level. In Ireland, Singapore, and the United Kingdom, government involvement was seen as an asset. In most of the other examples, political involvement was absent or negligible. Sometimes the university set up specialized funding and management partnerships with third party firms to assist or catalyze the process. KU Leuven and Kings College London provide examples of this. Some universities created seed funds, incubators, and science parks for new venture firms. Some did not.

Our studies show we find that top-down and bottom-up university initiatives, and even a combination of both, can all produce successful outcomes for regional economic development. Therefore we conclude that different universities manage technology transfer and commercialization differently and still achieve similar positive results in the local economy. Thus, there may not be one single pattern to serve as a

---

[2] Based on the results of a study that examined eight R&D organizations, Roberts and Malone (1996) found that both the policies implemented by the organizations and the environments within which they were based had direct effect of the results of the spin-off process. Roberts and Malone (1996) also state that selectivity and support are the two main dimensions of a technology commercialization process directed at facilitating the formation of spin-off ventures from an R&D organization. This means that an R&D organization or university must decide how severe to make its selection criteria for spin-off ventures and also decide on the degree of support to be offered through managerial and financial assistance.

general guide for "how to do it." Nevertheless, there are many interesting findings in these studies, and some general trends do emerge. We postulate that five core strategies can be identified that can improve a university's prospects for spin-off creation.

Although we argue that that university administrators and technology transfer professionals can learn from the studies in this book, it must be pointed out that efforts at transposing or replicating single elements of an entrepreneurial university model may only have limited success, given the interrelated nature of the drivers of spin-off activity.

1. Build "steeples of excellence"

Many entrepreneurial universities have pursued the "steeples of excellence" strategy, a "recipe for distinction" developed by Frederick B. Terman for science and engineering research. By focusing on the ability to attract and retain the scientific and engineering talent that is most capable of winning government funded research grants, it establishes a necessary technological foundation through which entrepreneurship can emerge. Without a distinguished faculty with the ability to generate innovation, there will be little basis for spin-off creation. Stanford, under Terman, initiated a policy of building academic steeples of expertise by recruiting and retaining a critical mass of faculty members in a selected niche or sub-discipline. According to Lenoir, the key to understanding Stanford policies in support of entrepreneurial activity is to see them as shaped fundamentally around attracting and retaining "star" academic researchers capable of winning research grants, and further enhancing the research profile of the university through their entrepreneurial activities and contacts with industry. UC San Diego also implemented this strategy to good effect. In Ireland and Singapore, this role of investing in excellent academics to build the capacity of the research community is now recognized as a central strategy in driving and harnessing a knowledge-driven economy.[3]

Furthermore, a necessary condition of a university's ability to create university spin-offs is its ability to attract large financial resources to fund leading-edge science and engineering research. Having access to strong financial R&D funds means that star scientists can undertake curiosity-driven exploration, conducted in an environment saturated in advanced technology. According to Lenoir, frontier research at Stanford played a

---

[3] For many policy makers the production of primary research information is not the end but the beginning of a process that continues until the usefulness of that information is realized.

central role in producing not only top tier publications, but also practical devices embodying the principles involved. From our findings on MIT spin-off companies, it also appears that much of the research activity that led to the creation of spin-offs is located in "Pasteur's quadrant" (Stokes, 1997, Tushman and O'Reilly, 2007) – being basic in nature but also of potential relevance to application.[4] For example, Professor Doug Hart's research efforts on 3 D-in-motion was the stepping stone in forming Brontes Technologies; Professor Eugene Fitzgerald's technological advances in strained silicon were a key factor in establishing AmberWave Systems; and Professor Anthony Sinskey and Dr. Oliver People's pioneering research in PHAs (polyhydroxyalkanoates) led to the formation of the bioplastics company Metabolix.

Faculty quality is an essential ingredient for spin-offs to emerge. University leadership targets areas of research expertise and promotes a high level of faculty achievement around them. Only by pursuing the steeples strategy and recruiting and developing world-class faculty and research staff in the targeted areas does the possibility of establishing effective new ventures become a reality. According to MIT Professor Robert Langer, one of the central components underlying a successful academic spin-off is a seminal academic paper on research that establishes the science underlying the product concept. The temptation to wander off the main research mission should be avoided. Stanford's provost, Frederick Terman, generally rejected research contracts unless there was a strategic fit with the university's established expertise and goals. He was critical of other institutions that sought contracts that they could fulfill with mediocre talent.

University administration should never forget that it is the faculty and the capabilities of that faculty that provide the foundation for academic commercialization to emerge. According to Lenoir, Stanford's core strategy was to focus on attracting and retaining the scientific and engineering talent most capable of winning federally funded research grants and contracts – steeples of excellence – and using those funds to support cutting-edge research that stimulates industrially relevant technology and high impact research. In China, Northeastern University is organizing internal faculty resources to engage in frontier research and address technological difficulties and societal problems in research fields such as green energy, computer science, and nanotechnology. One of MIT's academic steeples

---

[4] Stokes (1997) labeled "Pasteur's quadrant" after Louis Pasteur, whose work had significant theoretical and practical applications. In this quadrant, the researcher works to advance scientific knowledge, but remains acutely aware of the practical applications for his or her findings.

involves focus on helping transform the global energy system to meet the needs of the future and helping build a bridge to that future by improving today's energy systems. The structure of MITEI (MIT Energy Initiative) supports research that addresses key industrial concerns, including the development through basic research of enabling energy technologies that have the potential to overcome multiple energy challenges. Such initiatives give research universities the opportunity to build up areas of excellence, acquiring a local and global reputation along the way, benefiting the regional economy while advancing their international status.

2.   Cultivate leadership, support structures, and policies

Throughout the studies in this book, there is an emphasis on the role of leadership, support structures, and policies in fostering academic entrepreneurship. Academic leadership can add a strong sense of purpose to a university's character and establish an entrepreneurial heritage, either as a tacit presence or as a more proactive force that builds and celebrates a climate of entrepreneurial endeavor on campus. Creating a common leadership vision was important for MIT, Yale, the NUS, and University College Dublin (UCD), because it provided a clear sense of tacit support and direction when it came to promoting university-based entrepreneurship. Ideas emerged from the laboratories, guided by the commitment of supportive academic leaders who had a strong belief in what they were doing and what could be achieved.

The university mission is a precursor to improving technology transfer activities, informing the university on the structures and polices it will need to move forward. Drawing from its motto "Mens et Manus" (mind and hand), MIT's central mission for technology commercialization is to move technology rapidly to industry for societal benefit.[5] Similarly Yale saw itself as a "contributing institutional citizen" in economic development as opposed to being a passive observer. This vision was the catalyst for transformation and the emergence of academic entrepreneurial behavior at the university. The proactive leadership of Provost Frederick Terman at Stanford and MIT's Karl Compton in leveraging academic research played a key role in influencing all aspects of institutional life at their respective universities. Similarly, a series of interventions introduced by former President Hugh Brady of UCD helped promote an environment for commercialization. An innovation academy was developed to train postgraduate students in innovation and entrepreneurship;

[5] Nelsen, Lita and Thomas Ittelson. "Incubation without Walls." Nature Biotechnology Supplement 20 (2002): Be 26–27.

bio-incubation labs for start-ups were developed; a science park was established to enable spin-off ventures to grow and expand, and royalty distribution policies were formalized around intellectual property rights to provide greater certainty about the rewards associated with the technology transfer process.[6] MIT also developed a seed funding scheme[7] that enables academics to scope out commercial potential of research outcomes.[8] At UCD, an enterprising research commercialization scheme run by Enterprise Ireland offers funding to assist academics to bring a new product idea or business venture from a third-level educational institution to market. NUS established a seed funding scheme to provide very early stage seed funding to promising NUS spin-off companies. Similarly, KU Leuven invested in the creation of a fund to enable university start-up firms to access financial resources and managerial expertise for the transformation of a technology-based business idea into an organization with high potential. As at NUS, the founding of this fund was inspired by the absence of local venture capital willing to invest in companies operating close to scientific and technological frontiers. For countries to capitalize on their university research, technology transfer will be aided by the easing of restrictions against scientists turning their discoveries into companies.[9] In terms of incentive schemes, many universities discussed in this book adopted policies allowing university researchers to take a formal leave of absence to start a company, with the guarantee of jobs and tenure upon return.[10] Fini *et al.* (2011) also propose micro-level policies for universities in this area such as temporarily freezing the tenure clock, appropriate recognition in individual evaluations and compensation schemes or, pre-specified promotion tracks for faculty

[6] Science Parks are locations where academic entrepreneurs can operate but be in close proximity to a third-level institute in order to avail of their knowledgeable capabilities and resources. In a UK firm-level survey, Siegel *et al.* (2003) find that university science parks have slightly higher research productivity (i.e., generating new products and services, in addition to patent counts) than observationally equivalent firms not located in university science parks.

[7] Funded by a major grant from a successful entrepreneur, Gururaj ("Desh") Deshpande, along with his wife Jaishree.

[8] Universities face a number of resource constraints in creating successful spin-offs, but they cite access to venture capital as the most important, with access to other forms of financing also figuring highly (Wright *et al.* 2006).

[9] A number of recent studies suggest that universities need to improve their technology transfer structures if they are serious about promoting entrepreneurial development on campus (Litan *et al.* 2007).

[10] In the United States, Siegel (2004) also found widespread belief that there are insufficient rewards for faculty involvement in university technology transfer, especially for untenured faculty members, who continue to be rewarded almost exclusively on the basis of publications and grants. The issues arising from the reluctance of professors without tenure to market their ventures through the universities are evident.

who are willing to start a new business. Most universities in the United States tend to follow an "academic entrepreneur" centered model and typically do not interfere in the management and creation of start-ups. In contrast, Kings College London takes a more "investor centric" interventionist approach to technology transfer and has entered into partnerships with IP commercialization groups to provide funding and management teams to scale these companies. Rather than engaging in the commercialization process themselves, the university encourages its academics to allow an experienced management team to develop the technology. However, the academic can be involved in the process of CEO recruitment. The quality of the management team, and the team generally, is seen as important, if not more important, than the technology. Nevertheless, the technology has to be perceived to be robust enough to warrant creating a spin-out. In recent times, KCL has streamlined its processes, offering a new portfolio of innovative technologies and opportunities that can be licensed for free and put to use with easy access intellectual property (IP) agreements.[11]

Promoting a supportive environment for academic entrepreneurship is also about developing an entrepreneurial culture on campus, a commitment to entrepreneurship training, and a general willingness among academic staff to pitch in and contribute with all kinds of activity. Support programs and services need resources, but it is also important that programs and schemes be organized in an integrated and coordinated manner to ensure maximum effectiveness. To help achieve this, all of the universities in the study have tangible support services, such as the organized provision of training and a market-focused Entrepreneurship Center and Technology Transfer Office (TTO). Run effectively, the TTO can define roles and responsibilities, structures and processes that support the creation and development of new ventures. Typically these conform to a three-pronged governance model based around skills, organization, and alignment of key processes. The challenge for universities is to create a TTO with the right skill set. There is a danger that staff can lack the business acumen to deal with the commercial world and enable technology transfer. From a policy perspective, it is a balancing act. The TTO should drive proactive commercialization strategy, but not at the expense of a commitment to the core academic mission of education, basic (discovery) research, and dissemination of knowledge.

Professionalism and operational efficiency are essential for running a TTO because the office plays such a pivotal role in engendering academic entrepreneurship. The research of O'Gorman et al. (2006)

---

[11] www.kcl.ac.uk/innovation/business/easyaccessip/index.aspx.

on the knowledge spillover theory of entrepreneurship suggests several crucial reasons that technology transfer officers play a critical role as an intermediary and gatekeeper. The first is that scientists with new knowledge may underinvest in commercialization activity, as they do not see the benefits of commercialization; and second, those with the new knowledge may not recognize the commercial potential of the knowledge or may fail in their attempts to commercialize the new knowledge because of a lack of market understanding. Given that academics may not be aware of the viable opportunities that are available to them, it is imperative that the TTO professionals guide them and help them realize their full potential. However, Litan *et al.* (2010) and others questioned the effectiveness and efficiency of the TTO as a unit responsible for the commercialization of university technology. Siegel *et al.* (2004) also reported that firms expressed great difficulty in dealing with university TTOs on IP issues, citing the inexperience of the TTO staff, the TTOs' lack of general business knowledge, and their tendency to overstate the commercial value of patents. In addition, rather than actively recruit individuals with marketing skills, TTOs more often look for expertise in patent law and licensing or technical expertise. According to Breznitz, Yale experienced similar commercial capability deficits and recruited a senior Pfizer executive to restructure the Office of Cooperative Research and accelerate knowledge transfer between faculty and industry. At MIT, the TTO only hires technology transfer professionals with deep industry experience. Furthermore, most have worked in product development, marketing, and/or business development and understand the process of bringing new technology to market. These officers adopt a "can do" approach to technology transfer deals and a "get things done" attitude. Successful team staff, such as those at MIT, show a passion for seeking out new inventions, examining them quickly, and actively promoting them when they become commercial prospects.

Having the right TTO structure will enable synergistic networks to emerge between academics and venture capitalists and between advisors and start-up managers. The KCLE study provides evidence of the importance of the TTO in terms of developing effective governance mechanisms in young start-ups. KCLE's partnership with the IP Group is also seen as providing a mechanism that enables funding structures to develop the spin-off as fast as possible in order to obtain the upside gain. This collaboration has been successful in terms of enabling a number of spin-offs to be sold or floated on a stock market for significant capital gains.

With the right leadership team, innovative structures can be put in place that can influence the spin-off activity. Appointing the right people can drive positive change in organization alignment, as the NUS has shown. A new CEO was appointed who had a strong track record in managing venture capital investment and a prior background in running a biotech start-up. A more balanced organizational development approach with a stronger emphasis on management systems was quickly put in place. The NUS introduced major initiatives to make the office more "inventor-friendly," with less emphasis on maximizing licensing revenue, and a stronger focus on getting greater and faster deployment of NUS technology to the marketplace. Reaffirming the integrated NUS Enterprise approach, the new CEO emphasized greater coordination and cooperation among the units of NUS Enterprise by consolidating some of the separate units. In addition, NUS Enterprise introduced new processes to simplify negotiation on equity valuation.

There is also a need to develop integrated and coordinated structures to build an innovation ecosystem to support the rollout of engaged entrepreneurial programs across the entire institution. For example, to run a range of entrepreneurship programs, organized under one operating coordinating unit across the university, MIT and NUS have set up centers for entrepreneurship. The units are run with the aim of delivering entrepreneurship education to all disciplines across the university in a coordinated and seamless manner. Experience from MIT shows us that demonstrating to faculty at all levels and in all departments – and to students in all disciplines – the role of innovation and entrepreneurship can play a lead role in transforming lives and communities.[12] The Center's role is to drive innovation to empower students with the skills to push an idea through to implementation. By doing this, students will develop the entrepreneurial mindset to experiment, take risks, explore new opportunities, tolerate failure, and strive to overcome obstacles. Working with peers from differing disciplines, the center enables the universities to develop an entrepreneurship curriculum that provides students with a transformational experience based on action learning techniques. For example, MIT's recently launched course 10.S95/15.S70 "Ideas to Impact: Foundations for Technological Advances," delivered to students of the Skolkovo Institute of Science and Technology (Skoltech) and MIT, involved a cross-disciplinary effort from faculty at both MIT's Engineering School and MIT Sloan.[13] In the course, students applied key engineering principles

---

[12] Much of the existing literature on the nature of research that leads to university spin-offs has focused on science and engineering faculties. According to Wright et al., however, business schools within universities have an important role to play in the development of spin-off opportunities (Wright et al. 2009).

[13] Instructors: Dr. Luis Perez-Breva, Professor Ed Roberts, Dr. Rory O'Shea, Dr. Violetta Gerasymenko. For further details see https://entrepreneurship.mit.edu/news/new-half-semester-course-for-the-first-time-mit-and-skolkovo-students-toget.

and applications to evaluate and develop technological ideas into commercially viable concepts, and then built those concepts into viable commercial business propositions. Another example from MIT is the Innovation Teams (i-Teams) course (10.807/15.371), which brings together students from MIT Sloan and the MIT School of Engineering for a semester-long project assessing the commercial feasibility of novel MIT technologies.[14]

These centers should also support informal, out-of-class learning across campus, and encourage the entire community (academic and research staff, students, and alumni) to think about start-up opportunities. To make this model work successfully at MIT, the Martin Trust Center for MIT Entrepreneurship works in conjunction with academics from multiple disciplines and experienced entrepreneurs, emphasizing informal cross-disciplinary liaisons. The NUS also has integrated and coordinated structures to build an innovation ecosystem to support and sustain a culture of entrepreneurship and innovation across the entire institution. Beyond classes, the university provides a vast array of programs suited to meet the needs of emerging ventures, including networking functions, hackathons, mentoring, business competitions and more.

The MIT 100k business plan competition, a competition to promote campus entrepreneurship, has been a valuable way of engendering a real sense of entrepreneurial spirit among technical students. To fill the funding gap and accelerate the commercialization of university innovations, a new type of organization has emerged – the proof of concept center (PoCC). The PoCC enables inventors to evaluate the commercial potential of their research and makes it easier for inventors to obtain funding from outside investors, such as angel investors or venture capitalists, for further product development. For example, MIT's Deshpande Center has enabled the university to help fill the "valley of death" void between early stage research and a technology that is ready to commercialize. INRIA and IMEC have also played an important role in financing new inventions from the point where researchers recognize the potential for commercialization and help develop the idea to a stage where it is ready to be spun out of the research organization.

The policies and practices that foster spin-off success are an important driver for many universities. While there are numerous and various forms of policy employed to promote academic entrepreneurship, their success will depend on the institutional arrangements that encourage knowledge

[14] Instructors: Dr Luis Perez-Breva, Prof Fiona Murray, Dr Noubar Afeyan.

transfer to emerge. Careful evaluation of the local economic ecosystem will influence whether a "top-down" or "bottom-up" approach is best suited to the climate for economic development. While Yale, UCD, and Singapore chose top-down entrepreneurial programs, MIT and Stanford have traditionally relied more on their own entrepreneurial culture and a bottom-up policy. Yale and NUS chose their policies because there was little infrastructure in its region to support technology start-ups. The KU Leuven Research and Development (LRD) has grown into a significant portion of the university's total R&D portfolio employing over twenty support staff professionals. It offers space and managerial support for its spin-offs through its Innovation and Incubator Center, which is located on the campus. The Center mobilizes networks of partners and experts to interact with the spin-off company throughout its early stage development. In contrast, MIT did not develop a formal university incubator because the regional entrepreneurial infrastructure of Cambridge acts as the incubator to the university. UCSD combines institutional mechanisms such as CONNECT and the von Liebig Center to support entrepreneurship and drive technology commercialization efforts and new company creation.

Developing effective incentives for academics also requires careful policy consideration. MIT and Stanford do often take a small dilutable equity stake (5%) in the company but leave the running and management of the business to the academic entrepreneur. MIT does not look for a seat on the board of directors and allows its academics to devote an average of about one day per week to work on external entrepreneurial/consulting activities. In UCD, the process of starting up a company can be recognized as a "service contribution" in terms of academic promotion.

The need for good policies and the reason research universities need strong structures and conflict-of-interest policies around commercialization are reinforced by the John Hopkins experience and the Dalkon Shield and the Spectra patent controversy. According to Feldman *et al.*, these cases serve as a useful reminder of the reputational institutional risks that are involved with taking equity positions in ventures, especially science-based ventures. To avoid conflicts of interest, it is Stanford's policy to liquidate its equity investment in biotech spinoff firms prior to the commencement of clinical trials. Similarly, MIT's straightforward and "no exceptions" rules for keeping MIT and its startups separate actually aid the process of academic commercialization, because negotiations do not get bogged down while committees ponder over exceptions and risks. As such it is increasingly important that universities prepare for the "big disaster" and actively negotiate contracts that include sufficient safeguarding terms.

3.   Embed an entrepreneurial culture

Entrepreneurial universities demonstrate that the everyday life of the faculty is immersed in a culture that increases the chance of technology commercialization. Successful spin-off programs depend upon the actions of the staff and students of the institution, not solely on the sporadic attempts of a few top-down official leaders. There has to be an entrepreneurial ethos that permeates the character of university life. Creating an academic culture of commitment toward university entrepreneurship is essential for success. The universities in the study reveal that supportive campus environments do not exist in a vacuum. Tacit acceptance of entrepreneurial activity must exist outside the upper echelons of university administration – a real culture change has to occur across the entire campus.[15] In all instances the initiatives were successfully implemented because they generated significant interest and support from large numbers of students, faculty members, and alumni. Although particular programs and practices that contribute to entrepreneurial success may differ from one university president to another, the goal of providing a supportive entrepreneurial environment where academic entrepreneurship and student entrepreneurship are championed and nurtured by other senior leaders should not waiver. This view is supported by Professor Phillip Sharp, founder of Alnylam, and Professor Robert Langer at MIT, who both consider the creation of intellectual property and the commercialization of discoveries as complementary roles as academic teacher and researcher. Lita Nelsen, TLO Director of MIT, states that the greatest achievement of Professor Langer is the creation of 120 professors, who have graduated from his lab, and who now are trying to follow in his footsteps at other institutions (HBS 2007). She also states that the reason Professor Langer "is so successful is that his work is so central to what he believes is MIT's mission." The university as a whole must be entrepreneurially oriented and responsive to the start-up needs of academic entrepreneurs and must aim to embed positive cultural beliefs and assumptions about engaging in technology transfer. According to Henry Etzkowitz (2001), this entrepreneurial dynamic needs to be built into the U.S. academic research system by ensuring that both senior and junior faculty are responsible for obtaining their own research support.

---

[15] In the early years of biotechnology, the scientists who participated in private ventures typically risked the disapproval of their peers. Specifically, during this time in which academic entrepreneurship tested the boundaries of legitimacy, only prominent scientists at prestigious universities were able to attract the resources to establish new firms. Those who do so today typically act without concern for adverse professional consequences (Stuart and Ding 2006).

Another finding from the studies in this volume suggests that cultural change comes about in research groups where academics maintain a strong role model presence. Peers are also very important in helping students understand the "entrepreneurial norm" at an institution. By becoming involved with academics, students develop support networks that are instrumental in dealing with start-up challenges. This environment creates opportunities for students and academics involved in commercialization projects to work alongside academic entrepreneurs. Exposure to people who are passionate about moving their inventions out into the market helps instill the same qualities in fellow faculty and Ph.D. students. MIT also provides a free mentoring service for students, bringing real world experience to bear on university research that can sometimes suffer from a lack of clear commercial thinking. The Venture Mentoring Service adds immeasurably to the Institute's ability to spur innovation by providing the guidance and tools to help breakthrough research reach the marketplace. By forming working relationships between fledgling entrepreneurs and seasoned mentors, the service helps increase the likelihood that new ventures can succeed sooner in delivering the fruits of MIT research to the world. The NovaUCD Innovation Award is a way of increasing awareness of innovation, technology transfer, and entrepreneurship. The KU Leuven experience demonstrates "strategic orientation" toward entrepreneurship through installing appropriate incentive mechanisms and an appropriate support infrastructure. Given the nature of spin-off companies operating at scientific and technological boundaries, specific incubation processes have also been incorporated at Leuven.

4.   Let success breed success

Entrepreneurial role models will inevitably influence a university, and research shows that their interaction with faculty, staff, and students can make a big contribution to promoting academic entrepreneurship on campus. They can inspire those around them to aim for entrepreneurship goals and realize their ambitions.[16] Thus, in turn, creates a virtuous

---

[16] According to recent research, there are reasons to anticipate that a faculty member's transition to entrepreneurial science is easier in universities that have previously spawned academic entrepreneurs (O'Shea et al. 2005). Stuart and Ding (2006) estimate that one of the reasons behind this "contagion effect" is that it is easier to follow in another's footsteps. According to the authors, if someone down the corridor has been successful in bringing a new venture to commercialization, another academic might also be inclined to follow his or her lead. The first entrepreneur can provide much-needed advice on finding the right resources and how best to work with the TTO.

cycle of "success breeds success" innovation effect given that research has shown that as faculty become more knowledgeable about the firm formation process they are more likely to pursue commercialization if peers have already had some previous success. At Stanford and MIT, academic entrepreneurs provide support to peers before they embark on a technology transfer venture. This can lead to a cluster of commercial companies that rely on the involvement of key role models.

For example, Professor Fogarty at Stanford either founded or co-founded over thirty start-up companies in the period from 1980 to 2000. At MIT, Alex d'Arbeloff, founder and former CEO of Teradyne Corporation, first became Chair of the MIT Corporation and then, retiring from that position, began teaching in the Mechanical Engineering Department and the Management School. Having successful businessmen as course instructors brings students face to face with people who embody what can be achieved. According to O'Shea *et al.* (2005), once a university has established an entrepreneurial tradition and a number of successful companies, fellow faculty members can offer material, in addition to moral support to their colleagues who are trying to establish companies of their own. According to the authors, a previous stratum of university-originated firms and professors who have made money from founding their own firms creates a potential cadre of "angels" that prospective entrepreneurs can look to in raising funds to start their firms. Early faculty firm founders at MIT are known on campus for their willingness to supply capital to help younger colleagues.

The experiences of Yale and John Hopkins University show that if universities and department heads are not fully supportive of commercialization on campus, then it is difficult to foster an entrepreneurial culture. When a faculty comprises world-class science and engineering minds that have engaged in commercialization projects, there is a positive spillover effect for other academics who wish to pursue entrepreneurial careers. Without the support of their peers, there is far less motivation to form spin-off companies. The studies in this volume demonstrate that role models take different forms, but they can inspire those around them to aim higher and go for goals that they might have thought were beyond them. Working with an entrepreneur with a proven track record helps demystify what it takes to succeed. That is the principle underlying the MIT strategy of involving successful entrepreneurs and venture capitalists in teaching students.

Many of the studies in this volume show that when academics are exposed to successful role models and a culture that actively champions commercialization, they are more likely to engage in such activity themselves (O'Shea *et al.* 2005; Stuart and Ding 2006). Promoting an entrepreneurial culture is a way to overcome the chicken-and-egg problem that arises when academics look to each other for cues on how to start the virtuous circle of belief. Researchers and students can also feed off the success of their peers and predecessors. The Lemelson–MIT Prize is awarded to outstanding *mid-career* inventors, who have developed a patented product or process of significant value to society, which has been adopted for practical use. By recognizing and funding younger, mid-career inventors, the prize is designed to spur inventive careers and provide role models for future generations of inventors. The NUS "Immersion" program sends the brightest and most entrepreneurially minded NUS undergraduate students to five entrepreneurial hubs in the world to work as interns in high-tech start-up companies for one year, during which time they also take courses related to entrepreneurship at partner universities in each of the regions.

5.   Work with industry and government

The regional context of universities is another driver for spin-off activity. Local connections between the university, industry, and government can provide the university with increased research funds and access to market-related knowledge.[17] The studies in this volume show how trilateral relationships consistently emerge in regions where university entrepreneurship is successful, though they are at different stages of development and with different inherited socioeconomic systems and cultural values.[18] In some instances, we see that the university is expected to serve local innovation by helping industry resolve problems or jointly establishing R&D centers and science parks. In turn, industry is encouraged to rely on university research to renew existing or achieve new technological innovations and products. At the University of

---

[17] According to Walshock (1997), research universities have an increasingly significant role to play in regional economic development if they do three things: (1) embrace a wider and deeper understanding of the unique character and multiplicity of factors affecting economic development in a knowledge society; (2) see their role in society as mobilizing and making accessible campuswide academic resources – from the sciences to the humanities – relevant to the knowledge problems confronting advanced economies; (3) invest politically and financially in the development of institutional mechanisms whose central role is to facilitate, broker, and develop knowledge across the internal boundaries of academic disciplines and across the boundaries currently separating the highly valuable traditional research and teaching programs from the concerns and challenges confronting practitioners and decision makers in the larger society.

[18] Etzkowitz defines this dynamic relationship between government, industry, and universities as the "triple helix" model of innovation. According to the author, a triple helix of university–industry–government interactions is the key to innovation in increasingly knowledge-based societies.

California San Diego, the connections between the university, industry, and government-sponsored research programs unlocked increased research funding and access to market-related knowledge. In order to facilitate these collaborative activities, NEU developed a scientific park, an entrepreneurial park, and an industry park to allow university-industry partnerships to flourish. At MIT and Stanford, strong links with industry steered the faculty toward fertile new directions of research that would subsequently be absorbed into the university. UCD actively participates in the National Science Foundation Ireland Strategic Research Clusters (SRCs) and has adopted a "gateway" approach to facilitate partnerships between academia and industry to address crucial research questions, foster the development of new and existing Irish-based technology companies, and grow partnerships with industry that could make an important contribution to Ireland and its economy. This example demonstrates the active role governments can play in helping to generate innovation by funding innovation programs. Governments can also play a critical role by establishing appropriate legal frameworks and by facilitating partnerships and encouraging entrepreneurship. In Ireland, Enterprise Ireland, a semi-state agency, plays a central role in coordinating the technology transfer system. In China, the government acts as a "regional innovation organizer," playing the role of a leading institution of university–industry partnerships. The rise of Yale is also an example of how a university that works with the local environment/government, via its Office of Cooperative Research, can become a catalyst for local economic development. President Hennessy of Stanford, the founder of a number of high-tech start-ups, believes firmly in supporting Terman's vision of turning ideas into technology through close collaboration with industry.[19]

While there are no definitive rules, the guiding principle is that parties with a vested interest in regional economic development must communicate and collaborate. According to Walshock and Lee, in their analysis of the role of the University of California San Diego in the creation of industrial clusters, successive generations of San Diegans have learned that for the region to remain vibrant, all interested parties must "pool resources."[20] The university, government, and local industry

---

[19] President Hennessy, foreword in Dorf and Byers: Technology Ventures: From Idea to Enterprise, 2005.

[20] In contrast, while Johns Hopkins University developed some of the nation's embryonic leading edge medical technologies, the state of Baltimore did not have the regional entrepreneurial infrastructure in place (i.e., the entrepreneurial partnership, network events, and venture capital investment) to exploit the technology opportunities presented at the university (Feldman 1994).

work together to support new and uncertain ventures through shared agenda setting, shared investment, shared risks, and shared rewards. The region has developed two cultures in parallel, "entrepreneurial science" in the university and "entrepreneurial enterprise" in the community. They are linked through concrete institutional mechanisms that have contributed to the phenomenal growth of companies, jobs, and wealth in the area. San Diego is now renowned for world-class innovation and its thriving economy. KCL also illustrates the importance of partnerships and alliances with industry via the IP Group in terms of successfully incubating them for investment and various pharmaceutical, biotechnology, and medical device companies for developing research.

The five themes that emerge from this study can be molded into a normative model that will create an academic environment where spin-off activity is more likely to happen. The starting point is the science and engineering resource base of the university. By creating steeples of excellence and areas of research expertise, paths to the wider world of industry and government can open up, increasing access to research funds and to market-related knowledge.

Faculty quality will make this happen, but the challenge is to take the frontier work of star scientists and promote it properly, enhancing the research capabilities of the university and the likelihood of technology transfer. This approach highlights the importance of identifying and attracting star scientists to the university. Having a number of top tier academics means they can produce a vast range of invention disclosures with strong commercial potential. The importance of having a depth of expertise at the university also gives legitimacy in the eyes of potential investors.

Only through the cultivation of strong leadership and supporting structures and policies can a university hope to break down the walls between ivory towers of innovation and the commercial world. Setting out a vision and orchestrating its realization through the synchronization of operational resources will help embed commercialization entrepreneurship education in the culture of the university. Universities will be unable to develop successful spin-off programs without changing the mindset of "academics." To do this effectively, universities must ensure that an integrated and coordinated structure is in place to support culture change. Academics will not understand the legitimacy of commercialization unless it is supported from the top of the institution, as well as by proper communication structures, leadership, and performance measures. Simply sponsoring activities is not enough. There has to be a tangible strategy, redirecting, establishing new priorities, and reallocating resources to optimize the technology commercialization process.

Academic leaders must play their part in changing the status quo, helping overcome obstacles that inevitably arise in an institutionalized environment where there is resistance to change.

For policy makers to encourage academic entrepreneurship, an entrepreneurial and streamlined approach to the identification, protection, and commercialization of university intellectual property must be undertaken. The governance of the TTO is of central importance in achieving and sustaining technology transfer success and influencing stakeholders. Universities that achieve an entrepreneurial orientation will be more likely to succeed. A culture must be cultivated where start-up ventures are valued and peer support from fellow entrepreneurial academics is on hand, championing commercialization activity. Direct exposure to role models will heighten entrepreneurial activity. However, it must also be noted that the essential character of technology transfer lies not only in the formal structures and programs that universities construct, but also in the agency of academics in the entrepreneurial process. It is the sense of obligation and commitment from academic staff to engage in the entrepreneurial process that distinguishes top entrepreneurial universities from the others.[21] Therefore, it is important that the reward systems of universities must not act as a barrier to engaging in the entrepreneurial process.

While all these factors contribute to a workable model, every university is different and their progress will be dependent on other factors. The history of the learning institution and the context for its development will have influenced its mission and play an important role in how it adapts to an entrepreneurial strategy. There is a systemic process and a cycle of experience (Learn, Innovate, and Perform – see Figure 15.1). This knowledge accumulation inherent in the process of generating university spin-offs influences a university's future ability to produce spin-off companies (O'Shea *et al.* 2005).

Regional context provides another variable. Spin-off activity requires support from innovative customers and access to regional infrastructure and resources. From the studies in this volume, it can be seen that commercialization strategies relate to the regional institutional arrangements that enable knowledge transfer. Given its relatively low technopole environment, Yale and NUS chose high support–high selectivity infrastructure initiatives to accelerate transfer, while MIT

---

[21] According to MIT Professor Robert Langer, "Some academics feel science should be pure, so they avoid interactions with companies. But when done well, I think the benefits are enormous – in treatment of diseases, in new companies, in jobs" (HBS, 2005).

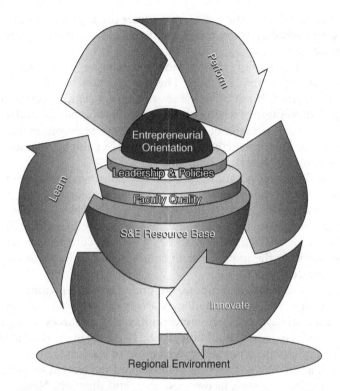

Figure 15.1: The development of a spin-off performance framework.

traditionally chose to adopt a more bottom-up perspective in terms of the creation and development of start-ups. However, both strategies have enabled the universities to contribute to the creation of a vibrant technology community in both regions.

Closing thoughts

The findings in this collection of studies echo other empirical work, highlighting how faculty quality and entrepreneurial activity reinforce each other in universities that successfully navigate the path to commercialization. Achieving institutional commitment and academic entrepreneurialism may require costly interventions, such as the recruitment of quality faculty and large investments in science and technology, but without a critical mass of faculty expertise, academic entrepreneurship will not occur at high rates. Investment in a TTO, entrepreneurship education, seed funding schemes, and incubator capabilities can help in many cases. Given the complex and time-intensive job of identifying, sourcing, and exploiting university technologies, the greater the capability of the TTO and its commercial partners, the greater the likelihood that the university will produce start-ups.

Retaining top-quality faculty and stimulating their interest in entrepreneurship is fundamental. The introduction of individual programs or policies will not by themselves change a campus culture or an academic's perception of whether the institution is supportive and affirming. The essential character of entrepreneurial research communities lies not only in the formal structures and programs but also in the underlying values that inspire their development.

Successful spin-off programs demand an enduring commitment from all of the university to promote academic entrepreneurship. It is a commitment that needs nurturing and is built upon incentives, rewards, and the investment of resources in the education of faculty. In contrast, unsuccessful attempts are frequently marked by the unwillingness of the institution to consider the importance of commercial development as either necessary or desirable.

Modern educational institutions are under growing pressure to provide a platform for high-technology start-ups and have to ensure that faculty and staff have sufficient opportunities and resources to engage in entrepreneurial behavior should they wish. There are many ways in which universities can make a positive contribution to economic development, but each institution must seek to organize and implement its programs in a manner that best suits its own resources and situation. Nevertheless, this chapter shows that despite all the variables, there are common strategies that can be pursued. Over time, a web of interlocking initiatives will create an institutional culture of academic entrepreneurship and increase the opportunities for spin-off success.

References

Bowen, H. Kent, Kazaks, Alex, and Muir-Harmony, Ayr. (2005). The Langer Lab: Commercializing Science. Harvard Business School Case.

Bradley, Samantha, Hayter, Christopher, and Link, Albert. (2013). Proof of concept centers in the United States: An exploratory look. *Journal of Technology Transfer*, 38(4), 349–381.

Bresnahan, T., Gambardella, A., and Saxenian, A. (eds.). (2004). *Building High Tech Clusters: Silicon Valley and Beyond*. Cambridge University Press.

Breznitz, S., O'Shea, R.P., and Allen, T.J. (2008). University commercialization strategies in the development of regional bioclusters. *Journal of Product Innovation Management*, 25 (2): 129–142.

Cunningham, J., and Harney, B. (2006). *Strategic Management of Technology Transfer: The New Challenge on Campus*, Oak Tree Press.

Dorf, R. and Byers, T. (2005). Technology Ventures: From Idea to Enterprise, McGraw-Hill Education. US.

Etzkowitz, H., Webster, A., Gebhardt, C., and Terra, B.R.C. (2000). The future of the university and the university of the future: Evolution of ivory tower to entrepreneurial paradigm. *Research Policy*, 29(2), 313–330.

Feldman, M. (1994). The university and economic development: The case of Johns Hopkins University and Baltimore. *Economic Development Quarterly*, 8, 67–66.

Fini, R., Grimaldi, R., Santoni, S., and Sobrero, M. (2011). "Complements or substitutes? The role of universities and local context in supporting the creation of academic spin-offs." *Research Policy*, 40(8), 1113–1127.

Gulbranson, C.A. and Audretsch, D.B. (2008). Proof of Concept Centers: Accelerating the Commercialization of University Innovation. Ewing Marion Kauffman Foundation.

Hockfield, Susan. (2007). Universities and the Global Knowledge Economy. Speech presented 20 November 2007, Confederation of Indian Industries (CII), Mumbai, India.

O'Gorman, C., Byrne, O., and Pandya, D. (2006). How scientists commercialize new knowledge via entrepreneurship. *Journal of Technology Transfer*, 33: 23–43.

O'Shea, R.P., Allen, T.J., Chevalier, A., and Roche, F. (2005). Entrepreneurial orientation, technology transfer and spin-off performance of U.S. universities. *Research Policy*, 34, 994–1009.

Roberts, E.B. (1991). *Entrepreneurs in High Technology: Lessons From MIT and Beyond*, Oxford University Press, New York.

Roberts, E.B. and Malone, D.E. (1996). Policies and structures for spinning off new companies from research and development organizations. *R&D Management*, 26(1), 17–48.

Rothaermel, F.T., Agung, S., and Jiang, L. (2007). University entrepreneurship: A taxonomy of the literature. *Industrial and Corporate Change*, 16(4), 691–791.

Shane, Scott. (2004). *Academic Entrepreneurship: University Spinoffs and Wealth Creation*, Edward Elgar, Cheltenham, UK.

Siegel, S.D., Waldman, A.D., Atwater, E.L., and Link, N.A. (2004). Toward a model of the effective transfer of scientific knowledge from academicians to practitioners: Qualitative evidence from the commercialization of university technologies. *Journal of Technology Management*, 21, 115–142.

Siegel, D.S., Westhead, P., and Wright, M. (2003). Assessing the impact of science parks on the research productivity of firms: Exploratory evidence from the United Kingdom. *International Journal of Industrial Organization*, 21(9), 1357–1369.

Slaughter, S. and Rhoades, G. (2005). From endless frontier to basic science for use: Social contracts between science and society. *Science, Technology and Human Values*, 30(4), 1–37.

Stokes, D.E. (1997). Pasteur's Quadrant, Basic Science and Technological Innovation. Brookings Institutions, Washington, DC.

Stuart, E.T. and Ding, W.W. (2006). When do scientists become entrepreneurs? The social structural antecedents of commercial activity in the academic life sciences. *American Journal of Sociology,* 112, 97–144.

Tushman, M., O'Reilly III, C.A. (2007). Research and relevance: Implications of Pasteur's quadrant for doctoral programs and faculty development. Academy of Management Journal, 50(4), 769–774.

Walshok, M. (1997). Expanding roles for research universities in regional economic development. *New Directions for Higher Education,* 97, 17–26.

Wright, M., Lockett, A., Clarysse, B., and Binks, M. (2006). University spin-out companies and venture capital. *Journal of Research Policy,* 35, 481–501.

Wright, M., Piva, E., Mosey, S. *et al.* (2009). Academic entrepreneurship and business schools. *Journal of Technology Transfer,* 34, 560–587.

Index

Printed in the United States
By Bookmasters